PLAY & CULTURE STUDIES
VOLUME 2

PLAY CONTEXTS REVISITED

PLAY & CULTURE STUDIES

Stuart Reifel, series editor

Volume 1: *Diversions and Divergencies in Fields of Play*
edited by Margaret Carlisle Duncan, Garry Chick, and Alan Aycock, 1998

Volume 2: *Play Contexts Revisited*
edited by Stuart Reifel, 1999

PLAY & CULTURE STUDIES
VOLUME 2

PLAY CONTEXTS REVISITED

edited by
Stuart Reifel
University of Texas at Austin

Ablex Publishing Corporation
Stamford, Connecticut

WB

Printed in the United States of America

ISSN: 1096-8911
ISBN: 1-56750-422-1 (cloth)
       1-56750-423-X (paper)

Ablex Publishing Corporation
100 Prospect Street
North Tower, 3rd Floor
Stamford, CT 06901

6/19/01 Vol 2

Contents

Introduction

I am pleased to present the second volume of *Play & Culture Studies*. With this volume, we intend to further discourse and understanding about the complex phenomenon we know as play. As with the previous edition, *Diversions and Divergences in Fields of Play*, our purpose is to provide a forum for new thinking about "play in humans and animals ... across various cultural, social, and activity settings" (Reifel, 1998, p. xi). Necessarily, this effort cuts across various disciplines, including biology, anthropology, history, psychology, education, leisure studies, sociology, and any field in which play theories contribute. The variety of the contributions to this volume, as with the last volume, reflects the breadth of this effort.

The 16 contributions that comprise this book are organized into five sections. Part 1 is titled "Adult's Stories of Play." The chapters in this section provide narratives that create differing stories about three understandings of play. In Chapter 1, "Play and Inventiveness: Revisiting Erikson's Views on Einstein's Playfulness," Cosby Steele Rogers and Dorothy Justus Sluss explore the psychoanalytic play theory of Erik Erikson, as applied by Erikson to the life's work of Albert Einstein. Kevin J. Sheehan contextualizes the early play-linked story writing of Brian Sutton-Smith in Chapter 2, "Playing with the Sacrificial Child: Brian Sutton-Smith's Boys' Story *Our Street*." In the last chapter in this section, "Toying with the Striptease Dancer and the First Amendment," Judith Lynne Hanna situates the stories of striptease dancers in larger legal and social contexts. In all cases, these chapters expand our thinking about the role of story as it connects to, and informs, differing forms of human play.

Much of the next two sections of the book deal with the ever-growing field of children's play. In Part 2, "Children's Play Contexts and Rules," contributions explore the thinking about our play beliefs (Chapter 4, "Kindergarten and College Students' Views of Play and Work at Home and School," by Robyn M. Holmes), play categorizations (Chapter 5, "Development Reflected in Chase Games," by Loretta J. Clarke), play rules (Chapter 6, "Rules in Children's Games and Play," by Carrie Freie), classroom play with young children (Theresa H. Escobedo's Chapter 7, "The Canvas of Play: A Study of Children's Play Behaviors While Drawing"), and parent participation in children's museum play (Chapter 8, "The Effect of the Physical and Social Environment on Parent-Child Interactions: A Qualitative Analysis of Pretend Play in a Children's Museum," by Stephanie Shine and Teresa

Y. Acosta). While the content of these chapters appears to be quite diverse, all deal with themes of play definition in social contexts, whether the defining is done by scholars or by play participants.

Most of Part 3 also deals with children's play, but all of the authors of these chapters reflect the belief that our understanding of play, whether children's or adult's, can be expanded by looking at play actions and meanings in diverse contexts. "Play in Other Cultures" includes three chapters that look at aspects of play in Japan (Chapter 9, "A Comparison of Playfulness Among American and Japanese Preschoolers," by Satomi Izumi Taylor, Cosby Steele Rogers, and Javid Kaiser), Taiwan (Sheng-Hsi Lin and Stuart Reifel's "Context and Meanings in Taiwanese Kindergarten Play," Chapter 10), and Germany (Chapter 11, "'Playing with Play': Germany's Carnival as Aesthetic Nonsense," by Felicia R. McMahon). All of these chapters acknowledge a theme of the uniqueness of play in different cultures, and how culture provides characteristic meanings and qualities that we must consider when we think about play.

Part 4, titled "Play in Other Species," reminds us that play is not only a human phenomenon. Maxeen Biben and Maribeth Champoux report on an experiment in Chapter 12, "Play and Stress: Cortisol as a Negative Correlate of Play in *Saimiri*." Chapter 13, "Play and Attachment Behavior of Peer-Only Reared and Surrogate/Peer-Reared Rhesus Monkey Infants in Their Social Groups" (by Maribeth Champoux, Courtney Shannon, Wendy D. Airoso, and Stephen J. Suomi), documents a number of variables linked to play in humans by means of studying monkeys. And Theia C. DeLong reports patterns of play in Chapter 14, "Observations of Free-play Behavior in Captive Juvenile Bottlenose Dolphins." These lenses on nonhuman play provide insights into our assumptions and definitions of human play.

The final section of this volume, "Other Conceptions of Play," includes two efforts to theorize about play. Clearly, all the contributors in Parts 1 through 4 of this book also deal with theory, but the final two chapters reflect a desire for more general models to guide our thinking. Moving beyond his "rhetorics" in *The Ambiguity of Play* (1997), Brian Sutton-Smith here proposes Chapter 15, "Evolving a Consilience of Play Definitions: Playfully." And Thomas S. Henricks contibutes Chapter 16, "Play as Ascending Meaning: Implications of a General Model of Play." Here, ideas about play are elaborated, and a tradition of "pure theorizing" continues.

The *Play & Culture Studies* series is linked with The Association for the Study of Play (TASP), an organization of scholars dedicated to promoting, stimulating, and encouraging the interdisciplinary study of play. It is worth noting that most of the contributions to this volume originated as presentations at annual meetings of TASP. Studies of play, especially studies that acknowledge play theory (or theories), have been encouraged by TASP, both at its annual meetings and in its previous publications. It is our intent that this intellectual tradition should continue, and it is my hope that such a tradition is reflected by the works presented here.

The work of preparing an edited volume is difficult to describe. That work is complicated when the range of submissions to the volume reflects the variety of disciplines and topics that appear within these covers. I could not have done my job as editor without the thoughtful contribution of numerous individuals who provided blind reviews for submissions and revised manuscripts. It is my pleasure to acknowledge those contributions here. Thanks to the following: Alan Aycock, Kendall Blanchard, Rosemary Bolig, G.-Dominique Bregant, Maribeth Champoux, Garry Chick, Loretta Clarke, Sue Dockett, Margaret C. Duncan, Joe Frost, Ann Marie Guilmette, Linda Hughes, Nechie King, David Lancy, Don Lytle, Grace Masselos, Alice Meckley, Melissa Park, Mary Rivkin, Warren Roberts, Cosby Steele Rogers, Lori Roggman, Olivia Saracho, Barbara Scales, Suzanne Seriff, Dorothy Justus Sluss, Peter Smith, Phillips Stevens, Jr., Brian Sutton-Smith, and June Yeatman. Also, thanks to Dottie Hershman and John Sutterby for their assistance with indexing and editing.

—Stuart Reifel, Series Editor
University of Texas at Austin

REFERENCES

Reifel, S. (1998). Series introduction. In M. C. Duncan, G. Chick, & A. Aycock (Eds.), *Play & culture studies: Diversions and divergences in fields of play* (vol. 1). Greenwich, CT: Ablex.

Sutton-Smith, B. (1997). *The ambiguity of play*. Cambridge, MA: Harvard University Press.

part I
Adult's Stories of Play

1

Play and Inventiveness: Revisiting Erikson's Views on Einstein's Playfulness

Cosby Steele Rogers
Virginia Tech

Dorothy Justus Sluss
East Tennessee State University

> "Anyone who has never made a mistake has never tried anything new."
> —Albert Einstein

Repetition, alternation, harmony, balance, and musical surprise fill my senses. I'm alive! I'm in flow. Body, mind, and spirit are united. Mozart plays in my headphones while I row my ergometer, varying the rhythm and tempo accordingly. My aging dog lies sleeping under the falling leaves of the trees, approaching the time to "let go" of her last season, only then to become a different part of the music of the cosmos. My vision is filled with the morning sunlight that reflects off the red, gold, and yellow leaves clinging desperately to the old maple tree. Winds shift speed and direction, returning to "surprise" the leaves, which finally "let go" to float, twirl, and waltz their way to the next season. My wandering mind hears them singing the words of the hymn "I Danced in the Morning," an adapation of the 19th century Shaker tune, "Simple Gifts":

> Dance, then wherever you may be;
> I am the Lord of the Dance, said He,
> And I'll lead you all, wherever you may be,
> And I'll lead you all in the dance, said He. (Carter, 1963/1990, p. 303)

3

There is a sense of joy, peace, and unity with nature and the universe. My ideas are mingling, dancing, playing with those of Schiller, Einstein, and Erikson. The spirit of the moment embodies Frederick Schiller's concept of aesthetic experience, described in his "Essays: Aesthetical and Philosophical" (1875a), captured in his poem, "Ode to Joy" (1875b), and understood by Beethoven, who gave it musical form in the "Ninth Symphony." As Levy (1978) postulated, my "body, mind, and spirit" (p. 188) are united in play. This experience is filled with play, as is every creative moment that elicits the birth of any new idea, image, or invention; like the traditional Gaelic melody:

Morning has broken,
Like the first morning,...
God's recreation
Of the new day! (Farjeon, 1931/1990, p. 469)

And so the circle comes anew. I return to the questions that stimulated my brief playful "amusement ride" (qtd. from Feldman, 1994, p. 106): What is the link between play and inventiveness? Did Einstein's inventiveness evolve as a function of play? Were his childhood experiences directly linked to his adult productivity? Are Erikson's views on Einstein's play and inventiveness congruent with current theories of play and creativity?

LINKING PLAY AND INVENTIVENESS

The relationship between play and creativity has been investigated by scholars from a variety of theoretical perspectives. Scientific inventiveness was the form of creativity that Erikson sought to explain in a short psychobiography of Albert Einstein. In this article, we will review briefly some of Erikson's basic ideas about play and playfulness. We then offer our analysis of one of Erikson's little-known papers, a psychobiography on Einstein. Finally, we will compare Erikson's ideas with more recent theories and research on play, inventiveness, and creativity.

Erikson's Views on Play

Erik H. Erikson's views on play (e.g., 1940, 1972, 1977) have influenced the work of practitioners in clinical and educational settings for many years. However, because play has often been relegated to a secondary role in human development, that is, as a facilitator of some other "more valued" developmental domain, such as cognition, the study of Erikson's work has seldom been given the attention it deserves by scholars who devote themselves to advancing the theory and research on play. In light of the current trends in the field of early childhood education, which rely heavily on play-based experiences (e.g., Rogers & Sawyers, 1988) for

Developmentally Appropriate Practice (Bredekamp & Copple, 1997), it seems prudent to carefully examine Erikson's contributions to our understanding of the role of play in the development of creativity, and to integrate Erikson's ideas with recent research and current theories of play.

Erikson's training in psychoanalysis influenced his view of play. Grounded in psychoanalytic theory, Erikson created a neo-psychoanalytic approach which expanded the realm of development to the psychosocial sphere. He found children's play to be the means to gain access to children's thoughts and feelings as they struggled with psychosocial issues (see Erikson, 1940). This theme can be observed in Erikson's early work, which focused on one aspect of play in the mastery of emotions (1940) and in his later studies, which reflected a broader, more aesthetic view of play and playfulness (1977).

According to Erikson (1977), the child's ever-widening social context is reflected in three arenas of play: autosphere, microsphere, and macrosphere. In his description of the ontogeny of play, the first play occurs in the *autosphere*, where children experience and experiment with the body and the first "self." During this time, the infants' and mothers' bodies are the primary sources of sensation and interaction. As a child's world expands, objects and toys are incorporated into the play arena, which is a *microsphere* representing the larger world. In this sphere, children use toys in two ways: (a) as props for acting out their emotions, and (b) as tools to discern the limits of rules established by guardians and society. In the microsphere, they gain mastery over their world as they gain control over their toys. When children enter the social realm, they enter the *macrosphere*, which involves interactions with others, contributing to a shared view of the world. Even after adults have participated in macrocosmic play, they may still exhibit microcosmic sphere with adult toys, such as cars, boats, and computers, thus engaging in play across the lifespan. Erikson proposed that the child's play, "...provides the infantile form of the human propensity to create model situations in which aspects of the past are re-lived, the present re-presented and renewed, and the future anticipated" (p. 44).

Erikson's early work on play as a therapeutic mode for the mastery of tension served as the basis for the development of the field of play therapy, and continues to wield an influence on practitioners in clinical and educational settings. As the field of psychology evolved, psychoanalytic theory fell into disfavor among psychologists, owing in part to the lack of empirical research to support assertions made by the theories, and, to alternative perspectives offered by feminist theories (e.g., Budd, Chance, & Simerly, 1985; Gilligan, 1979). Like Freud's psychoanalytic theory, Erikson's psychosocial theory contained constructs that were difficult to operationalize and, until recently, found more favor among clinicians than among empirical researchers. However, with improved research methods, many of Erikson's propositions are finding support in contemporary research (e.g., Adams, Bennion, & Huh, 1987; Bradley, 1997; Hamachek, 1994). Contemporary research on the sociodramatic play of preschoolers, which occurs during Erikson's stage of initiative versus guilt, focuses heavily on the development of social and cognitive skills, especially literacy. Less attention is being given to some of the basic functions of play, which Erikson helped document. Revisiting Erikson's psychosocial perspective on sociodramatic play might prove fruitful in extending our contemporary understanding of children's play.

Erikson's Views on Playfulness

The second theme in Erikson's views on play—i.e., differentiation of play versus playfulness—was implicit in his writing, but not articulated explicitly. For example, his major works on play (Erikson, 1940, 1972, 1977) included phrases such as "playful play," "playful exploration," and "playful mischief." For Erikson, playfulness differs from play in that playful rituals "formalize human playfulness." In his book, *Toys and Reasons* (1977), a compilation of a series of Godkin lectures presented at Harvard University, he included a stage-by-stage analysis of playful rituals that provide the opportunity for inventiveness. At each stage, Erikson captured the essence of playfulness by contrasting playful rituals (which contain repetition and surprise) and deadly ritualisms. The overall principle by which ritualizations are linked to playfulness is hard to conceptualize. It involves a dynamic pattern of alternating repetitive actions containing small increments of surprise or novelty. It is characterized by features common to Schiller's (1875) description of aesthetic principles that characterize play. Examples include rhythm, harmony, and balance. Playfulness is supported by successful resolution of psychosocial issues, such as trust versus mistrust, autonomy versus shame, and initiative versus guilt. This operating principle must be understood in order to recognize behavioral tendencies that reflect this disposition, and to provide guidance for those seeking to attain, or instill in others, a state of playfulness.

The first step in understanding Erikson's views on playfulness is to understand the role of ritualization in human experience. Rituals are a cultural phenomenon that serve some social function, such as facilitating the transition of a member of the culture from one social status to another. Baptisms, weddings, *bar mitzvahs*, and funerals are obvious examples of rituals that mark major transitions in social roles and developmental status. As such, they reflect macro-level developmental changes that comprise qualitatively different stages of development. At the level of microdevelopment, change is a more continuous process of repetition of rituals, accompanied by minute levels of adaptation that occur on a minute-by-minute and day-by-day developmental schedule. Over the long haul, these microdevelopmental adaptations culminate in major stage transitions that are marked by ceremonial rituals from the beginning to the ending of life, for example, christenings and funerals. In operation, the basic requirements for a ritual, according to Erikson (1977), include an element of repetition that is fairly predictable and is carried out with ceremonial detail. In animals, genetically controlled, fixed-action behaviors comprise a sort of ritual that enables members of a group or species to recognize others of its own kind. In humans, the rituals are less rigid, but no less important. Rituals which retain the features of repetition, but which contain no element of surprise or unexpected change, become, in Erikson's terms, "deadly ritualisms." Ritualisms may be invoked to provide a sense of stability when change threatens the individual. Hence, unable to negotiate an element of unexpected surprise, the anguished worker cries with a sense of urgency, "We've always done it this way!"

ERIKSON'S PSYCHOBIOGRAPHY OF EINSTEIN:
A CASE OF PLAYFULNESS

The essence of the spirit of play was, in Erikson's view, a "playful" approach to living. Einstein's life was used as an example by Erikson to provide a portrait of the playful individual and to show how one person's life could rendezvous with history to change the world. In March 1979, Erikson delivered an address at a Jerusalem symposium honoring Albert Einstein (Erikson, 1982). In May of the same year, he repeated much of that address in a colloquium sponsored by the Smithsonian Institution in celebration of the International Year of the Child and the Einstein Centenary. His Smithsonian presentation, titled "Play and Inventiveness," was filmed by the Smithsonian Institution and the negatives were stored in the Human Studies Film Archives. In 1990, the 16mm negatives of the film were loaned to Virginia Tech for the purpose of transferring them to video and making them available for educational purposes.[1] The authors transcribed the Smithsonian presentation and used it, along with the published Jerusalem paper, as a major source for this article.

Erikson's lectures on Einstein followed the psychobiography methodology used in his studies of Martin Luther (1958) and Gandhi (1969). This method involves examining Einstein's life and accomplishments within the social and historical context in order to understand his creative scientific accomplishments. He had referred to Einstein in several previous publications (e.g., "Play and Actuality," 1972; *Toys and Reasons*, 1977), but the Jerusalem and Smithsonian lectures provided him the opportunity to trace the life history of Einstein and to demonstrate systematically how playful negotiation of the stages of psychosocial development may have contributed, in part, to Einstein's scientific inventiveness. When the stages of psychosocial development are compared directly with Erikson's account of Einstein's development, they provide a congruent illustration of the play element in psychosocial theory, and indeed in sociocultural evolution.

Erikson (1972) attributes much of his understanding of Einstein to Gerald Holton, a noted science historian and biographer (see also Holton, 1978, 1986, 1995). Erikson, who viewed playfulness as a way of life, referred to Einstein's own assertion that his scientific creativity was due, in part, to the fact that he was child-like in the way he continued to ask "why" questions about the world even as an adult. Einstein's life provided Erikson with an example of a playful life—a life that produced the theory of relativity, which revolutionized humankind's view of the cosmos. The possible link between play and inventiveness was noted by Erikson in the Smithsonian presentation, "...it is in the early stages of life on which depend human playfulness and the challenges of creativity in later life" (Erikson, 1979, audio transcription).

Erikson referred to Einstein as "the victorious child" (Erikson, 1982, p. 151). This view emanated from his belief that Einstein's scientific inventiveness developed, in spite of his apparent battles with external pressures from society, and, in particular, from those charged with his education. Erikson attributed Einstein's victory to childhood family relationships which provided him with the foundations for trust, autonomy, initiative, industry, generativity, and integrity. One theme found throughout the presentation was that of a great sense of autonomy, which we interpret as a "playful" spirit or approach to life that enabled him to cope with stressful societal demands.

Ritualization and Playfulness: Erikson's Framework for Analyzing Einstein's Playfulness

Erikson's book, *Toys and Reasons* (1977), provides a systematic framework for analyzing playfulness across the lifespan. The book, an expansion of one of the 1972 Godkin Lectures given at Harvard University, includes a revision of a talk titled "Ontogeny of Ritualization in Man." Ritualization, according to Erikson, is the vital link between the ontogeny and the phylogeny of human playfulness. The six-stage framework includes rituals that are characteristic of the eight stages of psychosocial development (identity and intimacy were merged; generativity and integrity were merged). For each stage, the dominant ritualizations were described and linked to the experiences required for playful mastery of each stage. Each of the childhood ritual forms was purported to evolve into adult behavior patterns that become institutionalized. To understand the link between the ontogeny of ritualization framework, the psychosocial stages, and playfulness, it is first necessary to understand the defining characteristics of rituals. According to Erikson, the criteria are as follows: (a) meaningful regularity; (b) ceremonial attention to detail and the total procedure; (c) a symbolic sense of surpassing the reality of each participant and the deed itself; (d) a mutual activation of all concerned; and (e) a sense of absolute indispensability (p. 96).

At each stage, Erikson contrasted playful ritualization with nonplayful behaviors he called "deadly ritualisms." Ritualization, though marked by repetition, can also include an element of surprise which becomes a source of renewal and creativity. In his words, "...far from being merely repetitive ... any true ritualization, while onto-genetically grounded, is yet pervaded with the spontaneity of surprise..." (1977, p. 113). In contrast, deadly ritualism occurs, according to Erikson, when the focus is on maintaining the ritual without change. Preservation of the order precludes playfulness, creation, re-creation, and invention. In the section that follows, we will combine various sources from Erikson's work to show how Einstein's life provides an example of the link between one man's childhood play, lifelong playfulness, and scientific invention.

Erikson's Jerusalem (1982) and Smithsonian (1979) presentations were organized around narratives of specific episodes in the life of Einstein. Since the resolution of psychosocial issues is a lifespan process of resolving and revisiting those issues, the psychosocial struggles were experienced in various forms throughout Einstein's life. Therefore, to provide a systematic framework for this article, we arranged our analysis according to the critical issues that are normally central in the eight stages of psychosocial development, as proposed by Erikson in *Childhood and Society* (1950), in Chapter 7, "Eight Ages of Man."

Trust versus Mistrust

According to Erikson (1950), the first stage of psychosocial development focuses on the resolution of the issues of trust versus mistrust, and this theme occupies center stage during the period of infancy. Much of the establishment of trust occurs when parents and infants engage in reciprocal play as they form an attachment bond. The first form of playful ritualizations occur in infancy in what Erikson (1977) labels "mutuality of recognition." Daily rituals of caregiving associated with the infant's physical needs center around feeding, sleeping, touching, and looking. The caregiver alternates brief absence with reappearance, thus providing practice in separation and greeting. The infant game "peek-a-boo," for example, is a playful ritualization exemplifying mutuality of recognition. Adult caregivers know that once the infant has mastered simple facial recognition through repetitive exposure and absence, the game becomes boring. Variations of facial expression and position introduce an element of surprise that often results in squeals of delight. Mutuality of recognition is extended into adulthood through ritualistic greetings such as handshakes, chants, displays of symbols, and pictures of faces, all of which help us recognize others who belong to the same group. For example, ritualistic greetings of unseen family members often result in great surprise in recognizing the same, but very changed, cousin. A poignant example of ritualized recognition appeared in the movie *The Color Purple*, when two sisters, separated in childhood and reunited in adulthood, greeted each other with a childhood hand-clapping game and chant. According to Erikson, mutuality of recognition becomes a deadly ritualism if it is degraded to focus on unchanging or "idolized" images. For example, if statues or symbols of charismatic leaders replace the ideas which originally fueled the spirit of the ideology, it is an indication of a lack of openness to change.

In the Smithsonian presentation, Erikson (1979) speculated that the playful mother-child interactions surrounding the act of mutual recognition likely contributed to Einstein's sense of wonder. In Erikson's words:

> ...little Albert's open-eyed wonder was necessarily rooted in an early basic trust such as cannot emerge without the experience of that mutual recognition of mother and child

or what Joan Erikson has described as the "eye to eye" relationship which he expressed in many ways later on when he spoke about his relationship to the world of data. (audio transcription)

Einstein's basic trust received continued support in his school years when his mother permitted him the leeway to play classical music in his own way, thus developing initiative and industry. Erikson commented, "...one has indeed the strong impression that his mother, from the beginning had cultivated active trust by not trying to coerce him to learn what he mistrusted" (1979, audio transcription).

Autonomy versus Shame

The second struggle in Erikson's "eight ages," autonomy versus shame, is foremost in the life of the toddler. It is at this time of life that society, represented by the family, places demands on the child for compliance to standards of behavior that are sanctioned by the culture. It co-occurs with the child's newly discovered "self" as an independent, autonomous individual, capable of making choices and exerting one's "will." The power to exert one's will often takes the form of refusal to comply, as is characterized by the infamous toddler characteristic of replying "no" to a myriad of requests. Failure to comply generally elicits condemning looks (metaphorically speaking), which make it difficult for the child to "face himself" in others. Thus, condemning eyes and voices ("Shame on you") elicit a sense of shame in having not lived up to the expectations of significant others. In the socialization process, the toddler learns the boundaries—what is sanctioned, or "good," and what is forbidden, or "bad." Like all of the psychosocial stages described by Erikson (1950), the central issue of autonomy versus shame continues in altered forms throughout life.

The element of play in the stage of autonomy versus shame is in the interplay between the two polar entities. Autonomous players repeatedly test the boundaries at all ages. They dare to "leap" into new experiences, as Plato suggested, and if they leap too far, they go "out of bounds." Resilience is required to "leap back up" from experiences of shame. All this requires spiritual energy, which is apparently available to those who have leapt from a base which can be trusted to be available upon return, for example, basic trust.

Ritualization during early childhood involves training the child to become a member of a social community, necessitating discrimination between good and bad. The child must learn the boundaries of what is permissible and what is forbidden. Erikson (1977) labeled this form of ritualization "judicious" (p. 92). The adult ritual for testing the boundaries of the permissible is the courtroom trial. A playful approach to rules is to test the limits of what is permissible. When judicial decisions focus on the letter of the law rather than the spirit of the law, the deadly ritualism, which Erikson called "legalism" (p. 97), has occurred.

In his Smithsonian presentation, Erikson illustrated Einstein's autonomy with examples from various stages of his life. As a school-age boy, Einstein resisted learning, which was externally imposed. On one occasion, he expressed rage against a private teacher who came to his house by striking her with a chair. Though he resisted forced instruction, Einstein utilized his own methods of learning. Erikson commented that young Albert's resistance to militaristic teaching styles reflected a character trait which permitted him to remain free to learn in his own way. Einstein himself, in his 1950 book, *Out of My Later Years*, maintained passionately that education should evoke the spirit of play in children, rather than relying on "…methods of fear, force and artificial authority" (p. 33). Erikson was particularly impressed by Einstein's autonomous personality which enabled him to ignore taunts by peers, always ready to "laugh at any false authority" (1979, audio transcription).

Einstein's autonomous strivings evidenced themselves during his later schooling experiences. His experiences with classical German teachers, possibly influenced by a Prussian style of military training, heightened Einstein's resistance. Consequently, according to Erikson, he was asked to leave school because his presence spoiled the respect of the class. According to Erikson (1982), Einstein himself later wrote, "…fate, to punish me for my contempt of authority, made me an authority myself" (p. 156).

Erikson (1979) attributed Einstein's lifelong autonomy to the ability to preserve his "child" within, in spite of external pressures to conform.

> Thus, Einstein, we may conclude, succeeded in saving the child in himself, even when increasingly he had to accept, with a kind of non-violent resistance, isolation and even punishment, rather than submit to standardized formulations. (audio transcription)

Initiative versus Guilt

In the preschool stage of psychosocial development, referred to as "initiative versus guilt," Erikson (1950) notes that "a new hope and new responsibility" (p. 255) develops. The capacity for imagination and creativity results in the production of artifacts—stories, discovery of relationships, art, and ideas. Trust and autonomy provide the foundation for hope that a project can be attempted and finished. The negative counterpart of initiative is guilt over having gone too far with actions or imaginary deeds.

In the preschool years, playful ritualizations assume the form of drama. Dramas are stories with plots that depict human struggles as played out on various stages by various actors. Dramatic play reflects much of the range of themes in the human experience—conflict and resolution, love and hate, caregiving and aggression, power and helplessness. Playful dramatizations allow for creating possible future selves through role-play. If a playful spirit is retained in adulthood, it allows for flexibility in playing a variety of ever-changing family, career, and community roles.

The adult form of the dramatic is the theater. If drama becomes an inflexible impersonation of a role, it has, according to Erikson (1977), become a deadly ritualism. Erikson gave as examples adults who feel stuck in their career or family role, as well as those situations in which adults act as if they were playing without the flexibility of changing roles, for instance, playing their roles "in dead earnestness" (p. 102). He included in this category playing without the accompanying sense of joy or ego mastery.

Erikson believed that Einstein's tireless initiative affected his life. He cited here Maja's (Einstein's younger sister) reports of young Albert's persistence with puzzles, block building, and his construction of elaborate houses of cards. Erikson suggested a possible link between Einstein's constructive play and his theory of relativity because of Einstein's frequently quoted statement:

I saw it all first in forms, that means like jigsaw puzzles, and then I translated it into mathematics. (cited in Erikson, 1979, audio transcription)

Erikson (1979) commented on the relationship between the autonomous learning style described earlier and Einstein's initiative in creating new ideas and visualizing relationships not previously understood. The link is in the intuitive beholding of an idea, rather than rushing to premature completion. As an example of how imaginative thinking characterized Einstein's scientific creativity, Erikson recalled how, in 1944, Einstein declared that a combinatory play of a visual/muscular type occurred in his productive thought, before there was any connection with a logical construction that could be communicated to others.

Industry versus Inferiority

The fourth psychosocial struggle, industry versus inferiority, occupies the developing individual's energy most prominently during the school-age years. The capacity for learning the crafts of society, including academics, enables the child to develop a positive sense of industry, which is characterized by high levels of esteem and perceived competence (Harter, 1983). When attempts to master skills valued by society fail, a sense of inferiority ensues.

During the school age years, children attend to ritualization that involves formal procedures, proper methods, and the "right way" to play the game. Thus, nonplayful individuals attend obsessively to the "correct" way to use a recipe or a blueprint, unable to "let go" of the ritual. Erikson apparently believed that the successful negotiation of a sense of industry co-occurred with Einstein's consistent, continual playfulness. He indicated that Einstein was influenced not only by his mother's industriousness as demonstrated in her needlework, but also by her attitude and disposition. For example, after reviewing the written recollections of Einstein's sister, Maja, Erikson noted

...his mother inspired and cultivated his lifelong devotion to musical activity, here too incidentally, letting him find his own way to play Bach and Mozart, and as his sister suggests, to think musically on the piano. (1979, audio transcription)

Indeed, the postulation of a link between parental modeling of the disposition toward hobbies and leisure activity was recently borne out in research reported by Chick and Barnett (1995).

Identity versus Identity Confusion

Although the rudiments of identity exist at all ages, adolescence is a time for youth to begin to explore their identities (Erikson, 1968). Erikson (1956) proposed a moratorium, which allows the delay of commitment to occupation, religion, and political allegiance until playful exploration of a variety of roles permits choice and, hence, commitment to identities that are congruent with one's ideals.

The playful ritualizations of adolescence focus on solidarity of convictions, according to Erikson (1977). Adolescents create secret rites to signal fidelity and to mark initiation into a group. Spontaneously created rites allow for playful group processes. Solidity of conviction, if successfully carried into adulthood, evolves into ideological stances that characterize one's identity. Examples include religious conviction, political affiliation, and commitment to family relationships. In contrast, if group solidarity is symbolized by an unchanging ritual that becomes focused on the ritual itself rather than the ideological stance, the deadly ritualism which Erikson terms "elitism" is present. A poignant example was seen in recent years when it became public knowledge that initiation into a soldier's elite group involved a savage rite in which a metal pin was pounded into the chest of new initiates (McAllister, 1997).

Einstein's identity was formed by the sociohistorical context. Erikson noted that he was born to an enlightened and "free-thinking" Jewish family who had no hesitation in sending him to a Catholic public school. Yet, at one point in his development, Einstein is said to have been preoccupied with the diligent observance of orthodox Jewish practices. According to Erikson (1979), the family was so free-thinking that "they allowed Albert to take even religion seriously, at least for a while" (audio transcription). Apparently, Erikson was referring to Einstein's serious attention to meticulous observance of Jewish rules, for example, those governing dietary practices. It seems that Einstein was experimenting with a possible future role as a devout Jew, a role he later abandoned (Folsing, 1997) and then pursued in later life, albeit on Einstein's own terms.

The moratorium, which precedes commitment to identity, seemed to be characterized in Einstein by a choice to temporarily withdraw from certain roles. With the support of his father and physician, he obtained permission to withdraw from the highly restrictive military-style school. Later, he disengaged from Jewish religious affiliations, as well as from German citizenship (Folsing, 1997). Young Albert had a period of schooling in a Swiss institution with a Pestalozzian tradition, which permitted him leeway to think according to his "learning style." Erikson (1979, audio transcription) speculated that this experience may have been linked to Einstein's decision to choose his own identity as "a scientist, a universal citizen, and as an ethnic Jew."

If we accept recent views that lifespan identity development is a dynamic process of constructing, deconstructing, and reconstructing the self (Berzonsky, 1993; Kroger, 1989), Erikson's views of playfulness combine developmental identity to suggest that the adaptive personality is one that continuously reinvents the self. As such, the playful personality is one that is capable of bringing to work, family, and community roles the capacity for inventive problem solving and creative living.

Intimacy versus Isolation

Successful achievement of identity supports the possibility of establishing intimacy in young adulthood. Intimacy involves the willingness to reveal one's innermost self—the fears and hopes—to another. Erikson spoke of intimacy as an activity in which one finds one's self by losing oneself in another. Failure to achieve intimacy results in a sense of isolation and loneliness. Erikson did not give indepth coverage to the playful ritualizations of intimacy. Some examples of ritualizations that celebrate intimacy include engagement announcements and weddings. The maintenance of a lively relationship requires continuous renewal in daily rituals. Perhaps people who stay in relationships when genuine interest and lively renewal cannot be maintained are acting in what Erikson (1977) describes as a deadly impersonation of a role (the ritualism of the stage of identity).

Erikson provided an interesting interpretation of Einstein's resolution of the sixth stage, intimacy versus isolation. A popular image of Einstein is that he was lonely; biographers (e.g., Folsing, 1997; Hoffman & Dukas, 1972; Pyenson, 1985) consistently pointed out that Einstein was a loner, both in his childhood and in his adult years. While some project into this a possible lonely sense of isolation, Einstein seemed to have preferred solitude for the pursuit of his work. Einstein's capacity for solitude may have been a contributing factor in his ability to remain focused on his work. Indeed, Csikszentmihalyi (1997) noted that solitude is necessary in order to acquire skills that require concentration. He reported that adolescent participants in his research who felt that they must always be with friends tended not to have the psychic energy necessary for complex learning and to persist with complex problem solving tasks. Besides providing the opportunity for focused attention, Einstein apparently enjoyed his solitude. When he was ready to share his scientific insights and when he needed support and feedback from others, he frequently sought the company of some lifelong colleagues with whom he was willing to reveal his deepest thoughts—certainly a form of intimacy. Vera John-Steiner, in *Notebooks of the Mind* (1985), reiterated the importance of community and friendships for the development of creative work. She cited as an example the friendship of Einstein and the mathematician Marcel Grossman, with whom Einstein corresponded and tested some of his ideas. In 1912, when the two worked together, Grossman provided mathematical tools and contributed to final formulation of Einstein's gravitational theory. So, far from being lonely, Einstein experienced intimacy, but the focus remained on the creative challenge before him. Erikson contrasted the popular image of the "lonely" Einstein with the following perspective.

> Here I must say, however, when one reads some of his letters, and sees the reflection of some of the surviving members of his inner circle, one cannot doubt that this man

knew, and knew how to give to some selected individuals, some intense sense of intimacy. (1979, audio transcription)

Generativity versus Stagnation

Generativity occurs in mature adulthood when individuals take on the responsibility for nurturing the next generation, as in parenting or contributing to the evolution of the culture through one's accomplishments. Generativity's negative counterpart is stagnation or self-absorption. Acts of generativity, in the words of Csikszentmihalyi (1996), may include the transmission of one's own "genes or memes" (p. 199). Csikszentmihalyi used the term "meme" to refer to artifacts that are selected by the culture to be passed on to future generations. Great works of art, social structures, and scientific inventions are among the many possible creations which can become memes. Einstein's memes were advancements in the field of physics.

As for the stages of the ontogeny of ritualization, Erikson's framework (1977) combined the stage of generativity with that of integrity and formed the stage of ritualization called "Generational Sanction" (p. 114). In this role, the mature and generative adult echoes and reaffirms "...the informal ritualizations of childhood and youth" (p. 111). Erikson noted how old people and young children have an affinity for each other, a trait frequently attributed to Einstein's interactions with children. Reaffirming one's childhood ritualizations provides a unity of culture. In serving the function of generational sanction, the "...adult must act with an authoritative stance and reassurance, bolstered by a faith that they are acting in the image of 'God the Father, above all the kings, as a parent image ... who surely knew what He was doing when He created us in His image....'" (p. 111). Should the authority become obsessively power-focused, rather than care-focused, it will degenerate into the negative counterpart of generational sanction, for example, sapientism, a condition in which the unwise pretend to the next generation that they are wise. Folsing (1997) noted that Einstein refused to be classified as an authority and frequently engaged in playful self-derogatory remarked to avoid the image of authority. One of Einstein's generational acts of caring for the future generations was to write passionately about the need for educational practices that are free of sapientism. Einstein wrote:

> The development of science and of the creative activities of the spirit in general requires ... freedom of the spirit which consists in the independence of thought from the restrictions of authoritarian and social prejudices as well as from unphilosophical routinizing and habit in general. (1950, p. 13)

Integrity versus Despair

In the Smithsonian and Jerusalem presentations, little direct reference was made to the issue of integrity versus despair, the final stage in which the individual reviews life and confronts death as a natural part of it, or develops a sense of despair. Nevertheless, biographies of Einstein reveal that he had apparently confronted death. For example, when he was nominated for the Nobel Prize, Einstein was asked to write an autobiography to which he responded with the question of whether this was to be his obituary. The resulting autobiography was a listing of his scientific accomplishments, apparently his view of what comprised his life, his identity, and his own sense of integrity. Feldman (1994) seems to have made a stronger statement about Einstein's integrity than did Erikson (1979, 1982). After conducting a thorough study of Einstein's life and creativity, Feldman concluded "...Einstein's scientific genius, his aesthetic and religious sense, and his involvement with the world's problems may add up to a coherent human being" (1994, p. 130).

Einstein's Play: A Rendezvous With History

Erikson's major conclusion from his brief psychobiography of Einstein was that there were supportive conditions which coincided with the historical context, including the state of the field of physics, creating a "rendezvous with history." His conclusion is corroborated by current thinking in the field of creativity. For example, a framework proposed by Feldman, Csikszentmihalyi, and Gardner (1994), called the Domain Individual Field Interaction (DIFI) model, includes the interaction between the individual, the domain, and the field. The individual brings personal traits, skills, and experiences; the domain represents the area of creativity (e.g., art, music, medicine, science), and the field is the state of knowledge of a field of practice at a given time, including the individuals who decide what new inventions are admitted to the field for presentation to the next generation. In Einstein's case, the interaction between the mind and the domain was described by Csikszentmihalyi (1996):

> A domain generates novelty only when there is a convergence between an instability within it and the mind of a person who is able to cope with the problem. Therefore, even the most creative persons usually contribute only a few, sometimes only one, great new idea—the one they were prepared for, the one for which the timing was right. (p. 339)

Gardner (1994) described the totality of the relationship between the creative individual and a historically situated set of knowledge. This perspective is congruent with Erikson's psychohistorical approach. In his chapter, titled "The Creator's Patterns," Gardner noted: "Individuals are not creative (or noncreative) in general; they are creative in particular domains of accomplishment, and require the achievement of expertise in these domains before they can execute significant creative work" (p. 71). Holton, a science historian whose work influenced Erikson, describes further synchrony needed between an individual and a field in order for scientific advancement to occur. He wrote: "I conclude that in pursuing the documentable cases of 'impact' of one person or field on another ... there exists a mutual adaptation and resonance of the innovative mind with portions of the total set of metaphors current at a given time" (1986, p. 122). An amusement park ride was used by Feldman (1994) as a metaphor for the synchronicity between the creative individual, the domain, and the field. The metaphor represented the dynamic processes of "...coordination, change, adjustment, and new coordinations" (p. 109) between the individual and the total environment available.

The current perspectives on the conditions necessary for scientific inventiveness and other forms of creativity both reflect and extend Erikson's psychohistorical approach. At the minimum, all seem to agree with Erikson's (1958) assertion that "...you can't take the case history out of history..." (pp. 15–16). Einstein, it seems, was the right individual, in the right domain, in the right field, at the right time.

BEYOND ERIKSON: CONTEMPORARY PERSPECTIVES ON PLAYFULNESS

Erikson's approach to play and playfulness finds support in contemporary work, albeit, from alternative perspectives. Contemporary research on the link between play and inventiveness falls into the domain of play as a behavioral disposition (e.g., Barnett, 1990, 1991a, 1991b), playfulness as a personality trait (Rogers, et al., 1998), and theoretical paradigms for viewing the relationship between individual lives and creativity (e.g., Csikszentmihalyi, 1996; Gardner, 1994). While operating from alternative paradigms, current research and theory seem to not only complement Erikson's work, but also to provide confirmation for some of his assumptions and postulations.

Defining and Measuring Playfulness

One of Erikson's contemporaries, Nina Lieberman, pursued independently of Erikson's work the study of behavioral manifestations of the spirit of play. Although her perspective lacked sufficient grounding in previous theories, she provided the field with a focus on playfulness as a behavioral disposition, thus evoking a paradigm shift from the focus on discrete play behaviors. Lieberman (1965, 1967, 1977) defined playfulness as physical, cognitive and social spontaneity, manifest joy, and humor, and reported that playfulness in children was a unitary behavioral predisposition. Building on Lieberman's work, Barnett (1990, 1991a, 1991b) developed a more reliable measure of playfulness and provided data to support the proposition that playfulness is a unidimensional trait. Barnett (1991b) found the playful child to be characterized as imaginative, active, affective, confident, aggressive, and mischievous—all traits mentioned by Einstein's biographers.

Another approach to defining playfulness was reported by Rogers, et al. (1998). These researchers used the disposition dimension of the tripartite definition of play (behavior, context, disposition) put forth by Rubin, Fein, and Vandenberg (1983), which distinguishes play dispositions according to criteria related to (a) motivation source, (b) orientation to goals, (c) degree of domination by stimuli, (d) degree of nonliterality, (e) rule boundedness, and (f) degree of active involvement. Rogers, et al., developed a trait-rating instrument (Child Behaviors Inventory) to measure playfulness based on those criteria. Factor analysis of data obtained from parents' and teachers' ratings of preschool and elementary school children yielded a principle component called playfulness that was independent of gender and age. It is not known whether an adult extension of the trait-rating instrument will indicate that the playfulness trait demonstrates continuity across the lifespan.

Recently, Glynn and Webster (1992, 1993) used the Rubin, Fein, and Vandenberg (1983) criterion for the dispositions of play to develop an instrument designed to measure playfulness as a trait among adults. Their study of 550 highly intelligent individuals yielded a positive correlation between playfulness and innovative attitudes and intrinsic motivational orientation—traits which biographies of Einstein repeatedly mention (see Folsing, 1997). We can only speculate how Einstein's parents and teachers might have rated his playfulness, or how his colleagues and friends would have rated him as an adult, if an appropriate trait-rating instrument had been available. However, anecdotal data from biographies certainly suggest that his playfulness scores would have been high.

Even if we could demonstrate empirically that Einstein's disposition would yield a characterization of "playful" on a trait-rating scale, there is no definitive evidence that his childhood play contributed directly to his adult inventiveness. In fact, there was no reason to suspect in Einstein's childhood that he would become known for his scientific inventiveness. Though he was apparently a reasonably good achiever in school, he was not, in fact, precocious (Folsing, 1997). Attempts to draw links between specific childhood events or traits and adult inventiveness are often embellished in retrospect. Csikszentmihalyi (1996) put this in perspective in the following statement:

> But if the real childhood accomplishments of creative individuals are no different from those of many others who never attain any distinction, the mind will do its best to weave appealing stories to compensate for reality's lack of imagination. (p. 155)

Retrospective speculation about what Albert Einstein's playfulness scores would be if measured today represents a great "leap" from research grounded in reality. However, the modern measures do provide a new perspective through which to view history, and as such serve to help generate hypotheses worthy of researchers' attention.

Contemporary Views on Creativity Within the Sociocultural Context

Erikson's (1979, 1982) analysis of Einstein's psychobiography did not lead him to conclude that either extraordinary parenting, childhood play, or adult playfulness led directly to scientific inventiveness. For example, though Erikson described Einstein's parents as warm, supportive, and open to input by young Albert, the parenting was seen as a contributing factor, not a causal factor in Albert's basic trust, autonomy, and industry. Rather, the totality of Einstein's childhood experiences, combined with his strong autonomous strivings and sense of playful independence, were presented as supportive conditions that allowed the possibility of continual renewal in adulthood. That Einstein retained a sense of playfulness in adulthood is corroborated by Einstein's biographers, who mention frequently that Einstein attributed his success to his ability to continue to ask the questions that only children ask well into adulthood. Thus, we can conclude that Einstein experienced, at least, the conditions necessary for carrying a sense of autonomy and playfulness into adulthood—a condition corroborated by Csikszentmihalyi's (1996) study of the lives of creative people.

Csikszentmihalyi's (1996) recent research provides contemporary support that the factors proposed by Erikson as being important in inventiveness are were, indeed, important. Csikszentmihalyi interviewed 100 eminent creators and from his analysis of that qualitative data, enumerated 10 descriptors of the creative personality. Several descriptors appear on both Csikszentmihalyi's list and in biographies of Einstein. For example, Csikszentmihalyi lists the ability to use both convergent and divergent thinking and the flexibility to switch from one to the other. Einstein was able to play with images of the visual sensory type and to create imaginative scenes which were metaphors for problems he was seeking to solve (Holton, 1986, 1995). Yet, he was also able to separate irrelevant data in order to converge on specific facts essential in the problem solving process.

Another of Csikszentmihalyi's (1996) descriptors of creative personalities is the combination of playfulness and discipline, irresponsibility alternating with perseverance and hard work. Einstein's play with scientific ideas was achieved in the midst of disciplined research.

A third pattern attributed to creative individuals is an alternation between fantasy and reality, for example, "novelty rooted in reality," (p. 63). Einstein allowed himself to "let go" of traditional views of physics, but grounded his new ideas in the reality of knowledge available to physicists at the time. He avoided family responsibilities, yet demonstrated unusual discipline in his search for scientific truths. A fourth descriptor of the creative personality listed by Csikszentmihalyi is the tendency toward both extroversion and introversion, also reflected Einstein's pattern. Einstein did not care to join his childhood peers in play and shunned the public as an adult. In his 1950 book, *Out of My Later Years*, Einstein wrote, "I live in that solitude which is painful in youth, but delicious in the years of maturity" (p. 5).

Csikszentmihalyi (1996) also found that his famous creators were both proud and humble at the same time, a trait receiving commentary by Einstein's biographers. Further, Csikszentmihalyi commented on the tendency of creators to be both conservative and traditional at the same time. He cited the fact that even while Einstein was in the midst of revolutionizing physics, he nevertheless chose to play on his violin the most traditional classics of music. The artists/inventors/creators interviewed by Csikszentmihalyi were both passionate and objective about their work and had an openness and sensitivity, exposing them to suffering and pain, and yet experiencing a great deal of enjoyment. Examples of these sensitivities can be found in numerous biographies of Einstein.

Perhaps the one single feature of the lives of the great creators interviewed by Csikszentmihalyi (1996) that contrasted with the life of Einstein, yet confirmed one principle factor in the creative process, was that most of Csikszentmihalyi's interviewees reported stable, satisfying marriages. While, at first, this aspect of Einstein's life does not appear to fit the pattern of modern creators, he did in fact have the essential support from his colleagues.

Einstein took care to avoid family responsibilities that would have prevented him from pursuing his work, thus illustrating another of the traits of great inventors, i.e., the ability to focus and persevere in a task (Csikszentmihalyi, 1996). He attributed the necessity for focused attention to the need to preserve psychic energy. He pointed to the fact that people working two jobs and working women with children have little uncommitted attention left over to deal with novelty. In fact, in his book *Creativity*, Csikszentmihalyi referred to one of the popular images of Einstein—that he wore the same baggy pants and old sweater day after day. In Csikszentmihalyi's words, "He was just cutting down on the daily effort involved in deciding what clothes to wear, so that his mind could focus on matters that to him were more important" (p. 351). The opportunity to focus attention is limited to a privileged few, of which Einstein was one. According to Csikszentmihalyi (1997), "...most women in the world still have to devote a major part of their lives to keeping the material and emotional infrastructure of their families from collapsing" (p.11). According to his biographers, Einstein apparently viewed women, especially his second wife, Elsa, as a convenience that made it possible to live a comfortable life This lifestyle may have freed psychic energy for the pursuit of his overarching passionate goal—physics.

In listing characteristics of creative people he studied, Gardner (1994) stated, "All of them were quite prepared to use individuals and then to discard them when their utility was at an end" (p. 76). Einstein's first wife, Mileva Maric, collaborated with him while in school and later assisted his work by applying her mathematics skills. However, after a few years of seemingly happy marriage, Einstein found more comfort and joy with his cousin Elsa, whom he married after divorcing Mileva. He admitted to his second wife that he was not suited "...to the role of a faithful husband" (Folsing, 1997, p. 616) and he was seen frequently in the company of beautiful women. Folsing reported an incident in which Elsa and Albert Einstein had a confrontation when one of Albert's female companions arrived to pick him up for an evening out. Elsa refused to give Albert money for their activities. Sadly, it seems that Einstein might qualify for inclusion in Gardner's group of men who "use" others to their own utility.

One final match exists between Csikszentmihalyi's (1996) creators and Einstein's psychosocial development, and that is in the realm of generativity. Csikszentmihalyi's subjects, although utterly absorbed in their projects, became involved with historic and social issues. Einstein spent much of his time in later years writing, speaking, and contributing money to advance the causes of peace and Zionism. Folsing (1997) reported that Einstein gave generously to help Jews relocate from Nazi Germany. He spoke out as a pacifist in response to the onset of World War II and continued his protests against the development of nuclear weapons until the very end of his life. In fact, what became known as the Russell-Einstein Manifesto was the last letter signed by Einstein (April 11, 1955). In it, Bertrand Russell and Albert Einstein warned that "...in a nuclear war there would be neither victors nor vanquished, only total catastrophe" (Folsing, 1997, p. 738). Einstein's involvement in global issues exemplifies Csikszentmihalyi's conclusion that it is a "...myth that creators are too wrapped up in their own work to care about the rest of world" (1996, p. 201).

CONCLUSION

The major thesis of Erikson's psychohistorical approach is that childhood psychosocial experiences and personality dispositions must be coupled with expertise and must intersect with history in a very specific way in order to revolutionize the world. His view of Einstein's life was that it was "...a rendezvous in the here and now between man's scientific insight and the universal locus" (1979, audio transcription). Erikson's perspective is congruent with Holton's (1978, 1986, 1995) explanations of processes functioning in the evolution of science. "By acknowledging the role of history in Einstein's development, we gain the insight that, not only does one person's imagination transform history, but also that the individual's imagination is also formed, in part by history itself" (Lifton, 1996).

Feldman, Csikszentmihalyi, and Gardner (1994) pointed out that Erikson's psychohistories failed to provide either a coherent set of generalizations about the nature of creativity or a systematic framework for studying creativity. The model they proposed (DIFI) extends rather than replaces Erikson's view. All in all, we can only conclude that, while current research and theory on play offer a variety of paradigms from which to view play, the basic elements of the playful life, the aesthetic life, remain the same and each new paradigm provides, in Erikson's (1950) own words, "a way of looking at things" (p. 403).

NOTES

[1] Wilton S. Dillon, Director of Interdisciplinary Studies, Smithsonian Institution, is thanked for making the films available. Video copies of Erikson's presentation, titled "Play and Inventiveness," will be available soon through the Department of Human Development, Virginia Tech, Blacksburg, VA 24060. Contact the first author for more information.

REFERENCES

Adams, G. R., Bennion, L., & Huh, K. (1987). *Objective measure of ego identity status: A reference manual.* Unpublished manuscript, Utah State University.

Barnett, L. A. (1990). Playfulness: Definition, design, and measurement. *Play and Culture, 3,* 319–336.

Barnett, L. A. (1991a). The playful child: Measurement of the disposition to play. *Play and Culture, 4,* 51–74.

Barnett, L. A. (1991b). Characterizing playfulness: Correlates with individual attributes and personality traits. *Play and Culture, 4,* 371–393.

Berzonsky, M. D. (1993). A constructivist view of identity development: People as postpositivist self-theorists. In J. Kroger (Ed.), *Discussions on ego identity* (pp. 169–203). Hillsdale, NJ: Lawrence Erlbaum.

Bradley, C. L. (1997). Generativity-stagnation: Development of a status model. *Developmental Review, 17,* 262–290.

Bredekamp, S., & Copple, C. (Eds.). (1997). *Developmentally appropriate practice in early childhood programs* (Rev. ed.). Washington, DC: National Association for the Education of Young Children.

Budd, B. E., Clance, P. R., & Simerly, D. E. (1985). Spatial configurations: Erikson reexamined. *Sex Roles, 12,* 571–577.

Carter, S. (1990). I danced in the morning. In *The Presbyterian hymnal* (pp. 302–303). Louisville, KY: Westminster/John Knox. (Original work published 1963)

Chick, G., & Barnett, L. A. (1995). Children's play and adult leisure. In A. D. Pellegrini (Ed.), *The future of play theory* (pp. 45–69). Albany, NY: State University of New York Press.

Csikszentmihalyi, M. (1996). *Creativity.* New York: HarperCollins.

Csikszentmihalyi, M. (1997). *Finding flow.* New York: Basic Books.

Einstein, A. E. (1950). *Out of my later years.* New York: Philosophical Library.

Erikson, E. H. (1940). Studies in the interpretation of play: Clinical observation of play disruption in young children. *Genetic Psychology Monographs, 22,* 557–671.

Erikson, E. H. (1950). *Childhood and society.* New York: W. W. Norton.

Erikson, E. H. (1956). Ego identity and the psychosocial moratorium. In *New perspectives for research on juvenile delinquency* (pp. 1–23). Washington, DC: Children's Bureau, U. S. Department of Health, Education and Welfare.

Erikson, E. H. (1958). *Young man Luther: A study in psychoanalysis and history.* New York: Norton.

Erikson, E. H. (1968). *Identity: Youth and crisis.* New York: Norton.

Erikson, E. H. (1969). *Gandhi's truth.* New York: Norton.

Erikson, E. H. (1972). Play and actuality. In M. W. Piers (Ed.), *Play and development* (pp. 127–167). New York: W. W. Norton.

Erikson, E. H. (1977). *Toys and reasons.* New York: W. W. Norton.

Erikson, E. H. (1979, May). *Play and inventiveness.* Colloquium conducted at the Smithsonian Institution in observance of the International Year of the Child and the Einstein Centennial, Washington, DC.

Erikson, E. H. (1982). Psychoanalytic reflections on Einstein's centenary. In G. Holton & Y. Elkana (Eds.), *Albert Einstein: Historical and cultural perspectives* (pp. 151–173). Princeton, NJ: Princeton University Press.

Farjeon, E. (1990). Morning has broken. In *The Presbyterian Hymnal* (p. 469). Louisville, KY: Westminster/John Knox. (Original work published 1931)

Feldman, D. H. (1994). Creativity: Dreams, insights, and transformations. In D. H. Feldman, M. Csikszentmihalyi, & H. Gardner (Eds.), *Changing the world* (pp. 103–134). Westport, CT: Praeger.

Feldman, D. H., Csikszentmihalyi, M., & Gardner, H. (1994). A framework for the study of creativity. In D. H. Feldman, M. Csikszentmihalyi, & H. Gardner (Eds.), *Changing the world* (pp. 1–45). Westport, CT: Praeger.

Folsing, A. (1997). *Albert Einstein: A biography.* New York: Penguin.

Gardner, H. (1993). *Creating minds.* New York: Basic Books.

Gardner, H. (1994). The creators' patterns. In D. H. Feldman, M. Csikszentmihalyi, & H. Gardner (Eds.), *Changing the world* (pp. 69–84). Westport, CT: Praeger.

Gilligan, C. (1979) Woman's place in man's life cycle. *Harvard Educational Review, 49,* 431–446.

Glynn, M. A., & Webster, J. (1992). The adult playfulness scale: An initial assessment. *Psychological Reports, 71,* 83–103.

Glynn, M. A., & Webster, J. (1993). Refining the nomological net of the adult playfulness scale: Personality, motivational, and attitudinal correlates for highly intelligent adults. *Psychological Reports, 72,* 1023–1026.

Hamachek, D. (1994). Changes in the self from a developmental/psychosocial perspective. In T. M. Brinthaupt (Ed.), *Change in the self* (pp. 21–68). Albany, NY: State University of New York Press.

Harter, S. (1983). Developmental perspectives on the self-system. In P. H. Mussen (Series Ed.) & E. M. Hetherington (Vol. Ed.), *Handbook of child psychology: Vol. 4. Socialization, personality, and social development* (pp. 275–385). New York: Wiley.

Hoffman, B., & Dukas, H. (1972). *Albert Einstein: Creator and rebel.* New York: Plume.

Holton, G. (1978). *The scientific imagination.* Cambridge, England: Cambridge University Press.

Holton, G. (1986). *The advancement of science, and its burdens.* Cambridge, England: Cambridge University Press.

Holton, G. (1995). *Einstein, history, and other passions.* Woodbury, NY: American Institute of Physics.

John-Steiner, V. (1985). *Notebooks of the mind.* Albuquerque, NM: University of New Mexico Press.

Kroger, J. (1989). *Identity in adolescence: The balance between self and other.* New York: Routledge.

Levy, J. (1978). *Play behavior.* New York: Wiley.

Lieberman, J. N. (1965). Playfulness and divergent thinking: An investigation of their relationship at the kindergarten level. *Journal of Genetic Psychology, 107,* 219–224.

Lieberman, J. N. (1967). A developmental analysis of playfulness as a clue to cognitive style. *Journal of Creative Behavior, 1,* 391–397.

Lieberman, J. N. (1977). *Playfulness: Its relationship to imagination and creativity.* New York: Academic Press.

Lifton, R. J. (1996). Entering history: Erik Erikson's new psychological landscape. *Psychoanalysis and Contemporary Thought, 19,* 259–275.

McAllister, B. (1997, July 12) Discharge is recommended for sergeant involved in Marine wing-pinning ritual. *The Washington Post,* p. A7.

Pyenson, L. (1985). *The young Einstein.* Boston: Adam Hilger.

Rogers, C. S., Impara, J. C., Frary, R. B., Harris, T., Meeks, A., Semanic-Lauth, S., & Reynolds, M. R. (1998). Measuring playfulness: Development of the child behaviors inventory of playfulness. In S. Reifel (Vol. Ed.) & M. C. Duncan, G. Chick, & A. Aycock (Series Eds.), *Play & culture studies, volume 1* (pp. 151–168). Greenwich, CT: Ablex.

Rogers, C. S., & Sawyers, J. K. (1995). *Play in the lives of young children.* Washington, DC: National Association for the Education of Young Children. (Original work published 1988)

Rubin, K. H., Fein, G., & Vandenberg, B. (1983). Play. In P. H. Mussen (Series Ed.) & E. M. Hetherington (Vol. Ed.), *Handbook of child psychology: Vol. 4. Socialization, personality, and social development* (pp. 693–774). New York: Wiley.

Schiller, F. (1875a). *Essays: Aesthetical and philosophical.* London: George Bell.

Schiller, F. (1875b). Hymn to joy. In E. A. Bowring (Trans.), *The poems of Schiller* (2nd ed., pp. 63–66). London: George Bell.

2

Playing with the Sacrificial Child: Brian Sutton-Smith's Boys' Story *Our Street*

Kevin J. Sheehan, Ph.D.

Once upon a time there was a middle-sized boy named Brian, and he was called Brian. Now this is something quite unusual, because most boys are not called by their own name at all. Sometimes they are called "Snowy," and sometimes they are just called "Stinker," but they are hardly ever called what they really are. So Brian was a rather unusual sort of boy. (Sutton-Smith, 1949a, p. 174)

What precedes is the opening paragraph of a book entitled *Our Street,* the first chapter of which appeared as a story in the July 1949 issue of *School Journal,* a magazine brought out by the Education Department of New Zealand. The book was the work of a probationary teacher, Brian Sutton-Smith, who wrote it in order to provide the working-class boys he taught with realistic stories corresponding to their way of life. Because Sutton-Smith's own childhood had been similar to that of his students, he based the book on his experiences growing up in Wellington during the 1930s.

Sutton-Smith's use of the standard opening phrase of the fairy tale is ironic, for his book inverts the main features of that genre.[1] The plot of the fairy tale is typically a quest for identity, in which the hero leaves a place where his identity is secure, travels through a supernatural realm where his identity is uncertain, and arrives at a place where his identity is reestablished at a higher ontological level. Characters with magical powers assist the hero in his quest. The plot resolution hinges on the hero's transformation of identity; the conclusion reveals his new identity to be his true identity. In contradistinction to the fairy tale, *Our Street* is an episodic narrative about four ordinary boys. The action takes place in and around their homes, there are no characters with magic powers, and none of the boys undergo a transformation of identity. Because *Our Street* systematically deconstructs the genre of the fairy tale, it is essentially an anti-fairy tale.

The Education Department planned to serialize *Our Street* in subsequent issues of the *School Journal.* In an introduction to the series, Sutton-Smith instructs his young readers to evaluate the actions of the boys in *Our Street* from the standpoint of rule utilitarianism, the theory of moral value judgment dominant in Great Britain at the time. Rule utilitarianism states that the rightness or wrongness of any sort of action depends on the goodness or badness of its consequences; therefore, to act rightly one must act only on that maxim through which one can, at the same time, will to become a universal moral law. In short, this moral theory commands individuals to act only as they would like everyone in the same circumstances to act, their "liking" being determined solely by their feelings as benevolent human beings (Smart, 1967, pp. 206–207). Accordingly, Sutton-Smith tells his readers that the boys in his story

> haven't much time for anyone outside their own gang—or for boys they call "sissies," or boys that are in some way different from themselves.
>
> They haven't much time for grown-ups either. Perhaps they don't think about them much, except when they want money to go to the pictures, or when they begin to wonder whether or not they will be in trouble because of something they have done. And that is why they usually do get into trouble—because they don't bother to think whether the things they do will hurt other people, or what it would be like to live in a world where everyone acted as they do. (1949a, p. 174)

He then adverts to a specific incident in *Our Street:*

> In the second chapter, two of the boys slip in through the exit door of a picture theatre without paying for their seats. This meant that they had an extra shilling to spend on Eskimo pies and paper lollies.... If there is a fair chance of not being found out when you do a dishonest thing, do you still think it is a good thing to do? (1949a, p. 173)

Sutton-Smith concludes his introduction with this advice:

> There are a number of things like this that you could talk over. Try to think about everyone concerned, the boys in the gang, and the boys they teased and fought, and the people whose windows they broke. Could you still have as much fun if, at the same time, you tried to act sensibly, to be friendly towards the boys and girls whom you don't like much, and to be careful of other people's property? Well, that's for you to work out for yourselves. (1949a, p. 174)

Despite Sutton-Smith's introduction, the moral argument of *Our Street*—the set of moral judgments expressed by the story itself and capable of being expounded as a logical sequence of propositions—is radically inconsistent with rule utilitarianism.

A more appropriate introduction would have been an ironic warning "per Chief of Ordnance," such as Mark Twain (1884, 1996) had given the readers of *Adventures of Huckleberry Finn*:

> Persons attempting to find a motive in this narrative will be prosecuted; persons attempting to find a moral in it will be banished; persons attempting to find a plot will be shot. (n.p.)

Like *Huckleberry Finn, Our Street* conveyed a moral argument that was explosively dangerous to the social hegemony of its time.

The group of boys in *Our Street* include Brian's older brother, Smitty, and their neighbors, Gormie and Horsey. On Saturdays after doing their chores, they "make up their mind about what they are going to do" by a democratic process they call "bagzing":

> "I bagz we go to the football," said Smitty.
> "Aw, no," said Gormie.
> "Why not?" asked Brian.
> "Because," said Gormie.
> "Because what?" asked Smitty.
> "Because I bagz we go to the pictures."
> "I bagz we don't," said Brian.
> "I bagz the zoo," said Horsey.
> ...
> "Well let's see which two we bagz most out of the three," said Smitty. (Sutton-Smith, 1949a, p. 177)

When "bagzing" results in something that they all want to do, the boys spend their Saturday together. When it does not, they go their separate ways.

"Bagzing" is a leitmotiv that recurs throughout *Our Street* in support of a theme that the political scientist Timothy Cook has discerned at the heart of American children's literature: The "endorsement of unique, discrete individuals coming together on a voluntary basis to creatively form a political community in face of an always changing universe" (1988, p. 56). But unlike American children's books, which typically combine this theme with an ethics of self-realization, *Our Street* combines it with an ethics of power. This combination is patent in the "picture theatre" episode Sutton-Smith discusses in the introduction.

All four boys "bagz to go to the pictures" to see Hop-a-long Cassidy in *Bar 25 Range*. Finding themselves short of funds, they sneak two of their number through the exit, thereby conserving money for sweets. As soon as they are seated, they assess their financial situation:

> "How much have we got?" asked Smitty.
> "There's your sixpence, Horsey's sixpence, my fourpence, and Brian's and your pennies," said Gormie.

"That makes one and sixpence," said Horsey. Then the pictures started.

At half-time Brian went out and bought four three-penny Eskimo Pies, and Horsey bought sixpence worth of paper lollies. Brian and Smitty and Horsey and Gormie sat all through the Hop-a-long Cassidy picture eating Eskimo Pies and chewing paper lollies. Now and again they would cheer as Cassidy shot another Redskin, and Smitty would whistle when Cassidy kissed the girl. Every now and then one of them would throw a paper lolly down at the rows in the front where the last paper that hit them seemed to come from.

After the pictures they all galloped home.

Brian thought that he was Cassidy and the others were Redskins.

Smitty thought that he was Cassidy and the others were Redskins.

Horsey thought that he was Cassidy and the others were Redskins.

Gormie thought that he was Cassidy and the others were Redskins.

When they arrived at their street, the four Hop-a-long Cassidys left each other. Gormie went to his place, Brian and Smitty to their place, and Horsey to his place. They all shut their gates, climbed over them, and went inside, feeling very hungry because they had run all the way home. (Sutton-Smith, 1949b, pp. 216–217)

The political community described by Sutton-Smith in *Our Street* is a horizontal democracy whose members reject the universal benevolence of rule utilitarianism in favor of an egoistic gratification of the instincts, particularly the will to power.

The publication of the first chapter provoked outraged reactions from several local school boards and Headmasters associations. These protestations were met by various defenses in the popular press. The controversy increased as subsequent chapters appeared, ultimately reaching Parliament. Several Conservative members objected to the ungrammatical language and amorality of the characters and questioned the suitability of the work for the *School Journal*. In defense of the book, the Minister of Education replied:

> [*Our Street*] has an authentic New-Zealand background and the slang expressions are in keeping with the characters portrayed. On similar grounds exception could be taken to the publications in the journal of extracts from Dickens, Mark Twain, Marryat and other classic authors. (Sutton-Smith, 1996, p. 29)

In response to the growing number of complaints to the Publications Branch about the series, the Education Department discontinued *Our Street* after the third chapter.[2] According to Sutton-Smith, these complaints were, in part, "an attack by the opposition Conservative political party on the supposed moral slippage of the prevailing Labour party in power" (1996, pp. 29–30). But, more significantly, they may have represented an attempt by the middle class to conserve the myth by which they ratified their traditional system of educating boys.

Since the early Victorian period, the education of boys in Great Britain had devolved from a myth of self-sacrifice that had developed in the ascendant middle class during the Industrial Revolution. This myth identified the boy's innate will to power with concupiscence—an inordinate desire for the things of this world—and asserted that this inherited disorder could be corrected in the individual by the will willing its own extinction. Thus, through the sacrifice of his childhood, a man could become his own redeemer.

Although this sacrifice was envisioned as a voluntary self-surrender, it was thought to require the assistance of concerned adults. As the British children's book author C. S. Lewis (1948) has written:

> To surrender a self-will inflamed and swollen with years of usurpation is a kind of death. We all remember this self-will as it was in childhood the bitter, prolonged rage at every thwarting, the burst of passionate tears, the black Satanic wish to kill or die rather than to give in. Hence the older type of nurse or parent was quite right in thinking that the first step in education is to "break the child's will...." And if, now that we are grown up, we do not howl and stamp quite so much, that is because our elders began the process of killing our self-will in the nursery. (pp. 79–80)

Teachers continued the work begun by parents and nurses, steeling the boy to enter the innermost chamber of his soul and perform the necessary murder.

The ultimate purpose of the sacrifice of childhood was the production of the wise and virtuous man described by the political economist Adam Smith in *Theory of Moral Sentiments* (1948):

> The wise and virtuous man is at all times willing that his own private interests should be sacrificed to the public interest of his own particular order or society. He is at all times willing, too, that the interests of this order or society be sacrificed to the greater interest of the state ... of which it is only a subordinate part: he should therefore be equally willing that all those inferior interests should be sacrificed to the greater interest of the universe, to the interest of that great society of all sensible and intelligent beings, of which God himself is the immediate administrator and director. (p. 249)

The myth of the sacrificial child was basically a *laissez-faire* interpretation of the Jesus story. The British middle class believed that by killing his self-will, not only did a boy transform himself from a concupiscent child of Adam into the wise and virtuous capitalist described by Adam Smith, he repeated the Passion of Christ, thereby securing the Kingdom of Heaven for himself and his nation. Absurd as this belief was, it was no more absurd than the idea that a frog could be transformed into a prince by being hurled against a wall by a princess. Thus the fairy tale was the ideal form in which to express the faith of the British middle class.

From the 1860s until World War I, British publishing houses brought out a succession of children's books that conveyed the myth of the sacrificial child through narratives possessing the plot structure of the fairy tale. In these books, the act of the will willing its own extinction is symbolized by the suicide of a prepubescent boy. For example, in *The Water-Babies* (Kinglsey, 1863/1995), "poor little Tom" drowns himself in a river; in *At the Back of the North Wind* (MacDonald, 1871/1986), Little Diamond climbs a tree and prays to be raised up to heaven; and in *Peter-Pan* (Barrie, 1911/1987), the

Darling boys heed Peter's command, "Come," and follow him out their third-story bed-room window. All these self-immolations involve Christian imagery: Tom's, the sacra-ment of baptism; Little Diamond's, the crucifixion; the Darling boys', Simon-Peter and his brother, Andrew, following Christ's injunction, "Come follow me, and I will make you fishers of men." All illustrate the middle-class version of the paschal theme, "We die into life."

Following the war, bourgeois literary historians canonized these middle-class fairy tales as children's classics. Taken together, they functioned as a kind of gospel ratifying bourgeois educational practices. However, there was a crucial difference between the pre-war and the post-war interpretation of the sacrament that this scrip-ture prescribed. For the Victorian and Edwardian middle class, self-sacrifice repli-cated the self-surrender of God that occurred through the Incarnation; therefore, it *really* corrected the damage caused to human nature by Original Sin. For the post-war middle class, self-sacrifice was a fiction that kept them from despair in a world abandoned by God. The post-war middle class lived *as if* men could replicate the sac-rifice of Christ, *as if* they could free themselves by killing their self-will from the taint of the first man's transgression. During the interwar period, this morbid *as if* permeated the education of boys in Great Britain, giving it the tenebrous aspect of a passion play (Gregg, 1964; Sutherland, 1990).

Friedrich Nietzsche denounced the British myth of self-sacrifice as a decadent formulation of the English philosopher Jeremy Bentham's principle of utility, the doctrine that the individual should subsume his own interests to those of the collec-tive good, always acting on the principle that identifies "the greatest happiness of all those whose interest is in question, as being the right and proper, and only right and proper and universally desirable end of human action" (Bentham, 1967, p. 791, fn). "Man does not aspire to happiness," Nietzsche retorted, "only the Englishman does that" (1964, p. 2).

In *The Will to Power*, he argued that the only thing all men want is power; what-ever else men want, they want for the sake of power; therefore, when they want one thing more than another, it must be because it yields them more power (Nietzsche, 1969a; see also Kaufmann, 1967). The first British writer on education to accept this argument seems to have been Bertrand Russell. The horrors of World War I had con-vinced Russell that leading boys to kill their self-will only led them to kill one anoth-er. Caring for his first son, who was born in 1921, taught him that the education of boys consists in the cultivation of their will to power, not in its suppression (see Monk, 1996, chap. 21).

In his book *Education and the Good Life* (1926), Russell developed a theory of education based on the play of the self. According to Russell:

> In play, we have two forms of the will to power: the form which consists in learning to do things, and the form which consists in fantasy. Just as the balked adult may indulge in daydreams that have a sexual significance, so a normal child indulges in pretenses that have a power-significance. He likes to be a giant, or a lion, or a train; in his make

believe he inspires terror. (p. 125)

...

In games he is a king: indeed he rules his territory with a power surpassing that of any monarch. (p. 128)

Although Russell does not acknowledge his debt to Nietzsche, his theory of education is an adaptation of the German writer's notion of sublimation, by which Nietzsche meant the redirection of the will to power through life-affirming, rule-constituted activities. Russell writes:

The instinct of power, which in the child is crudely satisfied by identification with Bluebeard, can find in later life a refined satisfaction by scientific discovery, or artistic creation ... or any one of a thousand activities. If the only thing a man knows is how to fight, his will to power will make him delight in battle. But if he has other kinds of skill, he will find his satisfaction in other ways. (1926, p. 130)

Like most interpreters of Nietzsche since the advent of depth psychology, Russell mistook Nietzsche's concept of sublimation for the private, internal process described by Freud. However, for Nietzsche, because sublimation involved following rules, it was necessarily public and social. Nietzsche understood a fundamental point about the following of rules that would later be clarified by Wittgenstein (1970) in *Philosophical Investigations*: Following a rule entails *doing the same thing,* and what *the same* is can only be established through an activity in which two or more people participate (sec. 378). For Nietzsche, children's play was the model of sublimation because it was an activity in which children learned *to do the same thing.* Thus, children's play was both conservative and creative; it involved the reproduction of older cultural forms and the creation of new traditions. A truly Nietzschean theory of education would not view children's play as make-believe and adult life as real; it would recognize that child culture and adult culture alike are structures of the imagination, and would develop educational practices that emphasize the fundamental continuity between children's play and the rule-constituted activities that make up adult life (see Searle, 1969, pp. 33–42).

What sort of transformations of consciousness did Nietzsche believe were necessary to produce a society openly based on an ethics of power? To those who associate the doctrine of the will to power with Nazi Germany, the answer may come as surprise. In the opening section of *Thus Spoke Zarathustra,* Nietzsche (1969b) says that the creation of such a society requires three transformations of the spirit:

I name you three metamorphoses of the spirit: how the spirit shall become a camel, and the camel a lion, and the lion at last a child. (p. 54)

The camel is the weight-bearing spirit of metaphysical man, the spirit that posits a "true" world beyond the "apparent" world of experience in order to provide an "objective" justification for human values.

The lion represents nihilism—the negative form of human consciousness that succeeds the camel by exposing all tables of value as expressions of will that cannot be rationally justified. By becoming a lion, by giving "a sacred No even to duty" (Nietzsche, 1969, p. 55), man gives himself freedom and confers on himself the *right* to new values.

To *create* new values for himself, a third transformation of his spirit is necessary—the lion must become a child:

> But tell me, my brothers, what can the child do that even the lion cannot? Why must the preying lion still become a child?
>
> The child is innocence and forgetfulness, a new beginning, a sport, a self-propelling wheel, a first motion, a sacred Yes.
>
> Yes, a sacred Yes is needed, my brothers, for the sport of creation: the spirit now wills *its own* will, the spirit sundered from the world now wins *its own* world.
>
> I have named you three metamorphoses of the spirit: how the spirit became a camel, and the camel a lion, and the lion at last a child.
>
> Thus spoke Zarathustra, and at that time he was living in the town called The Pied Cow. (Nietzsche, 1969, pp. 55–56)

Heraclitus (1923) said that history is a child at play. Nietzsche wanted men to affirm this truth with their entire being. His cure for the mood of despair over the emptiness and triviality of existence that followed the death of God was not the morbid *as if* of the post-war British middle class, but "a sacred Yes"—a joyful affirmation of the human condition expressed in the spirit of children's play.

CONCLUSION

"And at that time he was living in the town called The Pied Cow." Doesn't that sound like a line from a fairy tale? Do you suppose that any British subject anywhere has ever written a children's story in the spirit of a child?

> Once upon a time there was a middle-sized boy named Brian, and he was called Brian. Now this is something quite unusual, because most boys are not called by their own name at all. Sometimes they are called "Snowy," and sometimes they are just called "Stinker," but they are hardly ever called what they really are. So Brian was a rather unusual sort of boy. (Sutton-Smith, 1949a, p. 174)

The boys Sutton-Smith wrote about in *Our Street* reject the principle of utility in favor of egoism. The gratification of the instincts, of the will to power, is the essence of their ethics. However, they do not express their will to power through the subjugation of others. Rather, they do so through play, in which it takes two forms: fantasy, like pretending to be Hop-a-long Cassidy shooting Redskins; and sublimation—the imposing of commands upon themselves and obeying them. These commands include rules they have learned from others, like those of football and cricket, and laws they make for themselves, such as the one that says that you must never go through an open gate—you must close it and then climb over it.

APPENDIX: RESPONSE TO "PLAYING WITH THE SACRIFICIAL CHILD"

First, a word of admiration for Sheehan's startling theoretical transcendence of my naive stories written for the eight-year-old children in my first teaching assignment 50 years ago. At the time, it was an amusing and enjoyable escape into my own childhood and a successful stimulant for the children's own writing. I emphasized the more dramatic episodes and childhood legends which we, as children, found exciting. My mother remarked, however, that I had left out most of the good behavior, which she felt was more typical of our lives at home, in school, and in church. The negative public reaction at the educational and parliamentary levels was my first personal experience of the power of conservative anger at nonconforming child behavior or speech. Conformity, in the New Zealand case, implied obeisance to authority and some mimicry of upper status BBC patterns of speech clarity.

Still, this political affront led me on to my Ph.D., an investigation into the play of New Zealand children. One might say that I have spent the rest of my life trying to clarify what it is about childhood play that got everyone so riled up. Or, alternatively, that I have spent the rest of my life justifying the character of childhood culture as itself a form of power politics and phantasmagorial mythology. I came to conclude that our major scholarly approach to childhood, as a form of standardized socialization (called child and educational psychology), was largely a Foucault-like management phenomenon for maintaining control over the potential rebelliousness of these inferiors. Sheehan speaks well to the hidden and public transcripts that the British used to rationalize their forms of childhood civilization.

My best accounts of what I think child culture is really about are reflected in: *A History of Children's Play* (1981b), which I had written in the early 1950s, but no one would publish for another 30 years; *The Folkstories of Children* (1981a); the edited work, *Children's Folklore: A Source Book* (1995); and, most recently, *The Ambiguity of Play* (1997).

—Brian Sutton-Smith

NOTES

[1] The fairy tale is a variant of the romance. My understanding of the structure and social function of the romance has been informed by Northrop Frye (1976). In addition, Max Lüthi's essays (1976) helped me see the special features of the fairy tale.

[2] *Our Street* was first published as a book in 1950 by New Zealand publishers A. H. and A. W. Reed. In 1975, an edition was brought out by Price Millburn and Company, in Wellington. In 1976, according to Sutton-Smith, *Our Street* was "serialized in a children's weekly column in the *Evening Post,* a Wellington newspaper (June, July, August 1976), and, in 1991, a chapter appeared in a Puffin New Zealand Story Book indicating at least some belated entrance to the canon of New Zealand children's literature" (1996, p. 30).

REFERENCES

Barrie, J. M. (1987). *Peter-Pan.* New York: New American Library. (Original work published 1911)

Bentham, J. (1967). *An introduction to the principles of morals and education.* In E. Burtt (Ed.), *The English philosophers from Bacon to Mill* (p. 791). New York: The Modern Library.

Cook, T. (1988). Democracy and community in American children's literature. In E. Yanarella & L. Sigelman (Eds.), *Political mythology and popular fiction* (p. 56). New York: Greenwood Press.

Frye, N. (1976). *The secular scripture: A study in the structure of romance.* Cambridge, MA: Harvard University Press.

Gregg, P. (1964). *A social and economic history of Britain, 1760–1963.* London: G. G. Harrad.

Heraclitus (1923). *On the universe.* In W. H. S. Jones (Trans.), *Loeb classical library, vol. IV* (pp. 449–509). London: William Heinemann.

Kaufmann, W. (1967). Nietzsche, Friedrich. In P. Edwards (Ed.), *The encyclopedia of philosophy* (p. 511). New York: Macmillan and The Free Press.

Kingsley, C. (1995). *The water-babies.* Oxford, England: Oxford University Press. (Original work published 1863)

Lewis, C. S. (1948). *The problem of pain.* New York: Macmillan.

Lüthi, M. (1976). *Once upon a time: On the nature of fairy tales.* Bloomington, IN: Indiana University Press.

MacDonald, G. (1986). *At the back of the north wind.* New York: New American Library. (Original work published 1871)

Monk, R. (1996). *Bertrand Russell: The spirit of solitude.* New York: The Free Press.

Nietzsche, F. (1964). The twilight of the idols. In O. Levy (Ed.), *Complete works of Friedrich Nietzsche* (p. 2). New York: Russell & Russell.

Nietzsche, F. (1969a). *The will to power* (W. Kaufmann & R. J. Hollingdale, Trans.). New York: Vintage Books.

Nietzsche, F. (1969). *Thus spoke Zarathustra* (R. J. Hollingdale, Trans.). London: Penguin Books.

Russell, B. (1926). *Education and the good life.* New York: Boni & Liveright.

Searle, J. (1969). *Speech acts.* London: Cambridge University Press.

Smart, J. J. C. (1967). Utilitarianism. In P. Edwards (Ed.), *The encyclopedia of philosophy* (pp. 206–212). New York: Macmillan.

Smith, A. (1948). *Theory of moral sentiments.* In H. Schneider (Ed.), *Adam Smith's moral and political philosophy* (p. 249). New York: Hafner.

Sutherland, G. (1990). Education. In F. M. L. Thompson (Ed.), *The Cambridge social history of Britain 1750–1950* (pp. 158–169). Cambridge, England: Cambridge University Press.

Sutton-Smith, B. (1949a). Our street. *New Zealand School Journal, 6*(43), 172–180.

Sutton-Smith, B. (1949b). Our street. *New Zealand School Journal, 7*(43), 212–217.

Sutton-Smith, B. (1981a). *The folkstories of children.* Philadelphia: University of Pennsylvania Press.

Sutton-Smith, B. (1981b). *A history of children's play.* Philadelphia: University of Pennsylvania Press.

Sutton-Smith, B. (Ed.). (1995). *Children's folklore: A source book.* New York: Garland.

Sutton-Smith, B. (1996). *Sutton-Smith play biography.* Unpublished manuscript.

Sutton-Smith, B. (1997). *The ambiguity of play.* Cambridge, MA: Harvard University Press.

Twain, M. (1996). *Adventures of Huckleberry Finn.* New York: Random House. (Original work published 1884)

Wittgenstein, L. (1970). *Philosophical investigations* (G. E. M. Anscombe, Trans.). New York: Macmillan.

3

Toying with the Striptease Dancer and the First Amendment*

Judith Lynne Hanna, Ph.D.
University of Maryland

Exotic dance is a lightning rod for American cultural conflicts over the First Amendment to the U.S. Constitution, religious morality, feminist morality, and economics. The exotic dance genre includes go-go, striptease, strip, topless, nude, table, couch, and lap dance. Exotic dance is adult business at the same time it is play: pretend and games, a mixture of pay for play and display outside "ordinary" life. There are different players in this ludic performance genre that is increasingly encapsulated in "enemy territory" with hostile opponents who want to eliminate it.

Exotic dance club participants vary by gender, sexual orientation, income, religion, and ethnicity. However, the focus of this article is primarily the White female dancer performing for the male patron in clubs that range from seedy strip bars to upscale gentlemen's clubs.

* This paper is a development of my presentation at The Association for the Study of Play (TASP), session on Adult Play in the 90's, April 2, 1997. I wish to thank planner R. Bruce McLaughlin and lawyers Gilbert H. Levy, Jack R. Burns, Bradley J. Shafer, Jeffrey J. Douglas, Dominic P. Gentile, Dayvid J. Figler, Jonnell Thomas, Luke Lirot, Clyde DeWitt, John Weston, Dick Wilson, Michael Murray, Charles J. Quaid, and Steven H. Swander, who introduced me to various aspects of exotic dance. To the many dancers, dance scholars, club owners, managers, staff, and patrons who generously shared their views, I am grateful. I appreciate helpful comments of Usha Charya, Katherine Frank, William John Hanna, and the *Play and Culture* series reviewers on earlier drafts of this paper.

My comments are based on dance research conducted since the 1960s, along with my experience as an expert court witness in First Amendment and other cases concerning exotic dance, beginning in March 1995. I became involved in the study of adult entertainment, community conflict, and legal processes when a planner in Tampa, Florida—working for a First Amendment lawyer in Seattle, Washington—found my name as an author of works on dance (Hanna, 1983, 1979/1987, 1988a, 1988b) in *Books in Print*. These individuals asked me to apply to exotic dance the semiotic paradigm I have used to study other forms of nonverbal communication. I analyzed how an ordinance of Bellevue, a Seattle suburb, would affect the communicative efficacy of the dancer's message. Additional court cases followed. The ordinances I analyzed include sections on the distance between the performer and the customer, lighting, body covering, and "obscene" behavior. I have even testified for dancers charged with prostitution and in a case against an exotic dance club involving a quadruple shooting, observing that the clubs have a climate of play, and not a climate of terror, as the plaintiffs charged.

ADULT PLAY

Although dancers compete amongst themselves for a patron's attention, there are two major games characterized by multiple realities and different combinations of strategy, chance, and skill (see Lytle, 1997). One kind of play is between dancers and patrons. The special allure of this game is the "presence," or charisma, of perceptive, performing erotic beings (both dancers and patrons) and the dynamics of dominance and submission. A second, and more serious, game is between exotic dance stakeholders (club owners, staff, dancers, and patrons) and cities, counties, and even states. In this game, forced private enterprise players risk high economic stakes, and even economic survival.

Each game has groups of players with their own primary motivation and game book. The rigidity of the rules depends upon the specific players. Economic considerations move dancers and clubs; the adult playground can be a lucrative business, and everyone is a winner. Groups pursuing religious and feminist moral dictates, on the one hand, and civil liberties beliefs, on the other, drive cities, counties, and states. In social drama (Turner, 1974), federal law, local ordinances, and house rules set by individual clubs provide the scaffold for the interplay between dancer and patron. When dancers and clubs allegedly run afoul of the existing laws, police and those in jurisprudence are cast as additional characters. The court plays a leading role when exotic dance clubs legally challenge local governments' attempts at restriction.

FANTASY PLAY

In conceptualizing exotic dance as play, it is noteworthy that the word *play* comes from the Old English *plegan*, meaning "to exercise oneself, move briskly," and that the Middle Dutch *pleyen*, "to dance," is a cognate term (Turner, 1982, p. 33).

Webster's Ninth New Collegiate Dictionary (1986, p. 902) tells us *play* can mean "sexual intercourse" and "dalliance." The word *entertain* derives from *entetenir*, meaning "to hold apart," that is, to create what anthropologist Victor Turner (1982) refers to as a liminal or liminoid (betwixt and between) space. Exotic dance takes place in this kind of space.

"Liminality is a temporal interface whose properties partially invert those of the already consolidated order" (Turner, 1982, p. 41). There is no subversion of the social status quo; rather, reversal of what usually transpires in the social order shows community members that chaos is the alternative.

Exotic Dance as Liminal

Between the everyday world and outlawed sexual behavior, exotic dance is liminal. It challenges mainstream behavioral patterns. Society stigmatizes this ludic activity for going against the grain of prescribed respectability. The morally controversial play of exotic dance is, as sociologist Gary Allen Fine (1991) points out, grounded in its contextual historical base and contemporary social status. The play decorum of exotic dance somewhat ameliorates the stigma for all participants in the liminal space. Moreover, in the United States, contrary to the situation in many other countries, exotic dance clubs are a sexual world where, as a rule, actual sex does not occur.

Stemming from the burlesque tradition, exotic dance makes fun of society's values and hypocrisy (Allen, 1991). Dancers caricature social mores, mock religious repudiation of the flesh, and play with cultural constructions of gender and ambiguity—independent from, as well as dominant and subordinate to, members of the opposite sex. Exotic dancers challenge the socially constructed definition of the role and behavior of women and the norms for modesty, shame, and secrecy (Hanna, 1988a). After all, to see an adult female's nude body has traditionally only been a man's conjugal right.

As a form of mental feedback, the creative improvisatory playfulness of exotic dance might in various ways nullify the rigidity that sets in after society adapts to a new situation (see Sutton-Smith, 1997). Fantasy is not rule-bound. Performance theorist and practitioner Richard Schechner explains the play/fantasy dynamic involved:

> In play and individual fantasy this world has not been institutionalized but remains the private privilege of each [person]. It is in fantasy that people break the rules—even the most rigorous. (1988, pp. 31–32; see also Hanna, 1986)

Patrons recognize adult play when they see the signage as they first enter an exotic dance club and then see stages. These actions frame the pretend play in which dancer and patron toy with each other. The exotic dancers become players after preparing themselves for the role. Many come to work wearing jeans and sweatshirt and no makeup, looking like the girl next door. In playing the role, a woman assumes a stage name and identity, often making up a life story to tell patrons. She dresses for the part with makeup, special grooming (removing body hair, getting a tan, etc.), an outfit to take off, and four-inch heels to keep on. She then improvises performances to feed patrons' fantasies (see Hanna, 1983).

> Intensity, passion, concentration, commitment: these are all part of the play mood. But this alone is not what makes play play. There is also the quality of acting out, of becoming another, of displaying a normally hidden part of yourself—and of becoming this other without worrying about consequences. Play implies getting away with it. (Schechner, 1985, p. 300)

The patron plays one or more of several roles. He may be the "naughty" man or "sinner" whose culture dictates he not view nude dancers. This is a mild form of rebellion with few, if any, negative consequences. Exotic dance is forbidden fun for some religious denominational adherents, husbands, and boyfriends. Upon entering a club, the patron pays a cover charge if required, stands at the bar or finds a seat, buys a beverage, watches stage performances, and may interact with a performer to purchase an individual patron-focused dance. This personal dance is a one-song performance intended for a patron at his table or couch, where the exotic dancer and patron can be close. Usually, she may touch him nonsexually, and he may touch her nonsexually at her discretion. After performing on stage, dancers circulate throughout the audience area to try to sell a "table dance" or "seat call." Weaving around the tables to indicate their availability for personal dances, they chat with patrons to allow requests.

These two phases of exotic dance split the sites of performance and the gaze of the participants between the stage(s) and audience area. In clubs where the dancers are independent contractors, earning their sole income through selling table dances, the disc jockey will periodically announce this fact to the patrons. He tries to encourage, even cajole, customers to empty their wallets.

A patron may play the role of someone other than his regular persona, escaping the usual routine of his everyday life. Because women have become more sexually and otherwise demanding of men, a patron can fantasize about a desired woman without having to cope with a "real woman."

At bachelor parties in the clubs, the groom's friends often arrange for him to be cast as a sex object on stage, where several dancers bestow real and pretend caresses. Similarly, for other celebrations, such as birthdays, patrons can request different scenarios of performances.

Exotic dance, as a form of play, is purposeful (Hanna, 1979/1987), primarily for dancers to earn money, but also for patrons to escape from the everyday routine and from stress. "Play borrows patterns that appear in other contexts where they achieve immediate and obvious ends" (Loizos, 1969, p. 228), such as sexual movements leading to reproduction.

Exotic Dance as Metaphor

Exotic dance performance is fantasy, metaphor, and arousal-seeking through novel charade, partly satisfying the human need to escape boredom (see Berlyne, 1971). Indeed, dance itself is a metaphor (Hanna, 1998d). *New York Times* critic Jennifer Dunning (1998) put it this way:

> Dance, like poetry, is an art of metaphor and abstraction, though it whisks by and cannot easily be reread. There are narrative dances, from "Swan Lake" to "Revelations," just as there are narrative poems. And nothing having to do with the human body can be truly abstract. Stillness and motion are inherently dramatic. But even the most clearly expressive phrase of dance is a distillation, whether the beating of a foot that suggests the beating of a heart newly and fearfully in love, or a raising of arms that approximates prayer. (p. B2)

"Eroticism," wrote Octavio Paz, a Nobel laureate, "is a representation that diverts or denies sex in action ... sexuality transfigured, a metaphor. The agent that provokes both the erotic act and the poetic act is imagination" (1995, p. 2). A patron can, inter alia, fantasize about an encounter with a dancer, including possession, foreplay, and consummation. The imagined relationship may be sexual, romantic, or loving, with commitment. The fantasy may be about dominance or submission. A customer can pretend to be desired, getting the personal attention of an attractive female who would not otherwise pay notice. In this pretend play, there is an inversion of traditional ideas of sexual satisfaction when a patron empties his wallet to look at a dancer who returns his gaze, or merely to converse with her.

The exotic dancer nonverbally conveys erotic messages (see Tiersma, 1993). For the same fee as a personal dance, she may also "sympathetically" listen to a customer confide his problems or give him solicited advice on how to rekindle his marriage.

Dancer and anthropologist Katherine Frank discovered a complex pattern of illusion and reality in the metaphoric interaction between a dancer and her regular patrons. "The service provided by the dancer to her regulars is an on-going performance of a relationship.... As these relationships may be long-term, they may engage more and more aspects of both parties' selves over time" (1998, p. 20). In an effort to "mitigate the psychological dissonance caused by the commodification of interpersonal interaction," some patrons will continually give gifts to the dancer—clothes, vacations, and cars (p. 21). The irony is that "if a dancer's performance is believable enough, the relationship between the dancer and her regular seems genuine; an exchange of money during the interaction, then, undermines that authenticity. It is the exchange of money, however, which always facilitated the interaction in the first place" (p. 22). Therefore, some regulars pay up front to get the monetary aspects out of the way.

Exotic Dance and Sex Roles

In studying numerous exotic dance clubs, dancer/scholar Katherine Liepe-Levinson encountered many ways in which exotic dance broke traditional female and male sex roles of control and surrender (1998, 1999). Protected by dress, men pay nude women to perform a sex-object role suggesting vulnerability, accessibility, and submission to men.

However, in most clubs, the "patriarchal commodification and objectification of females" presumption misses two key dimensions: the patron as performer and the dancer as subject. Often unintentionally, the exotic dance patron becomes part of the performance for other audience members who identify with the patron. Unpredictable spontaneous exchanges between performer and customer create entertainment value for everyone. This play encourages other patrons to request personal dances.

Some spectators not only pay to gaze at the dancer, and to solicit her gaze, smile, and whisper; "they also pay, and even tip extra, for the commodity of their own stage time." These are "moments in the spotlight where they can be seen by the dancers and their fellow spectators, where they can become the object of the gaze" and "experience the thrill of voluntarily exposing oneself to some sort of perceived external danger" (Liepe-Levinson, 1998, p. 6). New patrons to the club, especially, watch the performer-spectator performance.

"Onstage" (sometimes literally, such as at Omar's in Lansing, Michigan, where the patron sits on the stage, feet on the floor, and lies down on his back while the dancer performs over him), men enjoy the limelight in being before an audience. Depending upon a club's style of exotic dance, patrons can pay for stage-side seats, walk up to the stage for an individual patron-focused dance, or purchase a table dance that shifts the site of the performance into the audience area. Customers may gain attention through extravagant offerings of money.

"The position of being up close and not being able to touch at all reinforces the excitement-pain of sexual yearning that is for some, in and of itself, a profound source of sexual pleasure," states Liepe-Levinson (1998, p. 8). In our nation's capital, Washington, D.C., in such clubs as the 1720 Club, Good Guys, and J.P.'s, a patron who approaches the stage for a personal dance must control himself if a nude dancer raises her leg over his head or otherwise exposes "gynecological" views. The dancer may choose to facilitate the tipping game by graciously accepting a fee or tip, being still while the patron places it in her garter or tip box. Or, she may tease by moving, forcing the patron to wait, fumbling in anticipation, while other patrons watch (p. 9).

Schechner sums it up: "There is the performance, the performers, the spectators; and the spectator of spectators; and the self-seeing-self that can be performer or spectator or spectator of spectators" (1985, p. 297).

Each player in the erotic fantasy of exotic dance can perceive her or himself as dominant in a power game. Both patron and dancer can enter into and terminate an interaction at will.

A patron may win a sense of power through money, as well as ocular penetration. Knowing most dancers are economically dependent on a customer's spending, he has the power to bestow interest through buying attention, with no obligation beyond payment. He gazes upon her in eye-play; he has access to what is normally private. Dressed, the patron appears as patriarch in relation to the nude child-woman (Dragu and & Harrison, 1988, p. 123). "Some men," says former stripper Susan Hull (1980, p. 4), "feel powerful in their belief that their presence has stimulated the dancer's erotic state." The aggregation of men scrutinizing nude women may create a sense of male bonding that enables and institutionalizes the allusion of male dominance.

Of course, allusions of *female* dominance also exist. Many women look at male athletes, actors, and musicians as sex objects. And there are male strip clubs for women.

While one group of feminists sees the dancer as objectified and exploited, another group sees her as a subject in control. In this capacity, the dancer's empowerment comes through freedom to profit from control of her own appearance, sexuality, personality, conversation, and attraction. She teases with sexually titillating bodily disclosure and erotic movement. Defying prevailing male concepts of passive femininity, she controls the play of senses as she positions herself, especially her breasts, hips, buttocks, and pelvis, to center attention. The dancer may lure a male's penis into erection against his will and render him a "helpless slave of passion," says Liepe-Levinson (1998, p. 29).

When a woman walks down the street and men leer at her, she may feel violated. But when she is performing as an exotic dancer, she chooses to be gazed upon. "Of course it's a power trip," exotic dancer Monique Berry admitted (personal communication, June 1996). Many dancers feel psychologically and economically empowered when "crazy bastards pay money to goggle at your body" (Boles, 1973, p. 49). Nina Hartley, a feature dancer, said, "It's okay to be gazed upon. It hurts not to be gazed upon" (personal communication, April 1996). Nancy, an exotic dancer, said, "It is an interesting dynamic to have almost total control over a man and his wallet by manipulating him with your sexual energy" (personal communication, May 1996). Within the constraints of the law and club policy, which provide protective boundaries for free expression, exotic dancers choreograph their "vamping" strategy, direct their gaze, determine the degree and length of exposure of parts of the body (cf. Lewin, 1984, pp. 73–74), and choose with whom they will talk, sit, and try to sell a table or other personal dance.

Denying that patrons subordinate and sexually exploit them, some performers consider exotic dance to be antiestablishment, a feminist act, and a strike against patriarchy—making patriarchy pay. That is, men must purchase a personal dance for the eroticism of fleeting personal attention. Voyeurism is not done against the woman's will, but it is made possible through her willful power play. Of course, as in any kind of game, players can violate the rules, leaving others unhappy.

Not only is exotic dance somewhat antistructure, but it is also protostructure (cf. Sutton-Smith, 1974; Turner, 1969), both in challenging the norms of appropriateness and laying the groundwork for new patterns. Precursors to current exotic dance were pacesetters in bodily disclosure in mainstream society. The credit for some of the gain in sexual freedom for women over the past hundred years "must go to sexual entertainers, for it is impossible to make this kind of gain without women who are willing to work on the cutting edge of sexual change" (Dragu & Harrison, 1988, p. 55). As a recent minor example, I noticed exotic dancers were wearing high-heeled platform shoes a couple of years before they became popular among the broader populace.

AGGRESSIVE PLAY

A common response to exotic dance clubs is the Not-In-My-Backyard (NIMBY) sociopolitical drama. This pits segments of a community against exotic dance stake-holders and pushes them into a stressful life and death game (see Hanna, 1988b). Clubs in more than 85 localities throughout the nation are being attacked for alleged-ly being immoral, degrading women, and causing the adverse secondary effects of crime and depreciation of property values. Although exotic dance is protected expression ("speech" and "art") under the First Amendment (Hanna, 1996a, 1996b, 1997, 1998a, 1998b, 1998c, 1998d, 1998e), localities across the nation toy with the constitutional rights of exotic dance stakeholders. Local governments try to close exotic dance clubs by harassing them out of existence or by preventing their open-ing. The government game plan includes zoning limitations, regulating the sale of alcohol, restricting the amount of bodily disclosure, placing limits on the distance and physical contact between the performer and the patron, licensing of dancers and clubs, specifying signage, and making menacing vice squad raids.

Many adult entertainment ordinances are unconstitutionally vague, overbroad, cause irreparable harm, and serve no stated objective. Fort Lauderdale requires dancers to cover the buttocks. When asked where the buttocks issue began and ended, Michael Brasfield, Chief of Police, said, "I've never really thought about it" (*Carchio v. Fort Lauderdale*, 1996). Persons of ordinary intelligence must guess at the meaning of vague ordinances and differ as to their application, not knowing what conduct will subject them to violations.

In the United States legal system, precedent is important, so the resolution of a case in one locality reverberates elsewhere. The Supreme Court's 1991 five-to-four decision in *Barnes v. Glen Theatre* is the governing constitutional law in the area of government efforts to restrict or ban nude dancing.

The meaning of the decision, however, is vague. The court ruled that nude danc-ing is a form of expression entitled to a measure (whatever that means) of First Amendment protection. However, a four-judge plurality permitted the State of Indiana to strip the First Amendment-protected expression in the interests of "order and morality," requiring that dancers wear pasties and g-strings. *Barnes* upheld Indiana's application of its general law against public nudity to "nude barroom danc-ing" in the Kitty Kat Lounge and Glen Theater. However, Justice David H. Souter, who provided the fifth, and consequently deciding, vote in the case, asserted that only the harmful "secondary effects" of nude barroom dancing (which he presumed to include prostitution, sexual assault, associated crimes, and neighborhood blight) justified regulation of the constitutionally protected form of artistic expression.

The Twenty-first Amendment repealed prohibition, but permitted states to impose conditions on places in which alcohol can be consumed. At such venues, states have the power to regulate nude entertainment. However, the Supreme Court recently ruled, in *44 Liquormart v. Rhode Island* (1996), that the Twenty-first Amendment cannot override the First Amendment. So, new legal contests are imminent.

Subterfuge

The rules of democratic lawmaking require that lawmakers justify regulatory ordinances after deliberating arguments positive and negative. Many localities toy with this process. They engage in pretense to show that they enact ordinances to serve a substantial governmental interest. But the ordinances are a way to skirt the constitutional rights of the exotic dance stakeholders and hold them to a higher standard than the rest of society. Playing a game with exotic dance clubs (or acting earnestly) and using the ploy of following lawmaking rules, some localities get help from National Family Legal Foundation materials (including Len Munsil's *The Preparation and Trial of an Obscenity Case: A Guide for the Prosecuting Attorney* [1988], and *How to Legally Stop Nude Dancing in Your Community* [1994]). In defense, the clubs turn to members of the First Amendment Lawyers Association and American Civil Liberties Union.

Rationales for regulating exotic dance include preventing "adverse secondary effects." But, since 1988, R. Bruce McLaughlin, a member of the American Institute of Certified Planners, has investigated these charges in localities nationwide. For example, in California, Florida, Georgia, Minnesota, Missouri, New York, Ohio, South Carolina, Texas, Washington, and Washington, D.C., McLaughlin found no evidence of the anticipated pernicious consequences in exotic dance club locations. His findings contrast with the findings of approximately 50 local government "studies" that he examined. He found them to be not only outdated, but also unscientific. In these "studies," it is not known if the clubs were opened in areas already in decline, if they caused the decline, or some other factor was the cause. Of course, "In order to properly determine whether the Adult Use causes 'adverse secondary effects,' it is necessary to review comparative demands for police service, and comparative property values in the areas of the Adult Uses and in a series of control areas" (McLaughlin, 1994, p. 15; 1995). The "studies" proffered by local and state governments are rarely empirical, but usually consist of surveys of people known to disfavor the clubs (such as the religiously conservative National Law Center for Children and Families) on moral or lack-of-knowledge grounds, and are based on hearsay or single cases. Through its acceptance of localities' "studies" of adverse secondary effects or localities' reliance on "studies" conducted by other jurisdictions, irrespective of quality, time, place, and circumstance, the court perpetuates myth as fact. If exotic dance clubs caused problems, Loehmann's, an upscale women's clothing store chain, for instance, certainly would not have opened across the street from Solid Gold in Fort Lauderdale.

The city of Bellevue, Washington, charged exotic dance clubs with attracting crime. But the highest crime rate was in the high school environs! And, in 1994 and 1997, in this wealthy city of 103,000 people, there were even multiple killings by local teenagers. "For the sheer experience of killing," commented two 17-year-olds who slayed a family of four (Goldberg, 1997, p. A10).

Daniel Linz, Professor of Communication and head of the Law and Society Program at University of California, Santa Barbara, told the Lansing City Council that his research showed, contrary to city assertions, that female nudity decreased male aggression (see Pally, 1991a, 1991b.)

Local governments commonly try to regulate the distance between performer and patron (for example, *International Food and Beverage v. City of Ft. Lauderdale,* 1996). The rationale? Illustratively, the City Manager of Fort Lauderdale, Florida, claimed adult establishment ordinances needed to be updated to regulate new trends in the business, especially the growth of upscale exotic dance "gentlemen's clubs." Among other recommendations was the requirement that entertainers and patrons be four feet apart in alcoholic beverage establishments. Why? "This requirement would help curb lewd activity occurring when dancers are performing lap/friction dances" (Hanbury, 1996, p. 1). But why not just say no friction or no touching? What is the four-foot rationale?

One "whereas" clause of the ordinance refers to the use of the clubs for what are commonly called "unlawful and unhealthy sexual activities, including prostitution and sexual liaison or sexual conduct of a casual nature" (Hanbury, 1996, p. 1). Yes, some old-time clubs permit illicit sexual contact. But more clubs forbid prostitution, fire dancers who go out with patrons, and even refuse to admit unescorted women patrons for fear they may be soliciting. Statistics, appearing periodically in the media, report that large numbers of people—in high school and college, at work, in bars and restaurants, or through the Internet—have had, or are having, casual sexual relations. Where are the regulations for them? For the most part, the exotic dance clubs have the unique American feature of "look, but don't touch."

Another recurring "whereas" clause is "the concern over sexually transmitted diseases" as "a legitimate health concern" (Hanbury, 1996, p. 1). Yet, the Center for Disease Control has no evidence that proximity without the exchange of bodily fluids causes such problems. As the attorney for Club Roxanne's, in Fort Lauderdale, said at a city commission meeting concerning Ordinance C-96-8:

I don't believe there has been any case ever documented of anybody catching any type of disease through clothing. And that is what the dancers are wearing. They have bottoms on that cover up their genital areas—there is no possibility of any diseases being contacted between the people. (Hanbury, 1996, p. 17)

To which Mayor Jim Naugle replied, "There could be something airborne like tuberculosis or someone coughing on a customer or something like that!"

When asked about sexually transmitted disease from a close distance, Commissioner John Aurelius said he had no evidence "other than my common sense" (*Carchio v. Fort Lauderdale*, 1996). Are all service providers, from waitpersons to doctors, required to have a four-foot distance from their clients?

Another "whereas" clause in the ordinance states the four-foot distance only makes the entertainer's exotic message "slightly less effective" and that "the ability to engage in the protected expression is not significantly impaired" (Hanbury, 1996, p. 1). But nowhere are the process and efficacy of communication discussed. My analyses, and psychologist Edward I. Donnerstein's (1995) research, found such distance is significant in the context of club layout and industry norms for exotic dance.

The Fort Lauderdale case is not unique in its toying with a protocol. For example, in 1997, the Metropolitan County Council of Nashville and Davidson County passed an ordinance to its code of laws to further regulate exotic dance clubs. The Council's rationale lumped all adult entertainment establishments together, claiming: "At least fifty communicable diseases may be spread by activities currently occurring in these places, including, but not limited to, syphilis, gonorrhea, human immunodeficiency virus (HIV) infection, genital herpes, hepatitis B, hepatitis Non A, hepatitis Non B, amebiasis, and shigella infections." A full two pages of statistics on AIDS, syphilis, and gonorrhea in the United States, Tennessee, and then Davidson County followed. Yet the report has no evidence of where or how such diseases were contracted. Given the prohibition of patron-dancer physical contact, there is obviously no reason for the Nashville/Davidson County's three-foot distance requirement to prevent sexually transmitted disease.

The myth of "adverse secondary effects" became accepted as fact. In *Young v. American Mini Theatres, Inc.* (1976), the adult theaters argued the First Amendment grounds and did not challenge the "study" of the City of Detroit. The courts accepted local government studies on the grounds that the legislatures thought they were valid. As Steven H. Swander, a First Amendment lawyer, put it, "We have to play on a field that is already tilted" (personal communication, June 23, 1998).

Sting Operations

In a number of areas, the local police play the "predation game." In Las Vegas, when one of the clubs discovers in its midst the undercover vice squad pursuing its quarry, the disc jockey plays the song "Bad Boys," so that everyone is especially attentive. Sting operations lead to arrests, fines, new ordinances, and high expenditures of taxpayer and defendant money to litigate. Moreover, the police raids hurt exotic dance businesses by disrupting them during peak business hours, and by intimidating and driving away employees and patrons.

The City of Bellevue enacted a dancer–patron distance rule to facilitate vice-squad surveillance. On the witness stand, I was shown an undercover videotape in which a dancer was alleged to be putting her breast in a patron's face and massaging his penis. I described what I saw: A completely bare breast was not revealed. The dancer's covering was skirt-like, a loose flounce over the top that revealed the equivalent of what shows in ordinary décolletage. Police could have been filming from the floor, looking upward. The dancer's hand appeared to be moving up and down her thigh and massaging the man's enormous, Buddha-like belly. Her hand would have had to be completely out of sight to reach the man's organ (if, indeed, he had one).

Across the continent, Chief Mike Brasfield of the Fort Lauderdale police also claimed the patron–dancer distance regulation would facilitate his department's surveillance "work."

People get hurt in the vice squad games. A midday raid at Rick's, in Seattle, led to dancers traumatized over criminal obscenity charges. The dancers won the criminal case (*City of Seattle v. Darcy Poole*, 1996). Two subsequently filed a civil suit against the City of Seattle for wrongful arrest, unreasonable conduct, and intentional and/or negligent infliction of emotional distress. On November 20, 1995, following a previously arranged plan, Vice Detective Ken Swanson entered Rick's at approximately 1:20 p.m. to do a covert inspection. He reported: "After paying the cover charge, I sat down and purchased a soft drink. I positioned myself in front of the main stage." While seated, the detective watched the striptease routines of each of the 12 defendants. He recorded his observations on audiotape. In a later, brief, written report about each dancer, the detective noted the time he entered Rick's, the reason, seating, observation, and recording. He described the dancer's race, sex, hair color, type of clothing, tattoos and piercings, and where (if any), and stage name. Another two sentences stated purported illegal two- to three-*second* self-touching, in violation of a "standards of conduct" Seattle municipal code pertaining to live female nude dancing on stage—such as "rubbed her anus," "massaged her buttocks and anus," "massaged her vagina," "massaged her breasts," "pinched her nipples"—and also the number of times each act occurred. There was nothing pertaining to the dance as a whole.

The detective left, returning with cops who placed 12 dancers and the manager under arrest for "violating the adult entertainment ordinance." The arrestees were handcuffed and taken downtown to the King County jail. Each dancer was booked and her costume, along with the original tape and a copy, were placed into evidence. The police forced the dancers to take off their costumes in front of a male policeman (two female officers were also present). Elaine, who does not go nude onstage, asked if the male officer would leave. A female officer laughed, "Look what you do for a living. Think of him as your brother." Coincidentally, Elaine's brother had raped her as a child. The police displayed ignorance of the difference between play onstage and behavior in ordinary life, the separation of a working play persona and a private persona.

One of the dancers was so traumatized by the arrest, the false accusations, and the forced stripping in front of a male officer that she no longer dances. And she could not continue her studies to be a paralegal.

In the criminal "obscenity" court case, the jury ruled that the dancer (one case representative of the others was tried) did not engage in illegal behavior. According to the *Miller v. California* (1973) test, for work to be constitutionally obscene, all three of these criteria must be met: (1) The average person, applying contemporary community standards, would find that the work, taken as a whole, appeals to the prurient interest; (2) the work depicts or describes, in a patently offensive way, sexual conduct specifically defined by the applicable state law; and (3) the work, taken as a whole, lacks serious literary, artistic, political, or scientific value. I had explained to the jury how exotic dance meets the criteria of dance and art, as well as my analysis of videotapes of replicated dances at the time of arrest. With their hands flowing toward and away from the body, the dancers created designs on the body, covering parts in modesty, or pointing to them in seduction.

Having lost the representative criminal case against one dancer, the City of Seattle dropped the other cases. But the dancers lost their civil suit against the City (*Furfaro v. City of Seattle,* 1997), because Judge Carol A. Schapira gave the jury confusing instructions. She said the police did not need to consider part of the Seattle ordinance they acted under that deals with legal obscenity. The dancers are appealing (Hanna, 1998c, 1998d, 1998e).

In another contest of police/government against a club, Ben Zanganeh, the owner of an exotic dance club in Laurel, Maryland, closed it and then opened a rock-and-roll club on the site. "They set me up," Zanganeh said. "Police were there all the time. There was a memo at the station that said no problems at the club. But the captain told the cops to 'go find something wrong.' They got a stripper from Baltimore to dance and to violate rules and completely strip. I lost my license for a week and thought they'd keep after me" (personal communication, August 8, 1995).

Zoning and Bombing

Localities usually regulate where adult entertainment can be (for instance, a certain distance from schools). In its "generous" abatement zoning ordinance, Los Angeles offered "appropriate" sites for exotic dance clubs. The sites encompassed a local lake and harbor! Costly litigation for the city and clubs ensued. In *Topanga Press, Inc. v. City of Los Angeles* (1993), the Ninth Circuit Court said that certain conditions had to apply for a particular site to be considered part of the relevant real estate market. A property is "potentially" available when it is reasonable to believe that it might become available to any commercial enterprise; sites in manufacturing or industrial zones are part of the market if they are reasonably accessible to the general public, have the proper infrastructure of sidewalks, roads, and lighting, and are generally suitable for some form of commercial enterprise; and the site qualifies as part of the real estate market. Applying these criteria to relocation sites offered under the challenged Los Angeles ordinance, the Court concluded that much of the land "potentially available" for the relocation of adult businesses was not part of the real estate market and struck down the ordinance because it did not provide sufficient "reasonably available" sites for the relocation of adult businesses (Weinstein, 1997, pp. 395–396).

Some community members play with fire in the exotic dance game. A planned topless club was bombed in Fort Smith, Arkansas. Members of a nearby conservative religious congregation near the bomb site have repeatedly protested plans to open an adult nightclub, called Regina's Topless Bar. The owners said they would sue to overturn the city council's refusal to grant an operating permit (Reuters, May 29, 1997).

Changing the Rules

Local governments' tactics against exotic dance clubs include unfair play. They change the rules as soon as the clubs comply with the ordinances and amendments the governments enact, if the clubs thrive, in spite of restructuring their operations to meet the new requirements. The law is a mere toy to play with toward eliminating exotic dance. For example, the City of Dallas continues to amend its ordinances about attire, advertising, and zoning. First, it regulated no nudity. Skin-colored covering of the areola was permitted. Then the City redefined "simulated nudity." Dallas required nonflesh-colored, opaque pasties. Now the City wants every part of the breast below the top of the areola covered. (Yet, Janet Jackson's 1998 widely televised music video of the song, "I Get Lonely," shows all but the areola of the breast, framed by various costumes. Also, street and beach attire regularly show far more than what the city permits.) Dallas also requires exotic dancers to cover their buttocks. Through zoning, clubs had been separated from residences, churches, and schools. Then the City added additional facilities from which the clubs must be separated: historical districts, hospital zones, and child care facilities (these included registered and unregistered facilities interspersed throughout Dallas, including warehouse, commercial, and office building districts).

In 1994, the U.S. District Court, in *MDII Entertainment, Inc. v. City of Dallas*, ruled the City's regulation that the bottom half of the female dancers' breast be opaquely covered was unconstitutional as content-based restrictions on expression because it was not shown to be related to adverse secondary effects. So, in 1997, in a blatant end run around the ruling, Dallas changed the classification of the exotic dance clubs from dance hall to sexually-oriented business (SOB), with the very same breast covering restrictions, and added further regulations on contact between dancer and customer. Litigation is in process.

THE AGGRESSORS AND DEFENDANTS

The kinds of restrictive games that toy with exotic dance and the First Amendment result from the pressure of three groups: religious, feminist, and businesspeople and property owners. Some religious groups have made personal "lifestyle" issues central in contemporary political debate. Engaged in a moral crusade, they believe that expanding state control over sex and sexuality can reshape American culture along lines they prefer. Guardians of so-called "family values" strongly oppose exotic dance. Such ideological and religious fundamentalist groups as Pat Robertson's Christian Coalition, Donald Wildmon's American Family Association, and Washington Together Against Pornography spearhead assaults. They target the body as a surveillance zone central to the operation of power. Their agenda seeks to suppress all, or nearly all, information and entertainment about "sex," especially what they call the "petting zoos," "sexual assault parlors," and "rape cubicles." The "enemies of society," they believe, include exotic dancers.

It is hard to change the views of ideological religious groups that oppose exotic dance. However, there is legal recourse, albeit costly, to the new Puritans' legislative enactments against exotic dance.

A second contingent railing against exotic dance is composed of particular feminists who have, for contested terrain, allied themselves with the religious right, and some exotic dancers who had bad experiences (Holsopple, 1995). Some women have problems playing the game, finding it depressing, cynical, and overbearingly stigmatizing. Anthropologist Carol Vance (1993, p. 39) reports, "Fundamentalist and antiporn feminist attacks on art share more than rhetoric and tactics: both seek to reshape attitudes toward sexual imagery as part of a wide program of political, social, and legal reform."

Of course, feminists are divided amongst themselves (Jaggar, 1983; Jaggar & Rothenberg, 1993). Put simplistically, "neo-Marxist" feminists see a woman's choice to become an exotic dancer as the result of economic coercion: Dancers are held captive through high wages in exchange for abasement and abuse by men. "Radical" feminists believe that the basis of male dominance is male control of women's sexuality; "socialist" feminists view contemporary sexuality in terms of capitalism and male dominance. These feminists want to protect women from falling victim to male "lust," a perspective with 19th century roots, or exploitation, a 20th century view. Images in which women become the object of the rapacious male gaze in a patriarchal society are seen by some feminists as the principal cause of women's oppression (Ellis, O'Dair, & Tallmer, 1988). They consider dance intended for male sexual pleasure as degrading, subordinating, and allowing a woman to be vulnerable to violence.

Rebuttals to the feminist attacks on exotic dance come from some exotic dancers and civil libertarians, including certain other feminists. The exotic dancer, asserts Deborah Clipperton (1994, p. 13), a former stripper, displays her body "clearly also for her own pleasure," "viewing as well as being viewed." Exotic dancers have also defended their occupation on the grounds of values, art and entertainment, celebration of the female body and sexuality, self-empowerment, economic opportunity, and legitimate work. They rebut the charge of female dancers being subject to abuse any more than women in society writ large. Women commonly experience abuse within the military and in law offices, corporations, and automobile plants (see Grimsley, 1996).[1] Some exotic dancers say they learn how to handle verbal insults from customers while they perform, they look out for each other, and the club staff protects them against physical abuse.

Exotic dancers say the problem they face is neither degradation nor disempowerment. Instead, the problem is social stigmatization, the negative way their neighbors and family view them. Most people do not approve of exotic dance play. Interestingly, dancers rise in their esteem when they learn how much many earn.

Liberal feminists defend women's freedom to control their own exotic dance business without state interference, police harassment, or male dominance. Attacks against exotic dancing, they remind us, eerily recall the rationalization of totalitarian countries that eat away at human rights. "Looking historically and cross-culturally," Ellis, O'Dair, and Tallmer (1988, p. 8) say, "we see that when sexual expression is confined to the private sphere, women become more vulnerable to sexist practices, and women's concerns have a harder time claiming space in the realm of public discussion. Such silencing too easily serves, and has served in the past, to impose restrictions on women's behavior when it does not conform to the standards of a 'community' hostile to the development of women's autonomy and self-expression."

At the March 16, 1998, public hearing of the Lansing City Council on banning nudity, counsel Bradley J. Shafer concluded his remarks in defense of nudity in exotic dance clubs by quoting from Adolf Hitler's *Mein Kampf* (1943):

> Our whole public life today is like a hothouse for sexual ideas and stimulations. Just look at the bill of fare served up in our movies ... and theaters.... In shop windows and billboards the vilest means are used to attract the attention of the crowd.... If we do not lift the youth out of the morass of their present-day environment, they will drown in it. Anyone who refuses to see these things supports them, and thereby makes himself an accomplice in the slow prostitution of our future which whether we like it or not, lies in the coming generation. This cleansing of our culture must be extended to nearly all fields. Theater, art, literature, cinema, press, posters, and window displays must be cleansed of all manifestations of our rotting world and placed in the service of a moral, political, and cultural idea. Public life must be freed from the stifling perfume of our modern eroticism.... In all these things the goal and the road must be determined by concern for the preservation of the health of our people in body and soul. (pp. 254–255)

Members of Feminists for Free Expression note that women are exploited and harassed in all fields: "Exploitation will stop when it is vigorously prosecuted everywhere it occurs," stated McElroy (1995, p. 98). She goes on to ask two pointed questions. First, "Why is a naked female more of an 'object' than a clothed one?" And second, "If women's choices are to be trashed, why should radical feminists fare better than other women?" (p. 108).

CONCLUSION

Exotic dance is usually a pleasurable, gentle game played by the dancer and the patron. Exotic dance is also a hardball game with one side playing involuntarily. Caught in the culture war underway in our country, exotic dance clubs appear an easy target because of widely held negative stereotypes about them and their visibility in a huge sex industry ("The Sex Business," 1998; "The Sex Industry," 1998). There is little understanding of their transformation to upscale entertainment.

The war game pits exotic dancer, club, and patron interests in choice versus religious right, as well as certain feminist and businessperson interests in opposition. Each side has its organized efforts and how-to publications for the battle. The litigation is costly to both taxpayer and club stakeholder. Moralists, feminists, businesspeople, and local governments use laws against exotic dance to toy with the First Amendment and dancers', owners', and club staffs' livelihoods. However, the First Amendment is the overriding game book. The language we use to describe things affects the way we perceive them. Bifurcated in meaning, exotic dance is both business and adult play—fantasy and erotic dance art—on the bedrock of the First Amendment.

NOTE

[1] The U.S. Equal Employment Opportunity Commission accused the Mitsubishi Motors Corporation in Normal, Illinois, of allowing male employees to sexually harass hundreds of female workers—to engage in repeated "groping, grabbing, and touching," use abusive sexual language, require sexual relations as a condition of employment, and force women's resignations if they complained. This resembles what a few dancers, such as Kelly Holsopple (1995), say took place in exotic dance clubs but what most dancers vehemently deny. During my visits to over two dozen different clubs across the nation, I saw no such sexual harassment, although I heard reports of abuse in some clubs.

REFERENCES

44 Liquormart v. Rhode Island, 116 S. Ct. 1495 (1996).

Allen, R. C. (1991). *Horrible prettiness: Burlesque and American culture*. Chapel Hill, NC: University of North Carolina Press.

Barnes v. Glen Theatre, Inc., 501 U.S. 560 (1991).

Berlyne, D. E. (1971). *Aesthetics and psychobiology*. New York: Appleton-Century Crofts.

Boles, J. M. (1973). *The nightclub stripper: A sociological study of a deviant occupation*. Unpublished doctoral dissertation, University of Georgia, Athens.

Carchio v. Fort Lauderdale, No. 96-06697 (25), 96-06698 (07) (17th Cir., Broward County, Fl., May 1, 1996) (Justice Reporting Service, Inc. 523-6114).

City of Seattle v. Darcy Poole, No. 260398 (Mun. Ct. of Seattle, King County, Wash., 1996).

Clipperton, D. (1994). *Liberating the object: Representations of class, gender and high art in the work of two Toronto strippers*. Paper presented at the annual meeting of CORD, Denton, TX.

Donnerstein, E. I. (1995). Affidavit, State of Tennessee Public Indecency Statute Litigation (MDL Docket No. 1031).

Dragu, M., & Harrison, A. S. A. (1988). *Revelations: Essays on striptease and sexuality*. London, Ontario, Canada: Nightwood Editions.

Dunning, J. (1998, April 8). To see, even to enjoy, but perhaps not to understand. *New York Times*, p. B2.

Ellis, K., O'Dair, B., & Tallmer, A. (1988). Introduction. In K. Ellis, B. Jaker, N. D. Hunter, B. O'Dair, & A. Tallmer (Eds.), *Caught looking: Feminism, pornography and censorship* (pp. 4–9). Seattle, WA: The Real Comet Press.

Fine, G. A. (1991). Justifying fun: Why we do not teach exotic dance in high school. *Play and Culture, 4*, 87–99.

Fort Lauderdale Ordinance No. C-96-8 to Amend the Definition of Partial Nudity (1996), Code of Ordinances of the City of Ft. Lauderdale, Fl.

Frank, K. M. (1998). The production of identity and the negotiation of intimacy in a "gentleman's club." *Sexualities, 1*(2), 175–201.

Furfaro v. City of Seattle, No. 96-2-02226-8 (Mun. Ct. of Seattle, King County, Wash., 1997).

Goldberg, C. (1997, February 3). Bellevue journal: Family killings jolt a tranquil town. *New York Times*, p. A10.

Grimsley, K. D. (1996, April 10). EEOC says hundreds of women harassed at auto plant. *Washington Post*, p. A1, A13.

Hanbury, G. L. (1996). Memorandum no. 96-278, February 20, Agenda—Amendments to Adult Establishment Ordinances, February 15. Ordinance No. C-96. An Ordinance Amending Section 5-28.1, Nudity, Sexual Conduct Prohibited, of the Code of Ordinances of the City of Ft. Lauderdale, Fl.

Hanna, J. L. (1983). *The performer-audience connection: Emotion to metaphor in dance and society*. Austin, TX: University of Texas Press.

Hanna, J. L. (1986). Interethnic communication in children's own dance, play, and protest. In Y. Y. Kim (Ed.), *Interethnic communication* (Vol. 10, International and intercultural communication annual; pp. 176–198). Newbury Park, CA: Sage.

Hanna, J. L. (1987). *To dance is human: A theory of nonverbal communication* (Rev. ed.). Chicago: University of Chicago Press. (Original work published 1979)

Hanna, J. L. (1988a). *Dance, sex, and gender: Signs of identity, dominance, defiance, and desire*. Chicago: University of Chicago Press.

Hanna, J. L. (1988b). *Dance and stress: Resistance, reduction, and euphoria*. New York: AMS Press.

Hanna, J. L. (1996a). In defense of exotic dance. *Exotic Dancer Bulletin, 1*(3), 70, 72.

Hanna, J. L. (1996b). Exotic dance, the First Amendment, and court. *AnthroWatch, 4*(2), 12.

Hanna, J. L. (1997). Witness to injustice? *Exotic Dancer Bulletin, 2*(4), 80.

Hanna, J. L. (1998a). *Nudity—not nice?* Paper presented to Lansing City Council, Lansing, MI.

Hanna, J. L. (1998b, Summer). Undressing the First Amendment and corsetting the striptease dancer. *The Drama Review, 42*(2), 38–69.

Hanna, J. L. (1998c, Summer). Suing Seattle for wrongful arrest and conduct. *National Campaign for Freedom of Expression Quarterly*, 8.

Hanna, J. L. (1998d). Exotic dance in Seattle: The First Amendment and anthropology. *AnthroWatch, 6*(1), 4–6.

Hanna, J. L. (1998e). Defining dance in the courtroom. *Exotic Dancer Bulletin, 3*(3), 29.

Hitler, A. (1943). *Mein kampf* [My struggle]. New York: Houghton Mifflin.

Holsopple, K. (1995). From the dressing room: Women in strip clubs speak out! *WHISPER, 9*(1), 9.

Hull, S. (1980). *The psychology of stripping: A position paper.* Paper presented at Vancouver Community College, Langara, British Columbia, Canada.

International Food and Beverage, Inc. v. City of Ft. Lauderdale, No. 96-6577-CIV (S.D. Fl. 1996).

Jaggar, A. M. (1983). *Feminist politics and human nature.* Totowa, NJ: Rowman and Allanheld.

Jaggar, A. M., & Rothenberg, P. S. (1993). *Feminist frameworks: Alternative theoretical accounts of the relations between men and women* (3rd ed.). New York: McGraw Hill.

Lewin, L. (1984). *Naked is the best disguise: My life as a stripper.* New York: William Morrow & Co.

Liepe-Levinson, K. (1998). Striptease: Desire, mimetic jeopardy, and performing spectators. *The Drama Review, 42*(2), 9–37.

Liepe-Levinson, K. (1999). *Strip show: Performances of gender and desire.* New York: Routledge.

Loizos, C. (1969). Play behaviour in higher primates: A review. In D. Morris, (Ed.), *Primate ethology* (pp. 226–282). Garden City, NY: Doubleday Anchor.

Lytle, D. (1997). Problems, paradoxes and provocations: Defining play. In *Encyclopedia of exercise physiology* [On-line]. Available: database.rsnzgovt.nz/sportsei/encyc/index.htm/

McElroy, W. (1995). *A woman's right to pornography.* New York: St. Martin's Press.

McLaughlin, R. B. (1994, Summer). *Adult uses: Zoning and land use issues, a technical update.* Paper presented at the First Amendment Lawyers' Association Meeting, Santa Monica, CA.

McLaughlin, R. B. (1995, Summer). *Adult uses: Zoning and land use issues, a technical update.* Paper presented at the First Amendment Lawyers' Association Meeting, Chicago.

MDII Entertainment, Inc. v. City of Dallas, No. 393CV2093T (U.S. Dist. Ct. 1994).

Miller v. California, 413 U.S. 15 (1973).

Munsil, L. (1988). *The preparation and trial of an obscenity case: A guide for the prosecuting attorney.* Scottsdale, AZ: National Family Legal Foundation.

Munsil, L. (1994). *How to legally stop nude dancing in your community.* Scottsdale, AZ: National Family Legal Foundation.

Pally, M. (1991a). *Sense and censorship: The vanity of bonfires.* New York: Americans for Constitutional Freedom.

Pally, M. (1991b). *Sense and censorship: The vanity of bonfires resource materials on sexually explicit material, violent material and censorship: Research and public policy implications.* New York: Americans for Constitutional Freedom.

Paz, O. (1995). *The double flame: Love and eroticism.* New York: Harcourt Brace & Company.

Schechner, R. (1985). *Between theater and anthropology.* Philadelphia: University of Pennsylvania Press.

Schechner, R. (1988). *Performance theory* (Rev. ed.). New York: Routledge.

Seattle Municipal Code, Adult Entertainment Ordinance § 6.270.100(A)(2) (b) (1995).

The sex business. (1998, February 14). *The Economist*, 17–18.

The sex industry. (1998, February 14). *The Economist*, 21–23.

Sutton-Smith, B. (1974). Towards an anthropology of play. *Association for the Anthropological Study of Play Newsletter, 1*(2), 8–15.

Sutton-Smith, B. (1997). *The ambiguity of play*. Boston: Harvard University Press.

Tiersma, P. M. (1993). Nonverbal communication and the freedom of speech. *Wisconsin Law Review, 6*, 1525–1589.

Topanga Press, Inc. v. City of Los Angeles, 989 F.2d 1524 (9th Cir. 1993).

Turner, V. (1969). *The ritual process: Structure and anti-structure*. Chicago: Aldine.

Turner, V. (1974). Dramas, fields, and metaphor: Symbolic action in human society. Ithaca, NY: Cornell University Press.

Turner, V. (1982). *From ritual to theatre*. New York: Performing Arts Journal Publications.

Vance, C. S. (1993, September). Feminist fundamentalism—women against images. *Art in America*, 35–37, 39.

Webster's ninth new collegiate dictionary. (1986). Springfield, MA: Merriam-Webster.

Weinstein, A. (1997). Land use and the First Amendment: Recent developments in land use, planning and zoning law. *The Urban Lawyer, 29*(3), 387–398.

Young v. American Mini Theatres, Inc., 427 U.S. 50, 96 S. Ct. 2440 (1976).

part II
Children's Play Contexts and Rules

4

Kindergarten and College Students' Views of Play and Work at Home and at School*

Robyn M. Holmes
Monmouth University

At The Association for the Study of Play (TASP) Annual Meeting in 1997, a panel of past, present, and future TASP presidents noted that a precise definition of play has remained elusive. Numerous definitions and metaphors appear in play literature, and each is dependent upon the researcher's theoretical orientation and research agenda. Although most play researchers agree on the basic criteria essential to classify an activity as play, the concept is an amorphous one that possesses boundaries that are unclear, further highlighted when play is compared and contrasted with the seemingly polar activity of work.

As Baker (1977) suggested, the majority of Western children typically spend their days moving through designated segments of time such as "school time," "play time," and "work time." Such antithetical Western notions of play and work are appendages from the Puritan work ethic (e.g., Hughes, 1995; Overman, 1983), and have led to the creation of the play/work dichotomy, which has surfaced in both past and contemporary play literature (Blanchard, 1986; Hughes, 1995; Huizinga, 1955; Manley, 1986; Stevens, 1980). Although this dichotomy has served to define the concepts of play and work, it has also contributed to a limited, yet more profound understanding of these concepts.

* I sincerely thank the children and the college students who participated in this project, Dr. Bruce Cunningham for commenting on an earlier draft, and two of my students, Dennis Bott and Andrea Guzzo, for their help in coding the questionnaire data.

For example, in the past, play was often defined by what it is not. Huizinga's (1955) seminal work on the characteristics of play defined this activity as the antithesis of work and seriousness. Hence, play was viewed as fun, voluntary, and motivated intrinsically.

By contrast, work was perceived as serious, literal, and motivated extrinsically (see also Hughes, 1995). To this end, the objective of many past studies was to classify activities as either play or work (see, e.g., Vandenberg, 1984). Vandenberg argued that play should be viewed as essential to how one defines reality, rather than as a silly or superfluous undertaking. This latter view of play served only to reinforce the play/work dichotomy.

However, such categorical and comparative studies of play and work do not give much attention to how humans go about formulating their mental constructions or concepts of play and work. Hence, in the past, these terms were viewed as mutually exclusive, rather than as having extended boundaries. The latter notion is in line with the current thinking on human cognition and how people go about internally structuring their categories (see, e.g., Mervis, 1987; Rosch, 1973). Relatedly, Schwartzman (1978) has argued successfully that play may contain characteristics of work and visa versa. For example, Schwartzman contended that one can play at work and one can work at play (see also Abramis, 1990). In addition, play can be extremely serious—a characteristic associated with work. One needs only to observe two players involved in a fiercely competitive game to see how serious play can become.

The play/work dichotomy has received particular attention in studies aimed at improving educational practices, curricula, and learning environments (e.g., Cunningham & Wiegel, 1992; Hennessey & Berger, 1993; King, 1982). In the classroom, play and work are pervasive concepts for children and teachers. The importance of these concepts and the distinctions made between them in the classroom has led to the production of numerous studies that have examined both the teacher and the children's conceptions of these categories. For example, a study by Perlmutter and Burell (1995) suggested that when play and work are entwined in the classroom, this combination serves to help children manage time more effectively.

In a related work, Robson (1993) conversed with English nursery and primary school children to discover their notions about play, work, and learning. Her findings suggested that children categorized an activity as play by social criteria, whereas an activity was considered work if it was teacher-initiated (see also Marshall's 1994 study with kindergarten children that examined children's comprehension of their academic tasks).

Other researchers have conducted studies on children's emic conceptions of play, work, and play as work. In her germinal work, King (1979) utilized interviewing procedures to examine the teacher and the children's conceptions of play and work. In her sample, teachers classified more activities as play than the children did. In addition, the children classified activities as play if the activity was liked, selected voluntarily, and accompanied by free use of materials. By contrast, these children perceived work as any activity that was assigned by their teacher.

In a similar study, Smith, Takhvar, Gore, and Vollstedt (1986) examined children's emic conceptions of play and play as work. In agreement with King's (1979) previous study, children again categorized tasks as work if they were assigned by a teacher. This held true even if the work was given in the form of play. Similarly, King (1982) noted that children appeared to define work and play on the basis of particular social criteria. For work, these included assigned tasks. By contrast, for play, these included whether or not an activity was voluntarily selected, on an interrupted time span, and included free use of materials.

Cunningham and Wiegel (1992) studied teacher and children's emic perceptions of play and work by asking both groups to classify activities at school as play, work, or neither play nor work. In this study, children and teachers performed a picture-sorting task in which they classified activities, materials, and routines along the play-work continuum. Their findings suggested that children and teacher perceptions were congruent in the school context.

Finally, Wing (1995) also studied play and work from the children's perspective. This study revealed that children classify their activities at school along the play-work continuum, mirroring Cunningham and Wiegel's (1992) previous study. For example, activities were distinguished on the basis of criteria that included whether or not an activity was fun, voluntarily selected, and required cognitive effort among others. In addition, some activities were classified as "in between" play and work, providing evidence that these activities exist along a continuum rather than as mutually exclusive categories. Goodman (1994) also maintained a similar view of play and work as a continuum, rather than as polar opposites. In her study, Goodman found that at the center of this continuum, children placed activities that they initiated and found pleasurable, whereas other activities were placed at the end of the continuum.

Previous research on children's notions of play and work were conducted primarily in the context of the school about school-related activities. In order to gain a more complete understanding of play and work, it seems reasonable to investigate the views of children and adults in different contexts. The present study sought to examine and compare developmentally children and young adults' views of play and work as they occur in different contextual situations, that is, home and school. Operating under the premise that play and work are not mutually exclusive categories, this study planned to contribute to the existing literature by exploring the contextualized definitions of these concepts.

METHOD

Participants

This sample of participants was cross-sectional and contained two age groups. The children who served as participants were enrolled in a kindergarten class in a primary school that was located in a predominantly lower socioeconomic neighborhood. In the sample, there were 22 African American (9 boys and 13 girls), 2 European American (1 boy and 1 girl), and 2 Latino (1 boy and 1 girl) children. All of the children were at least five years old and some celebrated their sixth birthday while the data collection period was in progress.

The adult participants were all university students who were enrolled in an undergraduate psychology course. As part of their course requirements, these volunteers received course credit for participating in this project. In this sample, there were 47 European American (20 males, 27 females), 2 African American (1 male, 1 female), and 3 Latino (1 male, 2 female) participants. They ranged in age from 18 to 24 years. The rationale behind the selection of these two age groups was that these two groups represented arguably the beginning and end of the school experience for most children in the United States. Their shared educational experiences would serve as the basis for comparison of these two concepts in different contexts.

However, it is acknowledged that school experiences are subject to both intra- and inter-individual variation. A child's ethnicity and parental socioeconomic status are just a couple of the factors that can affect the school experience. However, school culture contains several core features (e.g., power and school structures, characteristics of the student-teacher relationship, adherence to class rules, completing homework, etc.) that serve to provide common core experiences for all students in which the concepts of play and work are employed. Shared educational experiences are discussed here in this light.

Finally, all proper names have been replaced with pseudonyms, and participants were treated according to the American Psychological Association guidelines for ethical treatment of human participants.

Design and Procedure

Data were collected from both samples via qualitative methods. For the kindergarten sample, data were collected using participant observation and unstructured interviewing. The children were interviewed both individually and in small groups during their indoor free play periods. In each situation, the children were asked a similar set of open-ended queries that were conceptually equivalent to the adult questionnaire, but were modified for developmental appropriateness. Informal conversations about play and work with individual children occurred throughout the school day at other opportune times, such as small group projects, developmental education class, and line formations.

The college participants were required to complete anonymously a four-page questionnaire that contained 15 questions on play and work. The original questions appear in Table 4.1 and Table 4.2. The completed questionnaires were returned to the researcher by dropping them in a box located in the psychology department. Participants were given the option of either completing the questionnaire on site or returning it to the researcher within a week's time.

Prior to coding the questionnaires, the author trained two student assistants how to code and categorize responses using completed sample questionnaires as a guide. Each question was categorized and coded independently by at least two coders to ensure reliability. Coders were in agreement in coding and categorizing all responses.

TABLE 4.1.
Adult Responses to Queries on Play

Responses	Frequencies[1]	
	Male	Female
1. What characteristics are necessary for you to define an activity as play?		
1. To have fun	5	12
2. Fun activities, not required or voluntarily selected	4	13
3. Physical movement	5	7
2. How do you define the word *play* at home?		
1. Social interaction	6	19
2. Relaxing	0	6
3. Doing what one wants	6	4
3. What kind of play activities do you engage in at home?		
1. Sports	12	19
2. Toys and video games	4	17
4. How do you define the word *play* at school?		
1. Social interactions and having fun	9	24
2. Physical activity/sports	5	12
5. What kind of play activities do you engage in at school?		
1. Social activities/parties	4	29
2. Sports activities	24	6
6. Does your definition of play change when you move from the context of home to school?		
Yes	6	20
No	11	10

[1] Frequency totals contain the actual number of responses. Responses for question #5 contained multiple category codings. These were counted as separate responses.

TABLE 4.2.
Adult Responses to Queries on Work

Responses	Frequencies[2]	
	Male	Female
1. What characteristics are necessary for you to define an activity as "work"?		
1. Something that has to be done	3	14
2. Not enjoyable	4	12
3. Goal-oriented	6	13
2. How do you define the word *work* at home?		
1. Helping parents around the house	6	6
2. Working around the house	5	8
3. Cooking, cleaning, laundry	1	4
4. School homework	1	21
3. What kind of work activities do you engage in at home?		
1. Domestic activities—cooking, cleaning, food shopping, laundry	9	38
2. Yardwork	10	6
3. Schoolwork	4	21
4. Childcare	0	5
4. How do you define the word *work* at school?		
1. Class assignments/homework/studying for tests	11	30
2. Unenjoyable time	3	3
5. What kind of work activities do you engage in at school?		
1. Class assignments	10	28
2. Studying	7	14
3. Homework	6	23
6. How does the context of work change from home to school?		
1. Home/help parents; school/career objective	1	6
2. Home/physical; school/mental	4	6
3. Home/less pressure; school/more pressure	4	11
4. No change	23	7
7. Please discuss the similarities and differences between play and work.		
Similarities		
1. Both activities	1	6
2. Both require energy	5	4
3. They can be fun	2	7
4. They complement one another	3	5
5. None	4	9
Differences		
1. Play is relaxing; work is stressful	3	9
2. Play is enjoyable; work is not	5	22
3. Play is voluntarily selected; work is not	2	8

[2] Frequency totals contain the actual number of responses. Responses for questions #3 and #5 contained multiple category codings. These were counted as separate responses.

TABLE 4.2. (continued)
Adult Responses to Queries on Work

Responses	Frequencies	
	Male	Female
8. What percentage of time, per day and per week, do you devote to play and work?		
1. 50/50	3	13
2. Play greater than 50	8	8
3. Play less than 50	3	11
9. What value do you place upon play in your life?		
1. Helps relieve stress	5	9
2. As important as work	1	7
3. Adds fun and excitement to life	2	7
4. A vital part of life	3	6

RESULTS

The Kindergarten Sample

Because data collection and subsequent analyses were performed individually for each of the age groups, the findings will be presented separately. Comparisons and interpretations of group findings will be revealed in the discussion. For the kindergarten children, interview data revealed the following trends regarding their conceptions of play and work activities at home and school.

For this sample of children, the word *play* was defined in the context of home and school as either playing with a friend or playing with a toy (see, e.g., Holmes, 1991). For example, I asked one child, named Rich, "When you use the word *play* at home, what do you mean?" He replied, "When you play with toys ... and play with your friends." I received similar responses when I queried the children about the definition of play at school. Classroom observations supported the children's notions that play was an activity engaged in with friends (notably peers), whereas an activity performed for and with the teacher was perceived as work. For all of the children in this sample, play activities were distinguishable from other activities because the former possessed the criteria of "fun" and were freely selected.

For this sample of children, "work" was defined in the context of home and school as something that they were asked to do by a "grown-up." At school, this grown-up was the teacher. For example, I asked Melissa, "What's the difference between play and work?" She replied, "When you play, you can do anything you want. Work is when you do everything the teacher says." At home, this adult was a parent, caretaker, or sometimes an older sibling. For example, I asked James, "When you use the word *work* at home, what do you mean?" He replied, "My mom makes me do work. She makes me clean my room."

The children's definitions of work and play remained stable when they were queried about these terms in the context of home and school. However, what did change, depending upon contextual situations, was the activities the children categorized as work. At school, work activities were those assigned by the teacher, and required a pencil and intense concentration. Observations of the children's facial expressions during work and play activities suggested that both activities at times required intense concentration. Depending upon the task, both play and work activities were also capable of eliciting smiles from the children. These observations served to support the notion that the boundaries of play and work concepts are blended.

Implicit in work activities was the notion that the children needed to provide the teacher with clear and predetermined responses that were judged by her as either correct or incorrect. For example, I asked Kevin, "When you're at school, what does the word *work* mean?" He replied, "Doing your math. You gotta answer all the things on your sheet the right way." Brian responded to the same query: "Do your math, writing, and do your homework." Almost all of the children's responses to this question listed mathematics, worksheets, and writing as work activities they performed at school.

Relatedly, work activities elicited from the children and performed at home by them contained activities that were also school-related. For example, Loretta and Emma's responses to the query, "What kinds of work do you do at home?" included "homework." However, when I asked Catherine the same question, she replied, "Clean up your room." David's response was similar to Catherine's, except he added, "raking the leaves." Thus, activities performed at home and categorized as work included both household chores and schoolwork.

Finally, given the recent debate over the position of recess in schools (see, e.g., Pellegrini, 1989, 1995; Sutton-Smith, 1990), the kindergarten children were asked how they would feel if they weren't allowed to play at school. Common adjectives received for this query were "sad" and "mad." Todd's response seemed to echo a sentiment held by most of the children: "I wouldn't like it [school]. All we do in school is work. I like to play." The children enjoyed their play time and wanted it to remain a part of their school day. For some of the children it was the "best part" of their school day "...cause we have fun when we play. We can do what we want." (see also Pellegrini, 1995).

The College Sample

Results from the sample university questionnaires revealed the following generalizations regarding conceptions of play and work in the context of home and school. Responses to queries for play and work appear respectively in Table 4.1 and Table 4.2.

The majority of respondents defined play as an activity that was voluntarily selected, fun, and not required of them. Approximately 84% of the females and 41% of the males noted these definitional criteria. The respondents were further asked to subdivide their general definition of play according to context. For example, approximately 70% of the females noted the following inclusive activities in their definition of play at home: social interactions with either family or friends and relaxing. By contrast, approximately 50% of the males defined play at home as playing games and enjoying the freedom to do whatever one wants.

When asked what kind of play activities they engaged in at home, the majority of female and male respondents listed games, toys, video games, and board games as play activities. Interestingly, almost an equal number of males and females listed sports as a play activity.

Definitions of play at school appeared to parallel the responses for play at home. More than half of the female respondents described play at school as those activities that involved social interactions with friends and that contained the element of fun. Both males and females included physical activities such as sports in their definition of play at school. Inclusive activities paralleled the responses for play activities at home: females reported social activities, whereas male respondents listed sports activities.

When asked whether their definition of play was dependent upon context more than half of the females responded affirmatively; whereas, approximately half of the male respondents, as well as a comparable number of females, reported that their definition of play remained stable across contexts. Responses to earlier questions appear to support these findings.

The sample was then asked a similar set of questions for the concept of "work." The majority of females defined work as mandatory, goal-oriented, and not enjoyable. Male respondents reported similar criteria. This concept was further subdivided into definitions of work in the context of home and school. Approximately 66% of the female respondents listed schoolwork in their definition of work at home. Approximately half of the male respondents included helping parents and working around the house. Inclusive activities of work performed at home for all female respondents were domestic activities such as cooking and cleaning and more than half included food shopping. Approximately 33% of the male respondents reported domestic activities and about 50% listed yardwork. Although the percentage was small, approximately 25% of the females reported childcare responsibilities, whereas no males reported this responsibility.

Definitions of work at school for all females and 50% of the male respondents included class assignments and homework at school. All male and female respondents listed either studying, class assignments, or homework as inclusive activities for work at school. When queried whether the context of work changed from home to school, over 50% of the females and 33% of the males viewed no change in work from home to school. However, an interesting dichotomy emerged: Approximately 20% of the males and 50% of the females viewed home as a less-pressured environment where you help your parents. By contrast, school was viewed as a pressured environment. The college sample was then asked to discuss the similarities and differences between play and work. Approximately 50% of the males and 60% of the females viewed play and work as both being fun, complementary, and requiring energy. Both males and females viewed play and work as being different in that play was enjoyable, relaxing, and voluntary; work was viewed as the antithesis of play.

Only the college sample answered the following question, "What is the percentage of time per day and per week that you devote to play and work?" (This question was not developmentally appropriate for the kindergarten children.) The majority of females claimed to devote an equal amount of time to play and work. However, a considerably higher proportion of males claimed to devote more time to play than work. Finally, the college sample was asked about the value they placed upon play in their lives. In this sample of males and females, play was viewed almost unanimously as a positive activity, a way to have fun, a way to relieve stress, and an integral part of life.

DISCUSSION

This sample of kindergarten children and college students agree upon the ingredients necessary to consider an activity play, that is, it has to be "fun." In addition, both children and adults classify an activity as play if it is not a required task. This confirms previous findings reported in literature which contend that play should be selected voluntarily (see, e.g., King, 1979; Robson, 1993; Wing, 1995). It seems plausible to suggest that such agreements may be associated with educational experiences shared by the two age groups.

However, an interesting gender difference arises between the two samples. In the context of home and school, the children offer a monosemic definition of play as either playing with a friend or playing with a toy. By contrast, the college sample's responses to the question "How do you define the word *play* in the context of home or school?" differed by gender.

For example, the female college students listed social interactions and events as play. In contrast, male college students listed play activities, such as sports and those involving physical movement. This finding supports the current literature on gender differences and play, that is, girls as more inclined to engage in activities that involve social interactions, whereas boys are inclined to engage in play activities that are more physical in nature and occupy large play territories (e.g., Crombie & Desjardins, 1993; Parker, 1984; Pellegrini, 1990, 1995). This finding also seems to suggest developmentally that girls choose to play with friends and remain people-oriented into young adulthood.

By contrast, boys choose to play sports and with toys, remaining object-oriented into young adulthood. One possible explanation may lie in the differential socialization experiences of boys and girls. Research suggests that girls are socialized around family and establishing and maintaining dyadic social relationships. In contrast, boys are socialized to be adventurous and independent and partake in group activities (e.g., Collins, 1984; Maccoby, 1990; Williams & Best, 1990).

It is also interesting to note that an equal number of males and females listed sports as a play activity. Another possible explanation for these responses is that male and female student athletes were included in the sample and were not isolated as a subsample.

Although the college respondents reported that their definitions of play changed when given a change in context, activities reported as play at home and school suggest that play definitions remain stable across contexts, and only the activities in which one engages changes. Similar findings appear for the children in both the context of home and school.

Both samples of kindergarten children and college students agree that the characteristics that are necessary to categorize an activity as work include nonvoluntary participation and whether it is enjoyable. The college sample, by virtue of increasing cognitive abilities and socialization experiences, also recognize that work is extrinsically motivated. This criterion is not a part of the children's classification scheme, however, striking similarities emerge between the kindergarten and college samples with regards to activities defined as work at home and school. Because they share membership in a similar sociocultural world—that is, school—both samples included school homework as work performed at home. Also, both children and college students report household chores as work activities performed at home.

Different criteria also emerge in the kindergarten children and college students' definitions of work at school. Both samples include class assignments and activities that involve learning, presumably because the school experience for both groups is governed by a similar rule structure. However, only the child sample included social criteria such as "doing what the teacher tells you to do." For the kindergarten children, the student-teacher relationship is one that implies authority. The teacher disciplines them to sit still and be quiet, insists that they follow class rules, and tells them to complete their work. In contrast, college students, by virtue of their extended experiences in school culture, have been socialized and internalized such behaviors and knowledge. Although authority is a characteristic of the student-teacher relationship, it presumably is not verbally expressed for the college student. Other factors are probably operating as well. For example, it seems reasonable to suppose that the college sample is aware that they must meet certain requirements in order to graduate and embark on their future career endeavors. Also, it would be nice to think that students are genuinely enthusiastic about what they are studying and learning at school.

In addition, the college sample was asked how the context of work changes from home to school. Although most reported there were no changes, several interesting findings emerge and seem to contradict reported adult responses. First, the college sample created an antithetical pair of physical work/mental work to describe the differences between work performed at home and at school. For example, one student stated, "Work at school is more mental and is required for power in the real world." Second, the dimension of pressure is introduced as a continuum with home having less pressure than that experienced at school. For example, pressure is experienced at school to "maintain a good GPA (grade point average)," and because of the "*stressful* task of trying to pass the semester with good grades" and "deadlines." Relatedly, the college students also reported that they experienced "relationship pressure" at school. No comparable findings emerge for the kindergarten sample since presumably they have not yet been socialized to experience pressure per se at school as it relates to one's future career.

When I asked the kindergarten children for the similarities and differences between play and work, the majority were able only to provide distinctions between the two concepts. The younger children do not perceive any similarities between play and work, perhaps because they view them as mutually exclusive categories. For the college sample, work and play possess both similarities and differences. In the former case, both activities require the expenditure of energy and are at times fun. Differences are more pronounced. To this end, the typical dichotomy of work/play emerges. Examples include play is relaxing/work is stressful; play is fun/work is not; and play is voluntary/work is not. Such patterns of thinking are typical of the way children at this age go about constructing their representations of the world. For children of this age, the world is comprised of absolute categories and distinctions (e.g., Holmes, 1995). One would expect the young adults of this study to exhibit more cognitive flexibility.

Also, the college sample received one question the kindergarten children did not. It asked about the percentage of time the college students devoted to play and work per day and per week. Interestingly, gender differences emerge. In this sample, the males claimed to devote more time to play than work, whereas the majority of females claimed to devote an equal amount of time to play and work. Finally, the kindergarten children and the college students both recognize the value of play in their lives.

CONCLUSION

The findings of this study suggest that these kindergarten children and college students are able to discuss play and work as they are defined and performed in different contextual situations. In addition, similarities in criteria for play and work are common across a wide age range. This suggests that criteria for structuring these categories remain stable over time. Differences in definitions and activities performed are dependent upon age (as a consequence of increasing cognitive abilities) and experience. However, I should be reluctant to extend these conclusions beyond this work. Both the kindergarten and college samples were relatively homogeneous with respect to ethnic and socioeconomic factors.

Future research may wish to further investigate the contextualized bases of these terms with different samples in terms of age, ethnicity, and socioeconomic status. One might also wish to investigate the stability and flexibility of these terms in different contexts. Such studies will prove fruitful in providing an explanation for how knowledge and structuring concepts develops and changes with age.

REFERENCES

Abramis, D. (1990). Play in work: Childish hedonism or adult enthusiasm? *American Behavioral Scientist, 33*, 353–373.

Baker, D. (1977) Worlds of play. *Childhood Education, 53*, 245–249.

Blanchard, K. (1986). Play as adaptation: The work/play dichotomy revisited. In B. Mergen (Ed.), *Cultural dimensions of play, games and sport* (Vol. 10, pp. 79–87). Champaign, IL: Human Kinetics.

Collins, W. (1984). *Development during middle childhood: The years from six to twelve.* Washington, DC: National Academy Press.

Crombie, G., & Desjardins, M. (1993, March). *Predictors of gender: The relative importance of children's play, games, and personality characteristics.* Paper presented at the Biennial Conference of the Society for Research in Child Development, New Orleans, LA.

Cunningham, B., & Wiegel, J. (1992). Preschool work and play activities: Child and teacher perspectives. *Play & Culture, 5*, 92–99.

Goodman, J. (1994). "Work" versus "play" and early childhood care. *Child and Youth Care Forum, 23*, 177–196.

Hennessey, B., & Berger, A. (1993, March). *Children's conceptions of work and play: Exploring an alternative to the discounting principle.* Paper presented at the 60th Biennial Meeting of the Society for Research in Child Development, New Orleans, LA. (ERIC Document Reproduction Service No. ED361084)

Holmes, R. (1991). Categories of play: A kindergartner's view. *Play & Culture, 4*, 43–50.

Holmes, R. (1995). *How young children perceive race.* Thousand Oaks, CA: Sage.

Hughes, F. (1995). *Children, play and development.* Boston: Allyn & Bacon.

Huizinga, J. (1955). *Homo ludens: A study of the play element in culture.* Boston: Beacon Press.

King, N. (1979). Play: The kindergartners' perspective. *The Elementary School Journal, 80*, 81–87.

King, N. (1982). Children's conceptions of work and play. *Social Education, 46*, 110–113.

Maccoby, E. (1990). Gender and relationships: A developmental account. *American Psychologist, 45*, 513–520.

Manley, K. (1986). Parody: Simultaneous work and play. In K. Blanchard (Ed.), *The many faces of play* (Vol. 9, pp. 133–140). Champaign, IL: Human Kinetics.

Marshall, H. (1994). Children's understanding of academic tasks: Work, play, or learning. *Journal of Research in Childhood Education, 9*, 35–46.

Mervis, C. (1987). Child basic object categories and early lexical development. In U. Neisser (Ed.), *Concepts and conceptual development: Ecological and intellectual factors in categorization* (pp. 201–233). Cambridge, England: Cambridge University Press.

Overman, S. (1983). Work and play in America: Three centuries of commentary. *Physical Educator, 40*, 184–190.

Parker, S. (1984). Playing for keeps: An evolutionary perspective on human games. In P. K. Smith (Ed.), *Play in animals and humans* (pp. 271–294). Oxford, England: Basil Blackwell.

Pellegrini, A. (1989). Elementary school children's rough-and-tumble play. *Early Childhood Research Quarterly, 4,* 245–260.

Pellegrini, A. (1990). Elementary school children's playground behavior: Implications for children's social-cognitive development. *Children's Environments Quarterly, 7,* 8–16.

Pellegrini, A. (1995). *School recess and playground behavior: Educational and developmental roles.* Albany, NY: State University of New York Press.

Perlmutter, J., & Burell, L. (1995) Learning through "play" as well as "work" in the primary grades. *Young Children, 50,* 14–21.

Robson, S. (1993). "Best of all I like choosing time": Talking with children about play and work. *Early Child Development and Care, 92,* 37–51.

Rosch, E. (1973). On the internal structure of perceptual and semantic categories. In T. Moore (Ed.), *Cognitive development and the acquisition of language* (pp. 111–114). New York: Academic Press.

Schwartzman, H. (1978). Introductory notes to Chapter IV. In M. Salter (Ed.), *Play: Anthropological perspectives* (pp. 185–187). NY: Leisure Press.

Smith, P. K., Takhvar, M., Gore, N., & Vollstedt, R. (1986). Play in young children: Problems of definition, categorization and measurement. *Early Child Development and Care, 19,* 25–41.

Stevens, P. (1980). Play and work: A false dichotomy? In H. Schwartzman (Ed.), *Play and Culture* (pp. 38-48) West Point, NY: Leisure Press.

Sutton-Smith, B. (1990). School playground as festival. *Children's Environments Quarterly, 7,* 3–7.

Vandenberg, B. (1984). Play, logic and reality. *Imagination, Cognition and Personality, 3,* 353–363.

Williams, J., & Best, D. (1990). *Sex and psyche: Gender and self viewed cross-culturally* (Vol. 13). Newbury Park, CA: Sage.

Wing, L. (1995). Play is not the work of the child: Young children's perceptions of work and play. *Early Childhood Research Quarterly, 10,* 223–247.

5

Development Reflected in Chase Games*

Loretta J. Clarke
University of Texas at Austin

INTRODUCTION

Play

Play is an integral part of most warm-blooded animals (Burghardt, 1984; Smith, 1984). While adults engage in playing, it is normally thought of as something for the young, or children. But, as Karl Groos said, "The animals do not play because they are young, but they have their youth because they play." (1898/1976, p. 76) There have been questions about why we play, as well as the functions it serves. In light of these questions, there have been some theories developed about play, including: a) the surplus energy theory; b) the relaxation theory; c) the preparation theory; d) the recapitulation theory; and e) the instinct theory (Ellis, 1973; Frost, 1992; Groos, 1898/1976, 1901; James, 1890/1950; Piaget, 1962; Schwartzman, 1978; Sutton-Smith, 1977a, 1977b, 1997). The surplus energy theory is most often used when explaining play (Burghardt, 1984; Ellis, 1973; Frost, 1992; Groos, 1901; Parker, 1984). It is believed that there is a surplus of energy pent up inside the animal or person, thus they engage in play. This theory has been refuted by some because it has

---

* I would like to recognize my classmate, Jeff Schneider, for all of his hard work in performing research and working on the Piagetian parallel with me. If it were not for him, the concept would not exist. I would also like to thank Dr. Joe Frost for his encouragement in researching chase games. Finally, I would like to thank Dr. Stuart Reifel and my blind editors for helping out with my text and final paper.

been observed that even when children are exhausted they will play (Burghardt, 1984; Ellis, 1973; Frost, 1992; Groos, 1901; Parker, 1984).

The relaxation theory purports that play behaviors occur in order to relax oneself. This seems more explanatory for adults than children, as children do not appear to have as much stress as adults do. Anthropologists and psychologists usually use the last three theories of recapitulation, preparation, and instinct to explain why certain play behaviors occur. For example, it is said that seeking games are played to prepare young children for hunting and gathering food. Then the instinct theory would say that since hunting and gathering food are essential for survival, the children have an instinct to play such games. This kind of goes hand-in-hand with the recapitulation theory, which says that because hunting and gathering were necessary for ancestors' survival, we play these games to recapitulate phylogeny for ontogeny (Groos, 1898/1976, 1901; James, 1890/1950; Piaget, 1962; Schwartzman, 1978).

Still others have similar ideas about why play behaviors exists. Brian Sutton-Smith (1977a) believes that playing is a preadaptive behavior. This means that play does not actually prepare for life in society, because the behaviors may or may not come into being beyond play. Thus, he says play preadapts children, it does not prepare children for society. Many believe that play is a preparation to live in society or culture in such a way that it allows freedom and rebellious behaviors to occur without any real consequences (Schwartzman, 1978; Sutton-Smith, 1977b).

More recently, Brian Sutton-Smith (1997) has refuted many of the existing theories about play, based on the lack of empirical evidence for their being. In his book, *The Ambiguity of Play* (1997), he even questions his own theory of play as being "preadaptive." He refers to play as rhetoric because there are so many interdisciplinary definitions and theories of it, each with their own insight. Sutton-Smith concludes in his book that play has developed in two stages: 1) reinforcement of synaptic variability, and 2) the organism modeling its own biological character.

There are many theories that explain play behaviors. Most of these mentioned are traditional theories. They have survived because they all have some credit to the explanation of play, but no one theory does so completely (Ellis, 1973; Sutton-Smith, 1997). There are also modern theories about play behavior (Frost, 1992), but they are less applicable to this search.

There is no clear-cut definition for play, but it appears that young humans and animals can differentiate between play and other behaviors without any definitions. It is researchers that require a definition of play in order to study the behavior. As such, there have been some characteristics of play that have been agreed upon by researchers. These play characteristics include that a) it is pleasurable; b) it is spontaneous and free, c) the players are active; d) it can be considered unproductive; e) it occurs separate from other activities; and f) it is voluntary (Burghardt, 1984; Ellis, 1973; Sack, 1977; Sutton-Smith, 1977b, 1997). Games are not believed to be the same as play because games involve rules and do not allow the freedom that is allowed by playing (Ellis, 1973; Frost, 1992; Piaget, 1962; Sack, 1977; Schwartzman, 1978).

Games

It is not unrealistic that there is a differentiation between play behavior and games. When a child is engaged in a game, she is playing. But just because a child is playing, she does not have to be engaged in a game. The characteristics of games are skill, chance, and strategy (Schwartzman, 1978; Sutton-Smith, 1972, 1977b). Some games involve one aspect, but many games include a combination of aspects. The games played by infants serve to develop the muscles and skills necessary for movement and survival in life (Frost, 1992; Groos, 1901; Piaget, 1962). As children get older, the games they play help them to deal with life and society. For example, games of "peek-a-boo" and "hide-and-seek" are thought to help children understand object permanence (Bruner & Sherwood, 1976; Phillips, 1967; Piaget, 1962).

While games are often categorized as separate from playing, in reality they are interconnected. It can be argued that even when toddlers are engaged in fantasy play, there are still inherent rules they must follow in order to participate. Also, even when older children engage in games with set rules, there is still the freedom of playing and possibly changing the rules according to the participants' culture. Thus, play and games are often used synonymously in writing and research.

Chase Games

There are categories of games that researchers have developed in order to help explain and study games and play. Chase games, which include tagging and hiding, come under a category that Brian Sutton-Smith (1972, 1977b) developed, which is "central person games." Chase games mostly involve physical skill, as one needs speed and agility to be successful (Brewster, 1976; Groos, 1901; Gump & Sutton-Smith, 1955). Chase games can also involve strategy, as in "hide-and-seek," where the players on both sides have to plan their strategy in order to catch or not be caught. And, as in any game, the element of chance is always present.

Children from cultures all over the world have been observed playing chase, tagging, and hiding games (Culin, 1976; Groos, 1898/1976, 1901; Gump & Sutton-Smith, 1955; James, 1890/1950; Kirchner, 1991; Maccoby, Modiano, & Lander, 1964; Opie & Opie, 1969; Phillips, 1967; Schwartzman, 1978; Sutton-Smith, 1972, 1977b). There are several theories about why children play these games. As mentioned earlier, "hide-and-seek" and "peek-a-boo" games are thought to be played so that children can learn object permanence. Others have said that hiding games are instinctual in children, for preparing them to practice the hunting and gathering skills that are necessary for survival. Groos (1898/1976) finds this to be true in animals: They play chase because of the instinct to hunt. Still others would say these games are recapitulatory for those cultures that no longer require hunting and gathering for survival. The problem with this theory is that, in most species, males do the hunting and gathering, while children and animals of either gender engage in chase games.

It is also believed that when children engage in tagging games, a stigma is passed around. This can include an illness, stupidity, "cooties," etc. (Thorne, 1993). Some believe that children engage in these games to master the anxiety associated with physical contact (Phillips, 1967), or to gain control (Groos, 1901; Gump & Sutton-Smith, 1955; Opie & Opie, 1969; Schwartzman, 1978). A less popular theory of chase games is that of courting, capture, and marriage, all of which are instinctual (Groos, 1898/1976, 1901; Schwartzman, 1978). With this theory, it is believed that chase games are engaged in as practice for the future hunt, chase, and capture of their mate, of which not much corroboration exists. Groos briefly mentions this aspect of chase games; he elaborates more on dancing and strutting as behaviors associated with courtship.

Play and games, in general, are enigmas (Ellis, 1973), but chase games are the ultimate enigma. As has been mentioned, they are widespread and popular for children all over the world, and they differ by culture. The four most common types of games include a) individual one-on-one chasing; b) an individual chasing a group; c) a group chasing another group; and d) a group chasing an individual (Brewster, 1976; Gump & Sutton-Smith, 1955; Kirchner, 1991; Maccoby, 1964; Opie & Opie, 1969; Sutton-Smith, 1972).

Many researchers group hiding games with chase games, with hiding as an extra element adding to the excitement of the game (Babcock, 1976; Brewster, 1976). Still others differentiate between chasing, catching, and hunting as separate games (Opie & Opie, 1969). Such strict categorization of games may be necessary in order to research them and for ease in listing them. But for most purposes, all of these games are encompassed in the single category of chase games, as chasing is inherent in each of them.

Piaget's theory of cognitive development (see Flavell, Miller, & Miller, 1993) has been used to study play development in children. Piaget devised four stages of cognitive development, which include: 1) the sensorimotor stage, from birth to around age two; 2) the preoperational stage, from age two to around age seven; 3) the concrete operational stage, from age seven to around age eleven; and 4) the formal operational stage, which occurs from around age eleven to well into adulthood.

In the sensorimotor stage, the child learns primarily through his or her senses, coordinating these through physical motions (e.g., looking, listening, feeling). In the preoperational stage, the child interprets the world through the use of words, images and drawings. When the child reaches the concrete operational stage, they can use operations. This means that they can perform logical thinking tasks, as long as they are concrete. According to Piaget, it is at the formal operational stage when one begins to think abstractly.

Using Piaget's stages in cognitive development (see Flavell, Miller, & Miller, 1993), the question is: Do hiding, chasing and tagging games tend to be played in a sequence that is parallel to cognitive, physical, and affective development?

METHODS

Participants

Two elementary schools in a school district in central Texas were used as sites to observe children during their recess times. The principals and teachers of each school gave their permission before the observations were performed. One researcher observed his first grade class, as well as the other first grade classes in his school. He also observed kindergarteners and second graders for the study. The other researcher observed third, fourth, and fifth graders at another school. Other participants included the researchers' own children, as well as the children of friends. There were three boys: one was observed at the age of three months, then again at the age of one year; the other boys were two and five years old. There was also a girl, age three.

Procedure

Both researchers observed and videotaped the chasing and tagging games that occurred during the recess periods, as well as interviewing some of the students about their games. There was no formal questionnaire that the researchers followed, as the interviewing performed was spontaneous according to each situation. Videotaping was also done in the home environment with the researchers' own children and their friends' children. The three-month-old was videotaped playing "peek-a-boo" and was videotaped again seven months later, at one year of age, playing chase games with the five-year-old. The two-year-old was videotaped playing chase with an imaginary chaser, plus with a peer, the three-year-old.

RESULTS

Developmental Sequence in Chase Games

Through the observations of free play at recess and the games of younger children at home, it was found that there is a developmental sequence in chase games that parallel Piaget's stages of cognitive development (see Table 5.1).

Adults initiate "peek-a-boo" games with children even in early infancy. While it helps the child to learn that the adult is perceptually gone and will always come back, it is also fun for the child to look for the adult, usually smiling and laughing in the process. This is a stationary game, as the child has not yet developed mobility. As the child gets older and has gained upper body mobility, they learn to move the object from between themselves and the adult to find the hidden adult, which is the beginning of chasing, although it is still stationary (Bruner & Sherwood, 1976). Also as infants get older, they begin to enjoy "I'm-going-to-get-you" games initiated by adults. This usually elicits loud laughs and screams and ends up with tickling and

TABLE 5.1.

Stage	Age	What actions are indicative of chase?	What is the outcome or consequence of the action?	What is the distinguishing factor of this stage?
1	Birth to age two	"Peek-a-boo" is like a stationary "hide-and-seek" game. The child's face is covered and the adult has to "find" them. The child learns to hide self.	The child laughs in surprise. The child learns to hide themselves and then learns to find the hidden adult.	There is not a clear chase involved.
2	Birth to age two	The adult is engaging the child in a stationary chase game initially. Then, when the child can crawl or cruise, they play chase. The adult verbally or nonverbally initiates the game.	The actions most often end in an embrace with hugging, tickling, and/or laughing.	This begins as a stationary game and evolves into a chase game when the child can crawl.
3	Birth to age two	The child moves away by crawling, cruising, or toddling and the adult pursues. Action is occasionally reciprocated with the child pursuing the adult.	Again, the action ends in embracing, hugging, tickling, and/or laughing. If the child is the chaser, there is not always a clear consequence.	Adult and child begin initiating the chase games. As children begin toddling, the game is not only played with the parents, but with peers.
4	Age 2–3	Children pursue or run away from one another in a reciprocal and random fashion.	There is no clear consequence. Children often run into each other and get hurt at this stage.	The reciprocity of the game. The game is still random, but the children will chase one another.

78

	Age			
5	Age 2–3	The game begins when one child moves toward or away from another child. A push toy may be used to pursue or an animal may be used to chase another child.	There is again no clear consequence. When one child nears or contacts the other child, the roles are often reversed.	There are clear intentions of chasing for the fun of it. Toys or animals are often used to initiate and play the game.
6	Age 4–5	The actions include pursuit by running after, or away from, another child. The chase game may involve a prop.	The game ends with a touch or capture of the other child. It may also end in a hug, tickle, tackle, rough-and-tumble, and possibly hitting.	The initiator is not only the chaser, but the chasee.
7	Age 4–5	Themes and fantasy play guide the chase game at this stage. Rules may be decided upon and role reversal is not random, but deliberate.	Outcomes vary according to theme. (i.e., jail, trapped by a monster, mommy and her babies)	Chase games become a plan of action and themes are often involved.
8	Age 6–11	The chase games are now organized games with rules. Still, the rules can be changed to suit the players.	Consequences depend upon the game. At this stage, arguments over rules often occur.	The chase games are now organized games with rules.
9	Age 12 through adulthood	There is an offensive player being chased by a defensive player. The games have definite rules that are not changed (basketball, soccer).	If the defensive player is successful, the offensive player does not score. The ultimate consequence is winning and losing.	Not only are the games organized with rules, but there are winners and losers.

* Stages 1–3 parallel Piaget's sensorimotor stage; stages 4–7 parallel the preoperational stage; stage 8 parallels the concrete operational stage; and stage 9 parallels the formal operational stage.

hugging. As the child begins to become more mobile, the adult still initiates "I'm-going-to-get-you," and they will crawl toward the baby, who will in turn crawl toward the adult. At this point, the infant does not flee from the adult, but they will chase the adult.

Around the second year, children will begin to flee from the adult, as they become initiators of the chasing games. These games often end in hugging and embracing, unless the child was the chaser, then the consequences are not always clear. When children become more social in the second year, they begin playing chase games with their peers. These games are usually random, without any clear consequence. Then, when fantasy play begins to develop, also in the second year (Piaget, 1962), toy animals and vehicles often become part of the chasing games. The consequences are still unclear until the end of the third year, when the roles are reversed and a child is touched or tagged, becoming either "it" or the chaser.

As the child improves in language skills, at around age three (Frost, 1992), the chase games are initiated using language. The intent is much clearer, and the chaser or the chasee can initiate the game. The game ends with a touch or capture, which can often lead to hitting. As the child gets closer to age five, his cognitive development is such that chase games now begin to take on simple strategy. The games involve loose organization, where players plan who will chase whom, if there is a base (for safety), if there are boundaries, and so on. At this stage, themes are often incorporated (i.e., jail, monster) and rules are decided upon not randomly, but deliberately.

Lastly, chase games are played that have definite rules and that have been learned either on the street, in school, or both (i.e., "Stuck in the Mud," "Freeze Tag"). Arguments over rules frequently occur at this level (Clarke & Schneider, 1996). Also, the chasing is incorporated into many organized sport games. For example, offense has the ball (e.g., basketball, football, soccer), and the defense chases him or her (and the ball) to keep them from scoring. Thus, chasing does not necessarily end in childhood, but for many extends well into adulthood.

CONCLUSION

It is interesting that in all of the research on play and games, there has not been much done on chase games. Most of the work is done broadly on play and/or games, but not usually on specific types of games. What makes this interesting is that in all of the research, chase games have been found prevalent in human and nonhuman play (Groos, 1898/1976, 1901; Smith, 1984), and they have been found, in some form, in many cultures (Culin, 1976; Groos, 1898/1976, 1901; Gump & Sutton-Smith, 1955; James, 1890/1950; Kirchner, 1991; Maccoby, 1964; Opie & Opie, 1969; Phillips, 1967; Schwartzman, 1978; Sutton-Smith, 1972, 1977b). Thus, if these games are so universal, why is there such limited work done on them? A possible answer is that it could only be theorized as to how chase games have evolved, and this has been researched. Another reason might be that there is not much interest in why chase games are played. This goes along with the enigma: Chase games are, and have always been, played by children of all cultures in some form, so why deal with it? They have just always existed, period.

I contend that if chase games are so popular, there has to be a reason that children have played them throughout the centuries. More empirical work needs to be done in this area to help solve the enigma identified regarding chase games. There are several theories that help explain how play and games have evolved. Depending on the discipline with which you are associated, you will believe one theory that best explains the phenomenon. Coming from the discipline of education with both a physical education and an early childhood education background, I see chase games as developmental. This background is evident in the description of the stages of chase games presented here, which parallel in general with Piaget's cognitive stages and the cognitive, physical, and affective development of children (Clarke & Schneider, 1996).

While these stages were observed in children, it was a small sample and it would be beneficial to perform observations of more children to allow for generalizations. Along with the observations, a questionnaire could be designed to ascertain from children reasons why they actually engage in chase games. Future questions might be: Can development of stages of chase games, as described here, be validated through consistency? Why do children play chase games? And why are such games so universal?

REFERENCES

Babcock, W. H. (1976). Games of Washington children. In B. Sutton-Smith (Ed.), *A children's games anthology: Studies in folklore and anthropology* (pp. 243–284). New York: Arno Press.

Brewster, P. G. (1976). Four games of tag from India. In B. Sutton-Smith (Ed.), *A children's games anthology: Studies in folklore and anthropology* (pp. 239–241). New York: Arno Press.

Bruner, J. S., & Sherwood, V. (1976). Peekaboo and the learning of rule structures. In J. S. Bruner, A. Holly, & K. Kylva (Eds.), *Play: Its role in development and evolution* (pp. 227–285). New York: Basic Books.

Burghardt, G. M. (1984). On the origins of play. In P. K. Smith (Ed.), *Play in animals and humans* (pp. 5–41). Oxford, England: Basil Blackwell.

Clarke, L. J., & Schneider, J. (1996, April). *Developmental stages of chase games.* Paper presented to Children's Play and Play Environments class, University of Texas at Austin.

Culin, S. (1976). Street games of boys in Brooklyn, N.Y. In B. Sutton-Smith (Ed.), *A children's games anthology: Studies in folklore and anthropology* (pp. 221–237). New York: Arno Press.

Ellis, M. J. (1973). *Why people play.* Englewood Cliffs, NJ: Prentice-Hall.

Flavell, J. H., Miller, P. H., & Miller S. A. (1993). Middle childhood and adolescence. In J. Tully (Ed.), *Cognitive development* (3rd ed., pp. 131–172). Englewood Cliffs, NJ: Prentice Hall.

Frost, J. L. (1992). Why children play. In C. Micheli, L. Reale, & J. Whitney (Eds.), *Play and playscapes* (pp. 1–21). New York: Delmar.

Groos, K. (1901). *The play of man* (E. L. Baldwin, Trans.). New York: D. Appleton.

Groos, K. (1976). *The play of animals* (E. L. Baldwin, Trans.). New York: D. Appleton. (Original work published 1898)

Gump, P. V., & Sutton-Smith, B. (1955). The "it" role in children's games. *The Group, 17*(3), 3–8.

James, W. (1950). *Principles of psychology* (Vol. 2). New York: Dover. (Original work published 1890)

Kirchner, G. (1991). *Children's games from around the world.* Dubuque, IA: Wm. C. Brown.

Maccoby, M., Modiano, N., & Lander, P. (1964). Games and social character in a Mexican village. *Psychiatry, 27,* 150–162.

Opie, I., & Opie, P. (1969). *Children's games in street and playground.* Oxford, England: Clarendon Press.

Parker, S. T. (1984). Playing for keeps. In P. K. Smith (Ed.), *Play in animals and humans* (pp. 271–293). Oxford, England: Basil Blackwell.

Phillips, R. H. (1967). Children's games. In R. Slovenko & J. A. Knight (Eds.), *Motivations in play, games and sports* (pp. 68–69). Springfield, IL: Charles C. Thomas.

Piaget, J. (1962). Explanation of play. In C. Gattegho & F. M. Hodgson (Trans.), *Play, dreams and imitation in childhood* (pp. 147–168). New York: W. W. Norton.

Sack, A. L. (1977). Sport: Play or work? In P. Stevens, Jr. (Ed.), *Studies in the anthropology of play: Papers in memory of B. Allan Tindall.* New York: Leisure Press.

Schwartzman, H. B. (1978). *Transformations: The anthropology of children's play.* New York: Plenum Press.

Smith, P. K. (Ed.). (1984). *Play in animals and humans.* Oxford, England: Basil Blackwell.

Sutton-Smith, B. (1972). *The folkgames of children.* Austin, TX: University of Texas Press.

Sutton-Smith, B. (1977a). Play as adaptive potentiation. In P. Stevens, Jr. (Ed.), *Studies in the anthropology of play: Papers in memory of B. Allan Tindall.* New York: Leisure Press.

Sutton-Smith, B. (1977b). Towards an anthropology of play. In P. Stevens, Jr. (Ed.), *Studies in the anthropology of play: Papers in memory of B. Allan Tindall.* New York: Leisure Press.

Sutton-Smith, B. (1997). *The ambiguity of play.* Cambridge, MA: Harvard University Press.

Thorne, B. (1993). *Gender play: Girls and boys in school.* Brunswick, NJ: Rutgers University Press.

6

Rules in Children's Games and Play

Carrie Freie

What is a rule? Responses from some third and fourth graders to this question were: "Something you have to obey," "Something you have to follow," "Something that you should follow," and "…something that somebody makes up and it's something that you have to follow." In many situations, rules seem to be unchanging standards of right and wrong ways to do things. It may seem that, especially for children, rules dictate what is right or wrong and separate what is acceptable from what is unacceptable. Yet children do not just obey or disobey rules that others have made. In games and play, they obey, disobey, change, modify, ignore, invent, adapt, interpret and reinterpret rules. In order to do this children rely on their own ideas of what is fun, boring, fair, unfair, right, wrong, and socially acceptable and unacceptable. In this chapter, I will explore how children use rules in game and play situations by explaining and interpreting some of the ways in which the third and fourth graders I observed used rules to construct their game, play, and social environments.

STUDIES OF PLAY

Scholarly studies of play are relatively new to the last century. This has been explained, in part, by the fact that Western culture did not, until the Victorian era, view children or children's behavior as unique or worthy of much attention. By the late 1800s, however, this trend began to change as theories of child development proposed that childhood experiences formed adult personalities (Cohen, 1993).

One trend of the 19th century study of play is the perception of children's play as mimicking adult culture. Groos (1912) believes play helps prepare a child for adulthood in this way. Groos discusses play as a stage of development; Spencer (1873) takes a similar approach, discussing play as a developmental stage in part of a social evolutionary theory.

At this time, some radical educators were also addressing play as a teaching tool; Froebel (1887) and Montessori (1917) were two proponents of this view. They proposed that children could best learn by incorporating play methods into educational approaches.

Functionalist approaches to play focus on its role in providing social stability. Turner's (1969) view of play (the play of adults) is that it reverses societal norms and, in so doing, helps balance social tension. Functionalist approaches to children's play highlight the imitative quality of play and its role in development of gender norms and culturally appropriate adult roles (Schwartzman, 1978).

The popularity of Freudian ideas had, and continues to have, a great influence on studies of children's play. Piaget incorporates this type of psychological theory into his work. Although Piaget focuses many of his play studies on the individual, some of his explorations analyze group behavior (Piaget 1962, 1972; Piaget & Inhelder, 1969). Specifically pertaining to this chapter is Piaget's (1962) theory concerning three types of children's games: 1) practice games, which focus on imitation and practice of social roles or situations; 2) symbolic games, which incorporate abstract symbolic representations; and 3) games with rules, which imply the existence of social relationships. He also points out that games with rules may be, at the same time, symbolic games. Games with rules, both symbolic and not, are the focus of the discussion that follows.

Furthermore, Piaget divides games with rules into those games in which the rules are handed down and those in which rules develop spontaneously (Piaget, 1962; Piaget & Inhelder, 1969). In my own observation, I did not find these categories to be mutually exclusive. Many games with handed-down rules also incorporated spontaneous rules.

Linguistic approaches to the study of play have also enjoyed popularity since the 1960s. Weir (1962) studies very young children's play with the use of sound. Kirshenblatt-Gimblett (1976) focuses on communicative play with sense and nonsense, and the contrast between the two. Bateson (1972) looks at play as a form of communication and studies how play space is framed, as well as how children learn communication skills through play. Goodwin (1985, 1990, 1993, 1997) also studies play and communication and observes the gender- and culture-based traits that are perpetuated in children's play groups.

Recent studies have also focused on gender and other aspects of difference that exist within play groups and how children define, interpret, perpetuate, or change societal norms within the play context (Alexander & Hines, 1994; Beresin, 1995; Goodwin, 1985, 1990, 1993, 1997; Hughes, 1991, 1993, 1995; Thorne, 1993). Hughes's work examines rules within girls' gaming from an ethnographic approach.

Thorne's work, taking a similar approach, examines gender-based behavior in school, particularly on the playground behavior of boys and girls. My own study uses a similar methodology based on observation and interviews. This is explained in more detail in the next section.

The study of children's play dates back to the 1800s, most of this work coming from a psychological perspective. The lives of children relating to other children are not commonly studied by anthropologists. "Despite Malinowski's early plea for documentation of children's lifeworlds, few anthropologists have taken as their mission the study of the linguistic, cultural and social life of children: children as subjects, actors and creators of culture" (Goodwin, 1997, p. 1). In a 1997 article in the *Anthropology Newsletter*, put out by the American Anthropological Association, Goodwin discusses the field of children's play studies and its strengths and weaknesses. Among other recommendations, she calls for more study on children's interaction in play. "Unfortunately we know very little about how children interact in the midst of actual play activities, subverting the rules for their own strategic interests. This is a very serious gap" (p.4). It is this gap that my research aims to study.

FIELDWORK AND METHODOLOGY

I conducted fieldwork with a group of approximately 48 third and fourth grade students of various ages, attending elementary school in an affluent school district near Albany, New York.[1] The group I worked with is team-taught by two female teachers, one White and one Black. Most of the students are from White, middle-class families.

The classroom where they spend most of their day is actually two rooms, connected by a sliding partition that is usually open. The rooms are colorful and welcoming. Student work is hung from the walls and ceiling and students' desks are clustered around learning centers. There are many books, three computers, a piano, and many other resources available for the students to use.

My role was that of an observer, rather than a participant or authority figure, although occasionally I did participate in play. I observed the children during lunch and recess time for about an hour a day, usually three times a week, over a period of five months. I chose these times because this was when the children were free to play games of their own choice or engage in spontaneous play.

I was first introduced to the children as "Miss Freie," and they were told that I would be with them during lunch and recess time. My hope was that I could be a "fly on the wall," watching the students without affecting their behavior. This of course was impossible. As I was not only a newcomer but also an adult, I represented an authority figure to the children. In the beginning, some of the children began to ask me if I was their new lunch monitor, to which I replied I was not. I explained that I was there observing, or watching, them because I was interested in the games they played. I explained that I was a student—like them—and I was going to write a paper about these games. My goal was to avoid their viewing me as an authority figure. I frequently helped with opening juice boxes or peeling oranges, but I did not take on a disciplinary role. When a conflict or complaint was brought to me, I referred the student to the lunch monitor or teacher. After about two weeks, I started to notice a few of the students breaking rules, for example changing seats at lunch or trading food while they were aware I was watching, realizing that I would not discipline them.

The lunch period is 30 minutes long, and after students finish eating, they often play card games. Sometimes the students will bring toys from home. Many of the girls trade stickers. The lunchroom is a gym, auditorium, and cafeteria all in one. The students I observed chose their seat from four, and later three, available lunch tables. An adult lunch monitor, assigned only to their class, watched the children, answered their questions, helped to open juice boxes and other tricky lunch items, mediated disputes, provided playing cards, and used a variety of strategies to keep the children seated and safe. Lunchtime activities are restricted by the rule that each student must stay seated at the lunch table. I found the lunch period very helpful for getting to know the children and looking at how they respond to adult-imposed rules of conduct.

However, the recess period provided me with the most interesting information. During this time, the children played outside on the playground. Located just outside the classroom, the playground is made up of a large field bordered on one side by an asphalt basketball court. Another side of the field is bordered by a playground station with slides, swings (including a tire swing), bars, rings, and more. There is also a jungle gym. Woods border the whole area on three sides.

On days when the weather was bad, the children stayed indoors. They played in both classrooms, and sometimes in a section of the hallway which could be closed off by two sets of double doors. Running and being loud were discouraged, and play was stopped by the teachers when it was considered too rambunctious for indoors. During this time, the children played board games, computer games, or engaged in spontaneous play.

Near the end of the five months, I conducted fifteen 35-minute interviews with groups of two, three, and four students. I interviewed a total of 18 students, of which were mainly groups of friends who played together. This method facilitated much discussion, and students were easily able to provide examples of the situations they described. However, I now realize that interviewing children who did not play together may also have been helpful in providing a difference in responses.[2] Only one of the groups interviewed was made up of three boys who did not frequently play or eat lunch together.

RULES IN PLAY AND GAMES

The focus of my study is on rules found in folk games and spontaneous play. "The distinguishing characteristic of a traditional folk game is that although it has rules, they are not written down" (Knapp & Knapp, 1976, p. 17). Spontaneous play, on the other hand, has no predetermined game rules. Most of the games I observed were what the Knapps call "folk games." Some card games, board games, and soccer may not exactly fit the definition of a folk game, but the children have adapted these games and, as a result, their rules are no longer the same as the written rules. In this chapter, I will examine how children change, interpret, ignore, follow, elaborate, or otherwise deal with rules in game and play situations.

Most approaches to children's folk games viewed rules as static or "set in stone" (Opie & Opie, 1969). Recent studies, however, have recognized the dynamic qualities of rules (Beresin, 1995; Goodwin, 1990, 1993; Hughes, 1991, 1993, 1995). The dynamic qualities of rules are what makes them usable and changeable. Rules have the ability to be transformed and adapted to different situations.

The types of rules I will be focusing on are what Hughes has called "higher-order gaming rules" (1991, 1995). Hughes lists three rule systems: game rules, social rules, and higher-order gaming rules. The game rules are the formal rules which outline how the game is "meant" to be played. The social rules consist of the rules of the society of which the game is a part. Higher-order gaming rules are the product of the interaction of the game rules and social rules and will be the focus of my discussion.

Rules in games and play are altered for many reasons, which are explained in the analysis that follows. I begin with a discussion of how rules are learned, as a newcomer into the group might be introduced to a game. The focus then shifts to specific rule-making behavior and it happened within the group I observed.

The ways in which rules are interpreted and applied are also important. Examining the process of learning, making, and applying rules illustrates how children take advantage of the plasticity of rules and are able to change or reinterpret rules to suit their situations. For example, the children I observed frequently changed a rule or rules of a game if they felt that the game was boring or unfair. Other motivations for altering rules included gaining a strategic advantage, including or excluding certain people, and adjusting to time or spacial constraints.

The section of this chapter called "How are Rules Used" addresses a similar theme, but specifically focuses on the invention of rules for controlling the makeup of the group. Cheating, rule breaking, and punishment are examined next. These concepts are defined and applied by the children during play. Lastly, this chapter touches on the relationships of the children and how social rules influence gaming rules and what happens on the playground.

GAME PLAYING DURING LUNCH AND RECESS

The children I observed played a variety of games during lunch and recess time. During lunchtime, both boys and girls played cards. Games such as "Blackjack" (or "Twenty-One") and "Spit" (in which players quickly arrange cards numerically) were popular. Card games were played daily during the lunch period by both boys and girls, usually in groups of two.

On days when the weather was bad, which were frequent, the children stayed inside during recess and played "Connect Four," card games, checkers, chess, computer games, reading, drawing, and other activities, as well as engaged in spontaneous play. "Connect Four," in which players take turns placing checkers in a grid, was one of the most popular indoor recess activities. Both girls and boys played this game. As the students played, a small crowd would often gather to watch. Students would call out to play the next winner. Checkers and chess were not played as regularly as "Connect Four," and hardly ever drew a crowd. Computer games were played by both boys and girls, usually with only one or two people at the computer.

Spontaneous play activities varied from day to day. Usually play groups ranged from two to ten students and were made up of primarily one gender.

Outdoors, the children played soccer, various forms of tag such as "Spider" (which is played on a jungle gym), basketball, and other games. Mostly groups of four or more girls played tag while larger groups made up of mainly boys played sports like soccer and basketball. Both boys and girls played on the swings, slides, climbing equipment, and sometimes with toys.

LEARNING THE RULES

Although the formal rules of games—text rules—may not be known to the students who play. They are only aware of the general characteristics of the game. Knapp and Knapp (1976) say that, "nobody knows exactly what they are [the rules of a folk game]" (p. 17). During my observation, if a student was unaware of the rules of a game, one or more of the children might attempt to explain them to him or her, but usually only the general goal was outlined and specific rules were learned during game play.

One way of making the rules known was to shout out an infraction when a player noticed a rule being broken. For example, during tag, "You can't tag the person who was just 'it'!". When specific infractions were identified, they were often stopped and the participating players thereby learned the rules (if they did not already know them). In cases where a player who already knew the rules broke them, he or she might be called a "cheater." The specific infraction was not addressed, but the player was expected to stop breaking the rules.

Also, newcomers are frequently given advantages while learning a game. More experienced players may be given a handicap to facilitate playing while players are in the process of learning the rules.

SPONTANEOUS RULE MAKING

In both game situations and spontaneous play, I saw children organize themselves by using rules. Higher-order gaming rules function as organizers of the game, play, and social situations and are usually invented during play activities. For example, I observed a group of girls who were playing with a rabbit in a room with the doors closed. The girls developed a password system in order to regulate who came in and out of the room. The password—"bunny, bunny, bunny, bunny, bunny," said quickly with sing-song intonation—was told to everyone already present in the room. These people could then come and go as they liked. One girl, Andrea,[3] guarded the door. A small group of boys came to the door, wanting to enter. Andrea asked the boys if they knew the password. The boys knew the password (they probably overheard it from outside of the room), but Andrea did not let them in, telling them it wasn't the correct password. Next, a girl came to the door, and she was asked for the password. She did not know the password, so Andrea told her, "Say bunny five times," and she was let in.

The password system that was developed functioned to control whom was let into the room to play. Gender was used as the basis for the inclusion of girls and the exclusion of boys. When the system failed and the boys found out the password, Andrea still did not let them in. The social function of the rule—its use as a device for controlling the gender makeup of the play group—was more important than following the actual rule. The children adapted the rule to the situation so that their purpose or goal was still served.

Another example of a spontaneous play situation in which rules quickly developed occurred when a hula hoop was brought out during recess. The children formed their own system to regulate how long each person was allowed to use the hula hoop (the third time it touched the ground a turn was over) and how it was to be passed on (the girls formed a line around the hula hoop).

HOW ARE RULES INTERPRETED AND APPLIED?

Large groups of boys often played soccer. Some of them played soccer outside of school on organized teams and knew official game rules. One 10-year-old boy, Paul, said when asked about the rules of the soccer game played during recess, "We just fool around." His friend added, "We just play, like, wildly and we don't care about the rules they have in soccer games." Another player added, "...we don't do penalties or anything." The official game rules were usually not applied during recess. Instead, children learned gaming rules (the intersection of game rules and social rules) as play happened, usually when perceived infractions of the gaming rules occurred. For example, in soccer, children discouraged touching the ball with one's hands (handball, a penalty by the official game rules of soccer). Yet in *moderation*, handballs did not carry penalties and were part of acceptable game play. When a handball happened only occasionally, it was ignored by the students. Yet when one student continually touched the ball with his hands, he was reprimanded by the others, who shouted that he was not allowed to touch the ball. I talked to some players about this particular situation, and one said, "We just don't care if somebody puts up their hand or touches the ball, we just keep playing." However, another player added, "But if you do it, like, too many times, then we won't let you play because sometimes it gets annoying."

The answer to the question of what is too many times is complex. Without following strict rules which dictate the game, the children must decide for themselves what constitutes "too many times." Factors such as who is performing the action, what the situation is, and the intentions or presumed intentions of the person in question all play a part in deciding if a handball or other potential infraction has happened too many times.

Certain players, especially those who disrupt games, acquire labels of being problem players, and potentially disruptive behavior from them seems to be less tolerated than equivalent behavior from a player who is not cited as causing problems or disrupting game play. For example, the boys discussed Jim, a player who consistently would touch the soccer ball with his hands. The boys knew that Jim was a frequent offender and so were less tolerant of his handballs. They frequently called out Jim's handballs, at the same time ignoring handballs made by other players who were not already labeled as frequent offenders.

The gaming situation may also affect the application and enforcement of rules. Generally, games with more players have less rule enforcement. The larger the group of soccer players, for example, the more tolerant the group was of traditional rule-breaking behavior. Enforcement of rules on such a large scale is more difficult than with a smaller, more controlled group.

The intentions, or presumed intentions, of the person suspected of breaking a rule are also important. For example, the boys who discussed Jim felt that when he touched the ball with his hands, it was not an accident. They had come to this conclusion because, although they had continually expressed their displeasure with his handballs, he continued to use his hands. Whether or not their perception of Jim's actions was accurate, it changed the way they treated him and how they decided he had touched the ball "too many times." The idea of perceived motivation or intent is further discussed in the section "Penalties, Consequences, and Punishments," in this chapter.

HOW ARE RULES USED?

According to Hughes, one trait of gaming rules is, "when and how the rules of the game ought to be applied, ignored or modified" (1991, p. 287). Most of the children in the group that I observed were already aware of how particular games were played before play began. Specific rules and decisions regarding rules were made while the game was being played. Before a game began, there was little or no discussion of how the game was to be played. "We sort of like just start playing because we know the rules," said Dave. Even teams were decided while playing. Rule making and rule changing became part of the process of playing. This may have been due to the time constraint the children were under, since recess was only 15 minutes long. This style of rule making does not separate making rules from play. These two events happen simultaneously.

While playing Spider, Cathy jumped off the jungle gym and called for "all girls" to join her. The girls formed a huddle and decided that the name of the person who was being chased would be called by the person who was "it" before the chasing began. The girls also quickly agreed that since one girl had not yet reached the huddle, she would be the next person to be chased. The rule making huddle became part of the fun of the game, and the girl who didn't make it there fast enough was next to be "it."

In the case of the password game, in which a password was required to enter the room, the focus and fun of the play was the rhetorical activity of rule construction and use. Changing the password, telling it to all those in the in-group, and guarding the entrance became the activity, thereby, the game.

WHY ARE RULES CHANGED?

Children could easily explain how they know if someone was not playing fairly, breaking the rules, or cheating, and what to do in that situation. They could not as easily explain cases in which rules were changed. These cases are difficult to explain because they are context dependent and each situation is unique. The changing of rules is motivated by a desire for fairness or strategic gain. Some situations in which rules might be ignored or modified are: if one player or team outperforms the other, if a player is constantly breaking a rule, if not enough people are included, if players want to exclude a certain person, and if the game is not running smoothly. Some players talked about changing rules in order to give one person or team a strategic advantage, which sometimes was concealed as fair.

In a situation in which one team outperforms another, players will often rearrange the teams to make the matchup more even. This is one reason for players, particularly better players, to change teams. "Usually one of our friends, he's also ten, he usually switches teams to the losing team," said Dave. Switching teams in order to keep the game exciting is common. Many of the players with whom I talked thought it was important to have a close match between the two teams so that the game would not get boring. Mark told me about giving points to the team with less experience. "But sometimes, at birthday parties when somebody who really doesn't play that game that much, they give them a lot of points...like if somebody has that game and the other person doesn't and they're just trying it, they give them like four points..." Another boy also talked about the idea of giving points to a disadvantaged team in order to make the match more equal: "...if people who just want to play and there's like about nine, ten people playing everyday ... there's these certain people who just like to play four on a team and they're all friends, against all the other people, sometimes we give them points, like only two for a head start."

If a player is constantly breaking a rule, it might also be changed. For example, a handball is against the text rules of soccer and carries penalties. The players adapted their rules so that a handball does not carry penalties. Handballs are common, and while they are generally avoided on the playground, in one player's words, "We just don't care if somebody puts up their hand or touches the ball. We just keep playing." The goal is to "keep playing," keep the game going, and to get as much playing time as possible out of a short recess period. As a consequence, not all game rules—especially those requiring time-consuming penalties, or those that are disputed—are enforced.

If not enough people are included in a game, the rules may be changed in order to accommodate a larger number of people. During one recess period, the class played a game called "Spud," a tag game using numbers or names and played with a ball. This game was organized by one of the teachers who, before the game, explained to the class that these rules were flexible, thereby allowing them to change the rules in order to accommodate their large group and include all of the students.[4]

Another example of game structure being altered in order to accommodate the group happened in the "Connect Four" games I witnessed. In this game, players take turns placing checkers in a plastic grid. The goal is to line up four checkers in a row, similar to "Tic-Tac-Toe." This is a game that comes in a box, with directions. The children did not have this box; they only had the checkers and plastic grid, which were kept in a large envelope. There were two game sets, and many children wanted to play on indoor recess days. A crowd would often gather around, and the students would call out if they wanted to play the winner of a game. The official rules of "Connect Four" state that it is a two-player game. The original rule of two players was sometimes changed to accommodate others who wanted to take part. In the games I watched, there were two primary players (usually at least one of these was a girl), often helped by another person, who gave them advice and sometimes even took turns placing the checkers. This team play was informal. Teams were not decided in advance; one player simply began playing with another. One or more additional players joining in a traditionally two-person game was common. Card games were also often played this way.

If the group playing wants to exclude certain players, rules might also be created for this purpose. The password game and the "all girls" rule in "Spider" are two examples of this. In each of these situations, the players used rules to develop strategies for controlling who was included in the game.

In situations where a game is not running smoothly—players perceive a problem, some rules seem unfair, or the players are not enjoying the game—rules will often be changed to solve the problem. Jennifer, a third grader, told me,

"Sometimes if you're not having fun with the rules you have, you could always change them."

Students also addressed changing the rules, or attempting to change the rules, for strategic gain. Jennifer discussed her desire to change rules, "When I was little and I would play with my dad or my mom or my big sister ... I would feel like, 'I really want to change these rules because the person I'm playing with, she always wins or he always wins and I don't like that.'" Attempts to change the rules to give one team an advantage—such as allowing a two-player team to compete against a single player in "Spit" or one team having three goalies in soccer—were usually not successful. These attempts did not result in a rule being changed because most players did not agree on the change. Some called the attempt to change "cheating" and those who began to use this new rule "cheaters." The majority of players, the more powerful players in particular, need to agree on a change in order for it to be considered fair and free of conflict. A girl in the third grade said, "If you want to change the rules a little bit, you've got to make sure the other rule is as fair as the one you already had.... People won't play with you if they don't think it's fair." She and her friends agreed that when rules are changed by only a few people, there may be an argument or players may quit the game.

Lauren explained that when rules are changed in a game, a new game is created. "Sometimes when me and my friends are, like playing outside, like sometimes...we make our own game. Like if somebody makes up a new rule like in the middle of the game." Although I did not witness this in my fieldwork, it is conceivable that over time and with continued adaptations, a game could change its character, and be reframed and viewed as a different game.

WHO CHANGES RULES?

A particularly skilled or popular player has more power to make or change the rules than those not as skilled or involved in the central action of the game. The person in the spotlight or in charge—for example, the player with the ball in soccer or the "it" in tag—will frequently be the one to make a rule. One reason for this may be that the other players are paying attention to this person more than to the other players of the game. The person who has the ball, for example, might stop and pick up the ball or kick it out of the playing area to attract the attention of the other players in order to make a rule.

However, the same players often have control of certain games day after day. These leaders frequently were the ones who made the rules. In my interviews, I asked a group of boys who played soccer, "Who makes or decides on the rules of a game?" They answered "Gary," who is an aggressive soccer player. This boy was established in their minds as a rule maker. In this group, certain students established themselves as rule makers in leadership roles. This same popular boy also claimed influential roles in the classroom and lunchroom settings, as well as on the playground.

WHEN RULES ARE BROKEN

Hughes (1993) describes cases in which the fairness of an action is often determined by the intent or perceived intent of the player or players. I found this assessment of cheating during my observation and interviews. Students told me that *intent* was the main factor separating cheating from changing or bending the rules. The motive for cheating is personal or team gain, frequently at the expense of the opposing player or team. Although the individual definitions for cheating vary, there are commonalities. Cheating is done with the intent of helping one person or team do well or win, or making an opposing person or team do badly or lose. This is accomplished by doing something which is "against the rules" or something which the other player or players are not doing. Hughes also found this same definition in her fieldwork with girls playing foursquare. Foursquare is a nonteam game played with a ball on a square court that is divided up into four equal squares, usually about 4 feet by 4 feet. Each square is numbered 1 through 4, and the fourth square is often called the king's square. The object of the game is to bounce the ball from square to square and get players "out." A player is "out" when he or she is unable to bounce the ball within the boundaries of another square. Within a playground setting, house rules are often applied during the game.

The examples of cheating that children cited highlighted selfish intent, sometimes containing malicious actions. Jennifer gave this example of cheating: "You have a game of cards, and someone looks away for a second, and you go ahead spaces or write down more points while they're not looking." Two other girls gave the example of peeking during a part of a game when one's eyes are supposed to be covered. The students did not agree that cheating was bad in every situation. Jennifer said, "But you know what? It's sometimes good [cheating], because if you really want to win and you never win, but people say that cheaters always lose, but sometimes they don't..." Justin said that cheating could be used for purposes other than to win or get ahead. Cheating, he explained, could be used to stop a game. Cheating is also done simply for fun, especially when there is more than one participant.

Children often changed the rules or bent the rules for the good of the game to keep the game moving, rather than for personal gain. Some reasons for changing the rules are to keep the game from becoming boring or to keep all the players involved. Most students agreed that "changing the rules" was not the same thing as "cheating." One third grade boy said, "...cheating is like, not following at all and bending the rules is kind of changing them." A third grade girl claimed, "We're like, all like, benders of rules." Not all students participate in cheating, but changing, bending, or adapting rules is something most players find necessary at one time or another for the reasons described above. Changing rules is also a group effort involving the agreement of all or most players in order to be successful.

PENALTIES, CONSEQUENCES, AND PUNISHMENTS

Hughes (1995) asks, "What are the limits and consequences of acceptable conduct in the game?" (p. 95). The group I observed did not verbalize the limits before the game began; instead, the children knew them before play or decided them during play. Most of the students shared understanding of the goals and gaming rules of the games they played, although these were unarticulated. The children could not say for sure that doing one thing would get someone kicked out of a game (except maybe starting a fight). Nevertheless, when it happened, each student could clearly recognize the situation. Children threatened others with expulsion from the game for repeated violations of a rule or continuation of unwanted behavior by the same person, for example, using hands in soccer. In one particular situation, the same student continually used his hands in soccer and was often threatened with expulsion. I never actually saw players make another player sit out, but apparently exclusion was common. A group of soccer players told me about one strategy they use when this situation occurs: Often they will allow the player to remain on the field, but ignore him and not pass the ball to him.

Breaking either the game rules or the gaming rules (rules integrating game rules and social behavior) had the potential to get a player kicked out of the game. However, breaking gaming rules was more likely to get a player expelled than breaking game rules. Picking up the soccer ball and taking it to the basketball court to play basketball in the middle of a soccer game is breaking a gaming rule and is likely to get the player excluded from the game. On the other hand, children may notice and verbally acknowledge breaking a game rule—for example, touching the soccer ball with one's hands—but will usually not result in a penalty. Yet, consequences may apply to a child who continually breaks a game rule that others generally follow. In these situations, the intentions and motive—or perceived intentions and motives—of the child who breaks the rule plays a part in the reactions of the other players. The consequence most frequently mentioned by the children was making a player sit out, or not letting him or her play the rest of the game. This may have happened in structured classroom or gym games, but I never actually saw this happen in the recess setting. More common was ignoring or excluding a player. Children told me particularly harsh violations of rules resulted in not letting the player play for a long period of time. I also did not see this occur. Instead, if the player continued to put himself or herself in the game, the children used strategies, such as not passing the ball to that player in soccer or basketball or not tagging the player in tag, as a method of exclusion and, in some cases, punishment.

Breaking rules which were continually broken by other players usually held no consequences unless the integrity of the game was threatened. A situation in which the same rule was continually not followed by the majority of the players led to the rule being changed, ignored, or simply forgotten. For the game Spider, the children changed the game by adding a penalty for jumping off the jungle gym while the game was being played. Originally, jumping off of the jungle gym in order to avoid being tagged was something the majority of players were doing, and there were no consequences. However, it made the game nonfunctional, since it was nearly impossible for the "it" to tag those who were not on the jungle gym. Lauren explained that this way of playing was not fun and also made the game unfair, "because it wasn't fair, because like when we were all bunched together, like everybody just jumped off and it wasn't fun anymore." Therefore, a penalty was invented for those who jumped off of the gym. Anyone who did this was automatically "it." This rule and penalty prevented players from jumping off the gym during the game, and, as a result, the game became functional again.

GENDER AND SOCIAL CONTEXT

Gender divisions in play settings are common among children in the United States (Goodwin, 1985; Hughes, 1995; Thorne, 1993). The children I observed separated into play groups which were composed mainly of members of one sex and played stereotypical "boys'" and "girls'" games. During recess, girls most often played on the playground equipment or played tag. The majority of boys played soccer or basketball. A few boys played on the playground equipment in both all-boy and boy-girl groups. Some boys joined in the girls' games, such as tag, and one girl consistently joined in the boys' soccer game. Hughes writes, "This reflects an important bias in children's experiences during the elementary-school years, when boys and girls tend to play in separate play groups and also to play stereotypically different types of games" (1995, p. 111).

Traditional theories about gender and play focus on differences between boys' and girls' play. Boys are supposed to be more aggressive, competitive, and play more team games. Girls are characterized as less aggressive and competitive, and prefer competition between individuals. Girls' games are also wrongly viewed as less complex than boys'. Hughes has done extensive work with girls' gaming and has found that girls compete quite aggressively, "but they did prefer certain ways of competing," which were not the same as the boys' (1995, p. 112).

On the playground, I witnessed a great deal of gender separation along traditional lines. Boys mainly played the sports-focused games which revolved around competing teams, while girls favored games such as tag and spontaneous play activities. Analyzing the dynamics of these play situations revealed some of the social ideas the children were using to construct their play worlds. On the playground, there appears to be a great variety of possible decisions a child can make. What game to play and with whom to play are just the beginning. Many of these decisions are determined by the social context, and gender is an important aspect of the social construction of play.

During my observation, I wondered why only one girl, Mandy, consistently played soccer with the boys. I saw two other girls come in periodically, but only she consistently played the whole game. The soccer games were traditionally competitive, although team solidarity was not strong. Players often did not know who was on their team and frequently changed teams for a variety of reasons. The aggressiveness of the game varied depending on who had control of the ball. Some players were more competitive and aggressive than others, and these were usually the players who had control of the ball most often. One of the players who often had control of the ball was Mandy. She was a good soccer player, and her enjoyment of the game led her to play even when other girls did not. She got as much playing time as she could each recess period. During one game, I observed Mandy's teammate was not passing the ball to her or anyone else. Numerous times she told him to pass the ball to her, but he continued to keep it for himself. She solved this problem by changing to the other team and taking the ball from him.

Tag games, played mainly by a group of girls, were highly structured and competitive. Again, the aggressiveness of the game depended on the aggressiveness of the individual players, particularly the person who was "it." The tag games the students played, according to traditional game rules, featured competition between individuals. However, in some cases girls would form alliances; the person who was last "it" would help to protect the other players. This person was called the "protector" and would physically put herself between the person who was "it" and the person she was protecting. This rule, which the girls brought to their tag games, added a greater challenge to the game. It worked in a similar way as "no touch backs" by insuring that the last person who was "it" would not be tagged next.

Hughes (1993) cites the rhetoric of "friends" used in foursquare, which is analogous to the concept of "protector." The girls use the rhetoric of "friends" and "protector" in order to establish to whom they are socially obligated to "be nice" and, as a result, to whom they are coincidentally forced to "be mean" in the course of the game. Their meanness is therefore not a result of actually being mean, but an unavoidable side effect of "being nice" or being a "protector" to one person.

Deciding who to play a game with seems to be greatly determined by established social relations within the group. Students I talked to mentioned shunning other students, usually for not observing gaming rules and social rules (rather than the rules of the game). Three boys, for example, told me that they often intentionally exclude a player who causes a fight or runs away with the ball so the others cannot play. The main goal in doing this is to keep the game going in order to take advantage of the limited recess time and stop someone who might prevent or interfere with game play.

I also observed a group of girls shunning a boy, Tom, with whom they determined it was undesirable to play. During the beginning of their tag game, the group of six girls attempted to use rules to exclude Tom. One of the girls jumped off of the jungle gym and yelled for "all girls" to come over to where she was standing. The girls huddled and decided on who would be tagged next. Throughout the rest of the game "it" would call the girl's name she was going after and then chase that person. At one point, Tom asked if someone would chase him, but he was ignored. The girls developed a rule of calling the name of the person who would be chased next. This was not something I had seen them do before. This name-calling rule made it obvious who would be tagged and who would be "it" next. It insured that everyone would get a turn, since players protested if they had not been chased in a few turns. It also insured that the excluded boy would not be included, since his name would have to be called by the person who was "it," and this would clearly go against the "all girls" group which had been established. The girls were choosing to exclude this boy from the game, although I have seen them include boys in their tag games before. In general, this boy was one of the students who is often excluded from play (by both boys and girls).

Sometimes gender is used as a basis for inclusion or exclusion either overtly (no boys/girls allowed) or subtly (playing a masculine or feminine stereotyped game). In the case in which Tom was shunned, the girls were using gender to exclude him. Although the actual reason they were refusing to play with him was probably because he was not well liked rather than the fact that he was a boy.

The girls and boys I observed had formed cliques. These cliques determined with whom the students would eat lunch and play during recess. A few students, like Mandy, were independent of the cliques and played with everyone in the class. Other students, such as Tom, were independent from the cliques because of exclusion rather than choice and tended to play with or sit with whichever group would accept them. Also, some cliques were more tightly knit than others. The group of girls who played tag, for example, played with each other in and out of school. Their teacher informed me that the girls had been in the same class for at least a year before I arrived and had become very close (in fact the teacher expressed a desire to encourage them to socialize more outside of their group).

CONCLUSION

The third and fourth grade children I observed used rules for many purposes. Gaming rules, defined by Hughes as a combination of official game rules and social rules, were followed, changed, ignored, enforced, and invented according to the context of the game or play, as well as the children's concepts of what was fair, fun, and acceptable.

Rarely, if ever, does one child have total control of the rules. In the groups I observed, successful changing of a rule required a majority of players to agree that the new rule was necessary and at least as fair as the old one. Children usually gave consent informally, for example, by following the new rule or telling it to other players. If players did not consent, they might disobey the new rule or quit the game.

One third grade boy said, "In the middle of the year we made rules and they stayed through the whole year, and sometimes we made rules and they didn't." Some rules are temporary and others are more permanent. Rules which players felt made the game more fun and fair were the ones that were often used the next time the game was played. There was usually no opportunity for rules invented in spontaneous play situations to be used again because the same play situation was not recreated.

The use, interpretation, social aspects, and consequences of rules play a part in structuring the game and the organization of play. They also are a part in establishing, maintaining, or challenging the social hierarchies that develop among children. Rules are not simply "something you follow." Rules are an important part of the way children relate to each other. They not only outline specific games but also reflect how kids structure social relations. Children do not seem to base their ideas of what is acceptable on rules, but they base the rules on their ideas of what is acceptable.

NOTES

[1] I would like to thank Linda Pershing for her help in introducing me to the teacher with whom I worked in this school and helping me to organize this fieldwork project.

[2] I would like to thank Linda Hughes for her helpful comments and suggestions on this paper.

[3] The names I use in this chapter are pseudonyms.

[4] This situation, in which one of the teachers determined the recess play, was unique. Usually the students determine their own games and play situations during the recess period. Nevertheless, this situation provided me with a unique opportunity to view a dynamic where both adults and children were involved in play and rule making.

REFERENCES

Alexander, G., & Hines, M. (1994). Gender labels and play styles: Their relative contribution to children's selection of playmates. *Child Development, 65*(3), 869–879.

Bateson, G. (1972). *Steps to an ecology of mind: Collected essays in anthropology, psychiatry, evolution, and epistomology.* New York: Ballantine.

Beresin, A. (1995). Double dutch and double cameras: Studying the transmission of culture in an urban school yard. In B. Sutton-Smith, J. Mechling, T. W. Johnson, & F. R. McMahon (Eds.), *Children's folklore: A source book* (pp. 74–91). New York: Garland.

Cohen, D. (1993). *The development of play* (2nd ed.). New York: Routledge.

Froebel, F. (1887). *The education of man.* New York: D. Appleton.

Goodwin, M. H. (1985). The serious side of jump rope: Conversational practices and social organization in the frame of play. *Journal of American Folklore, 98*(389), 315–330.

Goodwin, M. H. (1990). *He-said-she-said: Talk as social organization among black children.* Bloomington and Indianapolis, IN: Indiana University Press.

Goodwin, M. H. (1993). Accomplishing social organization in girls' play: Patterns of competition and cooperation in an African American working class girls' group. In S. T. Hollis, L. Pershing, & M. J. Young (Eds.), *Feminist theory and the study of folklore* (pp. 149–165). Urbana and Chicago: University of Illinois Press.

Goodwin, M. H. (1997, April). 1996–97 AN theme: The known, unknown and unknowable in anthropology: Children's linguistic and social worlds. *Anthropology Newsletter, 38*(4), 1, 4–5.

Groos, K. (1912). *The play of man.* New York: D. Appleton.

Hughes, L. (1991). A conceptual framework for the study of children's gaming. *Play and Culture, 3,* 284–301.

Hughes, L. (1993). "You have to do it with style": Girls' games and girls' gaming. In S. T. Hollis, L. Pershing, & M. J. Young (Eds.), *Feminist theory and the study of folklore* (pp. 130–148). Urbana and Chicago: University of Illinois Press.

Hughes, L. (1995). Children's games and gaming. In B. Sutton-Smith, J. Mechling, T. W. Johnson, & F. R. McMahon (Eds.), *Children's folklore: A source book* (pp. 93–119). New York: Garland.

Kirshenblatt-Gimblett, B. (1976). *Speech play.* Philadelphia: University of Pennsylvania Press.

Knapp, M., & Knapp, H. (1976). *One potato, two potato ... the secret education of American children.* New York: W. W. Norton.

Montessori, M. (1917). *The advanced Montessori method.* Cambridge, MA: Bentley.

Opie, I. A., & Opie, P. (1969). *Children's games in street and playground: Chasing, catching, seeking, hunting, racing, dueling, exerting, daring, guessing, acting, pretending.* Oxford, England: Clarendon Press.

Piaget, J. (1962). *Play, dreams and imitation in childhood.* New York: W. W. Norton.

Piaget, J. (1972). Some aspects of operations. In M. W. Piers (Ed.), *Play and development.* New York: W. W. Norton.

Piaget, J., & Inhelder, B. (1969). *The early growth of logic in the child.* New York. W. W. Norton.

Schwartzman, H. B. (1978). *Transformations: The anthropology of children's play.* New York: Plenum Press.

Spencer, H. (1873). *The principles of psychology* (Vol. 2). New York: D. Appleton.

Thorne, B. (1993). *Gender play: Girls and boys in school.* New Brunswick, NJ: Rutgers University Press.

Turner, V. (1969). *The ritual process: Structure and anti-structure.* Chicago: Aldine.

Weir, R. (1962). *Language in the crib.* The Hague, The Netherlands: Mouton.

7

The Canvas of Play:
A Study of Children's Play
Behaviors While Drawing[*]

Theresa H. Escobedo, Ed.D.
University of Texas at Austin

Drawing combined with talk can quite literally become a canvas for children's shared dramas.... As children grow as symbolic players ... they paint the canvas of play collaboratively with their friends. (Dyson, 1990, p. 54)

Humans have in common the ancient, universal, human urge to draw (DiLeo, 1970). It is possibly related to the equally ancient and universal human urge for social interactions and communications, by verbal or other symbolic means; and play is an important aspect of this interaction. The ability to create drawings, including symbols, allows humans not only to communicate their knowledge but also to become familiar with their environment; the emergence of symbolic representation is an important part of an individual's ability to know their world (Werner & Kaplan,

[*] This research study was supported in part by Project QUEST, Apple/ICEC Fellowship, and by the University Research Institute Summer Awards at the University of Texas at Austin. The laboratory facilities were furnished by the UT College of Education, the equipment provided by the college's Instructional Technology Computer Laboratory, and the technical assistance provided by the staff were essential in the implementation of this study.

We gratefully acknowledge the valuable assistance of Ambika Bhargava, as field observer; June Yeatman, as teacher and participant-observer; and Barbara Gilstad and Gloria Esco-Davidson as art table teachers and observers in the implementation of the study. Above all, we acknowledge the willing participation on the part of the parents and the children who were samples for the study.

1963). Symbols convey meaning by referring to a thing, idea, or feeling, and thus are the means by which humans express mental representations and images. In children, the emergence of symbolic representation, often in their play interactions, is an important step in the development of cognition, since it becomes not only an avenue by which children can express their knowledge, but also a means of integrating new experiences. They begin to separate the meanings of these experiences through play and its related substitution of objects (Berk, 1994). Thus, the use of play materials, such as dolls, blocks, and concrete art materials, helps children develop a greater and more accurate understanding of their environment by allowing them to reproduce the realities of their experiences (Maxim, 1985; Reifel & Greenfield, 1982). The influence of play on development has been shown in studies concluding that a child's mental skills are at a higher level during play than in other learning activities (Bodrova & Leong, 1996). Hence, levels of children's play are an important factor in developing their symbolic representational competence. Children possess an increasing reservoir of personal meanings about experiences, objects, and events, an important element that affects the degree to which they can symbolically represent their realities. Another factor affecting children's representational abilities for using drawing symbols is the gradual development of stages of art that all children systematically follow in predictable sequence, as in other developmental areas. In addition, through practice and repetition, children develop specific, recognizable symbols for particular mental images, or referents. In time and with experience, children's acceptance of appropriate referents begin to change, and symbols are then modified and become more complex (Smith, 1982).

It can be argued that the value of art lies in the contributions it makes to individuals' experience with, and understanding of, the world. However, research has shown that participation in art activities plays an important role in various areas such as development of visual perception, language, concept formation, emotions, writing and reading skills, and even play. In drawing, children transform emotionally significant experiences in order to express and interpret them, giving observable forms to their inner worlds; in play, children symbolize ideas and feelings through gestures and speech, which give them concreteness (Dyson, 1990). While drawing often is considered "constructive work" and separate from pretend play, there are those who study graphic symbolism and stress the interaction between children and their own products. This dialogue between children and their drawing often includes other people; thus, children's skills in collaborative play and story-telling infuses their drawings (Dyson, 1989; Golomb, 1988; Rogers & Sawyers, 1988). The interaction of art and play was demonstrated by a study conducted in a center-based environment in which art was an important area. Children could draw their own representations of the subjects they were studying; some viewed the art activities as play and used them in that way. This was shown in the answer of one child when asked about the experience: "'It be play.... Den you do your art.... It be fun. You be learning 'bout art and soft sculpture and tigers and books and stuff'" (Branscombe, 1991, p. 112).

There are differences in how children select certain media to organize and interpret their world. Some prefer storytelling and dramatic play and for them even drawing may serve as a dramatic medium. Children's understanding of the varied roles of people occurs in drawing as well as in more obvious activities like talk and play (Dyson, 1990). Dyson stressed the critical role of art and play in children's growth as symbol makers. Her observations of four- to eight-year-old children revealed them creating imagined worlds through drawing combined with talk, a combination that can "literally become a canvas for children's shared dramas" (p. 54). Though the children viewed themselves as drawing, they were involved in the complex negotiations of dramatic play. Thus, children can paint the canvas of play collaboratively with their friends. Others have reported examples of children's pretend play during drawing (Mathews, 1984) and have stressed the importance of children's talk as an essential component of early artistic development (Thompson, 1990). While there is documented evidence of children's play in drawing, there are few studies that have focused on specific types of play. Therefore, the purpose of this study was to analyze the drawings and the language of preschool children, describing possible play behaviors and types of play that are evident in their drawings, as well as related language episodes.

BASIS AND QUESTIONS FOR THE STUDY

In order to analyze the play behaviors evident in the language and in children's drawings produced with traditional art materials, the following questions were formulated for this study: What evidence was there that children engaged in play activities while drawing? What types of play behaviors were observed? What language episodes were associated with the play behaviors? To answer these questions, a descriptive design was utilized in the study. Certain parameters—a framework—were devised from which to view play behaviors and related language episodes.

The study was based on certain assumptions about children's development associated with the specific areas involved in the research: children's drawings, play, and language. Theories of children's art range from Piaget's (1955) cognitive development, to the psychoanalytic theory (Cole, 1966), to the perceptual theory posed by Arnheim (1954). However, the more comprehensive perceptual delineation theory (McFee, 1970) is more compatible with the view of children's art held by the researchers of this study. According to Mayesky (1990), this theory advances the idea that children's drawings are influenced by several factors, including children's physical and perceptual development, intelligence, and cultural dispositions; the emergence of distinct stages of art abilities are influenced by the child's maturational development. Also highly important is a psychological environment in which children work that embodies various degrees of support and rewards or threat and punishment. This would indicate that the most appropriate approach is a child-centered, play-oriented one (Bredekamp & Copple, 1997) that supports children in their artistic efforts and where punitive measures for discipline are not used. A final factor of the delineation theory deals with how children's drawings are influenced by the ability to manipulate art material as well as with individual skills of creativity and invention (Mayesky, 1990). Children's experiences, especially those that include opportunities for art, play, and discovery, would be influential aspects of this last idea.

In addition, included in the framework for this study was the idea of play as a creative activity, whether it is construction with objects, language, humor, imagination, or thinking and problem solving (Gottfried, 1985). Because of the general approach of the study—allowing the children involved to produce their drawings through play activities and self-initiated ideas—it was necessary to make a distinction from the play orientation found in the literature, which defines all pleasurable activity as play, even pleasurable work. The play theory used as the basis of the study is one that proposes that exploration and manipulation are prerequisite to meaningful play experiences. Play is not exhibited until exploratory activity has occurred; in exploration, children discover what the material does, and in play, they discover what they can do with the material (Fromberg, 1992; Rubin, Fein, & Vandenberg, 1983). Further delineated by the affordance concept, the sequence of extracting information from materials through exploration follows three phases: exploration of material through inspection, to manipulation (which may include experimentation), and then to play; "...the kinds of elaboration of reality that qualify as play, such as the transformation of objects for constructive purposes, or for the creation of an imaginary or pretend world, appear after exploration" (Wohlwill, 1984, p. 165). This sequence closely coincides with the sequence for development of stages of art abilities: Scribble, Basic Forms, then Pictorial stages. This progression also goes through exploration and manipulation, to mastery and control, and finally to meaningful representation (Mayesky, 1990; Mayesky, Neuman, & Wlodkowski, 1985; Smith, 1982).

There is support for the proposition that language is essential for artistic development; in addition, appropriate child–adult dialogue may provide understanding of artistic activity (Thompson, 1990). The shared cognitive basis for development in language and symbolic play is the ability to symbolize verbally or graphically; therefore, assessment of play can be used to judge a child's symbolic activity (McCune, 1985). This shared cognitive base is extended to include not only language and symbolic activity, but also cognitive development. Because play often includes or consists of purely symbolic activity, language is a possible indicator of a child's intentional play that is not evident from actions alone. Such symbolic activities can include pretend play, imaginary activities, and humor, which are usually oral interactions (Fromberg, 1990), as well as word games, play with words, and puns, which are based totally on language. By middle school, the arbitrary, or conventional, nature of words is fully realized and children can play with these abstractions in the form of jokes, puns, and riddles (Athey, 1988). The significance of children's play with language itself is considered an important aspect of play. Researchers have suggested that children enjoy playing with language because it makes them feel in control; also, playing with language for sound repetition, as well as in riddles, jokes, and metaphors, may have a poetic function (Fromberg, 1987).

Based on the orientation described above, the focus of this study was to examine children's drawings and related language episodes in order to differentiate those exhibiting play from those exhibiting exploratory behaviors. Those drawings categorized as play were further analyzed to identify possible different types of play: transformation of objects for constructive purposes or for imaginary purposes. Also included was identification of possible incidents of play with the language itself, such as puns and humor, as well as games, make-believe, pretense, and imagination.

METHODS AND PROCEDURE

The primary sources of data for the study were produced by four middle-class children: two males (a 4-year-old and a 5-year-old) and two females (a 4-year-old and a 5-year-old). The data included 36 hours of video tapes, extensive observation and field notes, and 120 drawings produced with traditional art materials. The setting included a drawing table arranged with concrete art materials corresponding to the drawing activities addressed on each specific session, as well as to the drawing and painting tools on the software available on each of two computers, which were to be used by the children as an alternate activity to the art table. This study of children's play behaviors at the art table was conducted in conjunction with one that investigated children's computer graphics skills in terms of stages of art, symbolic representation, and play (Escobedo, 1992; Escobedo & Bhargava, 1991). Therefore, computers, materials, videotapes, and audiotapes were arranged for the computer studies. The concrete art materials included drawing or scribble tools, such as crayons, marking pens, pads, and pencils. Others were added to correspond to the particular focus of that week, such as: patterned paper and wallpaper, template tracing shapes, solid-colored construction paper, and scissors to cut shapes for cutting and pasting, as well as different textured paper and textured plates.

The data were collected during eight 90-minute sessions, held weekly in an observation room of an education school. Videotapes were made of the activity at the art table and of the total environment. Through observations and field notes, careful documentation was kept of the process that took place at the art table with traditional art materials; the child's language was audiotaped and labels were recorded on the back of each depiction produced at the art table. Due to the nature of the correlated computer studies and the objective of collecting play data at the art table, it was planned to divide the children's time so that approximately half of the period was spent at the art table and half at the computers. The children's initial high interest in using the computers and the availability of only two computers during the sessions made it necessary to use a sign-up sheet of 15-minute intervals for the children to select their time at the computer. This resulted in a division of time so that the children played 15 minutes at each of the computers, with the remaining time spent at the art table, for a total of approximately 45 minutes at the computers and 45 minutes at the art table. This rotation resulted in approximately one 15-minute and one 30-minute period of uninterrupted time at the art table per weekly session. Once the children's initial curiosity with the computers became satisfied, they often chose to remain at the art table until their current art activity was completed. Four researchers were involved in collecting the data and writing notes after each session: One functioned as the main teacher, conducting the group orientations to the specific art materials and activities; these orientations lasted approximately five minutes per weekly session. She also provided student support for activities at one computer while a second researcher did the same at the other computer. Another researcher monitored the art table, while another observed and took field notes.

A constructivist, child-focused, guided-discovery approach was used to conduct the sessions and to introduce the children to the art activities. Due to the laboratory setting constraints, open centers selection was not possible. No specific tasks were required, as it was expected that the children would initiate their own graphic work through play experimentation and manipulate the materials to create their own artwork. Underlying this strategy was the belief that once given developmentally appropriate activities, children could construct their own knowledge. The major assumptions of the study were based on assertions that children's learning and acquisition of certain skills and concepts are conditional upon discovery learning, allowing the development and exploration of self-initiated projects (Bodrova & Leong, 1996; Bredekamp & Copple, 1997; Brooks & Brooks, 1993; Katz & Chard, 1995). The researchers followed weekly plans based on broad topics, formulated prior to the study and modified as needed, which guided the general direction of activities for the sessions. The topics were: scribble and pattern tools, shapes, background and foreground, overlapping, borders, and texture. The lessons provided hands-on demonstrations to introduce the children to the different concrete materials and to possible underlying art concepts that were involved. There was no selected curriculum and no attempt to teach formal concepts of Western art, as the list of topics might indicate to some readers. There was an attempt to organize the art table activities and materials to mimic the computer software key elements and to thus limit any possible confusion the children might encounter. For example, the computer screen can be made various colors and different-colored shapes, patterns, or drawings can be added, or overlapped. This computer activity corresponded to a simple cut-and-paste activity, commonly used with four-year-old children: To correlate the computer tools with the art materials, the children used different-colored construction paper sheets on which to paste their various colored cutouts, or to draw with colored markers. The other topics were similarly coordinated.

DATA ANALYSIS

This study was based on descriptive analysis which included frequencies and percentages as well as observational data. Preparation of the data prior to analysis included transcribing the videotapes, entering the data into a word-processing file, and checking the verbal transcriptions against field notes and videotapes, thus coordinating the language and actions of the children. The information was then coordinated with the appropriate drawings. The graphics were coded into designated categories as to evidence of nonplay, play behaviors, and types of play. Two coders independently reviewed and categorized both; interrater agreement was 97.5%.

The analysis of the data for play behaviors was based on comprehensive examination of field observations and field notes, careful review of the language transcriptions for evidence of play, and coordination of these with selected drawings. To answer the first question—What evidence was there that children engaged in play activities while drawing?—differentiation between exploration and play behaviors was made. The transcribed videotapes and the field notes were examined for evidence of intentional play behaviors that might or might not be evident in the graphics. The drawings were reviewed and classified into categories of Nonplay (Exploration and Manipulation) and Meaningful Play. These designations of the sequence of emerging play behaviors closely reflected the previously established stages of art (Escobedo & Bhargava, 1991): exploration and inspection were evident mostly in graphics categorized at the Scribbling stage, manipulation and experimentation were evident in graphics at the Basic Forms stage, and meaningful play behaviors (including construction with objects and fantasy) evident in those drawings at the Pictorial stage.

To answer the second question—What types of play behaviors were observed?—the drawings were coordinated with segments of the language transcriptions, organized into language episodes that gave indications of play behaviors and carefully examined for evidence of different types of play. For the third question—What language episodes were associated with the play behaviors?—the language episodes were examined carefully for intended purposes related to specific types of play behaviors, which might or might not be evident in any of the drawings; expected purposes were, for example, construction, fantasy, and play with the language itself.

RESULTS AND DISCUSSION

Analysis of the graphics and the descriptive data showed that 120 drawings were produced during the eight sessions. For Question 1—What evidence was there that children engaged in play activities while drawing?—differentiation between nonplay (exploration and manipulation) and play behaviors were made for evidence of play behaviors while drawing. Categorization of the drawings revealed the following percentages: 32.5% of the drawings were coded in the Nonplay category (21.7% in Exploration; 10.8% in Manipulation) and 67.5% in Meaningful Play. Table 7.1 shows these percentages for play categories by subject.

Further analysis of the descriptive data and the 81 drawings categorized as Meaningful Play (67.5% of total produced) were further coded to explore the different types of evident play behaviors in Question 2 (What types of play behaviors were observed?). This analysis of the drawings and the related language segments indicating play episodes showed evidence of transformation of objects for Constructive and Imaginative Play and resulted in the following percentage for the respective categories: 62.97% of the drawings were coded as Constructive Play and 37.07% as Imaginative Play. Table 7.2 shows percentages for types of play and totals for subjects.

Maturational levels, often exhibited by chronological age, are thought to affect the stages of art and also symbolic representational capabilities and levels of play (Smith, 1982; Werner & Kaplan, 1963; Wohlwill, 1984). The data coded for play categories evident in the drawings were analyzed by the two age levels represented by the subjects, two 4-year-olds and two 5-year-olds. Results revealed that graphics by the two younger children were categorized as 28.33% in the Nonplay category, while those by the two older children were 4.17%. In the Play category, the findings were reversed, with graphics by the older children accounting for 59.17% and those by the two younger for 8.33%. Further analysis of the data for differences in types of play episodes in relation to the age of the children also indicated that the older children's graphics were more often coded as exhibiting Constructive Play at 35.84% and

TABLE 7.1.
Percentage of Play Categories Exhibited in Drawings by Subject

	Nonplay			Meaningful Play	
	Exploratory	Manipulation	Nonplay Subtotal	Play Subtotal	Totals
Leila					
%	15.0%	4.2%	19.2%	0%	19.2%
(N=)	(18)	(5)	(23)	(0)	(23)
Walter					
%	5.0%	4.2%	9.2%	8.3%	17.5%
(N=)	(6)	(5)	(11)	(10)	(21)
Kiah					
%	.8%	1.7%	2.5%	27.5%	30.0%
(N=)	(1)	(2)	(3)	(33)	(36)
Jeremy					
%	.8%	.8%	1.6	31.7%	33.3%
(N=)	(1)	(1)	(2)	(38)	(40)
Totals	21.7%	10.8%	32.5%	67.5%	100%
(N=)	(26)	(13)	(39)	(81)	(120)

TABLE 7.2.
Percentage of Types of Play Episodes by Subject

	Constructive Play	Imaginative Play	Totals
Leila			
%	0	0	0.0%
(N=)			(0)
Walter			
%	9.88%	2.47%	12.35%
(N=)	(8)	(2)	(10)
Kiah			
%	28.40%	12.35%	40.74%
(N=)	(23)	(10)	(33)
Jeremy			
%	24.69%	22.21%	46.91%
(N=)	(20)	(18)	(38)
Totals	62.97%	37.03%	100%
(N=)	(52)	(29)	(81)

TABLE 7.3.
Percentage of Types of Play Episodes by Age

	Nonplay	Constructive Play	Imaginative Play	Totals
Four-Year-Olds				
Percent	28.33%	6.66%	1.67%	36.66%
(N=)	(34)	(8)	(2)	
Five-Year-Olds				
Percent	4.17%	35.84%	23.33%	63.34%
(N=)	(5)	(43)	(28)	
Totals	32.5%	42.5%	25.0%	100%
(N=)	(39)	(52)	(29)	(120)

Imaginative Play at 23.33%, as compared to the younger children's results of Constructive Play 6.66% and Imaginative Play at 1.67%. Thus, in this study there appeared to be age differences in that the older children had a greater number of graphics in the Play category, and used Imaginative Play more often than the younger children (see Table 7.3).

The elaborations of reality that qualify as play include the transformation of objects for constructive purposes or the creation of an imaginary or pretend world (Wohlwill, 1984). In Constructive Play, the child uses objects in attempts to create something, such as pictures, forms, or objects; in addition, object-oriented play involves not only what the child can do with an object, but also derivation or

TABLE 7.4.

Examples of Play Transformation of Objects per Subject

	Jeremy	Kiah	Walter	Leila
Construction Realistic	Envelope Paper airplane House	Heart Bird Dining	House with chimney, trailer, truck, and toaster; house with smoke	Explored
Imagination Make-believe	Marshmallow man, sun with face, snowman, invisible man			
Imagination Pretend	Tornado, a ghost, a treasure map, a ghost flying out of a haunted house, invisible man reading a book	Dribbles, a ghost, a ghost sound, a ghostly picture	A treasure map, confetti	
Imagination Play with Language	Tornado, label on table, people on people, scribble scrabble, table lose label, multimedia meteor	Lilly Leila, polka dot, making a dowse, squibble squabble, belly willy, willy silly, sparkle sparkle		Quack quack, willy silly, silly nilly, thanks for doing that
Imagination Games	A marshmallow man game, a ghost game, a maze game, TV's Pat Sajack	A ghostly game, a card game		
Imagination Humor	Teasing about picture and reminding him of nothing, multimedia called meteor shower			
Imagination Joking	An Easter joke			

imposing of novel meaning on objects and events. For Question 3—What language episodes were associated with the play behaviors?—language episodes were analyzed in order to identify play behaviors, including transformations and novel meanings that may or may not have been reflected in the drawings. Results of this study displayed such transformations as the children-created objects for Constructive and Imaginative purposes (make believe, pretend, language play, games, humor, joking); noted were everyday objects such as envelopes, birds, and houses, as well as transformations for pretending, games, and humor (see Table 7.4). Here, an age difference was also evident for transformation of objects. Under Constructive purposes, the youngest female's drawings and behavior showed much exploration with the materials and use of language play at a repetitive level only. The youngest male had various incidents of Construction at the realistic level and few at the Imagination, Pretend level. The two older subjects had examples of transformation for Construction as well as Imagination for the various level designations. This was especially evident in the work of the older male, who used Imagination, including humor and joking, as well as all the other level designations of Imagination.

The transcribed language correlated with corresponding drawings and associated with play episodes, the third question, confirmed not only the intentional play behaviors indicated in the graphics, but also the children's use of language for transformational purposes. Examples of the graphics and the associated language are presented below. This discussion is based on two major topics: transformation of objects for Construction, and transformation of objects for Imagination, or pretend, purposes; games, humor, play with words/language, pretense, and problem solving are incorporated when appropriate. Figure 7.1 is a drawing at the Construction level of play and was produced by the youngest male; associated language follows. As Walter discovered similarities between shapes in his drawings and familiar articles, he elaborated to construct other objects at the reality level with some imagination.

Language 1—Constructive Play, Reality Level and Imagination

(Walter had been scribbling with different shapes, resembling bricks.)

   Walter: I'm gonna make a whole city. *(Said as he discovers an idea)*

Teacher: A whole city?

Jeremy: I can make one too!

Teacher: Where is your city at?… Where is it gonna be?… Is it the city that we live in, or is it another city?… *(Asked at various points as Walter continues drawing)*

   Walter: It's the city that we live in.

Teacher: What part of the city?

   Walter: The part that we live in.

Teacher: Oh, I see. Are those buildings?

   Walter: Yup. All the buildings go up.

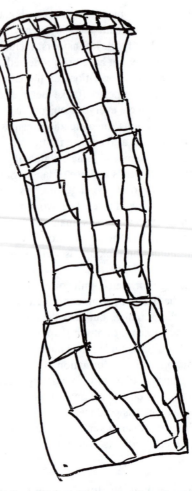

FIGURE 7.1.   Transformation of objects for construction of an imaginary city (Walter).

Teacher: Um-hum. How many buildings do you have?

Walter: One. I haven't built it... *(He starts to build)*

   (Later) I built my city, my city is almost finished.

Teacher: You built your city. Yes, you did...

Walter: My city is one city. Everybody lives in this building!

Teacher: Oh, it must be a pretty big building, huh?

Walter: Yes, that's why it has so many windows.

Teacher: Mmmm. Can I write on here that this is your city?

Walter: Yup.

Teacher: Should I put the city that we live in? Or just the city?

Walter: No, just put, a, just put this is the city that we live in and this is _____.

The incident began with Walter exploring with different shapes, as Figure 7.1 shows. Some of the shapes became the focal point for the Constructive Play that followed, when Walter discovered similarities between shapes and bricks and made the transformation from the objects to Construction activity; Imagination is displayed in that he installed a whole city in one building. Walter's explorations often elicited ideas that led to construction and transformation of objects to other objects. While not evident in this episode, he often demonstrated differentiation between reality and fantasy, a development that occurs through play (Fromberg, 1987).

The two older children often exhibited play that included transformation of objects for Construction purposes and for Imagination in creating pretend experiences and imaginary worlds. Evident also were play with words, humor, and games. The creation of an imaginary or pretend world is a significant characteristic of play and involves its transformational possibilities as related to objects, events, and activities; games are considered part of these possibilities for children, with the exception of games with rules, which are common in older children and adults (Gottfried, 1985). In addition, the verbal language associated with pretend play is important in that pretense is usually an oral interaction and the language provides powerful insights as to intentional behavior (Fromberg, 1990).

In the following dialogue, Kiah, the oldest female, exhibited her inclination to play guessing games with the teacher while constructing objects or scenes. On this occasion, she had been using her guessing game procedure which usually started with a comment such as:

Language 2—Constructive and Imaginative Play

Kiah: Bet you can't guess what I'm drawing.

Teacher: A flower. *(Kiah continues drawing)*

Kiah: Look! Now! Ba, it starts with a B. Now guess what this is. It starts with a B...

Teacher: (pause) A beetle?

Kiah: Nope.

Teacher: No?

Kiah: Cause look! It's not a beetle, it's not a bee.

Teacher: It's very colorful too.

Kiah: It's not a bee, it's not a, uhm, it's not the other one, so guess what it is.

Teacher: A BUTTERFLY!

Kiah: Yup!

Teacher: It's a butterfly, ooooh!

Kiah: Can you write butterfly?

Teacher: Oh sure, let me write it with my pencil! Can I borrow you pencil, and I'll give it right back to you? B-U-T-T-E-R-F-L-Y.

Kiah: Write it big ... so I can see.

FIGURE 7.2. Construction of object for playing a guessing game and related emergent literacy evidence (Kiah).

Kiah's drawing illustrates the transformational possibilities of play as related to objects and games. While the drawing is Construction, the language indicates games, part of the Imagination category. The language episode provides insight into her creation that involved not only the drawing and guessing game, but also exhibited her knowledge of letter sounds; emergent literacy evidence is clearly present.

In pretend play, children make assertions about important aspects of experience and illustrate their ability to explore invented worlds not constrained by the immediate situation or by actual experience. It is argued by some that the meaning of pretense consists of ideas and images retrieved from long-term memory and of novel combinations of these ideas and images. The player also makes mental claims about the reality of these images, denying they are inventions and insisting that they exist in the concrete reality of the here and now. The player simultaneously affirms the playfulness of these claims and indicates he is not to be taken seriously. Thus, children establish the play frame through metacommunications (Fein & Schwartz, 1986). Jeremy, the oldest male, often combined his drawings with humor and exhibited a preference for developing imaginary and improbable scenes.

Language 3—Imaginative Play, Pretend

Jeremy: Who's reading the book? Who's reading the book?

An invisible man! An invisible man is reading the book....

You see the book is in the air, and then the invisible man is reading it.

Teacher: Where, where is the invisible man?

Jeremy: You can't see him, he's invisible!

Teacher: But I think I see him.

Jeremy: Where?

Teacher: He's holding the book, isn't he?

Jeremy: Yeah, and he's reading it!

Teacher: He is? What's the name of the book?

Jeremy: The Haunted Lock-Nest.

Teacher: The Haunted Lock-Nest?

Jeremy: Yeah.

Teacher: That sounds like an interesting book.

FIGURE 7.3. An imaginary, improbable scene of an invisible man reading (Jeremy).

In the graphic and the language of this episode, Jeremy exhibited transformation of objects for Imagination in creating an imaginary scene that is totally improbable and included humor and play with the language itself. The first two lines of his dialogue show an inclination toward poetic verse and play with words as he initiates establishment of the play frame. Humor, considered a form of intellectual play with ideas, "…results from the playful production of fantasy incongruities when relatively greater attention is given to the impossibility or (at later ages) the improbability or inappropriateness of the imagined event" (McGhee, 1984, p. 221). Jeremy clearly indicates the playfulness and impossibility of the situation as the teacher responds and enters the play frame; this understanding is thought to occur typically in children 7 or 8 years old. However, in the episode, Jeremy, at age 5 years and 6 months, exhibits this understanding as well as play with the language in the reference to the name of the invisible book.

Early pretend play focuses on simple substitution of pretend objects for real ones. Later, children are able to rely more on their own imaginations and symbolic constructions. It is believed that there are several types of pretend play—including fantasy and sociodramatic play—and that pretense has positive effects on aspects of intellectual and social development, including creativity, imaginativeness, and problem solving, as well as on emotional development (Saltz & Saltz, 1986). The following language episode and related drawing illustrate Jeremy's facility in developing imaginary worlds.

Language 4—Imaginative Play

Jeremy: Haunted houses, houses really have ghosts in 'em! I'm going to make one flying out the window.
   (pause) See, see how the smoke is scribbles. It's like a ghost flying out…
   …Me stop, me heard ghost under table!
Teacher: You heard a ghost under the table?
Kiah: Oooooooooooooooo!
Jeremy: Ooooo, ah, ah, ah. *(Long while passes and teacher comes in)*
Teacher: Oh, what is this?
Jeremy: It's a haunted house.… See, this is a ghost.… And I'm gonna draw some more smoke coming out of the chimney. There's fire in the chimney.

Jeremy's drawings often indicated creations of imaginary or pretend worlds, a significant characteristic of play involving transformational possibilities. This is illustrated in this and his other imaginary depictions, which seem to rely almost totally on his imagination and symbolic constructions; these were much beyond the early substitution of pretend objects for real ones. This episode also indicates not only pretend play, including fantasy, but also sociodramatic play as both he and Kiah assume the role of the ghost, providing ghostly sounds.

Collaborative play in drawing, combined with children's talk, becomes a shared drama; for some children, drawing serves as a dramatic medium as they portray their

FIGURE 7.4. An imaginary scene of a haunted house (Jeremy).

understanding of the varied roles of people. The social interaction revolving around art and play provides a critical element in children's growth as symbol makers, and such verbalization is basic to emerging literacy, as reported by Dyson (1990) in her study; this was demonstrated by Kiah in the second language episode. In the following episode, Kiah initiated the action by drawing a house which turns haunted; the other children join the collaborative play/drama.

Language 5—Imaginative and Collaborative play

>*Kiah:* This is going to be something NEAT! *(She continues drawing)*
>*(long pause)*
>*(singing)* Me making a house. We're making a dowse.

>*Leila:* You did that! *(She refers to a mark on her paper)*

>*Kiah:* Me not do that. *(Walter enters argument about what Kiah did to Leila's paper)*

>*Leila:* When I did … the paper was like that! And I didn't want it like that!

>*Kiah:* I didn't put it like that either! A ghost did!

>*Leila:* Not it didn't, did it?

>*Kiah:* A ghost, oh weeeeeeeee!

>*Teacher:* A ghost?

Kiah: Oooooooooooooooh.

Teacher: Are you pretending to be afraid?

Kiah: Ooooooooooooooo. That doesn't make me scared. Oo oo oo ah ah ah ah!

Jeremy: (in baby talk) He behind me? He behind me!

Kiah: No not see nobody there!

Jeremy: Oh yeah, well you can look under the table, there's somebody there! *(All of a sudden he screams very loudly in fear of the ghost and the others join in, then they are giggling.)*

Walter: Jeremy really shouted!

Teacher: He's really loud. It hurt my ears.

Walter: Kiah too.

Kiah: When Jeremy did that it made me scream. I saw the ghost under the table.

Jeremy: (singing) Scardie cat you were afraid of me!

Leila: Auhhhh.

Jeremy: Scardie cat, you were afraid of me too.... *(pause)*

The drawing itself gave no indication of any ghostly happenings and the play purpose was evident only when the language episodes were examined. It served merely to initiate the language episode and the related collaborative dramatic play when Kiah pretended that she did not mark on Leila's paper, and that instead, it was a ghost that did it. Jeremy joins Kiah and Leila in the social drama while Walter comments on the action. There was much movement and loud verbalization. In play, gestures and noises make the situation explicit (Bodrova & Leong, 1996), as shown in this

FIGURE 7.5. Collaborative dramatic play of a ghost in their midst, evident in related language episode (Kiah).

episode. Thus, review of the descriptive data, including transcriptions of the language, indicated that the children engaged in collaborative play while drawing. In episodes such as this one, the children created imagined worlds through drawings combined with words, which in turn became shared dramas, as in Dyson's (1990) previous observations.

CONCLUSIONS AND IMPLICATIONS

In summary, the drawings and related languages demonstrated that the children in this study engaged in play behaviors while drawing, that these were reflective of different types of play, and that the language episodes indicated the children's transformations of objects for Construction and Imagination. Of the total drawings produced during the study, approximately one third (32.5%) were in the Nonplay category and two thirds (67.5%) in Meaningful Play. Thus, the data reviewed demonstrated children's use of materials through a progression of behaviors that included Exploration, Manipulation for the purpose of extracting information, and Meaningful Play behaviors. An important implication for teachers and parents of young children is that sufficient time be allowed for exploration and experimentation with art materials for children to perform at their own individual levels. It is important for children to interact with the materials, teachers, and with each other in order to benefit from the maximum levels of play. As reported here and elsewhere, benefits can include language, emergent literacy, collaborative play, and increased imagination.

Different types of play and transformations of objects for Construction and Imagination were evident in the children's drawings and related language episodes. As the children interacted in a supportive, child-centered atmosphere, they were free to engage in drawings that included transformation of objects for constructive as well as for imaginary purposes. They created depictions of various fanciful worlds containing games, play with words, pretense, as well as imagination and shared dramas. An important implication is seen for providing developmentally appropriate activities that allow for the development and exploration of self-initiated projects that lead to discovery learning. The importance of such an environment has been supported by many (Bodrova & Leong, 1996; Bredekamp & Copple, 1997; Brooks & Brooks, 1993; Katz & Chard, 1995).

The sample of this study was too small to make definitive contrasts between the two age groups. However, for these four children in this case, there was a noted age difference favoring the older two for Play versus Non Play behaviors, for types of play (Imagination versus Construction Play), and for Transformation of objects for Imaginary versus Constructive purposes. The products of the two younger children were more reflective of Nonplay and of Constructive Play, while those of the two older children indicated Play and Imagination with creations of various imaginary scenes such as ghost houses and the invisible man. However, the older ones also utilized Nonplay explorations to extract information when presented with different or new materials and activities. The age differences noted for the children in this study may be an indication of others' research findings, though the present small number of subjects prohibits generalizations: It has been suggested by some researchers that in pretend play older children rely more on their own imagination and symbolic constructions than on objects (Saltz & Saltz, 1986), that older children provide more verbal explanations about their actions in current and forthcoming play activities (Fein & Schwartz, 1986), that the play of older children is more diverse and complex (see Fromberg, 1987), and that older children spend a greater proportion of their time in higher forms of play. However, it may be that different children who engage predominantly in exploration and others in play are reflecting two modes of orientation towards the world: one based on seeking out information and the other on transforming reality at the level of fantasy. But when there is uncertainty or information to be extracted, exploratory activity will take precedence over play (Wohlwill, 1984), a finding noted in this study when different topics and activities that required distinct materials were introduced. Based on research findings in the literature, similar to those of this study, an important implication is that it is necessary to provide materials and activities for children that are appropriate for a wide range of developmental levels and interests and accommodate exploratory as well as play behaviors.

Findings from this study reflect those reported by others that given appropriate activities, children engage in various play activities while drawing. Further, through symbolic play the children were able to create their own reality, an important aspect of play (Reifel & Greenfield, 1982). Observations for children's transformation of objects resulted not only in Constructive Play and Imaginative Play, but also in collaboration among children. There was also an indication that for some children drawing serves as a dramatic medium; this was especially evident in the drawings and language episodes of the older male. These findings reflected those of Dyson's (1990): "As children grow as symbolic players ... they paint the canvas of play collaboratively with their friends."

In conclusion, the descriptive nature of this study prohibits generalizations. However, it can be implied from this study, and as reflected in other studies (Dyson, 1990; Mathews, 1984), that children can use art activities in playful and fanciful ways while learning different procedures and materials, when allowed to approach the experience in a child appropriate manner. Important implications for teachers are that child-centered, developmentally appropriate strategies are needed for children's art activities and to use children's drawing as support for other parts of the curriculum such as language and emergent writing. Attention should be given to providing sufficient duration of experiences and of time for children to explore the medium and materials, as well as to learn their uses. It can be implied from this study that young children, in drawing, depend on play and its various dimensions in the same ways as when learning about any other play materials. Adults and teachers should strive to maintain an atmosphere conducive to aesthetic responses, to sensory experiences and related language, and should exhibit positive, encouraging attitudes. As in any situation, artistic play should be fostered by an environment that encourages and supports playfulness through a child-centered, discovery approach. If activities provide open-ended materials that are seen as available for exploration and experimentation, children will be able to play with them and construct their own microworlds for imagination and constructive purposes, whether these be construction of substitute objects, of language, or of their own concepts and knowledge.

REFERENCES

Arnheim, R. (1954). *Art and visual perception: The psychology of the creative experience.* Berkley, CA: University of California Press.

Athey, I. (1988). The relationship of play to cognitive, language, and moral development. In D. Bergen (Ed.), *Play as a medium for learning and development: A handbook of theory and practice* (pp. 81–101). Portsmouth, NH: Heinemann.

Berk, L. E. (1994). Vygotsky's theory: The importance of make-believe play. *Young Children, 50*(1), 30–39.

Bodrova, E., & Leong, D. J. (1996). *Tools of the mind: The Vygotskian approach to early childhood education.* Columbus, OH: Prentice Hall.

Branscombe, A. (1991). "But, it ain't real!": Pretense in children's play and literacy development. In J. F. Christie (Ed.), *Play and early literacy development.* Albany, NY: State University of New York Press.

Bredekamp, S., & Copple, C. (1997). *Developmentally appropriate practice in early childhood programs* (5th ed.). Washington, DC: National Association for the Education of Young Children.

Brooks, J. G., & Brooks, M. G. (1993). *In search of understanding: The case for constructivist classrooms.* Alexandria, VA: Association for Supervision and Curriculum Development.

Cole, N. R. (1966). *The arts in the classroom.* New York: John Day.

DiLeo, J. H. (1970). *Young children and their drawings.* New York: Brunner/Mazel.

Dyson, A. H. (1989). *Multiple worlds of child writers: Friends learning to write.* New York: Teachers College Press.

Dyson, A. H. (1990). Symbol makers, symbol weavers: How children link play, pictures, and print. *Young Children, 45*(2), 50–57.

Escobedo, T. H. (1992). Play in a new medium: Children's talk and graphics at computers. *Play & Culture, 5,* 120–140.

Escobedo, T. H., & Bhargava, A. (1991). A study of children's computer generated graphics. *Journal of Computing in Childhood Education, 2*(4), 3–25.

Fein, G. G., & Schwartz, S. (1986). The social coordination of pretense in preschool children. in G. Fein & M. Rivkin (Eds.), *The young child at play* (pp. 93–141). Washington, DC: National Association for the Education of Young Children.

Fromberg, D. P. (1987). Play. In C. Seefeldt (Ed.), *The early childhood curriculum* (pp. 35–73). New York: Teachers College Press.

Fromberg, D. P. (1990). Play issues in early childhood education. In C. Seefeldt (Ed.), *Continuing issues in early childhood education* (pp. 222–243). Columbus, OH: Merrill Publishing.

Fromberg, D. P. (1992). A review of research and play. In C. Seefeldt (Ed.), *The early child-hood curriculum* (pp. 42–84). New York: Teachers College Press.

Golomb, C. (1988). Symbolic inventions and transformations in child art. In K. Egan & D. Nadaner (Eds.), *Imagination and education* (pp. 222–236). New York: Teachers College Press.

Gottfried, A. W. (1985). Introduction. In C. C. Brown & A. W. Gottfried (Eds.), *Play interactions* (pp. xvi–xiv). Skillman, NJ: Johnson & Johnson.

Katz, L. G., & Chard, S. C. (1995). *Engaging children's minds: The project approach*. Norwood, NJ: Ablex.

Mathews, J. (1984). Children drawing: Are young children really scribbling? In R. Evans (Ed.), *Early child development and care: Vol. 17* (pp. 1–39). New York: Gordon & Breach.

Maxim, G. W. (1985). *The very young: Guiding children from infancy through the early years*. Belmont, CA: Wadsworth Publishing.

Mayesky, M. (1990). *Creative activities for young children* (4th ed.). Albany, NY: Delmar.

Mayesky, M., Neuman, D., & Wlodkowski, R. J. (1985). *Creative activities for young children* (3rd ed.). New York: Delmar.

McCune, L. (1985). Play-language relationships and symbolic development. In C. C. Brown & A. W. Gottfried (Eds.), *Play interactions* (pp. 28–45). Skillman, NJ: Johnson & Johnson.

McFee, J. (1970). *Preparation for art* (2nd ed.). Belmont, CA: Wadsworth Publishing.

McGhee, P. E. (1984). Play, incongruity, and humor. In T. D. Yawkey & A. D. Pellegrini (Eds.), *Child's play: Developmental and applied* (pp. 219–237). Hillsdale, NJ: Lawrence Erlbaum.

Piaget, J. (1955). *The child's conception of reality*. London: Routledge and Kegan Paul.

Reifel, S., & Greenfield, P. M. (1982). Structural development in a symbolic medium: The representational use of block construction. In G. E. Forman (Ed.), *Action and thought: From sensorimotor schemes to symbolic operations* (pp. 203–233). New York: Academic Press.

Rogers, C. S., & Sawyers, J. K. (1988). *Play in the lives of children*. Washington, DC: National Association for the Education of Young Children.

Rubin, K. N., Fein, G. G., & Vandenberg, B. (1983). Play. In P. H. Mussen (Series Ed.) & E. M. Hetherington (Vol. Ed.), *Handbook of child psychology: Vol. 4. Socialization, personality, and social development* (pp. 698–774). New York: Wiley.

Saltz, R., & Saltz, E. (1986). Pretend play training and its outcomes. In G. Fein & M. Rivkin (Eds.), *The young child at play* (pp. 155–175). Washington, DC: National Association for the Education of Young Children.

Smith, N. R. (1982). The visual arts in early childhood education: Development and the creation of meaning. In B. Spodek (Ed.), *Handbook of research in early childhood education* (pp. 295–317). New York: The Free Press.

Thompson, C. M. (1990). I make a mark: The significance of talk in young children's artistic development. *Early Childhood Research Quarterly, 5*, 215–232.

Werner, H., & Kaplan, B. (1963). *Symbol formation*. New York: John Wiley.

Wohlwill, J. F. (1984). Relationships between exploration and play. In T. D. Yawkey & A. D. Pellegrini (Eds.), *Child's play: Developmental and applied* (pp. 143–171). Hillsdale, NJ: Lawrence Erlbaum.

8

The Effect of the Physical and Social Environment on Parent–Child Interactions: A Qualitative Analysis of Pretend Play in a Children's Museum*

Stephanie Shine
Texas Tech University

Teresa Y. Acosta
Houston Independent School District

Children's museums have joined traditional museums across the country as places where children and parents seek out information, novelty, and adventure, as well as quality time together. Unlike the hushed atmosphere of traditional museums, children's museums tend to be noisy, informal environments where serious purpose mingles with spontaneous play. Observing displays in traditional museums is replaced by direct experience with tangible objects to incite curiosity and allow children to make discoveries (Farmer, 1995; Koran, Morrison, Lehman, Koran, & Gandara, 1984). Exhibits in children's museums are constructed so that parents can structure

* The authors would like to thank the staff, parents, and children at the Austin Children's Museum for their helpful cooperation in this study.

the environment to "bridge the gap" between what is known and what is unknown to children, and eventually transfer responsibility of the learning experience to them (Cohen, 1989; Dockser, 1990; Kent, 1992; Wolins, 1989). Frank (1992) considers interactions between parents and children at the museum to be cooperative, describing mental representations that are "co-constructed" between individuals as they participate in museum activities together.

Research on parent-child interactions in traditional museums has focused on learning and teaching behaviors (Donald, 1991; Dunitz, 1985; Fialkowsky, 1991; Flexer & Borun, 1984; Henderlong & Paris, 1996; Hilke, 1989; Leichter, Hensel, & Larsen, 1989; Paris, 1994; Sabar & Shamir, 1988; Stevenson, 1991), while the exploratory, playful, and creative activities encouraged in children's museums have not been systematically described or evaluated. Although overlooked by researchers, these activities are nonetheless a major consideration in exhibit design in children's museums, notably in contextual exhibits. Participatory contextual exhibits are those which invite children to step into an environment, such as a jungle, construction site, or doctor's office, and participate in the activities suggested by the setting, often by taking on roles and engaging in pretend play (Finkelstein, Stearns, & Hatcher, 1985; Judd & Kracht, 1987). Goals of contextual exhibits are to promote concrete experiences with the exhibit topic, encourage multiple, open-ended responses, foster creativity, and provide a medium for learning through discovery, family interactions, and role-taking, in particular adult-child role reversal (Danilov, 1986; McNamee, 1987; Perrot, 1980).

Because parent-child interactions in museums have been shown to be limited when a scientific or mathematical concept is the subject of an exhibit (Ault, 1987; Gelman, Massey, & McManus, 1991; Laetsch, Diamond, Gottfried, & Rosenfeld, 1980; Sabar & Shamir, 1988; Shine & Acosta, 1994), we studied interactions in a familiar, contextual exhibit. When parents are not constricted by the academic content of a display, we wondered, how would they interact with their children? The purpose of this study was to determine the nature of interactions between parents and children in a familiar, contextual museum play exhibit and to generate a model of the influence of the physical and social environment on participant behaviors.

METHOD

Context and Participants

The familiar contextual exhibit reproduces everyday environments such as a grocery store, medical office, small business, post office, or fire station. The facsimile grocery store at a children's museum in central Texas was intended to provide a familiar setting for play and learning, allow multiple open-ended experiences, permit children to try on adult roles, give them the opportunity to do things on their own, and help them learn basic concepts such as counting, sorting, and classifying, according to the educational and exhibit planners at the museum (R. Alsup, personal communication, April 21, 1992; M. Yanez, personal communication, April 20, 1992).

We observed visitors to a children's museum as they visited this facsimile of a grocery store, which is a permanent exhibit in the museum. The store contained many of the familiar trappings of a neighborhood grocery: bins of artificial fruits and vegetables, boxed goods, a model dairy case, an actual cash register, a hanging scale, price guns, and small-sized replicas of a checkout counter, stocker aprons, cloth bags, and grocery carts.

Visitors to this exhibit consisted of 50 family units, observed over a two-week period. Family units at this exhibit most often consisted of a parent accompanying a child (17 mother–daughter dyads, 10 mother–son dyads, 13 father–daughter dyads, and 10 father–son dyads). The children ranged from around two to ten years old, but most of those observed were estimated to be four to five years old.

Data Collection

In order to study parent-child interactions in the familiar museum exhibit, observations of family units visiting the facsimile grocery store were conducted by both authors independently. We positioned ourselves in an unobtrusive spot in a corner at the entrance of the exhibit. When a family entered the exhibit, it became the focus of the observation until the family left the exhibit. We recorded the conversations between parents and children by hand, noting actions and nonverbal communications. Visits to the exhibit ranged from 2 to 15 minutes, noted by the observer who timed the visits with a watch; the average visit was 8 minutes in duration.

In order to understand the origin, design, and objectives of the exhibit, semi-structured interviews were conducted with the Director of Educational Services and the Exhibit Coordinator on the history, goals, and assessment of the targeted exhibit and the museum.

A third source of data was obtained from parent-focus groups. Fifteen parents visiting the museum were invited to fill out critical incident questionnaires, in which they gave detailed accounts of specific incidents of parent-child interactions (Neimeyer & Resnikoff, 1982). These parents then participated in a group discussion of their expectations, activities, and before-and-after visit conversations with their children, as well as their views on the role of play and learning at the museum. Knowledge of the goals and expectations that children bring to the museum would have added another dimension to our model of parent-child interactions, but because of the limitations of museum policy, interviewing the children was not possible.

Qualitative Analysis

Qualitative analysis was selected to most fully capture the nature and range of parent-child interactions in the contextual exhibits. Our data were analyzed according to the principles of grounded theory (Glaser & Strauss, 1967). The transcripts of parent-child interactions provided the data in the first stage of analysis. In the initial phase of open coding, four categories emerged describing parent-child interactions: *exploring materials, exploring concepts, self-regulatory guiding,* and *pretend playing.* Exploring materials referred to children manipulating the mechanical objects. Exploring logicomathematical concepts consisted of parents trying to engage children in classifying, counting, and weighing. Exploring social concepts included parents explaining the names and uses of items, as well as the sequence of shopping procedures. Self-regulatory guiding entailed helping children negotiate the exhibit, as well as helping them to share the materials and space with others. Indicators of pretend play were role-taking, object transformation, and variations in voice and language (Garvey, 1990; Smilansky, 1968). Because parents seemed to encourage role-taking and pretend play as a means of exploring concepts and self-regulatory guiding, the core category of pretend play emerged as the central phenomenon.

Having determined pretend play to be the central phenomenon characterizing interactions at the exhibit, we rewrote the parent-child dialogues into play narratives, reflecting how pretend play is initiated, maintained, and disrupted. We subsequently placed the narratives in a conditional matrix (Strauss & Corbin, 1990) in order to analyze the strategies parents and children used to maintain play and the reasons for, and consequences of, disrupted play. For an example of a play narrative placed in a conditional matrix, see Table 8.1.

Museum planner interviews and responses from the parent focus groups and questionnaires were also placed in a matrix and then coded for congruency. An example of the comparative matrix in which museum planners and parents offer differing views on the role of parents in joining make-believe play can be seen in Table 8.2.

TABLE 8.1.
An Example of Play Narrative in Conditional Matrix

Context	While 4-year-old girl selects items, weighs them, mimes eating them, and fills her cart, M browses, rearranging fruit, reading labels aloud. M comments on C's actions: "You're weighing eggs," and she informs her, "And remember where you got that so you can put it away." Sometimes M comments within play frame, "You're gonna buy out the store," "You got enough money?" When C mimes eating eggs, "Peel it, you're gonna be full." M attempts to get C to count eggs as she puts them away, one by one, still enacting eating.
Strategy	As child initiates play sequence, M attempts to teach C by naming, explaining, and classifying items.
Consequences of Play	As C continues play sequence, M attempts to guide C and enter play; C does not pick up on comments. As C continues to enact, M attempts to engage C in counting. C engages in solitary play, ignoring M's efforts to teach, guide, and enter play.

Note: M = mother; C = child.

TABLE 8.2.
An Example of Comparative Matrix of Museum Planner and Parent Views on Parent–Child Play

Exhibit Coordinator	"If parents just step away, if they let their children bring their stuff to an exhibit, it's wonderful."
Director of Educational Services	"The reason parent-child interactions are important is that we found out parents don't know how to play with their kids. One thing we do as staff is model what to do."
Parents	"If it [a sign at the exhibit] said 'Children Only' I would back off and let them play, but I want to be there to show and name fruit, to put words to fruit visually.

RESULTS

Results will be discussed in terms of the information obtained from the conditional matrix of play episodes, which reflect the context, strategies, and consequences of parent-child play at the exhibit (Strauss & Corbin, 1990).

Context: What Is Play Like?

A visit to the facsimile grocery store at the museum generally consisted of a sequence that involved the family unit entering and following a shopping script (Nelson & Seidman, 1984), in which the participants looked around, took a shopping cart, filled it with groceries, moved to the cash register, rang up and bagged items, and then restocked items. What varied was the interaction, that is, the manner in which parent and child expressed and responded to demands or cues. The interactions were seen in the strategies of play, or the ways that parents and children initiated, maintained, and disrupted the pretend sequence, as described below.

Strategies: How Do Parents and Children Play?

Initiating Play

Both parents and children who arrived at the facsimile grocery store usually responded to the physical context of the exhibit by acknowledging that it was a setting for pretend shopping. Parents generally encouraged children to play by inviting them to shop ("Would you like to get a cart and get dinner for tonight?"), by interpreting their child's actions ("Oh, you want to be a cashier"), or by invoking role-play ("I'll be the customer"). Children used the same tactics, but unlike their parents, they also entered into pretend play immediately, without explicitly organizing the roles, activities, or sequences of a play script (Nelson & Seidman, 1984). Therefore, while the make-believe grocery store elicited pretend play from children, the same context induced parents to *organize* or *frame*

(Bateson, 1976) play according to their knowledge of shopping procedures and vocabulary.

Maintaining Play

As the shopping sequence progressed, parents continued to encourage children to move along ("You better go cash out"; "Now it's time to put this back, we have to restock the shelves"), and to interpret their actions ("A crab? You wanna buy a crab?"), though they no longer specifically invoked role-play. However, they occasionally entered into the make-believe for brief moments by expanding upon the object transformation implicit in the child's play ("We'll have to get that home before it melts"; "Your fish is gonna stink"; "Put the eggs on top so they won't break"; "How much do you think this big ol' thing of salami costs?"), as if to maintain the play sequence. Parents rarely engaged in such pretend play for more than one exchange. More commonly, they offered short comments in keeping with their children's play, but consonant with their role of adult observer. For example, in the role of a shopper, a mother said, "Want some lemons and some fruit? This is nutritional food!"

Disrupting Play

Play interactions in the museum setting disintegrated when parents attempted to explore concepts with children or give them guidance about how to behave at the exhibit. Exploring concepts included getting the child to count or classify items such as toy fruit, and explaining shopping procedures or techniques, such as using the price gun. Parents in this setting were particularly didactic, ("Show me how you count these eggs"; "Can you say 'asparagus'?") and effectively triggered the ending of a pretend play episode. Once a parent made an effort to teach concepts or vocabulary, the thread of a make-believe scenario was not usually picked up again. The children either responded dutifully to their parents' requests to count or label or they declined to respond, occasionally continuing their own make-believe game.

While not all parents attempted to explore concepts, they all directed their children to restock the shelves, and they rarely couched this activity in play terms. Insisting on rearranging groceries and having to bring or call the child back to the grocery store to do so placed an even greater damper on pretend play. Indeed, cleanup inevitably signaled the end of a make-believe sequence, even though restocking the shelves took up a good portion of the time that the families were in the store. As Kerns and Barth (1995) point out, it may be difficult for a parent to be both an engaging playmate and a skilled caregiver in the same context; while the parent as playmate aims for affect in the relationship, the parent as caregiver seeks compliance—two goals which may be mutually exclusive.

Consequences: Play is Brief, Sporadic, and Noncontingent

As a result of the strategies parents and children employed while visiting the exhibit, we found three consequences to the play interactions. First, parent-child play was brief; that is, rather than having extended conversations, parents and children engaged in no more than one conversational turn while framing or enacting play. Further, the pretend play was sporadic; instead of engaging in a continuous play sequence, parents and children had isolated moments of pretend interactions during their time at the exhibit, particularly at the beginning, when play was initiated. Finally, and most importantly, we think parents and children did not participate in pretend play together, that is, their interactions were not contingent upon each other's (Garvey, 1976, 1990). Although both parents and children initiated play, neither successfully maintained it by responding to the other's cues. The children did not often respond to their parents' efforts to enter into their make-believe play, essentially engaging in solitary play. Parents attempted to respond to children's cues, but did not elicit elaborations that extended the play by adding new material (Haight & Miller, 1992, 1993). For example, no parent comment within the play frame elicited a verbal response, although children did follow some parental suggestions to act (take on a role, pursue an activity). When a father responded to his son's bids to join him in play as the store manager, his response of "I'm going to have to fire you" did not extend the ongoing scenario; on the contrary, the boy left the exhibit. Similarly, when a father commented on the expensive items his daughter was loading into her cart, she did not elaborate further or pursue the her father's statement.

Why did parents and children seem to have difficulty in responding to each other's cues in ways that could maintain and extend play episodes? One reason children did not respond to their parents' attempts to join the pretend scenario may be because the adult efforts were too thoroughly grounded in reality. In the imaginative object transformations described above, adults elaborated upon the characteristics of food items rather than suggesting inventive scenarios involving the materials. Parents also tended to follow a strict shopping script rather than an imaginary storyline. The children, on the other hand, did not necessarily follow reality-based scripts in pretend play, nor did they always view objects realistically. In the hands of one child, the plastic fruits turned into magical beings ("They're alive!"); another child was a dentist visiting the store from the nearby doctor's office exhibit; and other children were builders constructing the store.

Alternatively, it may be that the children did not respond to parental suggestions about shopping because they did not need this type of guidance. As O'Connell and Bretherton (1984) propose, children select from a "smorgasbord" of parental instructions those suggestions which coincide with the tasks they are trying to master. The children in our study may have already been very adept at the symbolic play transformations suggested by their parents.

Parents and children, then, had different interpretations of how to adhere to the play scenario suggested by the make-believe environment. Such interpretations are consonant with the differences between the 'as if' quality of mothers' play with young children, in which mothers guide play along lines of simulated reality, and the 'what if' quality of children's play, in which a fantasy is explored (Bretherton, 1984).

In our study, parents apparently took a realistic 'as if' approach to the pretend play environment, while the children seemed to take an inventive 'what if' approach.

Summary of Results

The results of our analysis of parents and children playing together in the museum grocery store reveal that while children engaged in pretend play, as suggested by the contextual exhibit, parents focused on exploring concepts and guiding their children in the context of pretend play, as suggested by the museum play setting. Despite the intent of the museum planners to establish an *interactive* museum setting to encourage open-ended responses and role-taking, parents and children appeared to follow relatively independent courses of action while they were at the exhibit. Interactions between parents and children were characterized by noncontingency rather than responsivity; the activities and interlocutions of one were not dependent on the other's (Garvey, 1976, 1990).

Influences on Parent–Child Interactions: A Model

To determine how the physical and social context of the museum visit led to noncontingent play interactions in parents and children, we developed a model of influences on the parent–child interactions. To develop the model, we triangulated the

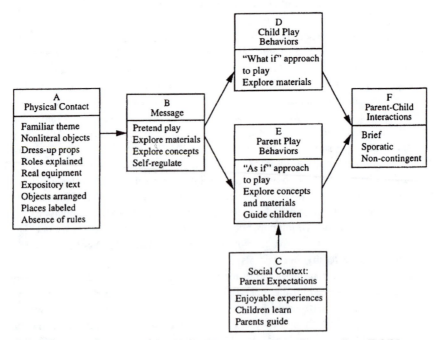

FIGURE 8.1. Influences on Parent–Child Interaction in the Grocery Store Exhibit

categories from the conditional matrix of play interactions with the responses from museum planner interviews and parent focus groups to discover the components that were associated with participant behaviors (see Figure 8.1).

Physical Context

Based on our observations and interviews with museum planners about the development and goals of the exhibit, we determined nine salient characteristics of the physical context as seen in Part A of Figure 8.1:

1. the familiar theme of the grocery store;
2. nonliteral objects, such as plastic fruits and vegetables;
3. dress-up props, including aprons and shopping bags;
4. written explanations of employees' roles on a wall mural;
5. real equipment, including a cash register and shopping carts;
6. expository text on the walls explaining procedures like restocking;
7. arrangement of items classified in boxes and bins, and on shelves;
8. food labels with the name of the food and a picture of it;
9. the absence of rules governing use of the exhibit (including the number of visitors, the amount of time, and the number of items selected from shelves).

Message Set

The salient aspects of the physical context of the exhibit contributed to cues or messages that encouraged participants to think or act in particular ways, depending on their expectations of the museum visit. Based on museum planner interviews, parent focus groups, and observations of visitor behaviors, we suggest that the nine salient characteristics of the physical context contributed to four messages to participants, as seen in Part B of Figure 8.1: *pretend play, explore materials, explore logicomathematical and social concepts,* and *self-regulation.*

Pretend play, involving role-taking and object transformation, was invited by the familiar grocery theme, nonliteral materials (plastic fruits and vegetables), dress-up aprons and bags, written explanations of employee duties, real equipment, and expository text about grocery procedures. Most of the salient aspects of the physical context contributed to a message of pretend play.

Exploring materials, referring to the manipulation of objects, was encouraged by the real mechanical equipment, such as the price gun, cash register, and scale.

Encouraging parents and children to explore logicomathematical and social concepts, such as classifying objects and shopping procedures, was communicated by the familiar theme, written explanations of employee duties, real equipment, expository text about grocery procedures, and arrangement and labels of items. Many of the aspects of the exhibit that communicated a message of pretend play also gave a message to explore concepts.

Self-regulation in the grocery exhibit, which involved sharing the space with others, was cued by the sign suggesting that shoppers restock groceries, by the laminated box tops showing where foods belong on the shelves, and by the deliberate lack of limits placed on the number of visitors allowed in the store, the amount of time to be spent at the exhibit, or the number of items to be taken from the shelves.

Social Context

The social context of the museum visit determines the cues or messages visitors respond to. We have defined the social context as the expectations visitors brought to the museum. Parents, for example—as revealed through focus groups and critical incident questionnaires—had the following expectations of their visit to the children's museum, as seen in Part C of Figure 8.1:

1. The museum should provide an enjoyable experience for their child.
2. Children should learn at the museum.
3. Parents should guide their children at the museum.

These expectations correspond to the exhibit messages of pretend play, explore materials and concepts, and self-regulation, and to the observed parent behaviors of framing play ("Why don't you be the checker?"), helping children explore materials ("Here's how this register works") and concepts ("Want to see how much the eggs weigh?"), and guiding children in self-regulating behavior ("Leave some for the other children"; "You need to be the stocker now and put all this stuff back").

We believe that the children, on the other hand, came to the grocery store exhibit to engage in pretend play and explore the materials. These probable expectations are in accordance with nine- and ten-year-olds' perceptions of children's museums as being fun as well as being places to learn (Jensen, 1994), corresponding to two messages sent out by the exhibit. Indeed, children's behaviors consisted of engaging in pretend play and exploring materials. The other two messages, explore concepts and self-regulation, as defined in this study, required adult guidance and presumably were not congruent with children's interests. This suggestion is similar to Jensen's finding that children prized autonomy in visits to museums.

Parent and Child Play Behaviors

The physical context, message set, and parent expectations led to independent and different parent and child play behaviors, as seen in Parts D and E of Figure 8.3. These behaviors were analyzed above and described in the Results:

1. Children explored materials and took a 'what if' approach to play as they engaged in inventive role-taking, object transformations, and play scenarios.
2. Parents attempted to explore materials and concepts with their children, guided them to self-regulate their social behaviors, and took an 'as if' approach to play as they followed a shopping script and simulated reality.

Parent-Child Interactions

Because parents and children independently engaged in different play behaviors, the resulting parent-child interactions were brief, sporadic, and noncontingent, as seen in Part F of Figure 8.3, and as discussed above.

DISCUSSION

Our analysis reveals that parents and children embarked on two different paths when they visited the children's museum. Based in part on differing expectations of the museum visit, parents and children responded differently to the message set of the exhibit. According to their own reports and our observations of their behaviors, parents set out to explore concepts and materials with their children and help them regulate their behaviors within a pretend play framework, while the children plunged into pretend play enactment. As a result, not only was the parent-child play brief, sporadic, and noncontingent, but also the conversations between parent and child were largely limited to questions and suggestions from the adult. At this point, we pose three questions about the significance of our findings.

1) Does it matter if parent-child play interactions at the children's museum are brief, sporadic, and noncontingent? One objective of contextual exhibits in museums is to invite children to learn about the physical and social world as they play and explore in the designed environment. The extensive literature on pretend play suggests that museum planners are on target to design environments that invite children to engage in pretend play. Importantly though, researchers have found that children benefit from pretend play at its best: engaged, committed, intensive, and persistent (Bornstein, 1989; Erikson, 1976; Jennings & Conners, 1989; Piaget, 1976; Singer, 1973; Smilansky, 1968; Vygotsky, 1967). According to Smilansky and Shefatya (1990), engaged social pretend play involves persistence in role-play for at least 10 minutes, interaction with co-players in the context of the play episode, and verbal communication within a role—activities which should take place during the construction and maintenance of a shared fantasy framework (Dunn & Dale, 1984). Parent-child play, at its best, has been found to consist of nondidactic, warm, verbally responsive, and light-hearted interactions (Göncü & Tuermer, 1994; Haight & Miller, 1992, 1993; Levenstein & O'Hara, 1993, Van der Kooij, 1989), parental modeling and inventive utterances (Lyytinen, 1989), turn-taking and reversal of roles (Van der Poel, de Bruyn, & Rost, 1991; Sutton-Smith, 1993), and mutual engagement (Howes, 1992).

Because the play episodes of the parents and children we observed were characterized by very brief duration and lack of mutual engagement, it is unlikely that the goal of facilitating discovery of social and physical worlds can be met when parent-child interactions consist of pretend play (role-taking and object transformation), but fall short of mutually engaged play episodes.

Another objective of contextual exhibits in children's museums is parent-child interaction, including role-play and role-reversal (Gallagher & Dockser, 1987; Regnier, 1987). Parent-child play is thought to have a positive effect on the levels of children's play and family play relationships (Fiese, 1990; O'Connell & Bretherton, 1984; Slade, 1987; Sutton-Smith, 1993; Van der Poel, de Bruyn, & Rost, 1991) as well as children's mastery of play functions, including the exploration of social relationships (Carson, Burks, & Parke, 1993; Carson & Parke, 1996; Howes, 1992) and development of specialized play language (Lyytinen, 1989). According to Sutton-Smith (1993) and Singer (1995), it is precisely the turn-taking and role-reversal parents and children engage in which may account for the benefits to children because in the reversed power relationship, children participate on equal terms with the adult. Given the lack of contingent play interactions we observed, the goal of parent-child role-play and role-reversal cannot be considered to have been met in the contextual exhibit.

2) What might the parental role consist of in a contextual museum setting? Although the parents in our study did not engage in contingent pretend play episodes with their young children, they did serve as organizers of the experience, both by framing pretend play scenarios (suggesting roles for role-play, explaining the use of props, and guiding the sequence of events) and by informing children about grocery store procedures, drawing their attention to equipment, and probing their knowledge of concepts (classifying, counting, weighing). In short, parents served as a type of scaffolder of their children's experiences in the contextual exhibit (Bornstein & O'Reilly, 1993; Wood, Bruner, & Ross, 1976). In this respect, parents engaged in the interactive and cooperative behaviors described by Hilke (1989) in her study of families visiting traditional museum exhibits. One parental role in the children's museum is therefore similar to the role parents may play in more traditional museums—that of a guide who interprets the exhibit artifacts for children and aids them in museum protocol.

Another possible role for parents is to observe their young children at play. Because children responded to the message conveyed by the make-believe play setting, the contextual exhibit provides an opportunity for parents to step back and observe their children in pretend play negotiation and enactment. Parents may learn about their children's knowledge of exhibit artifacts, their social skills with other children, and their inventive acts in the exhibit environment. It may be that in the context of the museum setting, parents would gain more from observing their children at play than in trying to engage them in pretend play. Indeed, Pellegrini suggests that while adults help very young children engage in social play, by the time children reach the age of three, adults may inhibit social fantasy play (Pellegrini & Perlmutter, 1989). Museum exhibits could be redesigned to allow for close but unobtrusive adult observation of children at play.

3) How can contextual exhibits be developed to reflect the multiple goals of children's museums, in particular, pretend play? First, the idea that familiar contextual exhibits such as the grocery store, doctor's office, or post office encourage parent-child role-play should be re-evaluated. Based on our findings, familiarity with the subject of the exhibit does not in itself prompt parents to engage in pretend play or in conversation that elicits responses from children. On the contrary, familiarity with a shopping script (Nelson & Seidman, 1984) may constrain parents to stick to a narrow set of play scenarios or to teach concepts that are not incorporated into children's ongoing play. Novel contextual exhibits, such as an ambulance or a recording studio, may elicit more playful behavior between parents and children (Acosta, 1997).

Second, to encourage varied pretend play, materials in the exhibit should elicit a variety of responses, that is, they should be open-ended and not designed so that only one script can be followed (Nelson & Seidman, 1984). Neither the theme of the grocery store nor the materials in the exhibit we observed allowed a wide variety of object transformations or play scenarios. Children accompanied by parents with a grocery script in mind were not encouraged to do more than fill the basket, tap the register, and restock groceries. While functionally explicit or realistic materials elicit play based on a theme, ambiguous objects elicit play that is more varied (Pellegrini & Jones, 1994). More open-ended props might include dolls to engage in a variety of make-believe scenarios, or paper and pencil, for children to invent lists, coupons, bills, money, notes, prescriptions, menus, recipes, grocery ads, etc.

Finally, the articulation of a message set to museum visitors should involve a clarification of museum goals based on knowledge of parent and child expectations. In this study, not only did museum designers express divergent views of parent-child play, but also the contextual exhibit gave different messages to parents and children who seemed to come to the museum with different expectations. Moreover, parents believed they were teaching through play, even though children were remarkably unresponsive to adult initiatives to engage them in didactic activities.

Before museum planners design contextual exhibits in the interest of fostering discovery of the physical and social world through parent-child pretend-play interactions, consideration should be given to the context of the environment (Christie & Johnsen, 1989). If the goal is to encourage parents and children to behave playfully, our evidence suggests that familiar settings, themed props, and scripted event sequences are not conducive to this goal. Novel settings, open-ended materials, and less scripted activities may elicit more playful behaviors (Acosta, 1997). If the goal is to encourage parents to teach children, our results suggest that when exhibits encourage role-play and object transformation, children do not respond to parental explanations; exploratory materials may elicit more interaction (Shine & Acosta, 1994). As children's museums and nature, science, and technology centers proliferate, and parent involvement in children's formal and informal education is increasingly called for, research on the effect of context on parent-child interactions becomes essential. Models of these effects can aid educators and museum planners to design settings which correspond to their goals.

CONCLUDING COMMENTS

In our analysis of parents and children playing in a children's museum, we found that the grocery store exhibit—a familiar setting with themed play materials and a scripted sequence of events—did not elicit the intimate, light-hearted, and responsive interactions often associated with play between parents and young children. Interestingly, while their children engaged in symbolic play, parents often adopted play strategies associated with mothers and younger children. The spectator role, in which parents offer pretend suggestions and comments (Dunn & Dale, 1984; Howes, 1992; Rogoff, Mosier, Mistry, & Göncü, 1991), the activities, including naming, labeling, questioning, correcting, instructing, directing, elaborating, and suggesting (Howes, 1992), and the 'as if' quality of mothers' play (Bretherton, 1984) have all been found in mothers playing with their 2- to 3-year-old children. Parents with their older children at the museum, it seems, do not adjust their play to meet their child's more sophisticated play. Therefore, the age of the child may also play a role in our findings, perhaps interacting with the public and educational constraints of the environment. Our study points to the need for continued investigation into the contextual influences on adult-child play in a variety of settings, particularly those involving older children.

REFERENCES

Acosta, T. (1997). *Contextual influences on parent-child play in a children's museum.* Unpublished doctoral dissertation, University of Texas at Austin.

Ault, C. R. (1987). The museum as science teacher. *Science and Children, 25*(3), 8–11.

Bateson, G. (1976). A theory of play and fantasy. In J. S. Bruner, A. Jolly, & K. Sylva (Eds.), *Play—its role in development and evolution* (pp. 119–129). New York: Plenum Press.

Bornstein, M. H. (1989). *Maternal responsiveness: Characteristics and consequences.* San Francisco: Jossey-Bass.

Bornstein, M. H., & O'Reilly, A. W. (Eds.). (1993). *The role of play in the development of thought.* San Francisco: Jossey-Bass.

Bretherton, I. (1984). Representing the social world in symbolic play: Reality and fantasy. In I. Bretherton (Ed.), *Symbolic play: The development of social understanding* (pp. 3–41). Orlando, FL: Academic Press.

Carson, J., Burks, V., & Parke, R. D. (1993). Parent-child physical play: Determinants and consequences. In K. MacDonald (Ed.), *Parent-child play: Descriptions and implications* (pp. 15–42). Albany, NY: State University of New York Press.

Carson, J. L., & Parke, R. D. (1996). Reciprocal negative affect in parent-child interactions and children's peer competency. *Child Development, 65*(5), 2217–2226.

Christie, J. F., & Johnsen, E. P. (1989). The constraints of settings on children's play. *Play and Culture, 2*(4), 317–327.

Cohen, S. (1989). Fostering shared learning among children and adults: The children's museum. *Young Children, 44*(4), 21–24.

Danilov, V. (1986). Discovery rooms and kidspaces: Museum exhibits for children. *Science and Children, 23*(4), 6–11.

Dockser, L. S. (1990). *Mothers in children's museums: A neglected dynamic.* Unpublished doctoral dissertation, University of Pennsylvania, Philadelphia.

Donald, J. G. (1991). The measurement of learning in the museum. *Canadian Journal of Education, 16*(3), 371–381.

Dunitz, R. J. (1985). Interactive museums. *Media & Methods, 2*(18), 8–11.

Dunn, J., & Dale, N. (1984). I a daddy: 2-year-olds' collaboration in joint pretend with sibling and with mother. In I. Bretherton (Ed.), *Symbolic play: The development of social understanding* (pp. 131–158). Orlando, FL: Academic Press.

Erikson, E. (1976). Play and actuality. In J. S. Bruner, A. Jolly, & K. Sylva (Eds.), *Play—its role in development and evolution* (pp. 688–704). New York: Plenum Press.

Farmer, D. W. (1995). Children take learning into their own hands. *Childhood Education, 71*(3), 168–169.

Fialkowsky, C. (1991). *Developing a learning model for museum education.* Unpublished manuscript.

Fiese, B. H. (1990). Playful relationships: A contextual analysis of mother-toddler interaction and symbolic play. *Child Development, 61*(5), 1648–1656

Finkelstein, J., Stearns, S., & Hatcher, B. (1985). Museums are not just for observing anymore! *Social Education, 49*(2), 150–154.

Flexer, B. K., & Borun, M. (1984). The impact of a class visit to a participatory science museum exhibit and a classroom science lesson. *Journal of Research in Science Teaching, 21*(9), 863–873.

Frank, R. E. (1992). *The mind in the museum. Creating mental representations: A developmental perspective.* Unpublished manuscript, Virginia Wesleyan College, Norfolk.

Gallagher, J. M., & Dockser, L. S. (1987). Parent-child interaction in a museum for preschool children. *Children's Environments Quarterly, 4*(1), 41–45.

Garvey, C. (1976). Some properties of social play. In J. S. Bruner, A. Jolly, & K. Sylva (Eds.), *Play—its role in development and evolution* (pp. 570–583). New York: Plenum Press.

Garvey, C. (1990). *Play.* Cambridge, MA: Harvard University Press.

Gelman, R., Massey, C. M., & McManus, M. (1991). Characterizing supporting environments for cognitive development: Lessons from children in a museum. In L. R. Resnick, J. M. Levine, & S. D. Teasley (Eds.), *Perspectives on socially shared cognition* (pp. 226–256). Washington DC: American Psychological Association.

Glaser, B. G., & Strauss, A. L. (1967). *The discovery of grounded theory: Strategies for qualitative research.* Hawthorne, NY: Aldine de Gruyter.

Göncü, A., & Tuermer, U. (1994). Multiple perspectives on parent-child play. *Educational Researcher, 23*(2), 38–40.

Haight, W., & Miller, P. J. (1992). The development of everyday pretend play: A longitudinal study of mothers' participation. *Merrill-Palmer Quarterly, 38*(3), 331–349.

Haight, W., & Miller, P. J. (1993). *Pretending at home. Early development in a sociocultural context.* Albany, NY: State University of New York Press.

Henderlong, J., & Paris, S. G. (1996). Children's motivation to explore partially completed exhibits in hands-on museums. *Contemporary Educational Psychology, 21*(2), 111–128.

Hilke, D. D. (1989). The family as a learning system: An observational study of families in museums. In B. H. Butler & M. B. Sussman (Eds.), *Museum visits and activities for family life enrichment* (pp. 101–129). New York: Haworth Press.

Howes, C. (1992). *The collaborative construction of pretend: Social pretend functions.* Albany, NY: State University of New York Press.

Jennings, K. D., & Conners, R. E. (1989). Mothers' interactional style and children's competence at 3 years. *International Journal of Behavior Development, 12*(2), 155–175.

Jensen, N. (1994). Children's perceptions of their museum experiences: A contextual perspective. *Children's Environments, 11*(4), 300–324.

Judd, M. K., & Kracht, J. B. (1987). The world at their fingertips: Children in museums. In B. Hatcher (Ed.), *Learning opportunities beyond school* (pp. 18–24). Wheaton, MD: Association of Childhood Education International.

Kent, S. S. (April 9, 1992). *New York City Museum Educational Roundtable Keynote Address.* Unpublished manuscript, Bank Street College of Education, New York, NY.

Kerns, K. A., & Barth, J. M. (1995). Attachment and play: Convergence across components of parent-child relationships and their relations to peer competence. *Journal of Social and Personal Relationships 12*(2), 243–260.

Koran, J. J., Morrison, L., Lehman, J. R., Koran, M. L., & Gandara, L. (1984). Attention and curiosity in museums. *Journal of Research in Science Teaching, 21*(4), 357–363.

Laetsch, W. M., Diamond, J., Gottfried, J. L., & Rosenfeld, S. (1980). Children and family groups in science centers. *Science and Children, 17*(6), 14–17.

Leichter, H. J., Hensel, K., & Larsen, E. (1989). Families and museums: Issues and perspectives. In B. B. Butler & M. B. Sussman (Eds.), *Museum visits and activities for family life enrichment* (pp. 15–50). New York: Haworth Press.

Levenstein, P., & O'Hara, J. (1993). The necessary lightness of mother-child play. In K. MacDonald (Ed.), *Parent-child play: Descriptions and implications* (pp. 221–237). Albany, NY: State University of New York Press.

Lyytinen, P. (1989). Effects of modeling on children's pretend play. *Scandinavian Journal of Psychology, 30*(3), 177–184.

McNamee, A. S. (1987). Museum readiness: Preparation for the art museum. *Childhood Education, 63*(3), 181–187.

Neimeyer, G., & Resnikoff, A. (1982). Qualitative strategies in counseling research. *The Counseling Psychologist, 10*(4), 75–85.

Nelson, K., & Seidman, S. (1984). Playing with scripts. In I. Bretherton (Ed.), *Symbolic play: The development of social understanding* (pp. 45–72). Orlando, FL: Academic Press.

O'Connell, B., & Bretherton, I. (1984). Toddler's play, alone and with mother: The role of maternal guidance. In I. Bretherton (Ed.), *Symbolic play: The development of social understanding* (pp. 337–368). Orlando, FL: Academic Press.

Paris, S. G. (1994). Children's explorations in a hands-on science museum. *Kamehameha Journal of Education, 5*, 83–92.

Pellegrini, A. D., & Jones, I. (1994). Play, toys, and language. In J. H. Goldstein (Ed.), *Toys, play and child development* (pp. 27–45). Cambridge, England: Cambridge University Press.

Pellegrini, A. D., & Perlmutter, J. C. (1989). Classroom contextual effects on children's play. *Developmental Psychology, 25*(2), 289–296.

Perrot, P. N. (1980). Children, museums, and changing societies: The growing interdependence of cultures. *Children Today, 9*(1), 17–21.

Piaget, J. (1976). Symbolic play. In J. S. Bruner, A. Jolly, & K. Sylva (Eds.), *Play—its role in development and evolution* (pp. 555–569). New York: Plenum Press.

Regnier, V. (1987). The children's museums: Exhibit and location issues. *Children's Environments Quarterly, 4*(1), 55–59.

Rogoff, B., Mosier, C., Mistry, J., & Göncü, A. (1993). Toddlers' guided participation with their caregivers in cultural activity. In E. Forman, N. Minnick, & A. Stone (Eds.), *Contexts for learning: Sociocultural dynamics in children's development* (pp. 230–253). New York: Oxford University Press.

Sabar, N., & Shamir, I. (1988). Evaluation of focused learning activities in the context of visiting museums. *Studies in Educational Evaluation, 14*(2), 261–267.

Shine, S. & Acosta, T. Y. (1994). *Children's experience with a museum exhibit on the human body: The role of materials and adults.* Unpublished manuscript, The University of Texas at Austin.

Singer, J. L. (1973). *The child's world of make-believe: Experimental studies of imaginative play.* New York: Academic Press.

Singer, J. L. (1995). Imaginative play in childhood: Precursor of subjunctive thoughts, daydreaming, and adult pretending games. In A. D. Pellegrini (Ed.), *The future of play theory. A multidisciplinary inquiry into the contributions of Brian Sutton-Smith* (pp. 187–220). Albany, NY: State University of New York Press.

Slade, A. (1987). A longitudinal study of maternal involvement and symbolic play during the toddler period. *Child Development, 58*(2), 367–375.

Smilansky, S. (1968). *The effects of socio-dramatic play on disadvantaged preschool children.* New York: John Wiley.

Smilansky, S., & Shefatya, L. (1990). *Facilitating play. A medium for promoting cognitive, socio-emotional and academic development in young children.* Silver Spring, MD: Psychosocial & Educational Publications.

Stevenson, J. (1991). The long-term impact of interactive exhibits. *International Journal of Science Education, 13*(5), 521–532.

Strauss, A., & Corbin, J. (1990). *Basics of qualitative research.* Newbury Park, CA: Sage.

Sutton-Smith, B. (1993). Dilemmas in adult play with children. In K. MacDonald (Ed.), *Parent-child play: Descriptions and implications* (pp. 15–42). Albany, NY: State University of New York Press.

Van der Kooij, R. (1989). Research on children's play. *Play and Culture, 2*(1), 20–34.

Van der Poel, L., de Bruyn, E. E., & Rost, H. (1991). Parental attitude and behavior and children's play. *Play and Culture, 4*(1), 1–10.

Vygotsky, L. S. (1967). Play and its role in the mental development of the child. *Soviet Psychology, 5*(3), 6–18.

Wolins, I. S. (1989). A case for family programs in museums. In B. B. Butler & M. B. Sussman (Eds.), *Museum visits and activities for family life enrichment* (pp. 7–13). New York: Haworth Press.

Wood, D., Bruner, J. S., & Ross, G. (1976). The role of tutoring in problem-solving. *Journal of Child Psychology and Psychiatry, 17*(2), 89–100.

part III
Play in Other Cultures

9

A Comparison of Playfulness Among American and Japanese Preschoolers

Satomi Izumi Taylor, Ph.D.
The University of Memphis

Cosby Steele Rogers, Ph.D.
Virginia Polytechnic Institute and State University

Javid Kaiser
Academy for Educational Development

INTRODUCTION

The increased attention to play in educational settings has been accompanied by an increase in the research on play (Gottfried, 1985; Jones & Reynolds, 1992; Trawick-Smith, 1994). The vast majority of play research has been concerned with educational outcomes such as the development of language, literacy, or improved social interaction. With the exception of Smith and Vollstedt (1985), few researchers have dealt with issues surrounding the definition and operationalization of play and its constituent components. One area of study which has promise for extending previous work on play is the disposition of playfulness. In contrast to studies of play behavior, playfulness is focused on the "how" rather than the "what" of play (Barnett, 1990). Its importance was underscored by Erikson (1972), who pointed to a sense of playfulness as a primary determinant of quality of life. If playfulness is a state of being that enhances the quality of life, then researchers should be interested in the definition and measurement of such a construct, as well as the determination of its etiology, facilitation, and development.

Research on playfulness has followed two lines of inquiry. First, the work of Barnett and her colleagues (e.g., Barnett, 1990, 1991) utilized Lieberman's (1965) definition of playfulness, which is comprised of physical, cognitive, and social spontaneity, manifest of joy, and sense of humor. Although Lieberman was a pioneer in research on playfulness, her theoretical and operational definitions of playfulness were based on intuitive notions of the construct. Thus, her rating scale did not have the benefit of a consensus among play researchers as to the definition of the construct. Likewise, more recent research by Barnett and her colleagues suffered the same disadvantage, even though Barnett was able to provide evidence for the existence of the five factors which comprised Lieberman's definition. The second line of research was by Rogers (Rogers, et al., 1998) who defined playfulness via the dispositions found in the theoretical and empirical literature reviewed by Rubin, Fein, and Vandenberg (1983). They defined play as "a behavioral disposition that occurs in describable and reproducible contexts and is manifest in a variety of observable behaviors" (p. 698). The following six criteria defined the dispositions of play: intrinsic motivation, attention to means rather than ends, player domination, pretense, freedom from externally imposed rules, and active involvement. The separation of play behaviors and playful dispositions brought attention to the way in which activities were performed. Thus, nonplay, or even work, could be carried out playfully. Playfulness, then, is the disposition to play and encompasses the attitude or spirit with which one goes about an activity, and it does not distinguish between work and play.

Recalling that the definition of play by Rubin, Fein, and Vandenberg (1983) included context as well as disposition toward behaviors, the logical next step in researching playfulness is to delineate the contextual factors which enhance or impede its development. One obvious context is cultural milieu. Parents and teachers in highly industrialized nations, where education is valued, may undermine the education of children if they do not appreciate the value of play. Educators held accountable for training students who can compete successfully in the world economy have been interested in comparing educational methods and outcomes of American and Japanese students (Azuma, 1986; Cummings, 1980; Inagaki, 1986; Vogel, 1979). However, because many studies were conducted primarily with school-age children, the image of Japanese education that has emerged is one of a highly structured "non-play" orientation. The philosophy which guides formal schooling after the age of seven years stands in sharp contrast to that of Japanese preschool education. According to Bacon and Ichikawa (1989) and Tobin, Wu, and Davidson (1989), Japanese preschools are more play-oriented than are American preschools. Indeed, the Minister of Education lists play as the basic component of early childhood education (Ishigaki, 1992).

The purpose of this study was to compare the disposition toward playfulness as it exists in samples of preschoolers in the United States and Japan. These two contexts differ markedly, in that Japanese preschool children are socialized for group orientation (Ishigaki, 1992), whereas American children are more likely to be socialized to maximize individual differences (Bredekamp, 1987). Playfulness is a trait that is defined in part by individual differences brought to the situation by the combined effect of genetic makeup and environmental experiences. However, these differences in personality interact with the context to determine the final expression of playfulness. A comparative study of the expression of playfulness in the two cultures would provide information on how such a trait is expressed in contrasting contexts. Specifically, this study was designed to compare preschool children's playfulness as rated by teachers in the United States and Japan. Additionally, factor analysis was used to determine whether the constructs are comprised of similar items in the two cultures.

METHODS

Sample

A total of 113 Japanese children (56 girls and 57 boys)—from 40 to 77 months of age—and their seven teachers participated in the study. All of the children were from middle-class, intact families. Permission for collecting the Japanese data from the kindergarten, in Kawasaki City, Japan, was granted by the kindergarten director and by the children's parents. The American sample included 85 children, ages 43 to 71 months, from middle-class families who attended preschools in a southeastern university town. The children's parents granted permission for their children to be rated by the teachers on behaviors observed at the school.

The Child Behaviors Inventory (CBI) was used to assess playfulness of children in both Japan and the United States (Rogers, et al., 1998). The CBI was translated into Japanese by the first author, then reviewed by three Japanese bilingual educational psychologists, who verified the accuracy of the translation. The 31-item trait rating form contains items that represent the six dispositions of play described by Rubin, Fein, and Vandenberg (1983). It is comprised of two factors: playfulness and externality. Data were gathered in the summer months in both countries. The first author gave instructions on the CBI to the teachers in Japan, who completed the inventory in one session. The first author was also available for the teachers to answer any questions that they might have.

RESULTS

Data from Japanese teachers' ratings of children's playfulness were compared with data obtained from the United States to assess group differences in scales for the two factors identified by Rogers, et al. (1998). Japanese data were then factor-analyzed separately to determine whether the items discussed were related in such a way as to construct a different factor. Means for the playfulness factor score were 4.27 (*SD* = .94) for the American children and 3.39 (*SD* = .68) for the Japanese children. Means for the externality score were 3.45 (*SD* = .92) for the American children and 3.50 (*SD* = .64) for the Japanese children. Differences between the scores of the American and Japanese sample were examined using *t* tests for independent samples. Playfulness scores for the American children were significantly higher than those of their Japanese counterparts (*t* = −7.29, < .001), but externality scores showed no significant differences between the two groups of children (*t* = 0.32, > .10). The Japanese children's scores were relatively homogeneous, while the American children's scores were heterogeneous, as reflected in the standard deviations of scores on both factors.

Since items on the CBI were structured according to factors that were derived from factor analysis that was performed on an American sample, it was not known whether the same items would cluster to form this personality dimension in data

TABLE 9.1.
Rotated Factor, Items, and Varimax Loadings for Japanese Children

Subscale, No., and Item	Varimax Loadings (Japanese)	Varimax Loadings (American)
Factor 1: Playfulness		
1. Always has ideas of things to do	.74	.71
2. Uses props in typical ways	−.51	−.16
4. Explores different ways	.60	.69
6. Invents new games	.66	.75
9. Uses things in own way	.71	.59
10. Looks to others to tell him/her what to do	−.38	.69
11. Enjoys learning new skills	.64	.44
12. Works well on his/her own	.31	.29
16. Starts activities for own enjoyment	.72	.69
20. Plays intently	.71	.58
21. Invents variations on stories	.69	.76
23. Rearranges situations to come up with novel ones	.70	.79
24. Creates own way to do things	.72	.76
26. Is imaginative	.70	.76
27. Uses toys/objects in unusual ways	.78	.67
28. Finds unusual things to do	.79	.74
29. Identifies with many characters	.54	.72
Factor 2: Active Involvement		
5. Needs reinforcement to continue activities	−.60	.73
8. Seeks approval frequently	.46	.75
15. Gets involved in activity/hard to get to quit	−.52	3.19
18. Uses toys/objects in way they were designed to be used	.51	.14
19. Plays eagerly	−.44	3.89
30. Gets very involved/forgets what is going on	−.64	3.09

based on Japanese children. Therefore, factor analysis was carried out on the Japanese data in order to assess the relevance of the factors originally identified by Rogers, et al. (in press). Varimax rotation based on ratings made by the Japanese teachers resulted in two principle factors (Table 9.1).

The factors did not consist of the same items found in the factor analysis conducted with the data from the American sample. Factor 1, in the Japanese data base, appears to measure *playfulness* and is comprised of 17 of the 28 original CBI items. Factor 2 is comprised of 6 of the 28 original items and seems to measure the child's *engrossment* in activities. Engrossment scores have moderately strong, positive correlations (+.80 and +.72, respectively) with item 30 ("Gets very involved/forgets what is going on"), and item 15 ("Gets involved in activity/hard to get to quit"). Item 8 ("Seeks approval frequently") and item 18 ("Uses toys/objects in ways they were designed to be used") show negative correlations (–.47 and –.58, respectively) with the Factor 2 scores.

CONCLUSION

The primary purpose of this study was to examine the group differences between Japanese and American preschoolers in terms of their disposition toward playfulness. American children were generally considered by their teachers to be more playful than the Japanese children. However, both Japanese and American children were similarly influenced by their dependency on external environmental factors, as indicated by scores on the externality factor. The fact that the Japanese children's scores were relatively homogeneous seems to suggest that individual differences are not salient for Japanese teachers participating in this study. This finding is congruent with the views of other researchers (Cummings, 1980; Nagagawa, 1991; Tobin, Wu, & Davidson, 1989; Vogel, 1979; White, 1984, 1987), who reported that Japanese tend to be insistent advocates of educational egalitarianism. Japanese egalitarian education holds that all individuals must be treated equally, whereas in American individualized education, each child is considered unique, and a valued pedagogical method is individualized instruction. The fact that the American children's scores were heterogeneous can be interpreted as meaning that American adults perceived greater individual differences in children. This finding coincides with other authors (Befu, 1986; Goodman, 1957; Nagagawa, 1991; Tobin, Wu, & Davidson, 1989; Vogel, 1979; White & LeVine, 1986), who found that Americans generally value individualism and independence.

Six criteria for the dispositions of play in the CBI did not represent separate factors in this factor analysis. Rather, two factors emerged for both the Japanese and American children. For the American children, one factor represented playfulness, and the other represented externality. For the Japanese children, one factor indicated playfulness, and the other represented the child's engrossment. The fact is that the six criteria of the play dispositions comprise one playfulness factor, instead of six factors corresponding to the six dimensions. This finding supports Lieberman's (1965) notion that playfulness is a unidimensional trait in children, and also coincides with Smith and Vollstedt's (1985) and Krasnor and Pepler's (1980) observations that when two or more specific criteria are met, an observable behavior is more likely to be considered playful. Both Japanese and Mexican teachers' perceptions of children influenced their ratings on the child playfulness trait. It is also plausible to suggest that different educational goals affected the teachers' perception of children.

The findings of this study has important implications for education. Since playfulness is a disposition, and inculcating dispositions in children is one of the primary goals of early childhood education (Katz, 1992; 1993), teachers should pay closer attention to the importance of playfulness as a disposition. According to Katz (1992), teachers cannot teach children to have certain dispositions, but children can learn from teachers who exhibit them. In her words, "It is unfortunate that some dispositions, such as being curious or puzzled, are rarely displayed by adults in front of children" (p. 1). The quality of children's lives can improve if they can observe playfulness in adults, as playfulness can determine one's attitude toward life (Erikson, 1972). By playfully approaching tasks or environments ordinarily seen as mundane or difficult, they can be made enjoyable. "Thus, even activities we don't think of as play—conversation, reading, and transitions—lend themselves to playfulness if a teacher or child wishes so" (Sawyers & Rogers, 1988, p. 49).

Bcause both Japanese and American children were influenced by external environmental factors, providing an environment that invites and allows children to be playful would foster this disposition. If children are to learn to be playful, they need ample opportunities to exhibit such behavior because: "A child who is to learn a particular disposition must have this opportunity to behave in a manner that is in keeping with the disposition" (Katz, 1993, p. 1).

Drawing further implications from this study for measuring playfulness in different countries must await replication of the findings on larger samples and on the extension of samples to populations of children in different countries.

REFERENCES

Azuma, H. (1986). Why child development in Japan? In H. Stevenson, H. Azuma, & K. Hakuta (Eds.), *Child development and education in Japan* (pp. 3–12). New York: W. H. Freeman.

Bacon, W., & Ichikawa, V. (1988). Maternal expectations, classroom experiences, and achievement among kindergartners in the United States and Japan. *Human Development, 31*, 378–383.

Barnett, L. (1990). Playfulness: Definition, design, and measurement. *Play & Culture, 3*, 319–336.

Barnett, L. (1991). The playful child: Measurement of the disposition to play. *Play & Culture, 4*, 51–74.

Befu, H. (1986). The social and cultural background of child development in Japan and the United States. In H. Stevenson, H. Azuma, & K. Hakuta (Eds.), *Child development and education in Japan* (pp. 13–27). New York: W. H. Freeman.

Bredekamp, S. (1987). *Developmentally appropriate practice in early childhood programs serving children from birth through 8.* Washington, DC: National Association for the Education of Young Children.

Cummings, W. (1980). *Education and equality in Japan.* Princeton, NJ: Princeton University Press.

Erikson, E. (1972). Play and civilization. In J. Jolly & K. Sylva (Eds.), *Play: Its role in development and evolution* (pp.690–703). New York: Penguin.

Goodman, M. (1957). Values, attitudes, and social concepts of Japanese and American children. *American Anthropologist, 59,* 979–999.

Gottfried, A. (1985). The relationship of play materials and parental involvement to young children's development. In C. Brown & A. Gottfried (Eds.), *Play interactions: The role of toys and parental involvement in children's development* (pp. 45–52). Skillman, NJ: Johnson & Johnson.

Inagaki, T. (1986). School education: Its history and contemporary status. In H. Stevenson, H. Azuma, & K. Hakuta (Eds.), *Child development and education in Japan* (pp. 75–92). New York: W. H. Freeman.

Ishigaki, E. (1992). The preparation of early childhood teachers in Japan: Part 1. *Early Child Development and Care, 78,* 111–138.

Jones, E., & Reynolds, G. (1992). *The play's the thing.* New York: Teachers College Press.

Katz, L. (1992). *What should young children be learning?* Urbana, IL: ERIC Clearinghouse on Elementary and Early Childhood Education. (ERIC Document Reproduction Service No. ED 290 554)

Katz, L. (1993). *Dispositions as educational goals.* Urbana, IL: ERIC Clearinghouse on Elementary and Early Childhood Education. (ERIC Document Reproduction Service No. EDO PS 93 10)

Krasnor, L., & Pepler, D. (1980). The study of children's play: Some suggested future directions. In K. Rubin (Ed.), *New directions in child development: Children's play* (pp. 85–95). San Francisco: Jossey-Bass.

Lieberman, J. (1965). Playfulness and divergent thinking: An investigation of their relationship at the kindergarten level. *Journal of Creative Behavior, 1,* 391–397.

Nagagawa, K. (1991). The Japanese and creativity. *Illinois Council for the Gifted, 10,* 11–13.

Rogers, C. S., Impara, J. C., Frary, R. B., Harris, T., Meeks, A., Semanic-Lauth, S., & Reynolds, M. R. (1998). Measuring playfulness: Development of the child behaviors inventory of playfulness. In G. Chick, & M. Duncan (Eds.), *Play and culture studies: Vol. 1* (pp. 151–168). Greenwich, CT: Ablex.

Rubin, K., Fein, G., & Vandenberg, B. (1983). Play. In E. Hetherington (Ed.), *Handbook of child psychology* (Vol. 4, pp. 693–774). New York, NY: Wiley.

Sawyers, J., & Rogers, C. (1988). *Helping young children develop through play.* Washington, DC: National Association for the Education of Young Children.

Smith, P. K., & Vollstedt, R. (1985). On defining play: An empirical study of the relationship between play and various criteria. *Child Development, 56,* 1042–1050.

Tobin, J., Wu, D., & Davidson, S. (1989). *Preschool in three cultures.* New Haven, CT: Yale University Press.

Trawick-Smith, J. (1994). *Interactions in the classroom: Facilitating play in the early years.* New York: Macmillan.

Vogel, E. (1979). *Japan as number one.* Cambridge, MA: Harvard University Press.

White, M. (1984). Japanese education: How do they do it? *The Public Interest, 76,* 87–101.

White, M. (1987). *The Japanese educational challenge: A commitment to children.* New York: Free Press.

White, M., & LeVine, R. (1986). What is an iiko (good child)? In H. Stevenson, H. Azuma, & K. Hakuta (Eds.), *Child development and education in Japan* (pp. 55–61). New York: W. H. Freeman.

10

Context and Meanings in Taiwanese Kindergarten Play

Sheng-Hsi Lin
National Tainan Teachers College, Taiwan

Stuart Reifel
University of Texas at Austin

Play is recognized as an educational and a sanctioned school activity. Developmental psychologists and educators conceptualized play as a significant force in various aspects of development, including cognitive, socioemotional, and language (Bruner, Jolly, & Silva, 1976; Erikson, 1963; Mead, 1934; Vygotsky, 1967), as well as a vehicle for learning (Vygotsky, 1967). Also, early childhood educators and professional organizations view children's play as the primary vehicle for, and an indicator of, their mental growth, and identify play curriculum as a developmentally appropriate practice for young children's learning (Bredekamp & Copple, 1997; Kagan, 1990).

Play is a remarkably important activity for children. Not only is it a means for expanding the self, but it is a major tool for self-preservation. Play is the province of the child. It is a "laboratory" where children can learn new skills and practice old ones, in preparation for adult life in society. Play is also a social workshop, an area for trying out roles, both alone and with other children. Play is also an area for expression; it is concerned with the themes and emotions that are experienced in everyday life. By studying children's play, we can understand what they think and feel about the world around them. We also can have a better understanding of all aspects of their development by studying play (Sroufe, Cooper, & DeHart, 1992).

There has been an outpouring of theoretical writings and empirical studies addressing the topic of children's play (Rubin, Fein, & Vandenberg, 1983; Smith, Takhvar, Gore, & Vollstedt, 1986). Many different aspects of research in this area have been explored. Social play (shared frames or metacommunication) is one aspect of play. The view of play as a form of communication has been a leap forward in the progress of play research (Kelly-Byrne, 1989). Studying the metacommunicative messages children use in play can contribute to our understanding of how children establish their play frame, as well as the meanings behind children's actions.

Play is also seen as a persuasive force in culture. Through play, social norms and cultural values are delivered and passed on. Thus, the essential nature of human play is culturally determined, and there is much cultural variation (Whiting & Edwards, 1988). More and more researchers are becoming aware of the importance of cultural or cross-cultural concerns in the study of play (Schwartzman, 1978; Suito & Reifel, 1993). The present study follows this trend.

For this study, pretend play is seen as an activity in which children create an imaginary world of roles and events. It involves role-playing and make-believe transformation. Role-play is an activity in which children pretend to be something or someone other than themselves, like pretending to be a mother, a doctor, or a monster. Make-believe play is an activity in which children transform objects and pretend real-life actions, such as giving an injection with a pen. Such play may become social, when children create a group activity in which they share with each other an imaginary world of roles and events (Fein, 1981).

Metacommunication is a term often used to indicate management messages that clarify how other verbalizations and behavior should be interpreted, or to establish the appropriateness of behavior in a particular play context (McLoyd, Thomas, & Warren, 1984). These messages may include statements about the organization of play (e.g., "I'll be the mother, you be the father"; "I'm not going to be the baby anymore"), components of play ("Pretend there is a rat in the cup"), or the rules that govern play ("You are a kid so you can't wear makeup, especially perfume") (Garvey, 1990).

Metacommunicative signals associated with social contexts are statements or actions with reference to the partner's previous utterances, or those that are directed to the play partner. For example, one child says, "Mom, I'm very hungry." The other child accepts the former child's attribution to her role by responding, "Be patient, I'm already cooking."

Metacommunicative signals suggested by nonsocial contexts are self-directed utterances or actions suggested by materials, past experiences with real-world objects or events, or a child's own decision (Reifel & Yeatman, 1993). For example, one child picks up a stethoscope and a bag, saying to the other child, "Let's go to see a doctor." In this case, materials (the stethoscope and bag) are influential elements contributing to their initiation of pretend play. In another example, a girl and boy are enacting an event of a wedding ceremony. The girl tells the boy, "You should hold my hand and walk very, very slowly." Here, the girl's past experience with a wedding ceremony guides her to correct the boy's performance and their pretend play.

By looking at the ways in which children metacommunicate with each other, the present study intended to describe the entry signals of Taiwanese children into pretend play and how they maintain their play frame. This report will focus on the physical or social contexts (see Schwartzman, 1986) suggesting metacommunicative messages for Taiwanese boys and girls.

RELATED LITERATURE

In a laboratory study, Matthews (1977) observed the dyadic social interaction of 16 four-year-old children (four boy-pairs and four girl-pairs) in a laboratory playroom. She examined the effect of the child's sex on preferred transformational modes in the initiation of fantasy play and found that boys use more material modes (object manipulation and reference to physical objects) than ideational modes (reference to magical events or situations) in initiating fantasy episodes. Girls use more ideational modes. On further examination, Matthews found that boys began with predominantly material modes, then steadily shifted to ideational modes until a balance was established. Girls, however, initially maintained a balance and then shifted to the ideational modes as the preferred means of initiating their fantasy activity.

In a laboratory study, Göncü and Kessel (1988) investigated the developmental differences in the organization and complexity of play interactions of three- and four-and-a-half-year-old children. They studied explicit metacommunication (negotiation) of pretend play and found that the girls expressed multiple dimensions of planning and symbolic representation more than the boys in their dyadic play; this finding is also consistent with McLoyd (1980). Göncü and Kessel explained that due to the play settings (kitchen, dress-up, and block play areas), girls may have had more ways of establishing a connection between existing objects and imaginary ones (i.e., reification) or of imagining that objects exist (i.e., object realism).

Suito and Reifel's (1993) findings, from a cross-cultural study of gender-role expectation in pretend play with Japanese and American children, showed that both Japanese and American girls seem to be concerned with role assignment and used kinship relationships like mother, baby, and father to address others in their play. On the other hand, Japanese boys did not discuss role assignment or overtly identify what roles they were playing. These observations on the gender differences of children in metacommunicative usage for initiating pretend play interaction need further exploration, especially with respect to different cultures.

Research on play in Taiwan has increased in recent years. Studies either tend to have general findings on developmental changes in social and cognitive types of play (Lee, 1973; Pan, 1991), or tend to explore the relationship between play and children's development and capacities. Mainly, those findings categorically indicated age-related play with Taiwanese children. Little knowledge of the content or context of their play forms has been recognized.

One study reported that the Taiwanese child's entry into the pretend world to some degree needs a teachers' instructions or guidance (Chien, 1993). However, some Taiwanese children spontaneously became involved in pretend situations without teachers' facilitation (Pan, 1991). Studies of children's play patterns in Taiwan mainly revealed evidence of quantity of play and rarely of quality of play (Lee, 1973; Pan, 1991). This was the researchers' concern in this study: What are the contextual sources, in terms of the influential elements within the play frame of pretending, that enhance the meanings of their metacommunicative signals?

The present study intended to describe the contextual factors, such as social or physical contexts, that influence children's frames of transformation. The study was built on Schwartzman's work on frames of reference, but, in some aspects, also departed from it. Accepting suggestions from Göncü and Kessel (1988), the present study also included information concerning nonverbal markers of play, to compensate for earlier studies in this respect (Giffin, 1984). Also, to minimize problems associated with unfamiliar play environments and unnatural social contexts, as shown in Matthews's (1977) study, this study was conducted in a natural setting—classrooms of playmates familiar to one another.

METHODS

Settings

Two five- to six-year-olds' classrooms in two different areas of Taiwan were each observed for four weeks during the middle of the first semester of the school year. One classroom is in a kindergarten affiliated with a public elementary school in northern Taiwan. There are two classes, each consisting of 20 five- to six-year-old children and two teachers. This school emphasizes a play-based curriculum and allows children to self-select (or self-direct) activity. The two classes interact with each other most of the time. They were separated only during group time and during afternoon activities. The two classrooms were divided into a total of 12 learning centers. The traffic flowed smoothly; each child took an assignment sheet and then went to a play area of choice. Before entering a play area, they were required to stamp a symbol representing the area on their sheet. However, a limited number of children were allowed in each area at one time, for example, the housekeeping area was limited to six children. All the materials around the classrooms were available and accessible to the children. Lin observed 10 of the children during free play from 8:10 a.m. to 9:00 a.m., since some children only attended school in the morning.

Another school, a daycare, was located in southwestern Taiwan. There were nine classes, consisting of two toddler classes, two junior classes (ages 3 to 4), three middle classes (ages 4 to 5), and two senior classes (ages 5 to 6). Most classes had 30 children and two teachers; the senior class had nearly 40 children and two teachers. This school included play, as well as academic work, in its curriculum. They allowed children to have self-selected (or self-directed) activity during free play. Their schedules were as follows: free play (exploring time), snack, group time, learning activity, outdoor play, lunch, nap time, learning activity, another snack, and another free play. The two senior classes only interacted with each other during free play in the morning. During the rest of the time, they were separated. All materials were available and accessible to the children in the learning centers during free play. The first author observed 10 of the five- to six-year-old children during free play from 8:30 a.m. to 10:00 a.m. because the schedule for free play in the afternoon occurred when the children were waiting to be picked up, and because the materials accessible to the children in the learning centers at the end of the day were limited.

Participants

Twenty children, ranging in age from five to six years old, were included, from both lower- and middle-class families; five girls and five boys were selected in each school. The children were selected by their teachers because of their familiarity with them.

Data Collection

The data for the present study were derived from two different sources. Notes were based on naturalistic observation of each target child, and tape recording of each child with a wireless microphone was done during the same period. Observations were made during visits to each school during morning free play for five days (or six days, if needed) every week. Note-taking and audiotaping were used during each observation. Target observations during free play were employed to develop an understanding of each child. One of the target children was followed and observed during the whole section of free play for a day twice a month; that is, each selected child in each school was observed and tape-recorded twice, for a total of two hours in that month. The observations for this study were a total of 40 hours.

The teachers introduced Lin to all the children during my earlier visits to the classrooms for three or four days in September and October. She had joined in their classes and played with them so that they were familiar with her. To minimize her presence affecting the children's play, the teachers told them that she was only an observer and not to feel compelled to invite her to play.

The techniques of tape-recording children during data collection were based on Suito's study (1991). A tie-pin style, battery-operated condenser wireless microphone and a receiver-recorder for audiotape cassettes was used in recording the target children. The microphone was attached to the child's clothes near the chest with a safety pin. The loose end of the microphone wire was secured at the child's shoulder with a safety pin, so that the incoming voice could be recorded at whatever direction the child is facing. The researcher followed the target child and spontaneously moved around with the child, taking anecdotal field notes.

The information recorded was integrated with field notes. The audiotaped recordings consisted of children's conversations with other children. The collected information included children's actions, verbal and nonverbal behavior, the objects they used, the circumstances in which their pretend behavior took place, and other children's reactions to the target children. The field notes were reviewed everyday. In case some utterances were not clear or occurred too quickly to be completely jotted down in the field notes, the audiotaped recordings then served as a supplement. At the same time, sole reliance on the recordings might provide utterances without clear indications of the whole play situation; the field notes compensated for this shortcoming. Summary notes were made from observations, focusing on individual utterances and actions for initiation and maintenance in pretend play. A sketch of each play-participant and his or her play activity was developed, forming a play file for each child.

Data Transcription and Analysis

Field notes included the setting, participants, and events, as well as a record of ideas, feelings, and interpretations written in the field or immediately after leaving the field. From these notes, metacommunicative signals—verbal or nonverbal—of each target child in interaction with peers and objects could be identified. Second, the individual child's conversation with peers during play were audiotaped. The tapes of the target children's utterances were fully transcribed. When the researcher used a tape recorder along with notes, she wrote down verbalizations, as well as behaviors, so that the notes and the tape corresponded.

Vocalizations directly associated with the sound properties of some real or imaginary objects, such as "vroom" (locomotive sound) or "choo-choo" (train whistle), were included. Some marks were used for nonverbal behaviors: an ellipsis for a pause (e.g., "You'd ... better") and brackets for voice levels (e.g., [loud] or [soft]) and tone of voice (e.g., [sweet] or [angry]), etc. Nonverbal cues consisted of actions children take and materials they utilize (e.g., a child picked up a rope to tie two stuffed animals together and placed them in front of her imaginary door). The researcher's commentary on data, which may be special terms in Chinese, or nonverbal cues related to our social customs contributing to children's play, was included for better understanding. For example, "Lau-Gung" is an intimate and sweet title that a wife might use with her husband, possibly like "Dear" in American. This term was used by a girl for defining her relationship to a boy when she intended to initiate pretend play. Such information concerning a description or explanation of a term for clarity was also included in the transcripts. Whenever possible, the transcription of observational data and a summary of each target child's transcription was completed the same day they were obtained.

In order to preserve the confidentiality of research participants, pseudonyms were used throughout, as were abbreviated initials for the participants' names and

TABLE 10.1.
Marks Used in the Transcription or Text

T	Indicates the teacher
TC	Indicates the target child
TG	Indicates a female target child
TB	Indicates a male target child.
TG1 (2, 3…)	Indicates the first (second, third…) female target child
TB1 (2, 3…)	Indicates the first (second, third…) male target child
G1 (2, 3…)	Indicates a girl interacting with the target child
B1 (2, 3…)	Indicates a boy interacting with the target child
Ex.1 (2, 3,…)	Indicates the first (second, third…) example.
.. (two dots)	Indicate a short pause
… (three dots)	Indicate a long pause
…. (four dots)	Indicate that the speaker's words are omitted
/	Means that the words re interrupted by the next speaker
/?/	Shows an inaudible utterance
( )	Indicate tones or stress
[ ]	Indicate the explanation or description of an action or material a child used, or of special meanings of some words or situations

related institutions' names. A list of remarks used in the text and transcripts are presented in Table 10.1.

Data Analysis

Qualitative analysis of the observational and audiotaped data focused on the comparison of the boys' and girls' verbal and nonverbal metacommunicative signals for initiating and maintaining their pretend play, and how they were associated with specific contexts to show transformation. For example, a child put on a hat, thus transforming himself into a fireman. The method of constant comparison was employed for analysis. The procedures for data analysis included unitizing, categorizing, and filling in patterns (Lincoln & Guba, 1985).

When unitizing the data, the researcher conceptualized each transcript sentence and paid attention to the metacommunicative signals the target children used for initiating or maintaining pretend play. Metacommunicative signals associated with social contexts were defined as those with reference to the partner's previous utterances or those directed to the play partner. For example, one child said, "Mom, I'm very hungry." The other child accepted the former child's attribution to her role by responding, "Be patient, I'm already cooking." Metacommunicative signals suggested by physical contexts will be defined as self-directed utterances or actions suggested by materials, past experiences with real-world objects or events, or the child's own decisions (Reifel & Yeatman, 1993), not related to peer stimulus. For example, one child picked up a stethoscope and a bag, saying to the other child, "Let's go to see a doctor." In this case, materials (the stethoscope and bag) were influential elements contributing to their initiation of pretend play. In another example, a girl and boy were reenacting a wedding ceremony. The girl told the boy, "You should hold my hand and walk very, very slowly." Here, the girl's past experience with a wedding ceremony guided her to correct the boy's performance and to joint their pretend play. There is another case of one "'drunken' patient" who came to see a "doctor," who took her alcohol bottle away to stop her drinking. When she asked the doctor to return the bottle, the doctor regulated her behavior by saying, "Use both your hands to receive it." Here, the social custom of using both hands to give and receive an object from another, a polite custom in Chinese society, serves as an influential element for maintaining their pretend activity.

The final tasks were to identify and integrate descriptive categories of metacommunicative signals associated with contextual factors. A comparison was made of the categories found for girls and for boys. The relationships of metacommunicative signals and contextual origins of girls and boys were also compared. Gender differences in metacommunicative signals for initiation and maintenance of pretend play were assessed by means of counting the frequencies of categories and explaining how they were associated with the contextual sources that enhance their meanings. Thus, the results of the analysis included explanations of how the contextual sources (physical and social) influence metacommunication.

RESULTS

Physical Contexts

The elements of materials, space, time, and experiences with the real world fell under the domain of physical context. How each element enhanced the meanings of metacommunicative signals is presented in the following sections.

Materials

Materials contributed to the boys' and girls' metacommunicative signals, whether in initiating or in maintaining their social pretend play. They used materials, such as blocks, to initiate their pretend play (such playing house or war). In addition, other materials contributed to their maintenance of pretend play over a period of time. For example, a target boy (TB8) treated a loaf of pottery as sugarcane and used a metal plane as a knife to peel the pottery clay. He transformed his action as "peeling a sugarcane" and later came up with the idea of selling the sugarcane. His idea stimulated another target boy (TB9) to "sell fried chicken" with the additional material of paper. The material (pottery clay) contributed to TB8's or TB9's interaction with the other silently "working" children, such as buying their product (sugarcane or fried chicken). The consumer, TB10, transformed some of the wrapping paper into a hat and directed his pretend event, assuming the role of an adult to distribute the hats to young children. Those materials also facilitated talk about their pretend play; to step in and out of the pretend frame, whether talking about the appropriate way of cutting sugarcane or suggesting a bowl of water as oil to fry a "drumstick."

Instead of the material itself, the degree and nature of the use of symbolism (based on the transformed material) was the key to initiate the children's interaction of pretend play. In some cases, symbolism was used to label the materials, rather than to direct the nature of their interactions in a scripted sense. In an example of boys' manipulating pottery clay, the pottery clay, because of its physical properties, was labeled "pancake," "egg," "teapot," or "snowman," respectively, by each child. Yet, this labeling by each child did not direct the development of a pretend scenario and did not initiate the talk about joint pretend. Rather, most of the remarks made by the boys were about what to do with the "pancake" or "egg," such as putting together the "pancake" and "eggs" and reconstructing them into a dinosaur. These remarks were about how to reach their goal of well-made products. Conversely, in the above scenarios of "selling sugarcane" or "selling fried chicken," the symbolism (sugarcane or fried chicken) was used to initiate a pretend action and develop a pretend event. These differences in the degree or nature of using symbolism reflected the differences in the boys and girls when they initiated their social pretend play.

Basically, both the boys and girls in this study seemed to simultaneously operate with the materials on four levels: a) working with the materials, b) talking about their work with the materials, c) talking about their pretend play, and d) actually pretending when they interacted with the material provided in the environment (Britain, 1992). However, there were some differences in the ways in which the materials in pretend were used, the talk about the transformed materials, and the use of symbolism with the transformed objects when the boys and girls metacommunicated in pretend play. Moreover, the differences showed evidence that the boys oriented more to materials than to relationship. However, the girls focused more on relationship over materials throughout their sessions of pretend play. In addition, these reflected big differences in metacommunicative messages, whether for initiating or maintaining their pretend play.

Initially, when using blocks as props in initiation or maintenance of their pretend interaction, the girls had the tendency to attribute human use to the plastic and unit blocks more than the boys. They tended to transform the blocks into food or utensils and the block structure as their house or a picnic spot in order to recruit everyone in the block area together. Their pretend plots were centered around daily life events or picture stories. At this point, the girls' focus of relationship over materials was significantly evident. Conversely, the boys in this study were more likely to attribute human figures or animals to the blocks. The individual blocks were portrayed as bombs, weapons, or equipment and the block structures as a house or park for the figures or animals. By adding miniature figures or animals, their play plots dealt in military battles, among dinosaurs, or in a zoo. Their pretend play was initiated by the interaction of those transformed objects according to individual needs. Although they sometimes role-played by speaking in the identities of the pretend figures or animals, they appeared to orchestrate the play interactions of these transformed objects. They acted either as a manager, instructing workers (playmates) to build a pretend structure, or as a director, directing the interaction of the pretend figures and animals. Here, the boys' orientation toward materials over relationship was seen.

Second, within the pretend frame, the use of the transformed objects significantly differed among the sexes. Girls were often heard to negotiate the identity of the transformed objects throughout the course of their pretend play. For example, the identity of substituted materials was changed and argued among the all-girl pretend play. In one case, a target girl (TG6) announced the theme of their play that day to be worshipping the ancestors. They started the procedures of worshipping by preparing the pretend food and wine, and setting up bowls and cups. They continuously argued about the substitution of the pretend objects and the correct amounts, the positions of the bowls and cups placed on the table, as well as the accurate proceeding order to adding wine to the cups. Their talk and negotiation of their pretend play dominated the majority of their play interaction.

However, the boys were more concerned about how to use the transformed objects, as well as finding toys as additional props for sustaining their play interaction during the session of pretend play. For example, once the boys entered the dollhouse, they began pretend actions by manipulating the utensils for cooking or looking for an additional prop (i.e., a stick) for sustaining their play interaction (i.e., assuming a beggar to be allowed in a house play). At the same time, the girls were still negotiating whether the stuffed animals were to be transformed as pets or babies. In another case of mixed-gender pretend play, the boys began by building a military camp. When the structures were all set, one boy kept asking, "Hey! Are you guys ready? Our soldiers [miniature toy figures] are going to invade yours. Open the door, quickly!" One girl in the play group shouted, "Hey! The soldiers need to have breakfast.... Hey! These [blocks] are the sandwiches for them rather than the bombs you used." The inference was that there appeared to be an agreed-upon goal (initiating a battle) between the boys. The goal that the boys agreed upon activated them to use the materials immediately. The boys' orientations to use the materials right away were significantly evident. Third, as mentioned earlier, the use of symbolism from the transformed materials differed among the boys and girls during their interaction of pretend play. When the girls used symbolism in their pretend episodes, the symbolism was the predominant force in directing the nature of their pretend play. The girls used symbolism, simultaneously developing a pretend plot with characters and events that directed their actions. Their talk about the pretend directed the majority of their interactions, regardless of the availability of the material. In addition, the complexity of their remarks about the pretend did not match the complexity of the materials they used. In the episode of the story of Cinderella, a target girl (TG3) started this play by putting on a tablecloth, then showing it to her playmate (G1). G1 commented on TG3's actions by saying that TG3 could be a princess. Continuously, TG3 looked for a volunteer for the role of servant. Under the circumstance that no one would like to be the servant, she assumed herself as the servant and later developed into Cinderella. In this session of play, TG3 and two other girls did not use many materials as props, except the tablecloth and a bunch of flowers. In addition, they used props only when the plot of the play required relevant objects. For example, when the stepmother in the play (depicted by G1) directed the servant to do chores, TG3 responded by wiping the tablecloth or mopping the floor. TG3 held the flowers when the plot of the pretend play went to the wedding ceremony. At other times, they only described and, sometimes, acted out the story. That is, their talk about the pretend and enacting the pretend directed the majority of their play interaction. The materials (the tablecloth and the flowers) were not the main characters in their pretense.

The boys of this study evidenced that they used symbolism more to label objects according to their properties than to direct the nature of their interaction in a scripted sense as they played. They were oriented more toward how to transform materials, then how to take action with the transformed materials. These appeared to be their main concerns, whether in initiation or in maintaining their pretend play. The case of clay, discussed previously in this section, as well as the above examples, would affirm this point. This pattern was used consistently in their other play episodes as well. For example, in the block center, most of the target boys' focus was on building the home or park rather than enacting events there, except playing war or acting out dinosaur and animal scenes.

In sum, the findings indicated that the boys were more focused on what to do with materials during pretend play. The girls were focused on who to be and what and how they should be related to each other during pretend play. These findings would explain why the girls were more likely to identify others' role identities and suggest enactment or ideas to others, whereas the boys used more self-reference to either join the ongoing pretend play or initiate a play frame. The fact that the girls' focused more on the relationship over the materials will be further discussed in the section entitled "Social Relations" in this chapter.

Space

In one of the classrooms in this study, access and control of interactive space appeared to be a greater concern of children, especially for the girls. As mentioned previously, once the girls got access to the block area or dollhouse, they often protected participants in interactive pretend episodes from other children (mostly boys) who might (potentially) either usurp their place, upset the balance of power, or change the pretend theme within an ongoing event of pretend play. The girls' tendencies to maintain a secure place in an ongoing episode of pretend play were often seen either in their initial pretend interaction or during the course of their play. Those who first had access to the place, the "host" girls, possessed the right to initiate the pretend theme (such as house play) and established it as a firm rule or "ticket" for the entry children (especially for the boys) into their ongoing pretend interaction. Besides the requirement for consent to play the same theme and the prohibited use of irrelevant objects in the initial play interaction, during the play, the girls carefully selected their participants, especially those amongst the boys. They either assumed others in the roles of tender pets or assigned the roles having heavy-loaded duties to limit the play behavior.

A possible element that might contribute to the access or control of play space is the issue of gender difference in orientation toward materials versus relationship throughout the play interaction. As presented above, the girls focused more toward relationships, resulting in everyone in the block area as participants in the attributed block play. To achieve the goal of incorporating everybody, the more space-controlled the built structure, the better.

The alternate explanation is that the spatial layout, with a limited number of players in each area, might hinder the children's tendency to include everyone and engage in extended episodes of pretend play, which may result in the infringement of other's space and thereby may contribute to the end of pretend play. Negotiation or argument about access to the popular play areas—such as the block area or the dollhouse—was a main concern for both the children and the teachers. Who could play in what location in the classroom was also a concern.

On the other hand, adequate space was a prerequisite for initiating and maintaining interaction of pretend play. In another scenario, the limited number of members in each play area may have contributed to the entry child's metacommunication outside the play frame in which the play group exists. A target boy (TB1) and two other boys wanted access to the dollhouse already accommodated by six players. The pretend talk used to enter the other group's (all girls) play was outside the frame of house play, and is worth noting, since it reveals the signals of pretend play. Their conversation was as follows:

TB1: We have three waiting to play for a long time here. Please let us in.

G1: No, there are only six people allowed in this area.

TB1: Please end your play soon, okay?

G2: Who told you to come late? We came first. I want to sleep now. Don't bother us.

TB1: Ding-Dong. Ding-Dong. *[Doorbell rings]*. Please open the door. P-l-e-a-s-e.

G2: Don't bother my sleep!

TB1: If you don't open [the door], then we'll break in.

G2: Hey! Don't be silly. The rule is already there, you should follow; otherwise, I'll call the teachers.

TB2: We already kneel down begging you. Please let us in.

G2: No, here is called "the Doll House" and we girls are here for playing with the dolls. This is not a place for you boys.

TB1: *[He walks sloppily, scratching a stick.]* Kind young lady, please give me some food and water, I've already not eaten and slept for three days.

G1: *[She gives TB1 a bowl and a tablecloth.]* There you go. Stay in front of our house only a while and leave soon!

Space limitations created a need for the boys to find a play frame that would allow some participation in a restricted space. The girls used classroom rules, as well as their own pretend play rules, to keep the boys away.

Time

Time issues also related to metacommunicative signals. This includes the elements of free time for child's play, the duration of play, and their past play experience. Whether children had free time to play with materials, discussion about their play with materials, or discussion about their pretend made a difference in their metacommunicative signals in sustaining the pretend interaction. The results indicated that when a signal indicating clean-up was heard, whether with music or by ringing a bell, the boys tried to creatively transform the signal into their ongoing play or altered their ongoing play into another to extend their play longer. For instance, they considered the bell ringing as a cue to explode their buildings (e.g., a zoo or a dinosaur park), cleaning up the "exploded" things to sustain their pretend interaction. The signal for clean-up, or for other transition activities, seemed to the children like an abrupt ending.

In addition, the play time in the teacher's daily agenda affected the duration of the children's play and became the heart of the play theme, which directed their play action and play talk. The two schools usually placed play time at the beginning or the end of a school day. The duration of play time for children was dependent on how early parents sent them to the school and how late they were picked up. Their play time was often terminated by either the teachers or their parents instead of at their own accord. In one instance, while a group was playing haunted house, one target girl (TG2) was scared by the darkness of the room and the ghost voices imitated by the other children, but felt excited and enjoyed the play. Upon termination of play, she commented, "I'm not ready to go home yet. I hope to stay here for play." One girl said, "I'll come early tomorrow to play haunted house." Another target girl (TG3) said, "Tomorrow, I'd like to play it again, too ... but my mom always gets up so late!" The episode of pretend play terminated by the children themselves revealed a different ending of the play. An example of metacommunication toward the end of the play is: "...then we got married and the end," or "All right, we finish the picnic and get ready to go home. What's the next thing we're going to play?... Oh, see the sky is dark now. I know ... we can pretend that it's dark ... late, and we camped here ... and the big wolf is coming." In these cases, they either had full closure of their play or altered an ongoing play frame to another. Therefore, having enough time for children to play and putting the play time in the heart of the daily schedule, rather than fitting it in at the beginning or end of the school day, may be important issues.

Moreover, the children's past play experiences with their playmates would affect their metacommunication when they initiated a play interaction or sustained their ongoing play.

Experiences Outside of School

Children were found to bring their past experiences with the real world of materials, roles, or events to their play interaction. This also influenced their metacommunicative signals during pretend play. Those experiences included gaining knowledge of natural science perhaps from a children's encyclopedia, perceptions of role appropriateness or role expectations, or their perceptions of adult and child as formed from their daily life experiences.

The children's experiences in gaining information or knowledge of natural science in the real world were brought to their play. This contributed to their play interactions in many ways. For instance, one boy (B1) and a target boy (TB4) were play fighting with toy dinosaurs. TB4 hit down B1's dinosaurs and stated, "Surrender as soon as possible! Your dinosaurs were all killed." B1 picked up a robot intending to substitute it for a dying dinosaur. TB4 protested, "Hey! You can't bring it into the war. There were no such robots in the world of dinosaurs." B1 maintained, "Yes, there is. In the contemporary century, the dinosaurs and the robots coexist. I learned it from the children's encyclopedia." B1's erroneous clarification by providing information from books made a contribution to the maintenance of their play interaction. His explanation convinced TB4 to allow the robot in their play theme, therefore continuing their pretend play.

Meanwhile, children's stepping out of their pretend frames to discuss the information concerning dinosaurs, robots, or other natural science became a interruption of their ongoing pretend play, particularly when the boys' play accidentally touched the "ground" of science (like dinosaurs or planets), it simply provided opportunities for the boys to discuss and correct information. This discussion and correction may initiate or develop competition of knowledge of habitation or physical properties of animals or of the force of weapons and bombs. Seldom did the boys simultaneously come back to the standpoint of their original pretend episode. Here, the children's understanding of information about science helped them to clarify, and sustain, play situations. However, it usually drew them to reality for discussion, which never allowed them to come back to their pretend state during the period of observation.

The children's social exchanges, which focused on concerns about the right way to represent reality, also affected their initiation and maintenance of pretend play. They had questions about knowledge of cooking procedures or of diagnosing a patient. For instance, girls were often heard to say: "You should put in oil before cooking food"; "Hey! You did not turn on the stove, how can the food be ready to eat?"; "You should put in butter and milk before the corn is done"; or "Hey! I don't need to have a shot. I just hurt my nose. Are you serious?"

As stated earlier, the concept of gender-typed role adoption and role appropriateness matters to the girls in their pretend play. This concept included what gender should play what role, as well as the manner in which it is played. The stereotyped expectation of role enactment was not only passed to the participants, it also made the girls step out of their pretend role and correct one another's role enactments during the course of pretend play. Such remarks included: "Girls play female roles and boys take male parts"; "You are not able to do anything here. How come you'll be the mom?"; or "Look! You keep the kitchen untidy and messed. You can't be the mom anymore!" They even identified a boy by saying, "The bad guy is coming! Papa, come on in and protect us." The boy was the one who was rejected (by the girls) because he intended to bring in toy dinosaurs and robots.

Expectation associated with adult roles were also a clue that contributed to the children's temporary termination in their play interaction with each other. In a typical example, three of the girls initiated family play, while the boys tried to get access to enter their play. The girls transformed the boys into bad guys and decided who should deal with them. TG3 talked to a girl who role-played as a mother, "You are the adult and you have to 'sweep' the bad guy."

Two close friends initiated "play twins," often stepping out of their role as a twin to explain what will happen next. Their talk about pretend follows:

TG3: Pretend that we are at the same age and we are twins.

 G1: Yeah, let's pretend to be close. And there's no fights between twins.

TG3: Pretend that I understand your words, and you know my sayings because we are twins.

From their metacommunication, there appeared to be a mutual understanding of what role should be played. However, the following indicates that each of them had different perspectives in mind for pretend.

TG3: Pretend I'm going to the potty.

 G1: Me too, because we are twins. We go to potty together.

TG3: Pretend I went to the potty for a long time.

 G1: I want to go with you.

TG3: You cannot always follow me everywhere.

 G1: Yes, I can because we are twins.

TG3: Oh no! Give me a break, please. I'll go to the restroom. Just a moment.

 G1: Me too.

TG3: Oh! Please not "Me too" anymore. I'm not your twin sister now. I REALLY want to go potty now.

Here, they seemed to have different ideas about the boundary of pretend and reality. For TG3, they both do not do the same thing at the same time out of the frame of playing twins. However, for G1, they can go together either in pretend or in reality. Finally, G1 said, "I want to go with you. Come on, we are good friends, right?" Their friendship was the strong force that bound them together. Mutual understanding of each other's perspectives was an important factor in this example.

The children's perceptions of low-status roles in reality would be passed on and used in their role assignment and role enactment on the pretend level. For instance, when other children in the dollhouse were busy with cooking or feeding, G1 had nothing to play with and was only lightly involved in their interaction, due to the low status of her role in the play. "I don't want to be the baby or the child anymore! It's too boring!" announced G1. A target girl (TG3) said, "Okay. You can be the younger sister, too." With their own experiences, they perceived (or conceived) a boy or a young child as a passive part in a family. Indeed, up to this date, this conception of a young child has prevailed in the adult world in Taiwan society.

The following example of house play also showed the role of a baby or a young child to be of low status. An all-girl play group was discussing who would be what role and what appropriate role was needed upon entering the block center. A target girl (TG1) said to another girl (G1), "You'll be the baby." G1 declined. TG1 stated, "You're supposed to be because you always sleep between us [TG1 and G2]. A baby always sleeps in between the adults." G1 insisted on being a sister instead of a baby. G2 reconfirmed, "My little brother sleeps in between my parents. Who told you to sleep in the middle of us? You have no choice." Consequently, G1 unwillingly took her role. The suggested role expectations in their play came from the children's experiences in their own families. An alternate reason is that friendship is at the heart of their play interaction. TG1 and TG2 are close friends and therefore think they are supposed to be doing everything together at school. Their separation by G1 at nap time does matter to them and they bring this to their play.

Additionally, their experiences with the media, such as television or storybooks, gave the children ideas to initiate pretend play. Examples are play "Bow Ching-Tien and Zhan Zhao," which is from a television program; play "Cinderella or Snow White," from storybooks; and play "Ling-Long Tar," which is simulated from a folk story.

Social Contexts

Social contexts involve classroom culture, children's social relations, and social conventions that contributed to the metacommunicative play signals in this study.

Classroom Culture

In this study, classroom culture (or classroom climate) was an important element in enhancing the children in joining others' pretend play, to initiate their interaction with others, and in developing mutual understanding to maintain pretend. It was apparent during sharing time (or group time) that play was the critical element shaping their imaginative work with real objects and establishing social habits. For instance, at sharing time, a teacher in one of the schools we observed asked the children to share their play experiences with the blocks. One of the children reported that their original idea was to build their own zoo, but there were only cars; no toy animals were available. So they changed their minds and built a military camp, which included an airport and a parking lot. When they used all of the blocks, they started with an episode of soldiers' flight training and of car racing. These multiple ways of transforming objects and creating many play frames contributed to their mutual understanding and their sustained group interaction.

Sharing time right after play also facilitates the boys' collaborative work in building blocks. One boy announced that even when someone in the other group accidentally hit their parking lot, knocking it down, they transformed the accident into a pretend earthquake. So they rebuilt their structure and decided to connect it with the zoo built by the other group. The two groups later invited guests (other children) to visit their modern zoo and airport with a parking lot. Unexpectedly, the accident became a facilitator, allowing the children to work collaboratively around the pretend scene. The teacher explained that their action was called a "collective creation." The value of collaboration and cooperation was realized by the children. From that day, the boys were often heard trying to reconcile with their partners by saying, "The teacher said that we should love and be kind to each other. Come on, let me play with you and help you strengthen your fort to repel the enemy."

On the other hand, efforts by the teachers at sharing time might hinder interaction during play time. In reality, the climate of competition for their final products might affect the children's interactions and reduce the collaborative or cooperative work during pretend play. One of the two teachers in either of the schools observed often showed the whole class the well-done work of a particular child to motivate the other children. This scenario of the teachers' efforts was most often seen when children manipulated the pottery clay or folded paper. Consequently, the children in these areas either played with materials individually or talked about their work with others. Some remarks included: "how pretty my snowman [made by folding paper] is"; "How much this looks like my dinosaur"; or "How fast I made a dinosaur with clay." Their talk did not often initiate the development of a play episode, due to competition about the quality of their pretend objects.

Social Relations

From the perspective of physical contexts, the boys focused more on what to do with the materials provided during play. The girls, however, focused on who to be and what or how they should be related to each other. From observations of the children's pretend play, it seemed that the girls often used very strong pretend roles to create a closeness out of activities that were more parallel or associative in their nature. For example, when the girls would draw together, they would often impose a theme of sisters drawing together or of students together in school. This was not observed in the boys' activities; they were not expressively collaborative about roles. Obviously, social relations predominated the heart of the girls' metacommunicative signals, whether in initiation or maintenance of pretend interaction. When the girls pretended collaboratively around familial roles and plots, their focus on relationships dominated over their focus on materials. This issue will be discussed by looking into several domains: friendship, host and entry play status, power and control, and conflict, negotiation, and agreement.

First, close, sustained friendships existing between two children tend to establish play patterns that are fairly constant in all their interactions together, both together in dyads and together with other children participating. TG3 and G1 were close friends and consequently they played together, entered into the ongoing play of the other children together, and role-played together. They usually role-played as sisters or twins, no matter who the other participants were in the pretend play. However, a mutual understanding of what one did not comfortably want to do together with the other was still important. In an example of playing twins, TG3 welcomed G1 to go potty together in pretend, but TG3 did not agree with this in reality.

Children who had been playing together for even a short period of time greet each other with the mutual assumption that they will play together. Whether this mutual assumption worked out sometimes depended on their early contact when they enter the classroom in the morning. Morning greetings between children upon arrival in the classroom played an important part in their subsequent play interactions for the day, affecting the patterns of problem-solving in conflict, or negotiation during play. When the children enter the classroom at the beginning of the day, they usually show new toys, stickers, or even candies to their friends until the teacher asks them to choose a play activity. Children were often heard saying not only, "I won't want to play with you anymore," but also "I won't give you my candy (or pretty stickers)," or "I won't let you see my picture book" when there was conflict or negotiation arising in play and the partners did not compromise. On another occasion, a girl brought her collection of fancy stickers and did not share with all the observers around her. She distributed her stickers to some boys and girls, saying, "You should be good to me." She did not share with one play group composed of four girls. At play time, her access to the group's play was denied. Although she protested to a teacher and successfully got in, she was unfortunately assigned a low-status role (a naughty and disciplined child) in the pretend play. This example represents the girls' focus on peer acceptance and relationship over materials in play.

Peer acceptance was a strong force used to solicit compromise while joining ongoing pretend play. For example, TB1 was playing in a predominantly female play group. This group decided to join another group's pretend play in the dollhouse. TB1 was denied participation with them because he refused to play house. TG1, a member of that group, announced that if TB1 was unwilling to play house, no one would be his friend and he would not play with him anymore. TB1 was upset about this but had no choice. He finally accepted the proposal and entered the dollhouse.

The interpersonal peer culture was used by all, however more extremely by the girls in order to regulate partners. This also became a threat to the ongoing interaction of pretend play between the children, which is discussed later. In this study, girls were more likely to identify the child (usually a boy) who looked on or passed by their play area and implicitly invited him into their play interaction. For instance, TB5 was passing by the block center where girls were initiating playing twins. He was stopped by a target girl (TG3), who called him, "Papa, come in quickly to watch our store. We want to go out for awhile." When the plot of their pretend play grew to a dangerous situation, such as a robber breaking in, TG3 asked TB5 to come to a corner, and said, "Papa, come hide here. Protect us. We're scared." The boys, on the other hand, were more likely to identify the partner's toys as characters of the play, which they enacted through object transformation. In an example of playing war, TB4 and B1 each held a toy dinosaur and pretended to fight together in the air. TB4 identified their ongoing situation, saying, "All your soldiers and guards were dead. Hey! Pick up the horse. He can fly and he is the final survivor." B1 responded, "No! The horse cannot fly." TB4 said, "I say he must be able to fly. Or just pretend he can fly, otherwise we have nothing to fight with in the war."

From the above examples, the girls' intention was to protect their participants in their pretend play, carefully selecting their playmates. They avoided the ones who refused to play twins, interrupted their pretend play, or would shift their pretend theme upon entering their area. For the boys in the above example, they intended to possess all of the blocks to keep their play going. These findings reflect that even when the girls and boys served as hosts during the play interaction, their orientations toward relationship versus materials dominated their interactions.

Second, the girls' orientation toward relationship over materials in play was also evidenced when either a host or an entry playmate during the ongoing pretend play. Access strategies can determine whether a child will be able to successfully enter into an interaction and/or influence the balance of power within a collaboration of pretend play. Also, when the children served as hosts in their play interaction, choosing which child may enter interactive pretend was a main concern for them.

The girls in this study were concerned about their ownership of the interactive space. Once they "possessed" the interactive space, they would protect participants from other children who might interrupt their play, or who might change their play plots for initiating or maintaining their pretend play. As the nonparticipating children approached, a participant usually carefully identified to the others a role to fit in the play interaction, keeping a balanced power within their play. For example, a target girl (TG3) identified a boy passing by the block center, saying, "Papa, come in quickly. The bad guy is coming. Come in to protect us." This was a reaction to a play group (consisting of three boys) who would come in for play; TG3 would try to invite another boy to repel them. Another possible reason for this exchange was that by implying a role to the other, they could make the role fit in their play, thus sustaining it over a longer period of time.

The girls, as hosts in play, tried to make a connection to a new, incoming playmate by specifying the ongoing theme, explaining the identities of the ongoing roles, or assimilating the new, incoming player into the ongoing play frame. A new, incoming playmate caused them to step out of their ongoing play frame to "examine" any irrelevant roles or objects within the frame. Also, it caused them to examine the need to redefine or reassign the role identities. Once these assessments were made and they were ensured everything was settled, then play resumed. They were very concerned with how to draw every playmate into the same play area together, thereby ensuing the ongoing interaction of pretend play.

As the above example noted, the girls incorporated all the children first, but the same was not evidenced with the boys. With regards to friendship, it was apparent that boys first thought about how to use the materials in a play area rather than about their playmates. A target boy (TB8) was heard saying, "…if you don't agree with how we transformed the object or what we were going to play with, then you don't need to play with us." If two play groups had a disagreement on how to play out the play theme or how to use the objects, they remained separate and played out their desired theme. This could have been the reason why they frequently switched their play themes.

The girls' discussions about pretend while out of a play frame were topic-related around play-sustaining roles and plots that included the entry child. Whereas, the boys had greater concerns as to how they would play with the materials; proceeding with their agree-upon play theme, regardless of who was or was not included.

Third, control and power were used as a means by which children directed or dominated the other participants or pretend plots during the interaction of pretend play. TG1 was the one who always directed the participants in their play interaction and the transition. In the example of "buying books at the bookstore," she directed the play interaction from "buying fairy tales" to "going home." Then she initiated "playing a mother teaching her child." In pretend play, she directed the play theme and specified the transformed place (bookstore and home). In reality, she was also a strong leader. She has served as a "daily monitor," demonstrating dancing activities in front of the class, distributing school supplies to the whole class at art activity time, and disciplining noisy children at nap time. However, she was occasionally either forced to lessen her control by the participants, or chose to back down for the sake of continuing the ongoing pretend play. For example, TG1 savagely shouted to TG3 to cook dinner quickly. However, TG3 retorted to TG1, "What a terrible, severe, and weird mom. I'm not your kid, don't ever speak to me this way again!"

In pretend, the possession or control of certain objects would become the main focus of the other playmates. For example, a pair of high-heeled shoes represented power to direct either the wedding ceremony role-play or the worshipping ancestors that coexisted in the dollhouse. In the play group simulating a wedding ceremony, the bride was the only one who could wear the shoes and direct other participants on what to do. Therefore, each of the girls often claimed ownership of the shoes, directing the others to cater to her, to put on clothes for her, and to clean up for her to be ready for the upcoming ceremony. In the group playing worshipping ancestors, the one who gained control of the shoes was the mother. The role of the mother had the authority to direct others to prepare the pretend food, dishes, and cups for the worship ceremonies. The role of the mother was also the only one who could direct the proceedings of the ritual (where to put the dishes of food and cups of wine, as well as when to add wine to the cups). (Interestingly, in a traditional wedding ceremony in Taiwan, the procedure is that a new couple should worship the ancestors of the husband's family.) These are examples of the power gained by possession of the shoes. Two possible reasons for these controlling behaviors could be that a) this was a direct result in the girls' sticking to the idea that only certain adults can wear high-heeled shoes, and that b) their perception of certain roles as they are associated with authority.

Note that whenever a child was allowed to play the "mother," she had more power on the pretend level, though not necessarily in reality (Schwartzman, 1978). The roles were mutually agreed upon during the pretend interaction. In an episode of house play, TG1, enacting a mother, severely beat the hands of her child (G1), due to her constant mistakes in counting numbers. G1 consented to this manner in pretend. Children use directives to indicate to the partner what to do in certain roles, which may be very authoritarian with children. Occasionally, some roles were used to give reasons for authority and directives to other participants in their pretend interactions. For example, TG7 announced, "I'm the big sister today, and you guys should listen to my words and commands,"; "She's more sharp, so she'll be the older sister."; or "Hey! Don't move my stuff. I'm the host who greets you guys. You are guests in my house and you should be polite and well-mannered. This is the tea with cream, not the papaya juice." TG7 used her role, giving the participants a good reason, as well as her power in specifying the play symbolism and directing what they did, all of which sustained their play interaction.

Power in pretend play is marked by possession or control of those materials that influence the children's play, either in initiation or maintenance, or by authority vested in social roles (Yeatman & Reifel, 1997). Lastly, conflict, negotiation, and agreement also served as elemental factors that suggested the meanings of children's initiation and maintenance of pretend play. An example of conflict involved an invasion of space between girls and boys. These instances were simply resolved by the girls claiming ownership and asserting themselves by verbalizing "Get out."

This study found that peer pressure was considered a facilitator as well as a threat, to children's pretend play. A threat to leave or to stop a friendship was used by the girls to negotiate who should be what role, what the play theme will be, or what plots were going to proceed. Remarks used by the girls included: "I don't want to play with you anymore!" or, "I don't want to play unless we play 'Snow White' and I'm the princess." In contrast, the boys made threats like, "You guys play with yours [blocks]! Why do you always play with ours?" or, "Get out, if you don't want to have the door here." These were used when they had disagreements on what to do with objects. In order to proceed with pretend play, there had to be a mutual agreement among the children. Consequently, the conflicts or negotiations among the children in pretend play would be considered productive conflicts.

Additionally, conflicts or negotiations in pretend play provided opportunities for the children to exchange different ideas and to reason with their playmates. In the analysis of the data, it was found that logic or reasons existed for their negotiation. The logic or reason presented was that the one who possessed the high-heeled shoes the time before could not be the role of the bride the next time. Also, the one who role-played as the mother could not also be the bride during their pretend play.

Variance of social convention shaped their different ideas about the possibilities of unconventional play. For example, what if a bride remarries and what if the unmarried woman had a child? This drew them together and they stepped out of their roles and play frame for productive discussion and mutual agreements in order to sustain their ongoing play interaction.

Social Custom or Social Convention

The children in this study were found to use stereotyped roles in their pretend play. Gender-linked concepts shaping play behavior were embedded in the social-cultural environment where the children's interaction took place. Consequently, social custom or social convention within the society was a main influential factor in the children's play.

For example, a target girl (TG6) and a boy were enacting a wedding ceremony. TG6 told the boy, "You should hold my hand and walk very, very slowly." Here, TG6's past experience with a wedding ceremony guided her to correct the boy's performance and to join their pretend play. In addition, this experience was shaped by social convention. There was another case in which one "'drunken' patient" came to see a "doctor" and the doctor deprived her of her alcohol bottle to stop her drinking. When she asked the doctor to return her bottle, the doctor regulated her behavior by saying, "Use both your hands to receive it." Here, the social custom of using both hands to give and receive an object from the other—a polite custom in Taiwanese society—regulated the partner's play behavior. Social convention served as an influential element for maintaining their activity.

Social customs led the children to step back to reality from the pretend state for correcting and specifying ongoing play. They also served as a means to facilitate the interaction of two play groups in a play area. Two play groups were playing parallel in the dollhouse. One group enacted a wedding ceremony, while the other group worshipped ancestors. TG6 announced, "Hey! The bride and bridegroom should come here to worship the ancestors after a while." Social custom drew two play groups together, as well as connected two play themes to a shared pretend theme. Social custom (worshipping ancestors during a wedding ceremony) served as a "social pivot" (Vygotsky, 1978) for the children to initiate a more complicated pretend theme. This theme involved more playmates, pretend roles, objects, and action plans than each of the two had done independent of each other.

Variances in the socialized children's perceptions of social custom and social convention made the children's play behavior different. Mutual understanding and perspective-taking of others' ideas became an important issue in initiating and maintaining children's pretend play. In an episode of playing house, a boy (B1) claimed for himself the role of a father in the play. His wife (TG7) addressed him with a title that was socially conventional. He did not realize there would be pretend talk between husband and wife when he first decided his role. Usually, the children have not initiated this kind of conversation in their past play episodes. Their conversation follows:

TG7: Lau-Gung…*["Dear," in an intimate and a sweet voice]*

  B1: Don't call me in this way. I most hate to be called "Lau-Gung."

TG7: But I always hear my mom call my dad in this way.

  B1: All right, you can call me "Lau-Gung," but not in such a sweet, intimate voice.

TG7: Okay, Lau-Gung *[in a plain voice]*, take this *[a basket]* away.

TG7 implied B1's identity and defined her relationship to B1 by addressing him with an endearing title. TG7's daily experiences of her mom calling her dad in this way suggested her pretend talk. However, B1 did not accept such an intimate calling. It may be because this was not the social convention from his daily life experience. TG7 continued their play interaction by adjusting her voice and assigning a job to others.

DISCUSSION

Researchers indicated that, other than the degree of social participation that is evidenced in pretend activities, children's pretend play tended to be influenced by materials, ideas or reactions of others, personal motivation, and past experiences (Reifel & Yeatman, 1993). This study, focusing on physical and social contexts, supported the above findings, but other, different elements were found in the contexts. In addition to materials and playmates, social custom and social conventions served as the "social pivot" (Vygotsky, 1978) to make children's metacommunicative signals possible and suggest their meanings in play. Social custom facilitated a connection of two ongoing play themes together and provided a way of seeing the complexity and organizing process of children's pretend play.

Materials seem to be an important means to initiate and maintain pretend play interaction, especially for the boys. The girls used materials (high-heeled shoes) as symbols of certain roles (bride or mother) and possession of power (directives and authoritarian) in play. However, it is also considered a source of the negotiation and conflict among children, interrupting the play sustenance or initiating a new play frame (Yeatman & Reifel, 1997). In this study, the access and ownership of the symbolized objects became a source of conflict in the boys' and girls' play.

Consistent with the works of Britain (1992), the girls in this study were found to focus on relationship over materials; whereas, the boys oriented toward materials over relationship. When the girls included playmates for role assignment or action suggestion, their focus on social relationships dominated over their focus on materials. They tended to find materials to support their focus. However, the boys had more tendencies to convey their metacommunicative signals by transforming materials, and were concerned with how to use the transformed object to develop and define their pretend play. It is difficult to say whether gender, or other issues, is at the heart of this different orientation. What can be said, however, is that these different orientations (play choice) provide somewhat different experiences for the children involved in each and that these experiences can impact children's development.

The girls in this study were more likely to identify others' role identities and suggest enactment or ideas to others, whereas the boys had relied on self-reference to either join the ongoing pretend play or initiate a play frame of pretending. This may be because the girls were more likely to join in the activity of playmates, whereas the boys were more likely to pursue their own ideas for play. It seemed that this orientation toward connections for girls was so strong that they would often use pretend roles to create a closeness out of activities that were more parallel or associative in their nature. Gilligan's (1982) portrayal of interpersonal style possibly interpreted that. However, there is need for evidence to support this study from different cultural perspectives. It also fails to explain boys' emphasis on materials as they play.

Pretend topic marks roles and materials as relevant to the frame (Reifel & Yeatman, 1993). The girls employed the pretend topic as shaping rules for protecting the participants or entering playmates. That is, the rules within pretend frames were topic-related around roles, transformed objects, and plots to regulate the participants and entering playmates for participating and ensuing their play interaction. Meanwhile, the boys tended to test the rules by adding irrelevant props or roles into the play, and to find the opportunities to play out their own ideas of pretend themes related to objects.

Power in pretend is marked by possession or control of these materials (Yeatman & Reifel, 1997), themes, and access to the interactive place, which occurred in the girls' play interaction in this study. Much of the time and interaction in the girls' play was spent addressing who is to control what materials and what space. Conflict within the pretend frame characterizes most of the duration of this pretend episode (Yeatman & Reifel, 1997). The findings of this study supported this standpoint. The girls in this study were concerned with the control of the access and ownership of the interactive place and certain symbolized materials. The boys, in contrast, made threats when they had disagreements on what to do with the materials.

There is much social pretend through enacting the transformation of replicas in boys' play, usually as a director, actor, or narrator. As a director, they metacommunicate how to arrange the toy dinosaurs, robots, or other animals, as well as how to act, and how to control the will of the animals. As actors, they imitate the voices of the replicas they enact. As narrators, they describe what the animals are doing, giving the rationales to the actions of the animals. It's interesting to find gender differences in the roles they enacted by their use of the blocks. The girls in this study enacted human roles in the block structure; whereas, the boys let the toy figure or animals come alive, living within the transformed block structure. The girls used the symbolism from the blocks as a setting to enact the adult's role, initiate play events around everyday experiences, and later develop the pretend plot with the characters and event.

Meanwhile the boys act out the role of the replicas and initiate the event according to the transformation of the replicas. Their pretend talk predominantly centered around the transformed objects. This made different girls' and boys' pretend talks both within and out of the play frame. There were not only gender differences in the content of the messages, but also in the metacommunicative signals; the boys conveyed nonverbal signals when enacted through object transformation. The boys' play, in this case, is what Erikson (1963) called microplay, which involves taking a real world and shrinking it to a smaller level. Through play, children do a number of things: recreate experiences from the past, represent the reality, and anticipate the future. Microplay and nonverbal behavior through enacting in toys or replicas needs more exploration in further studies.

The pattern of findings appears to suggest the benefit of a contextual view of classroom play (Reifel & Yeatman, 1993). Issues of material and social influences on play can be discerned from the descriptive analyses of how boys and girls make different play uses of the classroom, with the boys demonstrating an orientation toward their own play ideas and materials, while the girls oriented toward playmates. While it might be possible to interpret some of these findings in terms of Gilligan's (1982) female orientation toward connectedness, such a theoretical formulation cannot explain the boys' patterns. A contextual theory, building on Vygotsky (1978) and Bateson (1972), might more adequately deal with issues of represented meanings that appear in play within a given cultural context. This study demonstrates that unique cultural meanings surface in Taiwanese classroom play, suggesting the merits of further studies in different cultural contexts.

REFERENCES

Bateson, G. (1972). *Steps to an ecology of mind.* New York: Ballantine Books.

Bredekamp, S., & Copple, C. (1997). *Developmentally appropriate practice in early childhood programs* (Rev. ed.). Washington, DC: National Association for the Education of Young People.

Britain, L. (1992). *Having wonderful ideas together—children's spontaneous collaboration in a self-directed play context.* Unpublished doctoral dissertation, University of Oregon, Eugene.

Bruner, J. S., Jolly, A., & Sylva, K. (1976). *Play—its role in development and evolution.* New York: Basic Books.

Chien, C.-Y. (1993). Dramatic play in teaching and learning: An observational research. *Journal of Early Childhood Education, 2,* 247–262.

Erikson, E. (1963). *Childhood and society.* New York: W. W. Norton.

Fein, G. G. (1981). Pretend play in childhood: An integrative review. *Child Development, 52,* 1095–1118.

Garvey, C. (1990). *Play.* Cambridge, MA: Harvard University Press.

Giffin, H. (1984). The coordination of meaning in the creation of a shared, make-believe reality. In I. Bretherton (Ed.), *Symbolic play* (pp. 73–100). Orlando, FL: Academic Press.

Gilligan, C. (1982). *In a different voice: Psychological theory and women's development.* Cambridge, MA: Harvard University Press.

Göncü, A., & Kessel, F. (1988). Preschoolers' collaborative construction in planning and maintaining imaginative play. *International Journal of Behavioral Development, 11*(3), 327–344.

Kagan, S. L. (1990). Children's play: The journey from theory to practice. In E. Klugman & S. Smilansky (Eds.), *Children's play and learning: Perspectives and policy implications* (pp. 173–185). New York: Teachers College Press.

Kelly-Byrne, D. (1989). *A child's play life: An ethnographic study.* New York: Teachers College Press.

Lee, F.-T. (1973). A study of preference of play in Taiwanese children. *Reports of Taipei Municipal Teachers College,* Taipei, Taiwan.

Lincoln, Y., & Guba, E. (1985). *Naturalistic inquiry.* Newbury Park, CA: Sage.

Matthews, W. S. (1977). Modes of transformation in the initiation of fantasy play. *Developmental Psychology, 13,* 212–216.

McLoyd, V. (1980). Verbally expressed modes of transformation in the fantasy play of black preschool children. *Child Development, 51,* 1133–1139.

McLoyd, V., Thomas, E., & Warren, D. (1984).The short-term dynamics of social organization in preschool triads. *Child Development, 55,* 1051–1070.

Mead, G. H. (1934). *Mind, self, and society from the standpoint of a social behaviorist.* Chicago: University of Chicago Press.

Pan, H.-L. (1991). Chinese children's play behaviors in the Republic of China. *Bulletin of National Taiwan Normal University, 37,* 111–131.

Reifel, S., & Yeatman, J. (1993). From category to context: Reconsidering classroom play. *Early Childhood Research Quarterly, 8,* 347–367.

Rubin, K. H., Fein, G. G., & Vandenberg, B. (1983). Play. In P. M. Mussen (Series Ed.) & E. M. Hetherington (Vol. Ed.), *Handbook of child psychology: Vol. 4. Socialization, personality, and social development* (pp. 694–774). New York: Wiley.

Schwartzman, H. B. (1978). *Transformations: The anthropology of children's play.* New York: Plenum.

Smith, P. K., Takhvar, M., Gore, N., & Vollstedt, R. (1986). Play in young children: Problems of definition, categorization and measurement. In P. K. Smith (Ed.), *Children's play: Research developments and practical applications* (pp. 39–55). New York: Gordon & Breach.

Sroufe, A., Cooper, R., & DeHart, G. (1992). *Child development: Its nature and course.* New York: McGraw-Hill.

Suito, N. (1991). *Case study of four-year-old children's gender-role expectations and gender-related differences and similarities in Japan and in the USA.* Unpublished doctoral dissertation, University of Texas at Austin.

Suito, N., & Reifel, S. (1993). Aspects of gender role in American and Japanese play. *Play Theory & Research, 1,* 26–54.

Vygotsky, L. S. (1967). Play and its role in the mental development of the child. *Soviet Psychology, 5,* 6–18.

Vygotsky, L. S. (1978). *Mind in society.* Cambridge, MA: Harvard University Press.

Whiting, B. B., & Edwards, C. P. (1988). *Children of different worlds: The formation of social behavior.* Cambridge, MA: Harvard University Press.

Yeatman, J., & Reifel, S. (1997). Conflict and power in classroom play. *International Journal of Early Childhood Education, 2,* 77–93.

11

"Playing with Play": Germany's Carnival as Aesthetic Nonsense*

Felicia R. McMahon
Syracuse University

INTRODUCTION

Whether known as *Fasching, Fasnacht, Fastnacht,* or *Karnival* (Straube, 1904), depending on the region, the German carnival reaches its zenith during the pre-Lenten season throughout the country and now takes place in the former-Communist East Germany. The most "traditional" *Fasching* (meaning "fifth season") celebrations are said to be celebrated in the Catholic regions of southwestern Germany, where townspeople don wooden masks unique to their individual communities. A bonfire in each village square is built at sunset, and an effigy of one of the masked figures is burned, which participants say signifies *Winteraustreibung,* or the "driving away of winter." The celebration continues until midnight, when all festival play ceases. In the predominantly Catholic areas throughout southwestern Germany, this is when the Lenten fast begins. In large northwestern cities like Cologne, the celebration takes the form of parades that are quite grand in scale, resembling the Macy's Day Parade in the United States.

In north Germany, where it is predominately Protestant, *Fasching* is not celebrated at all. However, in eastern Germany, which is Protestant, and, until 1989, was a

* Research for this essay was conducted in the former West Germany during 1985–1987, and again during a Fulbright grant in East Germany in 1995–1996.

separate Communist country for forty years, *Fasching* has been celebrated in some communities for over a decade, and even prior to the fall of the Berlin Wall.

Coupled with the highly structured presentation of "chaos," the continued existence of this form of carnival in German society, and its recent popularity in eastern Germany, calls for further indepth study. One line of investigation in the past included research into what German scholars termed "mythic codes" as evidence of pre-Christian survivals (Stahl, 1981). For example, it is known from writings of Church prohibitions that a mid-winter, pre-Christian festival in many German towns was banned by the clergy in the Middle Ages, only to resurface after the French Revolution. During the latter period, the Church was secularized and the strictures against the festival were disregarded. Later periods, such as the German Romantic Movement in the 19th century, the reigning of the Third Reich during World War II, and, most recently, the reunification of Germany, experienced many renewed carnival celebrations.

FESTIVE PLAY IN SOUTHWESTERN GERMANY TODAY

I first encountered the German carnival tradition in the former West Germany in 1985. As we walked along an unlit street in the town of Elzach on a frosty February night, individual shapes began to appear out of the darkness: expectant festival participants huddled along the narrow streets. We heard the faint sound of flutes in the distance. We suddenly saw firey torches held by demon-like bears hopping out from nowhere. Hundreds of red- and green-costumed figures appeared, their faces invisible behind wooden demon masks, their heads covered with tricorn hats bedecked with thousands of snail shells and trimmed with giant red balls. I pulled away from the torches waved in my face by the garish, red figures. My ears reverberated at the hollow thud of inflated pigs' bladders bound to slender switches and wielded weapon-like by the prancing figures at curbside. The effect was electrifying, and I reeled, disoriented, hurled backward to some primeval consciousness.

The *Narren*, as the masked figures are called, repeatedly yelled to the crowd, "*Narri!*," the crowd responding "*Narro!*," meaning "foolish" or "crazy." A band of clowns continued the music as the demons built a bonfire and burned a monstrous demonic effigy. The lilting, hypnotic music pierced the dark night air as the flame-silhouetted revelers pranced about. With death-defying adroitness, they leapt over the fire, soaring above it to the cheers of the clustered onlookers. This ritual continued until the flames died. Then, sweeping the ashes aside, some satyr-like creatures turned their attention to the enthused crowd and chased squealing young girls into the late-winter night. Others strode into the restaurants, encouraging us to spend the evening in revelry. Precisely at midnight, all merrymaking abruptly halted, and the crowd made its way homeward through the dark, and now quiet, streets. Completely stunned and emotionally exhausted, I made my way back to my hotel room. My brain pleaded for an answer to a question: What was the meaning of all of this?

I later learned that the opening of "High Carnival" is the Thursday before Ash Wednesday. In the town of Offenburg, also in western Germany, the *Hexenzunft*, modeled after the guilds of the Middle Ages, is an organization of men who work in the community. Men are allowed to join the group after they have performed two years of community service. They are then granted the honor of dressing as *Hexen* ("old hags"). Only members are allowed to wear the *Hexen* costumes, and wooden masks, carved by a special German woodcarver who creates them only for Offenburg, cannot be bought or sold. People are reintroduced into the community this way. The least frightening are introduced first, which are the unmasked *Alti*, the older, married women of the community, also having performed two years of community service. Although they do not mask their faces, they wear the 18th-century costumes that were once the daily attire of the women of that region.

Then the *Büttel*, or "messengers," arrive on the scene ringing bells to warn the crowd of the evil eye of the *Hexen*. These are the young, unmarried men of the community who will one day apply for membership in the *Hexenzunft*. Next, the younger women, dressed as *Spättlehansel*, or bird-like figures, make their appearance. Their costumes are ragged, and although they approach the crowd, they will usually just pat heads and fondle faces, not meaning to frighten anyone.

At the center of this festival play is the "presentation of strangeness," which is heightened by the role of the *Hexen*. During the German carnival, men are often dressed as women, or, as in Offenburg, as a form of the *Hexe*, a human-eating creature that can also be playful. The *Hexe* is said to be a parody of fecundity or the old priestess in German fertility rites. Invented in the recent past, the use of the *Hexe* mask dates back to only 1936.

The last to be introduced is the *Hexenmeister*, which is a devil-like creature with horns and the most terrifying figure of the festival. Torches or inflated pigs' bladders are used to tease the crowds and to keep the pitch of *Fasching* elevated. Simulated pigs' bladders are now used in Germany; but, as late as the early 1900s, *real* bladders, tied to poles, were used in this manner. After World War II, the festival was "reinvented," the *Hexe* remaining the central figure.

In Offenburg on *Schmutzigerdonnerstag*, the Thursday before Ash Wednesday, it is traditional to call the villagers to the *Stadtmittel* ("town square") at 6:00 a.m., liminal in regards to time, to serve *Fasnachtbohnesuppe* ("*Fasching* bean soup"), which the *Hexen* say will make the children grow into strong *Hexen*. Children and *Hexen* are known to tell the truth, although at most times the *Hexen* will not speak, but will growl or gesture. The community also plays a role in this event by selling food at ridiculous prices, for example, something that would cost 3 marks might be sold for 3 pfenning. A *Hexenbaum* ("old hags' tree") is erected on a roof and decorated with shoes and other unlikely objects, drawing attention to the concept of "things out of place." The *Hexen* literally take the keys of order and are given authority to create chaos. Spontaneous dramatizations are improvised by the *Hexen*, and the street becomes a stage for a theater performance. There is intense participation between the *Hexen* and the spectators. In fact, I was singled out several times as a "foreigner" and pulled into the arena. Because I did not know what was going on, I tried to get away. The *Hexen* invariably chased me and dragged me back to the center of the street. Once, they chased me completely away from the crowd and down the street, leaving me there, to the intense amusement of the spectators.

I didn't know it at the time, but my "role" of naivety was merely to disrupt. When there is little distance between the audience and the performers, the particulars of village life are highly dramatized. During the skits later performed onstage in halls, there was a great distance, so the particulars of everyday life were more realistic. These were the times when the masks were sometimes removed for dialogue.

During the week, the *Hexen* continue to shake the people trying to "drive out winter." At night, there is be a *Hexenball*, during which time politicians are "honored." Friday is *Ruhetag* (a "day of rest"), when in some towns *Fasnachtkuchen* (pan cakes) are fried. On Saturday the farmer's market becomes the *Hexenmarkt*. At all other times, fresh vegetables are bought here, but at *Hexenmarkt* the vegetables that the *Hexen* "dress up" are rotten. Here, the *Hexen* try to sell their crazy, rotten vegetables to the crowds to raise money for next year's activites.

Hexen continue to play pranks on the people until the *Hexenfraß* ("witches' feed") on Shrove Tuesday. This afternoon is reserved for the children. *Hexen* line the balconies and throw *Blutwurst* ("sausages"), oranges, and candy to the crowds, and the children will tease the *hexen* by calling, "*Gizig, gizig, gizig isch die Hex. Wenn sie nicht so gizig wär, gäb sie au ebbes her*" ("Greedy, greedy is the witch. If she wasn't so greedy, she'd give us some."). One festival participant informed me that the throwing of treats was for "*Glück*" ("luck"). Alcoholic beverages, such as *Glühwein* and *Schnapps*, are sold to the adults. The *Hexenmeister* will make an appearance. Then the *Hexen* disappear until 6:00 p.m., once again a liminal time.

All is quiet until the band reappears, playing marches and other military music. Then the crowd gathers around the bonfire over which the *Hexen* spring. The bonfire is the most profound symbol of self-canceling behavior, for the very thing that is built is destroyed. This is the *Hexensprung*. The *Winteraustreibung* begins amidst fireworks and cheering. During this time and throughout *Fasching*, the *Hexen* yell "*Narri!*" and the crowds respond "*Narro!*," signaling a crazy scene where space is dislocated, and everything is called into question. During the entire ritual, the crowd repeatedly yells, "*Schelle, schelle, Sechser, alli alti Hexe, Narro! Wir sind froh!*" ("Shake, shake a sixpence, all old hags. Crazy! We are merry!"), the loud music from the band continually echoing throughout the entire town. Normally, the street is subject to fixed town rules, but during *Fasching* there are none.

THE "NEW" CARNIVAL TRADITION IN EASTERN GERMANY

Although the government of the former East Germany did not collapse until 1989, *Fasching* was taking place even in censored times. Censorship still existed in May 1989, when Erich Honecker, the former Communist dictator of the former East

Germany, announced during an annual political celebration, "The wall will still stand in 100 years!" However, less than six months later, the Berlin Wall that had divided Germany for 40 years came crumbing down. Before I arrived in the "new" Germany in 1995, I had been told by Germans living in the west that *Fasching* was never celebrated in eastern Germany because it, like northern Germany, was largely Lutheran and that public performances had been banned by the Communist government. I discovered that neither was true. On November 11, 1995, at 11:11 a.m., *Fasching* opened in the city marketplace in Chemnitz. Five *Fasching* groups, unmasked but wearing various sequined or feathered hats and costumes, marched with their bands through the city streets until they gathered at the City Hall. There, the *Bürgermeister* was summoned, and the *Elfenrat* ("Council of Eleven"; a group who organizes *Fasching* each year) demanded that he turn over the key to the city. After a series of satirical speeches, the groups sang and then marched away until evening.

I quickly introduced myself to one of the members of the *Elfenrat*, who was dressed in a green-and-white sequined jester hat, and asked if I might join the group to take photographs. That night, I was invited to the celebration, designated as the "guest of honor," and seated at the *Stammtisch* ("reserved table"). From my perch above the crowd, I had a bird's-eye view of all that went on that night.

Although February would be the month when Fasching reached its peak, tonight was not only the opening of the "fifth season," but also the anniversary party of this particular *Fasching* group, which had been publicly celebrating *Fasching* for 10 years—in spite of censorship by the former East German Communist government. For two hours, the 11 men and women became "quick-change artists," costumed in various disguises such as ballet dancers, belly dancers, and "tribal women" with large pink balloons as bouncing "breasts." Then, they formed a band and began playing "music" by blowing on watering cans and rubbing washboards. The group paraded, mimed, sang, and danced as the crowd joined in. At one table, spectators dropped their pants. Whenever the *Elfenrat* entered or left the room, the group marched in a circle, their arms extended in a military salute, and yelled, "*Verziehung!*" ("Excuse us!") three times while military music played.

During "High *Fasching*" which takes place before Ash Wednesday, the group performed in a local restaurant for 11 nights. The performances ranged from the men dressing as "Heidi" in long, blond wigs and short, aproned dresses and singing a pop German song by that title, to skits about insignificant daily events, to a scene with a large piece of cardboard across the front of a room and the word *Pissoir* ("toilet") painted on it. Two men entered this public "toilet" and stood behind the "wall" to urinate. The second man motioned with his head that he was armless and pleaded for some help. Grimacing, the first man unzipped the other's pants and supposedly, on the other side of the wall, held the man's penis so he could urinate. When both men had finished, the first man tried to light a cigarette, only to discover that he had no lighter in his pocket. Suddenly, the second man's arms appeared and, with lighter in hand, lit the other man's cigarette.

Another skit involved a tourist and an East German customs officer before the Reunification. The officer, oblivious to the tourist, is cleaning the toll gate with a tiny dustcloth:

Tourist: [*riding a bicycle, singing*] Going by bicycle to foreign countries, how I like that, it's great.... Hello, is anybody here? Nobody. Well, I have to hide my new GDR money. Hello, is there anybody here?

Officer: [*turns around*] Don't shove!

Tourist: What do you mean? I am not shoving, but I have been here for half an hour now, waiting...

Officer: I'm supposed to say "Don't shove!" It's a regulation.

Tourist: Is it also a regulation that we have to queue and wait everywhere?

Officer: Customs examination! Customs Officer Zöllemann. [*Here the two engage in lengthy word play with their names.*] Shut up! I want to see your passport!

Tourist: Wait a minute. Here it is—I'm a friendly guy, right?

Officer: Don't move! We are looking for you! [*Goes to telephone.*] Hello, boss! Do you have somebody on your wanted list with the following description: cabbage head with the ears of a pig, the neck of a goose, a chicken breast, a pig's belly, frog's legs, veal knuckles, an oxtail, and the eggs [balls] of a quail.

Tourist: That's not my passport—that's a menu!

Officer: Sorry, boss, it wasn't his passport, it was a menu. [*Turns to tourist.*] What do you mean? Where can one find such a menu? Not here. I guess, this man comes from abroad.

Tourist: Here you have my passport.

Officer: Uh...your passport photograph? Normally you have your *face* photographed!

Tourist: Do you always have a good day?

Officer: You have 12 children?

Tourist: Can you imagine that? I have been married for 12 years and I have 12 children. Wouldn't you say that I should write a book about that...

Officer: You should read one at night instead. Where do you come from?

Tourist: [*continues*] Can you imagine... I didn't sleep with my wife before I married her... and you?

Officer: I don't even know your wife!

This skit continued for another 10 minutes. In another routine, the men entered barechested, wearing huge, black top hats that covered their heads and arms. On each man's chest, eyes and a nose were painted and his navel was outlined with red to represent a mouth, which appeared to open and close as each man gyrated to the music. After two hours of these absurd dances and songs, the men, now dressed in their green *Elfenrat* costumes, ate, sang, and danced with the rest of the crowd until long past midnight.

THE RELATIONSHIP BETWEEN THE WESTERN AND THE EASTERN GERMAN FESTIVALS

Although *Fasching* has ambiguous origins, southwest Germans claim that their form of the festival is "authentic" and that the eastern German festival is "invented." However, as Stephen Nissenbaum (1997) has elucidated in his indepth study of the carnival roots of present-day Christmas celebrations around the world, all festivals are invented at some time and some place. Furthermore, even when images remain the same, meanings may change. A major difference between east and west carnivals is the noticeable lack of tourists at the eastern *Fasching*. However, in western Germany, a staged and highly stylized *Fasching* attracts many foreign tourists each year and has become a tourist industry. This is not the case in eastern Germany. The festival there is performed by eastern Germans *for* eastern Germans. My presence at the festival was highly irregular, indicating that in this respect, eastern Germans could also claim that their carnival is more "authentic."

Also, masks are not worn by the eastern German men, but in southwestern Germany, the villagers pride themselves on their use of "ancient" masks. However, these masks today may be historically coded, but are not mythic. There is no record these masks and costumes were worn by pre-Christian tribes or in Germany before Reunification. Rather, Bausinger (1990) points out that until the 19th century, *Fasching* masks and costumes were not "frozen," but differed from year to year. It is possible that images from pre-Christian festivals that took place in the early spring have been incorporated into modern-day festivals like *Fasching*, but the motivation behind all festivals changes just as historical periods change, and pre-Christian beliefs have little bearing on the modern functions of *Fasching*.

The highly staged parades and community events performed by the *Hexen* are relatively recent inventions in southwest Germany and although the content has changed, the skits are said to resemble those described in written historical references to the *Fastnachtspiel*. This was the carnival skit banned by the Pope because it parodied Christian practices adapted from heathen cults. The *Fastnachtspiel* was a Shrovetide play that emerged in the 15th century, the first secular drama of pre-Reformation Germany. The farces, mixed with satirical attacks on greedy clergymen and themes from pre-Christian German literature, were considered as threats by the clergy and banned until the 18th century. The present-day skit topics are not survivals of earlier times, but rather chosen images that towns select to represent certain "past" references, real or imagined, and endow them with political significance. During the World War II, for example, *Fasching* served as a tool for propaganda and was a socially sanctioned form of "play" during which hostility could be directed against "enemies" of the Third Reich. In other words, a community member could dress up as a stranger and intimidate and frighten others, while the community likewise could act out feigned fear of the masked figure. The use of festival "hostility" became acceptable in a officially sanctioned manner. The manner in which festival play was used as a tool for National Socialist propaganda during World War II is apparent from existing written evidence in the form of *Fasching* satirical skits:

> When someone today in Germany gets the creeps [or terror]
> He feels hot and cold [the jitters]
> Then it's certainly because he has shit on the stick [a guilty conscience]
> Because he starts smelling the prosecuting attorney [on his heels].
> He picks all his belongings up,
> Becomes quickly a political emigrant,
> Grabs secretly in the night the walking stick [leaves the country]
> and moves to the Promised Land. (Stahl, 1981, p. 194)

Hobsbawm and Ranger (1983) believe that modern countries construct ways of communicating to their citizens the relationship between government and people, and the labile aspect of play makes it possible for play to be co-opted by dominant forces to target victims. It is important to realize that references and selected images can always have new significance because, for example, nonsense can be used to disguise victimization. Furthermore, the nonsense is dependent on the relative sense of the situation in which it is embedded (Stewart, 1979).

There are other important aspects: Nonsense in *Fasching* can serve practical festive functions when, for example, laundry is hung across city streets and trees are decorated with shoes, thus indicating "time out of time," as well as where the festival is localized. In addition, the new "ritual criticism" (Grimes, 1990) considers the aesthetic process as a central component in the experiential side of ritual and festival. Applying this approach, a critique of the older structural concepts of "order and disorder" and festival as trope for culture, suggests that the reality is much more disorderly than this neat dialectic of structure and antistructure or a simple "carnival semiotic." After the concept of structure and anti-structure was introduced by Victor Turner (1969), many anthropologists and folklorists (Babcock, 1978; Falassi, 1987) later considered carnivals as cultural rites of inversion. Geertz (1973, 1987) argued that festivals in general are metaphors of our group identity on a grand scale and Fernandez (1986) suggested that the "meaning" of these performances is to convince not only others, but our own members as well, that we are indeed a distinct group. The potential for negative events to occur is only mentioned briefly by Fernandez, who idealizes festivals without accounting for the degraded amusements that sometimes occur during or after festivals. While he does suggest that in carnival "we can suspend belief in ourselves and celebrate incongruities" (p. 290), he says nothing about festival bending back on itself as a kind of "playing with play." And, most importantly, Sutton-Smith (1997) has shown us that most of these explanations of play are embedded in the rhetorics of theorists like those mentioned above.

DEEPER INSIGHTS

In southwest Germany, uniform costumes are carefully created to give a ragged appearance, and the mood of the festival is brought to a peak by characters jumping over a bonfire. It may appear that this is "antistructure," but the introduction of the strangest figure or most spectacular event planned to occur at a certain time demonstrates that an "ordered chaos" underlies *Fasching*. The design and sequence of these events is determined by festival aesthetics, not necessarily an "antistructure." Festival aesthetics vary from culture to culture because as Roger Abrahams (1970) points out, festive play must be situated in a context that is similar, yet at the same time different, from the "real world" in order to be effective.

This is not to say that the "ordered chaos" cannot serve as more than a stylistic element of the festival tradition, recreated in a manner exemplifying a "reinvented tradition in an on-going present" (Handler & Linnekin, 1984). Nonsense in a potentially dangerous situation illustrates the notion of the "hidden transcript" (Scott, 1990). For example, the former East German *Elfenrat* group recalled that during the carnival in 1989, before anyone knew that the demise of the Wall was near, their *Fasching* party was attended by "unknown guests" who were actually secret police known as *Stasi*. By luck, someone noticed the *Stasi* and the *Elfenrat* members, who were playing "music" on a washboard, became especially noisy and crazy, thus breaking up any conversation among festival participants. In 1995, a kind of "playing with play" from the past took place as the "history" of the washboard band incident was created and set to rhyme by the group:

> The carnival speech made by the new-landlord "hollerbach" was "not half bad"
> [after all we still lived in the "zone"]
> One saw quite "strange characters"
> who didn't laugh at our jokes!
> It was good luck that they "overlooked"
> and nobody had to go off with them.
> It was a miracle that nothing happened,
> otherwise we would have had to go to our next carnival-party
> decimated! A group of three would have had to rule.
> At the end there was a "riot"
> [conversations suddenly stopped in the hall]:
> The Washboard band-really dextrous-
> wielded their loud instruments.
> With loud colors, washboard-rubbing
> Glasses and panes rattled!

When the *Elfenrat* marches today in the washboard band, they are demonstrating a kind of "playing with play" in which nonsense from the past is recounted playfully in the present. The same nonsense has an entirely different significance having become celebratory as well. Recognizing this, it is possible to interpret this type of performance as "acting out of a pun," and likewise, the two men urinating and the top hat routines are dramatizations of a "carnival aesthetic" where each participant tries to gain a dominant voice by becoming the biggest fool. Certainly this applies in the "upside-down" world of carnival. While some theorists may see the use of a pig's bladder tied to a pole to slap people over the head during the southwest German *Fasching* as a rite of incorporation, from a carnival aesthetic, the *Narren* are employing the pig's bladder because it is a comical object with dirty connotations. While the border-crossing skit can be both a parody of life in the former East Germany or, as memories of the former government fade, it may represent nostalgia for a former way of life, routines may disintegrate into utter nonsense without reference, elucidating nonsense as "the infinity of nothingness" (Stewart, 1978, p. 148) where "the system itself provides the rules for giving meaning to itself, beginning with no content, ending with no content, pure process which has no end other than itself. It does what it is about" (Holquist, 1972, p. 159).

Thus, we must remember that since festival is experiential, it is assessed on many different levels by individuals who judge how well "play is played with." Rituals and festivals "are subject to ongoing assessment. They can be judged wanting. They can be improved upon. They can fail" (Grimes, 1990, p. 9). The play is well played when ambiguity and incongruity exist in the right tension; sequence and timing are critical; festive play is situated in a context that is similar, yet at the same time different, from the "real world." All of these are aesthetic components of nonsense, but novelty seems to be the key. For this reason, the introduction of males masked as females from other countries may be selected for novel considerations, rather than for racist connotations. It is in culturally specific creative combinations of nonsense for nonsense's sake that experiential significance for participants is born. By avoiding reductionist theories, which ignore the importance of nonsense for nonsense's sake, we can then account for the craziness of festival amusements.

REFERENCES

Abrahams, R. D. (1970). Folk drama. In R. Dorson (Ed.), *Folklore and folklife, an introduction* (pp. 351–362). Chicago: University of Chicago Press.

Babcock, B. (1978). *The reversible world: Symblolic inversion in art and society*. Ithaca, NY: Cornell University Press.

Bausinger, H. (1990). *Folk culture in a world of technology*. Bloomington, IN: Indiana University Press.

Falassi, A. (1987). *Time out of time: Essays on the festival*. Albuquerque, NM: University of New Mexico Press.

Fernandez, J. W. (1986). *Persuasions and performances: The play of tropes in culture*. Bloomington, IN: Indiana University Press.

Geertz, C. (1973). *The interpretation of culture*. New York: Basic Books.

Geertz, C. (1987). Interpretive anthropology. In H. Applebaum (Ed.), *Perspectives in cultural anthropology* (pp. 520–526). Albany, NY: State University of New York Press.

Grimes, R. L. (1990). *Ritual criticism: Case studies in its practice, essays on its theory.* Columbus, SC: University of South Carolina Press.

Handler, R., & Linnekin, J. (1984). Tradition, genuine or spurious. *Journal of American Folklore, 97*(385), 273–290.

Hobsbawm, E., & Ranger, T. (1983). *The invention of tradition.* Cambridge, England: Cambridge University Press.

Holquist, M. (1972). What is a boojum? Nonsense and moderism. In P. Brooks (Ed.), *The child's part* (pp. 145–164). Boston: Beacon Press.

Nissenbaum, S. (1997). *The battle for Christmas: A cultural history of America's most cherished holiday.* New York: Vintage Books.

Scott, J. C. (1990). *Domination and the arts of resistance.* New Haven, CT: Yale University Press.

Stahl, B. (1981). *Formen und Funktionen des Fastnachtfeierung in Geschichte und Gegenwart.* Bielefeld, Germany: B. Kleine Blitzdruck.

Stewart, S. (1979). *Nonsense: Aspects of intertextuality in folklore and literature.* Baltimore: Johns Hopkins University Press.

Straube, M. (1904). *Manual of German etymology.* New York: Albright.

Sutton-Smith, B. (1997). *The ambiguity of play.* Cambridge, MA: Harvard University Press.

Turner, V. (1969). *The ritual process: Structure and anti-structure.* Ithaca, NY: Cornell University Press.

part IV
Play In Other Species

12

Play and Stress: Cortisol as a Negative Correlate of Play in *Saimiri**

Maxeen Biben
Maribeth Champoux
National Institutes of Health

INTRODUCTION

Play is a commonly observed, but poorly understood, behavior that is seen almost universally in young mammals, but less frequently in older animals (Fagen, 1981). It is generally considered "normal" and even essential for young mammals, including humans, to spend a considerable amount of time in play, play being a chief means of social interaction, exercise, and learning (Chivers & Einon, 1982; Rubin, Fein, & Vandenberg, 1983; Smith, 1982).

Despite the acknowledged importance of play in mammalian life histories, little attention has been paid to conditions that foster playful interaction, or to the motivational or emotional states conducive to play. Observation of the occurrence (or, more to the point, the nonoccurrence) of play has led to the belief that it is very responsive to stressors of both a long-term (e.g., malnutrition, social harassment) and short-term (e.g., alarming stimulus) nature (Baldwin & Baldwin, 1976; Chepko, 1971; Dunbar & Dunbar, 1992; Moodie & Chamove, 1990; Muller-Schwarze, Stagge, & Muller-

---

* The authors acknowledge the assistance of R. Brown, D. Bernhards, and M. Haines, as well as the help-ful comments of S. Suomi and J. Brown. This research was supported by the Intramural Research Program of the National Institute of Child Health and Human Development.

Schwarze, 1982; Wolff, 1981). Yet, little is known about the extent of the relation-ship, and even its direction, whether positive or negative, is unclear.

The assumption of a negative relationship is implicit in the interpretation of playfulness as an indicator of psychosocial well-being in captive animals. If young animals kept in a captive situation do not play, this is generally taken to be a sign of poor health, poor adjustment to the housing situation, or impoverished play opportunities, such as lack of appropriate partners, space, or play objects (Caine & O'Boyle, 1992; Wemelsfelder, 1993). If such a relationship has validity, then play-fulness could be a useful construct for the animal care professional in assessing well-being. For animals in more naturalistic settings, the presence of play has been interpreted as a means of signaling vigor, as well as the health status of a youngster to a parent, or of a suitor to a potential mate, courtship being one of the more reli-able places to find playful behavior in adult humans and animals (Cummins & Suomi, 1976; Fagen, 1981, p. 361).

Evidence for a depressive effect of environmental stress on play can be found in some of the classic play deprivation studies, where drought and food shortages were associated with sharp declines in play, presumably because it is energetically too cost-ly to maintain (Baldwin & Baldwin, 1976; Muller-Schwarze, 1968; Muller-Schwarze, Stagge, & Muller-Schwarze, 1982). Historically, and even today, children in subsis-tence societies have little opportunity or energy for play (MacDonald, 1993).

Nonetheless, despite the evidence for a negative relationship, it is not uncommon to encounter youngsters who persist in playing even under the most impoverished and stressful conditions. Indeed, play deprivation studies typically fail because this behavior can be so difficult to extinguish (Chepko, 1971). In their zeal to play, young primates can exhibit considerable flexibility in overcoming obstacles, such as a lack of appropriate play partners (Biben, 1989; Biben & Suomi, 1993).

In some circumstances, brief stressors may even have a stimulating effect on the occurrence of play (Moodie & Chamove, 1990), perhaps by introducing novelty. Young rhesus monkeys in a captive troop played more frequently when the group was under stress than when it was not (O'Neill-Wagner, Bolig, & Price, 1994), sug-gesting that play itself may reduce stress or act as a coping mechanism (Coe, Franklin, Smith, & Levine, 1987). However, there is little evidence to support this compelling idea (Crepeau, 1989).

It is evident, therefore, that the relationship between play and stress is far from clear, and that environmental stressors may have quite different effects. In addition, individuals may vary markedly in their responses to these environmental contingen-cies. We have observed that, for squirrel monkeys housed under seemingly identical environmental conditions, some will play and some will not. Generally, pairs will play either robustly or negligibly within a few weeks of pairing, and will remain at this level for months or even years.

Some factors known to influence the likelihood of play in primates as well as other animals include the absolute and relative ages and/or sex of partners (Boulton, 1991; Govindarajulu, Hunte, Vermeer, & Horrocks, 1993; Hass & Jenni, 1993;

Watson, 1993). Play emerges as one of the first social behaviors exhibited by infants and persists as the most frequent peer-directed social activity throughout youth, diminishing sharply at sexual maturity, particularly for females. Females also typically play in different ways, or at a lower frequency, than males (primates: Biben, 1986; Cheney, 1978; Symons, 1978; humans: Smith & Connally, 1972; Whiting & Edwards, 1973). In most species, notably in squirrel monkeys, play is most likely to occur and be sustained between youngsters of the same sex and comparable in age, weight, and/or abilities (Baldwin, 1969, 1971; Boinski, 1986; Humphreys & Smith, 1987). Other probable factors that have received less attention are compatibility with the partner and familiarity or security of the environment. However, the effects of any of the above factors are hardly formulaic; animals, and primates in particular, respond as individuals and the success of their play relationships with other individuals may be highly idiosyncratic. Whereas age and sex are readily observed, the effect of other, less evident factors affecting readiness to play (for instance, stress) may still be manipulated and measured by indirect means, such as cortisol levels.

Squirrel monkeys demonstrate a robust adrenocortical response to social separations, with age and sex being important variables influencing the magnitude of the response (Mendoza, 1991; Mendoza, Lyons, & Saltzman, 1991). In the present study, we examined the relationship between the incidence of play behavior and plasma cortisol levels in juvenile squirrel monkeys under two conditions: Animals with a familiar, age-matched partner of the same sex in familiar, quiet surroundings; and, separated from their original partner and re-paired with a new partner with whom he or she has not previously been housed.

We proceeded under two assumptions: first, that the change from a familiar partner to a new, unfamiliar partner would, in most cases, act as a stressor. Interactions between individuals having no prior experience with each other are characterized by uncertainty, novelty, lack of predictability, and aggression, all of which are known to elicit a physiological stress response (Hennessy & Levine, 1979; Mendoza, Lyons, & Saltzman, 1991). However, in time, animals may adjust to a new partner, even prefering the new partner to the previous partner. In addition, we hypothesized that the level of play exhibited with a partner would vary with the level of stress experienced as a result of being paired with the new partner, and that this level of stress would be reflected by the plasma cortisol level. If play is inversely correlated with stress, and cortisol is an indicator of stress, then cortisol levels should be inversely correlated with measures of play.

METHODS

Subjects

The study was conducted during 1991 and 1993, using four pairs of juvenile, laboratory-bred squirrel monkeys each year. A third group was studied during 1992, but illness and death in that group compromised the comparability of the data; therefore, the 1992 data were discarded. The 14 males and two females were 21 to 35 months of age (mean age = 24.6 ± 0.9 months). Squirrel monkeys show their highest frequencies of play from about 6 months of age to 2 years of age (Baldwin, 1969), and prefer partners of the same age and gender. Because we desired to see evidence of preferences for play, we elected to study animals slightly older than the optimum play range, using both sexes. For the age range used in this study, we judged our subjects to be young enough to still be very playful, but past the age when they are so playful that they will accept almost anyone or anything as a playmate (Biben, 1989; Biben & Suomi, 1993). Original pairs, including the two females, had been housed together as pairs for several months before each year's study. Some had been housed together, in the company of other animals, from birth. During the period of study, animals were housed two pairs to a room in 2 × 1 × 2-meter wire mesh cages. Animals were housed in two rooms in two separate buildings. This allowed us to avoid stressing animals in one room (and thus affecting cortisol levels) when capturing animals in the other room.

Blood Collection and Analysis

A volume of 0.3 milliliters of blood was drawn from the femoral vein of each monkey by experienced personnel using 25-gauge needles and heparinized syringes. Blood was immediately transferred on ice to polypropylene tubes for centrifugation. Plasma was stored at −70° C. To control for circadian fluctuation in plasma cortisol level, all blood was drawn at the same time of day, at 11:00 a.m. The unavoidable stress caused by the capture of an animal, or its neighbors, appears to not cause an elevation in cortisol levels in squirrel monkeys for at least a 5-minute period after the onset of the stressor (Coe, Mendoza, Davidson, Smith, Dallman, & Levine, 1978). We therefore used a team approach with amply trained, rehearsed personnel to ensure that all four animals in a room were captured and bled within 5 minutes of personnel entering the room. Use of rooms in separate buildings also helped us to meet the 5-minute goal. Most animals were bled within 3 minutes of room entry. All blood samples from a single year's study were sent as a group for analysis. Samples were assayed for plasma cortisol at a 1:25 dilution by radioimmunoassay at Hazleton Laboratories, in Vienna, Virginia.

Behavioral Observations

Behavioral (play) observations were recorded remotely on ½-inch videotape for 2-hour periods at 10:00 a.m. and 1:00 p.m. 4 or 5 days per week. Using the videotaped data, the following play and compatibility behaviors were scored for each pair:

Play. Squirrel monkey play is exclusively social and is of the type known as play-fighting, or rough and tumble. Using the definition of Biben (1986), play bouts included wrestling, beginning with recognizable play initiation behaviors and ending with animals' final interaction, followed by at least 10 seconds of noninteraction. Only the duration of play bouts was recorded, in seconds per hour observed. All play was social, involving the participation of both partners; therefore, both partners received the same play score.

Huddle. Huddling is an upright resting or sleeping posture assumed by squirrel monkeys seated in contact with each other, each with its tail curled over its shoulder. In social groupings, time spent huddling (here, in seconds per hour observed) with various individuals is a robust indicator of affiliative preferences. Huddling is an easily observed and generally useful measure of affiliation in squirrel monkeys (Biben, 1986; Smith, Newman, & Symmes, 1982; Strayer, Bovenkerk, & Koopman, 1975).

Aggression. Any instances of fighting or other aggression were noted. Play fighting and aggression are easily distinguished on a number of criteria in most species (Pellis & Pellis, 1987).

Experimental Procedure

Original pairs were observed informally for at least one month prior to formal observation, to assure that they did not fight and appeared compatible. Three weeks of baseline data with original partners were collected before re-pairing animals. Behavioral data were collected daily during weeks 1–3 to determine baseline values for play and huddling, and any evidence of aggression or fighting by each animal in the original pairs condition. Levels of cortisol for this baseline condition were obtained by two blood draws, one done at the end of week 2 ($CORT_1$) and one at the end of week 3 of the study ($CORT_2$). Behavioral data for weeks 1 and 2 were summed as $PLAY_1$ and $HUDDLE_1$; data for week 3 were summed as $PLAY_2$ and $HUDDLE_2$.

At 7:00 a.m., 1–2 days after $CORT_2$ was obtained, animals were re-paired with a new partner. The new partner was chosen from the animals housed in the same room, but the two animals had never shared a cage. Thus, compared to original pair members, new partners were less familiar and shared less social history, although they had had some visual, auditory, and olfactory contact. Because two youngsters were females, two of the re-pairings also involved a change in sex of partner. All animals remained in their original rooms following re-pairing.

At 11:00 a.m. on the day of re-pairing, four hours after meeting the new partner, animals were bled again ($CORT_3$). Delaying blood collection 4 hours from the time of re-pairing allowed the stress response to restraint and handling to abate, leaving any evidence of elevated cortisol the result of the re-pairing only. Daily behavioral data collection then resumed on the new pairs for a 4-week period. Blood was drawn from all animals at 1 week ($CORT_4$) and 4 weeks ($CORT_5$) after the re-pairing, at which point the study was concluded for that year. Behavioral data collected in the week after re-pairing, before $CORT_4$, were summed as $PLAY_4$ and $HUDDLE_4$; data collected in the subsequent 3 weeks, up to the final $CORT_5$ blood draw, were summed as $PLAY_5$ and $HUDDLE_5$.

RESULTS

Cortisol Levels with Original Partners

In 1991, $CORT_2$ values for both members of one pair were > 2.5 times greater than their $CORT_1$ values, and more than 2 standard deviations higher than the mean $CORT_2$ values for the remaining 1991 animals, suggesting a disturbance in the room before collecting that sample. The $CORT_2$ values for these two animals were discarded as being outliers. Correlation between $CORT_1$ and $CORT_2$ for the remaining 14 animals was r (12) = 0.942, $p < 0.0001$. We therefore used the mean of $CORT_1$ and $CORT_2$ (referred to as $CORT_0$, an estimate of cortisol levels in the original pairs condition) in subsequent analyses.

Cortisol Values After Re-pairing

The animals' $CORT_3$ values, obtained four hours after being paired with a new partner, showed an average increase of 25.5% from $CORT_0$ values (see Figure 12.1). A repeated measures ANOVA was significant for the effect of re-pairing on cortisol levels $[F (3, 45) = 2.95, p < .05]$; however, a post hoc Student-Newman-Keuls pair-wise comparison of means revealed that only $CORT_0$ and $CORT_5$ differed significantly.

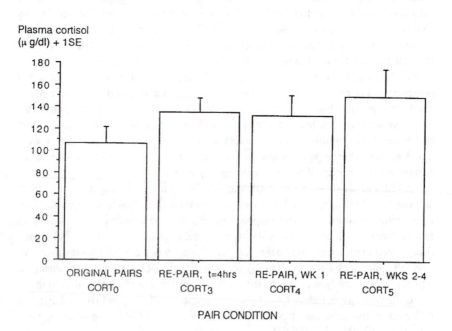

FIGURE 12.1. Time- and pair condition-dependent changes in plasma cortisol levels, $N = 16$ individuals.

Play with Original Partners

Play was a frequent activity for many, but not all, pairs in the original pairs condition. The percentage of observed time spent in play varied from zero for one pair to 16% (565 sec/hr) for another pair, with a mean of 5% (174 sec/hr). As is typical for play behavior, there were large differences within pairs from day to day, although the $PLAY_1$ and $PLAY_2$ scores were highly correlated [r (6) = 0.88, p = 0.002]. The mean of $PLAY_1$ and $PLAY_2$ (referred to as $PLAY_0$, a measure of playfulness in the original pairs condition) was used for analysis.

Play After Re-pairing

In the first week after being paired with a new partner, play scores dropped an average of 53% from those seen with the original partners (Figure 12.2). The effect of re-pairing on play scores was significant [F (2, 30) = 6.08, p < .01].

Newman-Keuls comparison of means showed $PLAY_0$ to be significantly greater (a = 0.01) than $PLAY_4$ or $PLAY_5$, which were not significantly different from each other. The first week after re-pairing was a period of behavioral unrest for some of the subjects. One pair fought. In another pair, one partner tried frequently, aggres-

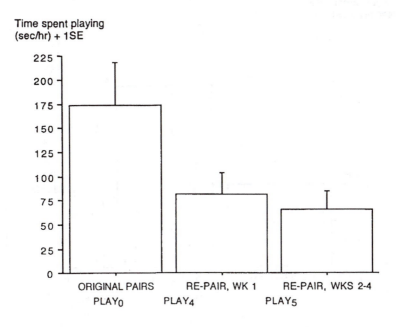

Time spent playing
(sec/hr) + 1SE

| PAIR CONDITION |
| ORIGINAL PAIRS $PLAY_0$ | RE-PAIR, WK 1 $PLAY_4$ | RE-PAIR, WKS 2-4 $PLAY_5$ |

FIGURE 12.2. Time- and pair condition-dependent changes in amount of observed time spent playing, N = 8 pairs.

sively, and unsuccessfully to get the other to play. In a third, one partner initiated and dominated the play so overwhelmingly that his partner eventually withdrew.

Time did not significantly affect the animals' play scores after re-pairing. The animals quickly established and maintained their level of play with a new partner: The correlation between the $PLAY_5$ scores (weeks 2–4 after re-pairing) and $PLAY_4$ scores (week 1 after re-pairing) for the 8 new pairs was $r\,(6) = 0.965\ (p < 0.0001)$.

Huddling with Original Partners

The eight original pairs averaged about 6 minutes of huddling per hour observed, with a high degree of correlation $[r\,(6) = 0.895, p = 0.0012]$ between $HUDDLE_1$ and $HUDDLE_2$ scores. The combined score, $HUDDLE_0$, was used for analysis.

Huddling After Re-pairing

Time spent huddling more than doubled during the first week with a new partner, with 13 of 16 individuals showing an increase (Figure 12.3). The increase was short-

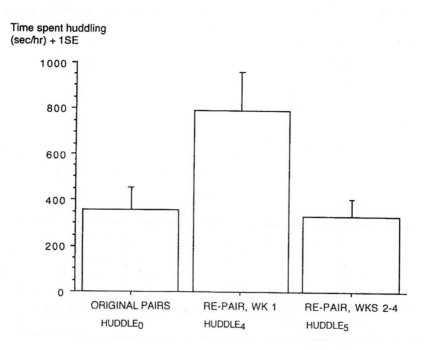

FIGURE 12.3. Time- and pair condition-dependent changes in amount of observed time spent huddling, $N = 8$ pairs.

lived, however, as HUDDLE scores returned to baseline levels in weeks 2–4 after re-pairing with new partners. The ANOVA was significant [F (2, 30) = 17.75, p < .01].

Relationships Among Variables

The previous analyses looked independently at the effect of pair condition (original pairs versus re-pairing) on play, huddling, and cortisol, finding a persistent decrease in play and increase in cortisol level when animals were re-paired, and a transitory increase in huddling. To look at the more direct relationships between any two of these variables, simple linear regression models were used.

Play and Cortisol

Averaged over all individuals and all conditions, the correlation between play and cortisol values was negative and significant, $r = -0.437$, $df = 47$. Examination of the regression plot (Figure 12.4) revealed that, at cortisol levels over 200 μg/dl, play was all but eliminated.

Table 12.1 lists each correlation between play and cortisol at each time point. In the original pairs (baseline) condition, cortisol and play were the most poorly corre-lated; during weeks 2–4 after re-pairing (for play) and at 4 weeks after re-pairing (for cortisol), they were the most strongly correlated.

Huddle and Cortisol

Huddle and cortisol showed an overall negative and significant relationship of $r = -0.312$, $df = 47$, somewhat lower than that for play and cortisol (see Figure 12.5).

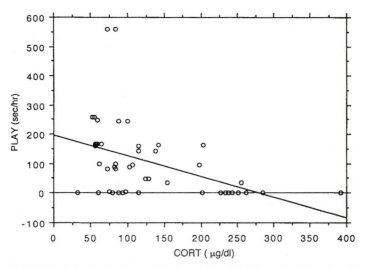

FIGURE 12.4. Regression plot of variables PLAY and CORT, for all pair conditions, Y = 198.011 – .699X.

As with the play and cortisol relationship, levels of cortisol greater than 200 $\mu g/dl$ were associated with depressed (but not eliminated) levels of huddling. Negative relationships were obtained between huddle and cortisol at each time point, but none was significant. These relationships are presented in Table 12.2.

TABLE 12.1.
Correlation of Measures for Play and Plasma Cortisol

Pair Condition	Measures	r	N	p
Original pairs	$CORT_0$, $PLAY_0$	−0.254	16	0.3500
Re-pair, week 1	$CORT_4$, $PLAY_4$	−0.562	16	0.0220
Re-pair, weeks 2–4	$CORT_5$, $PLAY_5$	−0.703	16	0.0017
All conditions	All of the above	−0.437	48	0.0017

TABLE 12.2.
Correlation of Measures for Huddling and Plasma Cortisol

Pair Condition	Measures	r	N	p
Original pairs	$CORT_0$, $HUDDLE_0$	−0.438	16	0.0907
Re-pair, week 1	$CORT_4$, $HUDDLE_4$	−0.405	16	0.1219
Re-pair, weeks 2–4	$CORT_5$, $HUDDLE_5$	−0.280	16	0.3002
All conditions	All of the above	−0.312	48	0.0303

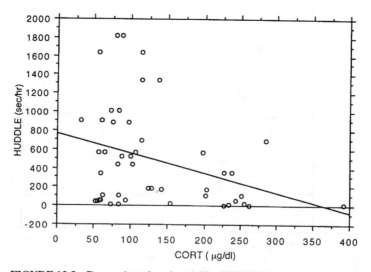

FIGURE 12.5.   Regression plot of variables HUDDLE and CORT, for all pair conditions, $Y = 763.457 - 2.09X$.

Play and Huddle

No significant correlations were obtained between the play and huddle variables.

DISCUSSION

Stress and Play

Examination of the relationship between play behavior and plasma cortisol levels (as an indirect measure of stress) was the main objective of this study. The hypothetical stressor was separation from a familiar peer and subsequent re-pairing with a similar but unfamiliar peer.

The adrenocortical response we observed with this paradigm bears inspection. Although the loss of a social companion and forced cohabitation with a stranger might reasonably be considered stressful for most species, cortisol levels obtained from the animals 4 hours after re-pairing were, on average, not significantly higher than baseline values, although the animals varied considerably in their stress responses. This somewhat counterintuitive finding is not unusual for squirrel monkeys (Mendoza, 1991). In several studies with both juvenile and adult squirrel monkeys, little change from basal plasma cortisol levels was seen in separations from familiar peers or introductions to strangers (Coe, Smith, & Levine, 1985; Hennessy, Mendoza, & Kaplan, 1982; Mendoza, Coe, Lowe, & Levine, 1979). Indeed, if animals were previously held in isolation, introduction to a social partner often resulted in a *reduction* in cortisol from basal levels, indicating that such social manipulation was perceived in a generally benign light, as befits a species where individuals separate and regroup repeatedly as they forage (Boinski, 1986). Over time, generally a matter of weeks, cortisol levels did gradually rise, and remained at a higher level than basal levels as newly paired animals established dominance relationships (Coe, et al., 1985; Mendoza, et al., 1979). These patterns are similar to those seen in the present study, with the highest cortisol levels occurring at 4 weeks after re-pairing. We had expected that the animals might adjust to each other after a few weeks together, but this did not happen. Instead, the highest cortisol values, lowest play scores, and by far the best negative correlation between play and cortisol were in the $CORT_5$ and $PLAY_5$ values. The failure of several of the pairs to adjust and the length of time needed to reach the highest observed cortisol levels suggest that, as in the previously mentioned studies, behavioral occurrences—such as polarized dominance relationships—may have developed as a result of interactions or fights that were not observed by us. Large differences in dominance are stressful under confined conditions and are not conducive to play (Biben, 1986, 1989; Imakawa, 1990).

The main effect of interest here, the observed correlation between plasma cortisol and playful behavior, was negative and linear for the data over all conditions. The weakest association was found in the baseline condition, for youngsters who had been housed together for many months, or from birth. In this condition, cortisol and play showed only a weak, nonsignificant negative relationship. We may speculate that the good negative correlation between play and stress in the re-paired animals, and the poorer correlation in those of long acquaintance, may derive from a certain level of accommodation that one may expect to find in a highly social primate such as the squirrel monkey. Although our baseline conditions were designed to provide as unstressful a situation as possible for the original pairs, there was a broad range among individuals in their cortisol levels, indicating that some animals were nonetheless stressed, or simply reflecting individual differences in physiology or stress response. The distribution of play among these familiar partners also showed much interindividual (or, more accurately, interpair) variability, reminding us that, as with human children, "personal compatibility" or "liking" is a largely unquantified, but still significant, factor influencing the frequency of play between any two individuals (Boulton, 1991).

Young primates generally choose play partners of similar age, size, sex, or motivation, but may be forced by circumstances to play with less well-matched partners (Cheney, 1978; Clarke, 1990). Their choices are ultimately based on the costs and benefits of play with particular partners, and the availability of alternative partners (Fagen, 1981). Captive animals who are forced to cohabitate may simply "go along to get along," and the disassociation of their expressed behavior from their emotional state may reflect this. It has been our observation that animals housed in pairs sometimes differ considerably in their apparent motivation to play, as evidenced by the frequency of each animal's play initiation behaviors. It is not uncommon to see one animal in a pair initiate nearly all the play bouts and to expend considerable effort to get only a fairly weak play response from the other. In such cases, it appears that the reluctant partner, like a beleaguered human parent or older sibling, may play with the insistent youngster just to get some peace. Thus, the inverse relationship that is so clear in the re-paired animals is probably the truer expression of the relationship between these two variables. In the re-paired animals, play was all but eliminated from the repertoire of those exhibiting the highest levels of cortisol, whereas long-time cagemates showed only a modest reduction in play when their cortisol levels were very high.

Young primates who are under stress exhibit depressed levels of many behaviors (Suomi, Collins, Harlow, & Ruppenthal, 1976; Suomi, Harlow, & Domek, 1970), regardless of the origin of the stress (e.g., separation from a social partner, poor health, poor nutrition, environmental danger, etc.). In the present study, levels of cortisol exceeding 200 μg/dl appeared to indicate an animal undergoing sufficient stress as to eliminate play and depress huddling.

Animals who are not experiencing high levels of stress are free to express any number of behaviors, but may not be motivated to do so. The strength of the linear relationship between play and cortisol is perhaps surprising in this respect, as it indicates that it is not simply the removal of stress that enables play to occur, but that animals feel ever more playful as stress is reduced. This apparent linearity of the relationship between stress and play is, of course, valid only if we know where on the continuum of stress response we have sampled. Specifically, it is the low stress situation that is in question.

Particularly boring environments or those with little or no social interaction possible may appear to be the least stressful ; however, it actually can be very stressful for an active, social species like the squirrel monkey (Mendoza, Coe, Lowe, & Levine, 1979) and their effect on later play is difficult to predict (Ikemoto & Panksepp, 1992). The failure of some, but not all, animals to show play after being raised in impoverished conditions suggests that some minimal level of stimulation, interaction, arousal, or stress is needed for play to occur—in other words, an inverted U-shaped relationship rather than a linear one. Aldis (1975) summarized several anecdotal reports, in a diversity of species, of temporary increases in play occurring in apparent response to some environmental event having slight fear or novelty value. Since both frightening and novel stimuli are stressors, we might conclude that a small dose of stress was beneficial for play, particularly if it was temporary. This describes a rather short-term relationship, usually stimulating play immediately (but sometimes delayed by a few hours [Moodie & Chamove, 1990]), with little information provided as to the relative overall playfulness of the involved animals, and does not necessarily conflict with the more basic, long-term relationship studied here.

It is difficult to assess whether a species that thrives in captivity, as *Saimiri* does, is more or less stressed in a captive versus a wild environment. In the present study, we made every effort to keep the environment low in stress, by, for example, housing subjects in a room where other squirrel monkeys were present and limiting entry to the holding rooms, except for routine maintenance. The subjects' housing conditions provided an environment suitable for play—a large cage, a young partner of similar age, and plenty of leisure time. Still, one can no more force animals to play than one can force human children to do so, and it is a testament to the robust nature of playful behavior that we did observe it, albeit in varying amounts, at such a range of measured stress response.

Stress and Huddling

The overall negative relationship between huddling and cortisol makes sense if stressed individuals are not relaxed enough to huddle. However, in the first week after re-pairing, at a time when cortisol levels rose and one pair fought, huddling time nearly doubled from baseline values (although the animals with the highest cortisol values had depressed levels of huddling). It thus appears that the fact of separation and re-pairing was viewed by most individuals in a more benign light than we had expected, at least to the point that they were able to rest in contact with the new companion and perhaps even find comfort in his or her presence. Play, on the other hand, may have been seen as a riskier encounter, as most were not willing to engage in it. After a few weeks had elapsed, social relationships became more polarized: those characterized by low stress were playful with a return to baseline levels of huddling, while highly stressed animals did not play or huddle with each other.

CONCLUSION

Exploring the relationship between stress and play is an investigation with both practical and theoretical ramifications. As a practical matter, anyone working with captive primates must, as the result of humane considerations and recent and pending legislation, assure the well-being of the animals in their care (Mason, 1989; Mendoza, 1991). Yet, few adequate assessment measures exist (Vandenbergh, 1989). One intuitive measure useful for, but not restricted to, young animals is the presence of play behavior. Because play is known to be quite sensitive to stressors, for example, play may be greatly curtailed in response to nutritional or environmental stress (Baldwin & Baldwin, 1974, 1976, 1978; Dunbar & Dunbar, 1992; Muller-Schwarze, Stagge, & Muller-Schwarze, 1982; Poole & Fish, 1975; Wolff, 1981), and, in some cases, to emotional stress like the loss of the mother, the presence of playful behavior is considered to be a sign of general well-being (Dukelow & Dukelow, 1989; Fagen, 1981, 1992). The present data support this assumption, and establishes a linear and negative relationship between the amount of play behavior and a potential measure of an animal's stress level. This may provide primatologists with an expedient and supportable measure of well-being, which is particularly useful, considering new mandates requiring pair housing of primates wherever possible. Pair housing acknowledges that primates, as social animals, need the companionship and social support of compatible partners to function optimally, both physiologically and behaviorally.

In the squirrel monkey, a species living in large social aggregations, affiliative relationships range from long-term, close friendships to more casual aquaintances (Biben, Symmes, & Masataka, 1986; Smith, Newman, & Symmes, 1982). We began the present study with established pairs who showed evidence of close affiliation and had expected that separation from the compatible partner and re-pairing with a new and relatively unfamiliar partner would be stressful for these animals. However, the pattern of cortisol changes after re-pairing revealed a more complex response than we had anticipated. While most individuals showed a modest increase in cortisol level immediately after re-pairing, levels continued to rise over the next several weeks for some, while declining in others. In a species where individuals encounter and interact with many others, the company of a relatively unfamiliar conspecific may be viewed with equanimity, becoming stressful only after the two fail to establish a closer affiliation, with no alternative outlet available for their affiliative needs. Thus, it is probably wise to monitor compatibility of pair-housed animals for at least several weeks after their introduction. If cagemates are not compatible, their inability to escape from each other may adversely affect their health and behavior—and the outcome of research endeavors.

On the theoretical side, our understanding of the motivational basis for play, and our ability to predict where and how play will occur, are still inadequate (Panksepp, Siviy, & Normansell, 1984; Pellis, 1991). Despite the ubiquity of play in young mammals, and its role as the chief means of social interaction between youngsters, play remains a poorly understood behavior with no clear "adaptive value" yet established. In humans, developmental and functional analyses of play have been the subject of clinical interest, particularly as a symptom and early predictor of psychopathology. Comparable studies of play in animals have been few, despite the common assumption that play in animals is an indicator of good mental as well as physical health. Therapists know that "play ... cannot be produced on demand,..." rather, it "...flourishes in environments that are experienced by the players themselves as familiar, safe, and nonthreatening" (Wood, 1996). The present experiments give us a better understanding of how an animal's physiological response to environmental conditions is likely to affect its play and may help explain and remedy situations where youngsters fail to show appropriate play.

REFERENCES

Aldis, O. (1975). *Play fighting.* New York: Academic Press.

Baldwin, J. D. (1969). The ontogeny of social behaviour of squirrel monkeys (*Saimiri sciureus*) in a seminatural environment. *Folia Primatologica, 11*, 35–79.

Baldwin, J. D. (1971). The social organization of a semifree-ranging troop of squirrel monkeys (*Saimiri sciureus*). *Folia Primatologica, 14*, 23–50.

Baldwin, J. D., & Baldwin, J. L. (1974). Exploration and social play in squirrel monkeys (*Saimiri*). *American Zoologist, 14*, 303–314.

Baldwin, J. D., & Baldwin, J. L. (1976). Effects of food ecology on social play: A laboratory simulation. *Zeitschrift fur Tierpsychologie, 40*, 1–14.

Baldwin, J. D., & Baldwin, J. L. (1978). Exploration and play in howler monkeys (*Alouatta palliata*). *Primates, 19*, 411–422.

Biben, M. (1986). Individual and sex-related strategies of wrestling play in captive squirrel monkeys. *Ethology, 71*, 229–241.

Biben, M. (1989). Effects of social environment on play in squirrel monkeys: Resolving Harlequin's Dilemma. *Ethology, 81*, 72–82.

Biben, M., & Suomi, S. (1993). Lessons from primate play. In K. B. MacDonald (Ed.), *Parent-child play: Descriptions & implications* (pp. 185–196). Albany, NY: State University of New York Press.

Biben, M., Symmes, D., & Masataka, N. (1986). Temporal and structural analysis of affiliative vocal exchanges in squirrel monkeys (*Saimiri sciureus*). *Behaviour, 98*, 259–273.

Boinski, S. (1986). The ecology of squirrel monkeys in Costa Rica (Doctoral dissertation, University of Texas at Austin, 1986). *Dissertation Abstracts International, 47*(05), 1893B.

Boulton, M. (1991). Partner preferences in middle school children's playful fighting and chasing: A test of some competing functional hypotheses. *Ethology and Sociobiology, 12*, 177–193.

Caine, N. G., & O'Boyle, V. J. (1992). Cage design and forms of play in red-bellied tamarins (*Saguinus labiatus*). *Zoo Biology, 11*, 215–220.

Cheney, D. L. (1978). The play partners of immature baboons. *Animal Behaviour, 26*, 1038–1050.

Chepko, B. D. (1971). A preliminary study of the effects of play deprivation on young goats. *Zeitschrift fur Tierpsychologie, 28*, 517–528.

Chivers, S., & Einon, D. (1982). Effects of early social experience on activity and object investigation in the ferret. *Developmental Psychobiology, 15*, 75–80.

Clarke, M. (1990). Behavioral development and socialization of infants in a free-ranging group of howling monkeys (*Alouatta palliata*). *Folia Primatologica, 54*, 1–15.

Coe, C. L., Franklin, D., Smith, E., & Levine, S. (1987). Hormonal responses and accompanying fear and agitation in the squirrel monkey. *Physiology and Behavior, 29*, 1051–1057.

Coe, C. L., Mendoza, S. P., Davidson, J. M., Smith, E. R., Dallman, M. F., & Levine, S. (1978). Hormonal response to stress in the squirrel monkey (*Saimiri sciureus*). *Neuroendocrinology, 26*, 367–377.

Coe, C. L., Smith, E. R., & Levine, S. (1985). The endocrine system of the squirrel monkey. In L. A. Rosenblum & C. L. Coe (Eds.), *Handbook of squirrel monkey research* (pp. 191–218). New York: Plenum Press.

Crepeau, L. J. (1989). The interactive influences of early handling, prior play exposure, acute stress, and sex on play behavior, exploration, and H-P-A reactivity in juvenile rats (Doctoral dissertation, Bowling Green State University, 1989). *Dissertation Abstracts International, 51*(03), 1133B.

Cummins, M. S., & Suomi, S. J. (1976). Long-term effects of social rehabilitation in rhesus monkeys. *Primates, 17*, 43–51.

Dukelow, W. R., & Dukelow, K. (1989). Reproductive and endocrinological measures of stress and nonstress in nonhuman primates. *American Journal of Primatology* (Suppl. 1), 17–24.

Dunbar, R., & Dunbar, P. (1992). Environmental influences on play behaviour in immature gelada baboons. *Animal Behavior, 44*, 111–115.

Fagen, R. M. (1981). *Animal play behavior*. New York: Oxford University Press.

Fagen, R. M. (1992). Play, fun, and communication of well-being. *Play and Culture, 5*, 40–58.

Govindarajulu, P., Hunte, W., Vermeer, L. A., & Horrocks, J. A. (1993). The ontogeny of social play in a feral troop of vervet monkeys (*Cercopithecus aethiops sabaeus*): The function of early play. *International Journal of Primatology, 14*, 701–719.

Hass, C. C., & Jenni, D. A. (1993). Social play among juvenile bighorn sheep: Structure, development, and relationship to adult behavior. *Ethology, 93*, 105–116.

Hennessy, M., & Levine, S. (1979). Stress, arousal, and the pituitary-adrenal system: A psychoendocrine hypothesis. In J. M. Sprague & A. N. Epstein (Eds.), *Progress in psychobiology and physiological psychology, vol. 8* (pp. 133–178). San Diego, CA: Academic Press.

Hennessy, M. B., Mendoza, S. P., & Kaplan, J. N. (1982). Behavior and plasma cortisol following brief peer separation in juvenile squirrel monkeys. *American Journal of Primatology, 3*, 143–151.

Humphreys, A. P., & Smith, P. K. (1987). Rough and tumble, friendship, and dominance in schoolchildren: Evidence for continuity and change with age. *Child Development, 58*, 201–212.

Ikemoto, S., & Panksepp, J. (1992). The effects of early social isolation on the motivation for social play in juvenile rats. *Developmental Psychobiology, 25*, 261–274.

Imakawa, S. (1990). Playmate relationships of immature free-ranging Japanese monkeys at Katsuyama. *Primates, 31*, 509–521.

MacDonald, K. (1993). Parent-child play: an evolutionary perspective. In K. B. MacDonald (Ed.), *Parent-child play: Descriptions & implications* (pp. 113–143). Albany, NY: State University of New York Press.

Mason, W. A. (1989). Primatology and primate well-being. *American Journal of Primatology* (Suppl. 1), 1–4.

Mendoza, S. (1991). Sociophysiology of well-being in nonhuman primates. *Laboratory Animal Science, 41*, 344–349.

Mendoza, S., Coe, C., Lowe, E., & Levine, S. (1979). The physiological response to group formation in adult male squirrel monkeys. *Psychoneuroendocrinology, 3*, 221–229.

Mendoza, S., Lyons, D., & Saltzman, W. (1991). Sociophysiology of squirrel monkeys. *American Journal of Primatology, 23*, 37–54.

Moodie, E. M., & Chamove, A. S. (1990). Brief threatening events beneficial for captive tamarins? *Zoo Biology, 9*, 275–286.

Muller-Schwarze, D. (1968). Play deprivation in deer. *Behaviour, 31*, 144–162.

Muller-Schwarze, D., Stagge, B., & Muller-Schwarze, C. (1982). Play behavior: Persistence, decrease, and energetic compensation during food shortage in deer fawns. *Science, 215*, 85–87.

O'Neill-Wagner, P., Bolig, R., & Price, C. (1994). Do play activity levels tell us something about psychosocial welfare in captive monkey groups? *Communication and Cognition, 3*, 261–272.

Panksepp, J., Siviy, S., & Normansell, L. (1984). The psychobiology of play: Theoretical and methodological perspectives. *Neuroscience and Biobehavioral Reviews, 8*, 465–492.

Pellis, S. (1991). How motivationally distinct is play? A preliminary case study. *Animal Behaviour, 42*, 851–853.

Pellis, S., & Pellis, V. (1987). Play-fighting differs from serious fighting in both target of attack and tactics of fighting in the laboratory rat *Rattus norvegicus*. *Aggressive Behavior, 13*, 227–242.

Poole, T., & Fish, J. (1975). An investigation of playful behaviour in *Rattus norvegicus* and *Mus musculus* (Mammalia). *Journal of Zoology, London, 175*, 61–71.

Rubin, K., Fein, G., & Vandenberg, B. (1983). Play. In P. H. Mussen (Series Ed.) & E. M. Hetherington (Vol. Ed.), *Handbook of child psychology, vol. 4. Socialization, personality, and social development* (pp. 694–774). New York: Wiley.

Smith, H. J., Newman, J. D., & Symmes, D. (1982). Vocal concomitants of affiliative behavior in squirrel monkeys (*Saimiri sciureus*). In C. T. Snowdon, C. H. Brown, & M. R. Peterson (Eds.), *Primate communication* (pp. 30–49). Cambridge, England: Cambridge University Press.

Smith, P. K. (1982). Does play matter? Functional and evolutionary aspects of animal and human play. *Behavioral and Brain Sciences, 5*, 139–155.

Smith, P. K., & Connally, K. (1972). Patterns of play and social interaction in pre-school children. In N. Blurton-Jones (Ed.), *Ethological studies of child behaviour* (pp. 65–95). Cambridge, England: Cambridge University Press.

Strayer, F., Bovenkerk, A., & Koopman, R. (1975). Social affiliation and dominance in captive squirrel monkeys (*Saimiri sciureus*). *Journal of Comparative and Physiological Psychology, 89*, 308–318.

Suomi, S. J., Collins, M. L., Harlow, H. F., & Ruppenthal, G. C. (1976). Effects of maternal and peer separations on young monkeys. *Journal of Child Psychology and Psychiatry, 17*, 101–112.

Suomi, S. J., Harlow, H. F., & Domek, C. J. (1970). Effect of repetitive infant-infant separation of young monkeys. *Journal of Abnormal Psychology, 76*, 161–172.

Symons, D. (1978). *Play and aggression: A study of rhesus monkeys.* New York: Columbia University Press.

Vandenbergh, J. G. (1989). Issues related to "psychological well-being" in nonhuman primates. *American Journal of Primatology* (Suppl. 1), 9–15.

Watson, D. M. (1993). The play associations of red-necked wallabies (*Macropus rufogriseus banksianus*) and relation to other social contexts. *Ethology, 94*, 1–20.

Wemelsfelder, F. I. G. (1993). The concept of animal boredom and its relationship to stereotyped behaviour. In A. Lawrence & J. Rushen (Eds.), *Stereotypic animal behaviour: Fundamentals and applications to welfare.* Wallingford, UK: CAB International.

Whiting, B. B., & Edwards, C. P. (1973). A cross-cultural analysis of sex differences in the behavior of children aged three to eleven. *Journal of Social Psychology, 91*, 171–188.

Wolff, R. J. (1981). Solitary and social play in wild *Mus musculus* (Mammalia). *Journal of Zoology London, 195*, 405–412.

Wood, W. (1996). The value of studying occupation: An example with primate play. *American Journal of Occupational Therapy, 50*, 327–337.

13

Play and Attachment Behavior of Peer-Only Reared and Surrogate/Peer-Reared Rhesus Monkey Infants in their Social Groups[*]

Maribeth Champoux
Courtney Shannon
Wendy D. Airoso
Stephen J. Suomi
National Institutes of Health

The integral interaction between the development of play behaviors and infant rearing condition has been amply demonstrated in laboratory-reared nonhuman primates. For example, infant rhesus macaques reared with no exposure to peers during the first six months of life exhibit inappropriate play behaviors upon their initial introduction to agemates. Animals which are raised with only a mother, and no peers, are hyper-aggressive and overly cautious toward agemates (Alexander & Harlow, 1965). In contrast, monkeys reared in isolation respond to peers with fear, submission, and total

* We would like to thank Carilyn Aleman, Alan Dodson, Amit Garg, Chip Hamilton, Mariken Hasert, Jo Hess, Ted King, Jr., and Alyssa Rulf for their assistance in data collection. We are grateful to Dr. Dee Higley for his support and encouragement, and to two anonymous reviewers for their suggested improvements on the manuscript. This research was conducted as part of the Intramural Research Program of the National Institute of Child Health and Human Development.

inhibition of play behavior (Harlow, Rowland, & Griffin, 1964). Access to peers during infancy does not guarantee normative play development, however: Rhesus monkeys reared *only* with peers exhibit delayed maturation of species-typical play patterns (Chamove, Rosenblum, & Harlow, 1973). The optimal laboratory environment for rhesus monkey play development includes mothers, adults, and other peers; rhesus infants raised in these environments exhibit the most sophisticated play repertoires (Ruppenthal, Harlow, Eisele, Harlow, & Suomi, 1974).

Experimental protocols, or maternal rejection or illness, occasionally necessitate nursery rearing of primate infants. Nursery rearing involves balancing the requirements of animal husbandry with the desire to facilitate optimum social development. Although primate infants have been reared in nurseries for decades, debate still continues regarding the "best" method of socialization. Infants have been reared in individual housing with controlled access to peers (Rosenblum, 1961; Ruppenthal, Walker, & Sackett, 1991), in peer dyads (Chamove, Rosenblum, & Harlow, 1973; Ruppenthal, et al., 1991), in peer groups (Chamove, et al., 1973) and in peer groups containing inanimate "surrogate mothers"(Duijghuisen, Timmermans, Voctheloo, & Vossen, 1992).

Full-time peer access, whether in a dyad or in a larger peer group, tends to promote intense attachment to the social partner(s) (Higley, Hopkins, Thompson, Byrne, Hirsch, & Suomi, 1992; Ruppenthal, Walker, & Sackett, 1991). This attachment is manifested by the hallmark "choo-choo" clinging arrangement observed in peer groups and by mutual ventral clinging in peer dyads. It is likely that the clinging of full-time peer-reared monkeys contributes to the well-documented delay in development of play and sexual behaviors (e.g., Chamove, Rosenblum, & Harlow, 1973; Ruppenthal, et al., 1991), due to the competing motor demands of clinging and peer play. In contrast, animals reared with inanimate surrogate mothers or with controlled peer access develop behavioral repertoires that are more similar to those exhibited by mother-reared monkeys (Chamove, et al., 1973).

In this study, we compared the social and nonsocial behaviors of monkeys in two rearing conditions: group peer-only reared, and individually housed with an inanimate surrogate mother and controlled peer access. Whereas in previous studies animals were observed outside their home cages in primate playrooms, we observed animals in their home cages or home rooms. We believed the familiarity of the home cage/home room environment would allow a more accurate assessment of their behavior unconfounded by the effects of novelty. In addition, the animals in this study were provided access to peers for 2–3 hours daily, which differs substantially from the 30-minute socialization period utilized in most other studies (e.g., Chamove, Rosenblum, & Harlow, 1973; Rosenblum, 1961; Ruppenthal, Walker, & Sackett, 1991). On the basis of previous findings, we anticipated that the surrogate/peer-reared monkeys would engage in higher levels of play, and less clinging and proximity, than would the peer-only reared infants.

METHOD

Subjects

Subjects were 56 nursery-reared rhesus macaque infants. The infants were separated from their mothers on days 1–3 postpartum and reared according to the procedure described by Ruppenthal (1979). From days 1–15 of life, animals were individually housed in plastic cages measuring 51 × 38 × 43 centimeters. Each cage contained an inanimate "surrogate mother," 25 centimeters in height, composed of a polypropylene cylinder, 16.5 centimeters in circumference, attached to an 11.5-centimeter-wide circular metal base by a flexible metal component. The surrogate mother was covered with an electric heating pad, which was itself covered with fleece fabric. Loose pieces of fleece fabric covered the floor of the cage. The internal temperature was maintained at approximately 27° C. Infants could see and hear, but could not have physical contact, with other infants. At 15 days of age, the infants were moved to another, larger room into individual wire mesh cages measuring 64 × 61 × 76 centimeters. The animals retained their surrogate mothers covered with fleece, albeit minus the heating pad. As in the earlier housing condition, the animals were in visual, auditory, and olfactory contact, but not in tactile contact with other infants. Lights were on from 7:00 a.m. to 8:00 p.m. Room temperature was kept between 22–26° C, and humidity was maintained at 50–55%.

The animals were provided with a 50:50 mixture of Similac (manufactured by Ross Laboratories, in Columbus, Ohio) and Primilac (Bio-Serv, Inc., Frenchtown, New Jersey) formulas. They were hand-fed until they were old enough to independently feed themselves. Formula was administered ad libitum until 4 months of age, at which time the animals were placed on a ration of 300 ml/day of formula. At age 5 months, they received 200 ml/day, and at 6 months they were weaned from the formula. Purina High Protein monkey chow (#5038) and water were provided ad libitum when they reached one month of age.

Socialization commenced when the animals reached 37 days of age. All animals were housed and socialized in the same large colony room. Peer-only reared monkeys (PR; $n = 29$, seven groups) were permanently placed into groups consisting of 4–5 similar-aged infants in 71 × 81 × 152-centimeter cages. Surrogate/peer-reared infants (SPR; $n = 27$, six groups) were housed individually with their surrogates in 64 × 61 × 76-centimeter cages for 21–22 hours each day, receiving 2–3 hours of interaction each day within groups of 4–5 peers in a 71 × 81 × 152-centimeter cage in the home room. Animals were hand-caught by nursery personnel and carried to and from the socialization cage. The SPR infants had access to their surrogates during the socialization and individual cage conditions. Apart from the differences in the housing and socialization procedures, PR and SPR monkeys were treated identically.

Data Collection and Analysis

Behavioral data collection commenced when the animals were approximately 2 months old and continued until the youngest group member was approximately 6 months of age. Behavioral data were collected twice weekly, for 5 minutes per animal, using a portable laptop computer. Animals were observed between 10:00 a.m. and 3:00 p.m. SPR monkeys were observed while in the social group after being placed into their group by the nursery personnel and given at least 5 minutes to adapt before behavioral observations were initiated.

Using a focal animal scoring system, we assessed total duration and total frequency of 14 social and nonsocial behaviors, listed in Table 13.1. Operational definitions of behaviors were derived from Hansen (1962) and Rosenblum (1961), and are described in Harlow and Harlow (1965). All observers were trained to a reliability criterion of 0.95 agreement (Pearson product-moment coefficient) across all behavior categories.[1]

TABLE 13.1.
Definition Of Behaviors

Ventral cling	Ventral contact with another animal.
Self-groom	Grooming of one's own body, self-scratching, biting or cleaning nails.
Self-clasp	Firm manual or pedal gripping of self which is not a component of an ongoing behavior, i.e., self-groom.
Self-mouth	Sucking (not biting) at own bodily appendage or fur.
Environmental exploration	Any manual, pedal, or oral examination, exploration, or manipulation of the physical environment. Includes manipulating or playing with chow while eating, and also drinking.
Locomotor stereotypy	Any repetitive, patterned, and rhythmic locomotor movement across the substrate. Includes changes in location through walking, running, dropping from ceiling to floor, rolling, hopping on all fours, bouncing around the cage, and "displays." Only scored after 3 repetitions of the act; thereafter scored whenever it occurs.
Nonlocomotor stereotypy	Idiosyncratic nonlocomotor stereotyped actions such as repetitively saluting, picking the teeth, or strumming the mesh. Only scored after 3 repetitions of the act; thereafter scored whenever it occurs.
Passive	Absence of all social, exploratory, and locomotor behavior. May be scored with self categories and vocalization only. Includes sleeping, resting, bouncing in place, and cage shakes.
Locomotion	Any self-induced change in location. Includes changes in location through walking, running, dropping from ceiling to floor, rolling, hopping on all fours, bouncing around the cage, and "displays."
Proximity	Includes proximity (sitting, standing, locomoting, or lying within arm's reach of another animal), groom, and receive groom. Also includes any oral, pedal, or manual exploration of another animal; and receiving any such exploration/grooming from another monkey.

TABLE 13.1. (continued)
Definition Of Behaviors

Play	Performance of any social play behavior, including: initiating play by "play face," nonaggressive chasing, tagging, swatting, bobbing, biting, pulling, lunging, mouthing, wrestling (rough and tumble), or receiving play from another animal. Quasisexual behaviors such as mounting another animal, whether appropriately or inappropriately oriented, with or without thrusting. Mount attempts and presenting or receiving a mount from another animal are also included.
Aggression	Performance of aggressive behaviors, such as bites, hair pulls, aggressive chases, threats, hitting, or slapping.
Receive aggression	Receipt of aggressive behaviors.
Vocalizations	Any vocal sound emitted by the monkey, except coughing and sneezing.

The data from weeks 11 through 26 of life were averaged into four 4-week blocks for analysis (before week 11, not all animals had been observed). The averaged values were analyzed using 2 (Rearing: Peer versus Surrogate Reared) by 4 (Block) repeated measures univariate analyses of variance. Univariate analyses were performed to allow analysis with missing data points (e.g., due to animals leaving the study before 6 months of age). Significant interactions were analyzed by t-test. Behaviors of aggression, receive aggression, locomotor stereotypy, and nonlocomotor stereotypy occurred too infrequently to be analyzed.

RESULTS

There were significant effects of rearing condition for behaviors of ventral cling, self-mouth, locomotion, proximity, social play, and vocalization. As shown in Table 13.2, PR animals spent more time clinging and in proximity to other monkeys than did the SPR animals. They also self-mouthed more often and vocalized more frequently than did the SPR monkeys. In contrast, the SPR infants engaged in more locomotion and play activity than did the PR monkeys. In addition, there was a Block by Rearing interaction for passive behavior. As Figure 13.1 demonstrates, SPR monkeys spent more time in passive behavior than did PR monkeys during Blocks 1 [$t(50) = -1.95, p = .055$] and 2 [$t(48) = -2.11, p < .05$] only. Both groups spent equivalent amounts of time in self-groom, self-clasping, and environmental exploration.

TABLE 13.2.
Behavior of Peer-only Reared and Surrogate/Peer-Reared Monkey Infants

Behavior	Rearing Condition		F (1,54)
	Peer-only	Surrogate/peer	
Ventral cling	29.5 (3.9)	10.6 (1.6)	7.72**
Proximity	162.8 (5.0)	81.2 (3.2)	84.4**
Self-mouth	75.0 (5.1)	17.0 (1.9)	37.06**
Locomotion	44.5 (1.8)	88.5 (3.7)	40.87**
Play	7.9 (1.1)	35.0 (2.0)	64.58**
Environmental explore	60.7 (2.8)	63.5 (2.4)	0.19, n.s.
Self-clasp	2.06 (0.4)	0.8 (0.3)	1.66, n.s.
Self-groom	7.2 (0.8)	5.3 (1.3)	0.60, n.s
Vocalization	6.3 (1.1)	1.6 (0.4)	5.64*

Note: Values represent mean duration (sec) except vocalization. Vocalization values represent average frequency (5 min session). Standard errors in parentheses.
* $p < .05$. ** $p < .01$.

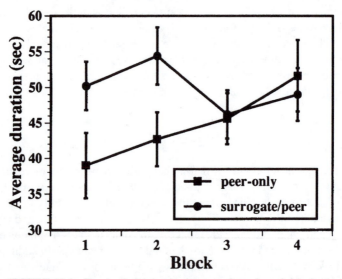

FIGURE 13.1. Passive behavior (sec) across four 4-week blocks in peer-only reared and surrogate/peer-reared infant rhesus monkeys.

DISCUSSION

The results of this study demonstrate that the nature of the social relationships between SPR monkeys in their social group differs from that of PR monkeys. As anticipated, the SPR monkeys engaged in more social play than the PR monkeys.

Additionally, as expected, the SPR monkeys displayed less ventral clinging and less proximity to peers than did the PR infants. It should be noted that although the inanimate surrogate mothers were present in the socialization cage, the SPR infants spent very little time clinging to them (or to each other). SPR infants in the individual cages do cling ventrally to the surrogate, but engage in very little play behavior with the surrogate (personal observation). They are therefore effectively partitioning their social behaviors between filial attachment to the surrogate and play behavior with peers. A similar pattern is not observed in the PR monkey infants. It therefore appears as if the nature of the relationships of SPR infants is more similar to that observed in mother-reared monkeys than are the relationships of PR infants, in that they have developed separate maternal attachment and peer play motivational systems (as outlined in Harlow & Harlow, 1965).

It has been demonstrated that peer-only reared animals develop an attachment relationship to their peer partners (Higley, et al., 1992). This relationship has been characterized as anxious attachment, because peers are not effective sources of response-contingent feedback and therefore do not promote attachment security. Animals that are individually housed with surrogates direct their attachment to the surrogate, as has been demonstrated in several species using animate and inanimate surrogate figures (squirrel monkey: Kaplan, 1974; rhesus monkey: Mason & Capitanio, 1988; cynomolgus monkey: Timmermans, Röder, & Kemps, 1988). It should be noted, however, that these attachment relationships appear to differ from the attachment relationship with the mother (e.g., Hennessy, Kaplan, Mendoza, Lowe, & Levine, 1979; Meyer, Novak, Bowman, & Harlow, 1975). When surrogate-reared animals are socialized, they should be free to engage in species-normative play behaviors with peers, as they are not regarding their peers as their attachment figures.

Some nonsocial behaviors differentiated the SPR and PR monkeys as well. The SPR infants exhibited twice as much locomotion as the PR monkeys. Locomotion in the social context incorporates elements of motion play, such as hopping, twisting, and bouncing. In addition, the PR monkeys exhibited more self-mouthing and vocalizations than the SPR monkeys. These behaviors are often considered indices of stress or arousal (Mineka & Suomi, 1978). It is possible that the anxious/ambivalent nature of the PR monkeys' attachment relationships are being reflected in higher levels of these putative distress behaviors, even under baseline (nonchallenged) conditions.

An implication of the results of this study is that the presence of a secure attachment base facilitates play interactions with peers in rhesus monkey infants. Parallel findings have been reported for human infants (see Cassidy & Berlin, 1994): inhibited environmental exploration and peer play have been correlated with insecure attachment. Although not a part of the present study, formal assessment of attachment classification using a version of the Strange Situation has differentiated mother-reared and peer-only reared juvenile rhesus monkeys, with peer-only reared animals showing clear evidence of insecure attachments (Higley, et al., 1992). We therefore anticipate that the consequences of differential rearing conditions will continue to be expressed in future years as the PR and SPR animals mature and forge their affiliative and parental relationships.

NOTE

[1] Because behavioral observations were conducted as they occurred (i.e., were not scored from videotape), it was necessary for observers to make rapid judgments differentiating behaviors that may have resembled each other motorically. In particular, discriminating between social play and certain other behaviors (e.g., social aggression, locomotion) requires extensive training (see Bekoff, 1976, for a review of this issue). When training new personnel to observe infant social play, particular emphasis is placed on such metacommunicative signals as play faces, relaxed posture, and a "bouncy" quality of locomotion, as well as role reversal.

REFERENCES

Alexander, B. K., & Harlow, H. F. (1965). Social behavior of juvenile rhesus monkeys subjected to different rearing conditions during the first 6 months of life. *Zoologische Jahrbucher Physiologie, 60*, 167–174.

Bekoff, M. (1976). Animal play: Problems and perspectives. In P. P. G. Bateson & P. H. Klopfer (Eds.), *Perspectives in ethology, vol. 2* (pp. 165–188). New York: Plenum Press.

Cassidy, J., & Berlin, L. J. (1994). The insecure/ambivalent pattern of attachment: Theory and research. *Child Development, 65*, 971–991.

Chamove, A. S., Rosenblum, L. A., & Harlow, H. F. (1973). Monkeys (*Macaca mulatta*) raised only with peers: A pilot study. *Animal Behaviour, 21*, 316–325.

Duijghuisen, J. A. H., Timmermans, P. J. A., Voctheloo, J. D., & Vossen, J. M. H. (1992). Mobile surrogate mothers and the development of exploratory behavior and radius of action in infant long-tailed macaques (*Macaca fascicularis*). *Developmental Psychobiology, 25*, 441–459.

Hansen, E. W. (1962). The development of maternal and infant behavior in the rhesus monkey (Doctoral dissertation, University of Wisconsin). *Dissertation Abstracts International, 23*, 2219.

Harlow, H. F., & Harlow, M. K. (1965). The affectional systems. In A. M. Schrier, H. F. Harlow, & F. Stollnitz (Eds.), *Behavior of nonhuman primates* (pp. 287–334). New York: Academic Press.

Harlow, H. F., Rowland, G. L., & Griffin, G. A. (1964). The effect of total social deprivation on the development of monkey behavior. *Psychiatric Research Report, 19*, 116–135.

Hennessy, M. B., Kaplan, J. N., Mendoza, S. P., Lowe, E. L., & Levine, S. (1979). Separation distress and attachment in surrogate-reared squirrel monkeys. *Physiology and Behavior, 23*, 1017–1023.

Higley, J. D., Hopkins, W. D., Thompson, W. W., Byrne, E. A., Hirsch, R. M., & Suomi, S. J. (1992). Peers as primary attachment sources in yearling rhesus monkeys (*Macaca mulatta*). *Developmental Psychology, 28*, 1163–1171.

Kaplan, J. (1974). Growth and behavior of surrogate-reared squirrel monkeys. *Developmental Psychobiology, 7,* 7–13.

Mason, W. A., & Capitanio, J. P. (1988). Formation and expression of filial attachment in rhesus monkeys raised with living and inanimate mother substitutes. *Developmental Psychobiology, 21,* 401–430.

Meyer, J. S., Novak, M. A., Bowman, R. E., & Harlow, H. F. (1975). Behavioral and hormonal effects of attachment object separation in surrogate-peer-reared and mother-reared infants. *Developmental Psychobiology, 8,* 425–435.

Mineka, S., & Suomi, S. J. (1978). Social separation in monkeys. *Psychological Bulletin, 85,* 1376–1400.

Rosenblum, L. A. (1961). The development of social behavior in the rhesus monkey. (Doctoral dissertation, University of Wisconsin). *Dissertation Abstracts International, 22,* 926–927.

Ruppenthal, G. C. (1979). Survey of protocols for nursery rearing infant macaques. In G. C. Ruppenthal (Ed.), *Nursery care of nonhuman primates* (pp. 165–185). New York: Plenum Press.

Ruppenthal, G. C., Harlow, M. K., Eisele, C. D., Harlow, H. F., & Suomi, S. J. (1974). Development of peer interactions of monkeys reared in a nuclear-family environment. *Child Development, 45,* 670–682.

Ruppenthal, G. C., Walker, C. G., & Sackett, G. P. (1991). Rearing infant monkeys (*Macaca nemestrina*) in pairs produces deficient social development compared with rearing in single cages. *American Journal of Primatology, 25,* 103–113.

Timmermans, P. J. A., Röder, E. L., & Kemps, A. M. L. J. (1988). Rearing cynomolgus monkeys (*Macaca fascicularis*) on surrogate mothers with bottle feeding. *Laboratory Animals, 22,* 229–234.

14

Observations of Free-Play Behavior in Captive Juvenile Bottlenose Dolphins (*Tursiops truncatus*)*

Theia C. DeLong
Millersville University

Dolphins have fascinated and captured the imagination and curiosity of humans for centuries. They are of particular interest to behavioral researchers because of their social complexity, large brain size, and capacity for learning. Observing dolphins in the wild is difficult due to poor water clarity, weather conditions, and the behavior of the dolphins themselves. Observations in a zoo or aquarium environment cannot be used in place of observations in the wild to determine dolphin behavior patterns because a captive environment may constrain and/or modify behavior and social patterns that typically occur outside of captivity. However, there is evidence that species-typical behaviors are present in the captive environment (Dufran & Pryor, 1980). Captive observations can provide useful insight and details on behavior and activity patterns, such as parental care, that are almost impossible to collect in the wild (Reid, Mann, Weiner, & Hecker, 1995; Reiss & McCowan, 1993; Renjun, Gewalt, Neurohr, & Winkler, 1994).

---

* Funding for this research was provided by the Alex Henderson Scholarship, Millersville University. Thank you to Nedra Hecker and Drs. Samuel J. Ha, Julie W. Ambler, Guy L. Steucek, Alice M. Meckley, and Susan P. Luek for their help and support. A special thank you to the mammalogists at the National Aquarium in Baltimore's Marine Mammal Pavilion for their time and the use of their facilities.

This study examines the behavioral patterns and interactions of two *Tursiops truncatus* juveniles: one male named Cobie, and one female named Chesapeake (Chessie) at the National Aquarium In Baltimore (NAIB), in Maryland. These two juveniles belonged to a nursery group of five bottlenose dolphins that also included their two mothers—Hailey and Shiloh—and the dominant female—Nani. Five questions were used to develop the study and were chosen to be the focus of the study after all observations were gathered: Are there differences between the two juveniles in 1) activity patterns throughout the day; 2) activity patterns from day to day; 3) amount of time spent in different activities; 4) selection of interaction partners; and 5) instigation of interactions? Initial observations of the dolphins resulted in the following hypotheses:

1. The majority of the juveniles' time is spent in some form of play behavior.
2. More play behavior occurs between the juveniles themselves and Nani than with their mothers.
3. More play behaviors occur between the two juveniles and Nani than just between the two juveniles.

Development of social behaviors is essential to the development of juvenile dolphins. As in the majority of mammalian species, social play behavior is the first non-mother-directed form of social behavior (Vanderschuran, Niesink, Spruijt, & Van Ree, 1993). While the majority of their resting time is in the company of their mothers, the calves will spend increasingly more time away from their mother as they grow older (Reid, Mann, Weiner, & Hecker, 1995). This time away is spent socializing with other calves and adults in their group. Bottlenose dolphins mature enough to leave their mothers at about five years of age (Slijper, 1976). Both juvenile males and females leave the nursery group at approximately this age to join a coalition of young adults: males join a group of subadult males, and females join a group of females who are without young (Johnson & Norris, 1986). The males will eventually form a pair bond with one other male; these pairs may form loose "coalitions" once the males mature, at about 13 years of age (Ridgway, 1986). Females return to the original pod with their mothers, taking their place in the dominance hierarchy. In captivity, where there are groups of both sexes, males dominate. Therefore, young dolphins' abilities to relate socially with other dolphins is crucial, and must be developed before they can mature and join the adult hierarchy. This social ability in mammals is intricately related to, and developed through, play behavior between the juveniles and other juveniles or adults in their nursery group, or later on, in their peer group (Hughes, 1991).

For human children, play and peer social interaction (nonmother) are preferred and predominant activities. During social play, children use both verbal and non-verbal signaling to maintain social play construction (Meckley, 1995). Like human children, the play behavior of animals is characterized by an element of pretense through signaling. The most distinctive feature of animal play is that it "involves taking skills ordinarily displayed in one context and applying them in contexts in which their true function cannot be achieved" (Fagen, 1984, p. 160). It is a simulated type of activity that allows a player to experiment with behaviors without having to face serious consequences, and to practice skills that may be of use in other areas of life. Chalmers and Locke-Haydon (1985) found a relationship in small mammals between the amount of play and the possession of various skills, such as agility and the ability to compete for food.

The structure and context of play suggests its use as a form of skill development through practice. An individual's creation of training sequences under these non-threatening conditions allows for the testing of combinations of behaviors and learning from mistakes made. For the observer, interpretation of behavior and context combinations in play that are not directly associated with the skill being perfected can be difficult to explain. Fagen (1981) has compiled principle subroutines in play that are utilized in skill development hierarchies, and that may prove valuable in interpretation of those subroutines.

One of these principles states that "sometimes, effective practice, even for skills not involving social interaction, must involve other organisms" (Fagen, 1981, p. 321). This principle is true in bottlenose dolphins. Play behaviors are observed in both young and adults of this species, as well as in other cetaceans both in the wild and in captivity. Play behavior is only a characteristic of those species whose predatory pressures are not great, and who do not have to spend all their available energy gathering food and surviving (Breland & Breland, 1966). Animals in captivity do not need to search for or capture prey. This may explain why they engage in many forms and high frequency of play (Schusterman, Thomas, & Wood, 1986). Play may involve members of its own species, other species and material objects (Slijper, 1976). Juveniles commonly take part in social play behaviors that may look aggressive, but may actually be practicing "the real thing." Another principle states that "movements should be broken down and practiced in parts" (Fagen, 1981, p. 321). These "practice" behaviors for dominance may include tail slapping, head butting, and jaw snapping (Slijper, 1976). In mammals, play is often linked with elements of aggression, such as chasing, hitting, and biting.

Play aggression may indicate the maturity of an animal, since it increases as the animal matures. This increase is especially true at the time when the individual matures enough to establish a position in a dominance hierarchy. Play fighting promotes higher social interaction and cognitive skills, which are positive characteristics in a social situation. Since males are usually higher in the dominance hierarchy in captivity, the observation that males engage in more play fights than females is not surprising (Hughes, 1991). This holds true in all species of apes and monkeys studied thus far, as well as in other animals. This could be a genetically-based difference, because exposure to increased levels of male hormone during pregnancy seems to predispose a variety of species (such as monkeys and rats) to enjoy rough and tumble play (Meaney, 1988; Symons, 1978). In children, play aggression (rough and tumble play) includes such categories as "hit at," "play fight," and "chase" (Pellegrini, 1989).

In dolphins, real aggression behaviors include the snapping of jaws, a sharp jerk of the tail, biting, swatting, and ramming (Johnson & Norris, 1986). Mouthing, chasing, and tail slapping are three categories that are used in real aggression, but are also used as play aggression by dolphins. These categories are sometimes accompanied by bubble blowing with the blowhole in both marine and river dolphins (Johnson & Norris, 1986; Renjun, Gewalt, Neurohr, & Winkler, 1994; Slooten, 1994).

Two scales used to categorize play behavior in children may be of interest to those studying the play behavior of juvenile bottlenose dolphins. In 1962, Jean Piaget proposed a theory of children's intellectual development that included four categories of play on the cognitive level (Piaget, 1962; Rubin, Maioni, & Hornung, 1976; Rubin, Watson, & Jambor, 1978): functional play (repetitive muscle movement with or without objects), constructive play (using objects or materials to make something), dramatic play (role-playing and make-believe transformations), and games with rules (recognition and acceptance of and conformity with pre-established rules). Parten, in a 1932 study, developed three main categories of play on a social level (Parten, 1932; Rubin, et al., 1976; Rubin, et al., 1978). These categories include solitary, group, and parallel play, the last of which involves children playing with objects or engaging in activities similar to those of other children in close proximity, but not interacting with those other children. These cognitive and social levels of play development may also be relevant to analyzing developmental patterns of juvenile bottlenose dolphin play behavior if the juveniles can be identified as exhibiting some or all of these categories.

METHOD

Participants

The nursery group consists of five dolphins: one dominant female and two mothers and their calves. Nani, the dominant female, is 24 years old, and weighs about 580 pounds. Hailey, mother of the male juvenile, is second in the dominance hierarchy and is 18 years old. Cobie, the male juvenile, gains his dominance position from his mother. Born on March 26, 1992, he is four years old, and weighs 300 pounds. Shiloh, the mother of the female juvenile, is below the other two adults in dominance, 18 years old, and weighs about 385 pounds. Chesapeake, the female juvenile at the bottom of the dominance hierarchy, was born on March 7, 1992, and weighs about 301 pounds. Both calves are near the age where they would leave the nursery group to join a group of mixed young. Cobie would eventually form a pair bond with one other male, and Chessie would eventually go back to her mother's group (N. Hecker, personal communication, February 1, 1996).

Nani came to the NAIB in 1990. Hailey and Shiloh have been together since they were both collected in Mississippi Sound in 1982, and came to the NAIB in 1990. Both juveniles were born at the NAIB.

Facilities

The NAIB pool system is a circular, 1.3 million-gallon (100 feet in diameter) marine mammal pool system made up of three main pools, listed in order of decreasing size: the main exhibition pool (ExP), comprising half of the entire area; the back left holding pool (HP1), two-thirds of the remaining half; and the back right holding pool (HP2), making up slightly less than the remaining third. Dolphins in HP2 also had access to a fourth, smaller medical pool (the gate between the two pools was usually open). Observations were made from an underwater viewing area in the center of the entire pool system, and from the public exhibition window of this system in ExP. All observations in the main exhibition tank were made from the public window, and those in the other pools were made from the underwater observation area. No direct view into the small medical pool was available, so all of the observations of behaviors in that pool were made from the underwater observation area through the gate that connected it to HP2.

Each of the two pools was divided into sections for the sake of determining general placement in the pools for each behavior. ExP, the main exhibition pool, was divided into six sections; the semicircular area was divided lengthwise into two sections, and then again crosswise into thirds (#1–6). HP2 was divided into four quadrants (#1–4), with the connecting medical pool being labeled as section #5.

Apparatus

All observations in this study were recorded on paper, using an ethogram designed specifically for this study. This ethogram recorded the animal observed, the date, the pool, the number of respirations during the five-minute period before observation began, the time, the numbered location in the pool, the activity, and any additional comments. Activity categories utilized in this study included "play" (P), "chasing" (C), "mouthing" (M), "touching" (T), "infant" (I), "quiet" (Q), "tail slap" (TS), "other" (O), and "could not see" (CNS) (see Table 14.1). Multiple activities could be recorded in one observation. Video recordings, made on January 25, 1996, February 1, 1996, and February 29, 1996, were used to review certain behaviors again in more detail. A Nikon Action-8 VN-350 8mm video camera recorder was used to make these recordings on Maxell 8mm 120 GX-MP videotapes. Footage was then transferred to Scotch performance high grade T-120 videocassettes. Photographs of behaviors were taken on Kodak 400- and 1000-speed film using a Nikon N6006 camera.

Procedure

Observations were recorded on every Tuesday from September 7, 1995, to November 28, 1995 (except on November 7), and on January 25, 1996, and February 1, 1996. On October 10, 1995, only Cobie was observed. A continuous method of

Table 14.1.
Definitions of Behaviors Observed During the Study

Behavior	Definitions
Play (P)	Juvenile activities with things in the environment (may also include other animals), including objects (things in the environment other than animals to play with, i.e., hoop, sprinkler, ball), bubble-blowing, and "King-of-the-Mountain." "King-of-the-Mountain" usually occurred in the main exhibition tank (place play). This beaching of a dolphin out of the water onto a platform may also include other individuals' attempts to beach themselves and/or attempts to push whichever dolphin is on the platform off into the water.
Chasing (C)	Pursuit or following of one dolphin by another at speeds faster than that of mother/juvenile pairs infant swimming or Nani swimming around the pool alone.
Mouthing (M)	Contact or attempted contact between the open mouth of one dolphin and any part of another dolphin (or object). Mouth warring is when two dolphins are positioned face to face, sparring with open mouths.
Touching (T)	Any physical contact between any body part of one dolphin and any body part of another dolphin (not including mouthing or prenursing touching of the juvenile's melon to its mother's abdomen).
Infant (I)	Activities between only the mother and her juvenile. Swimming with the mother (below, above and back, or next to—not forward of), any attempt or successful nursing, or touching of juvenile's melon to its mother's abdomen (prenursing).
Quiet (Q)	Juvenile swimming slowly or resting at the surface alone, swimming forward of its mother, or swimming slowly with its mother and other individuals.
Tail slap (TS)	One dolphin bringing its tail down forcefully on some part of another dolphin, frequently the head. Can produce a loud noise if done at the surface of the water.
Other (O)	Any behavior or activity not included in any other category (i.e., sexual play).
Could not see (CNS)	When the individual being observed was out of the viewing range of the observer.

Note: Behaviors observed during the study. The activity category names were developed for use in this study only, and may not correspond to behavior names used by other authors.

sampling was used, recording location, behavior, and interactions every two minutes. All observations were made between 10:00 a.m. and 4:00 p.m., broken up by shows. Observations were collected during the dolphins' free time, with no trainers immediately present and when all five individuals in the nursery group were together. A juvenile was randomly chosen for each period of observation. Total observation time was 666 minutes (333 observations) for Chessie, and 656 minutes (328 observations) for Cobie. The total observation times, in minutes, of the juveniles in each pool were as follows: Chessie ExP-354, HP2-312; Cobie ExP-282, HP2-374.

Data Reduction

Due to a show involving the males in the main pool, observations of the nursery group in HP2 were not used in calculating results, since the presence of the trainers in the immediate vicinity and the responses of the audience to the show may have affected the behavior of the nursery group. Each show was about 30 minutes in length, and show times varied by month. September and November shows within the observation period occurred at 11:30 a.m. and 2:00 p.m. October shows within the observation period occurred at 11:30 a.m., 1:00 p.m., and 3:00 p.m.

Observations made while the nursery group was in HP1 (January 25, 1996) were not used in the calculations, because the males are usually kept there when they are not in the main tank (ExP). This may have affected the behavior of the members of the nursery group; being at the age where he is challenging his dominance position, the juvenile male was observed doing some behaviors not observed in other pools, such as forcefully slamming himself up against the platform edge as he swam by. Also, because of construction (jack-hammering) in the building housing the marine mammals that may have possibly disturbed the dolphins and influenced their behavior, observations made on February 1, 1996, were not used.

RESULTS

Differences in activity periods during the day were examined by dividing the observation time between 10:00 a.m. and 4:00 p.m. into six 1-hour periods. The proportion of the total number of activity observations in each time period for that activity

Table 14.2.
Observations of Chessie and Cobie Each One-Hour Time Period Between 10:00 a.m. and 4:00 p.m.

Activity	X^2	df	P	Results
Chessie (female)				
Infant	6.39	5	> 0.10	No sig diff
Quiet	10.22	5	> 0.05	No sig diff
P,C,M,T,O	6.08	5	> 0.10	No sig diff
Cobie (male)				
Infant	8.64	5	> 0.10	No sig diff
Quiet	12.08	5	< 0.05	Sig diff
P,C,M,T,O	20.21	5	< 0.005	Sig diff

Note: The number of observations in each one-hour time period between 10:00 a.m. and 4:00 p.m. were noted, and the play, chase, mouth, touch, and other (P, C, M, T, O) categories values were combined because of small sample size. The expected frequency for a given activity category at a time period was P(A) x number of observations for a time period. The proportion of time devoted to a particular activity did not vary significantly between the hours of 10:00 a.m. and 4:00 p.m. for Chessie. Cobie did not show any significant variation in infant activity between the hours of 10:00 a.m. and 4:00 p.m. However, he did exhibit a significant increase from the expected values in quiet activity between 1:00 p.m. and 2:00 p.m. He also exhibited significant differences in P, C, M, T, and O behavior categories combined. The most significant differences from expected values for P, C, M, T, and O were a decrease in these activites between 11:00 a.m. and 12:00 p.m., and an increase between 3:00 p.m. and 4:00 p.m.

was calculated, and the P, C, M, T, and O categories' values were combined because of small sample size. An alpha level of $P = .05$ was used for all stastitical tests. Chi square tests confirmed that there was indeed no significant difference in the proportion of time Chessie engaged in different activities during the day (see Table 14.2). There was a significant increase in the proportion of time that Cobie spent in all activity categories between 12:00 p.m. and 2:00 p.m., except for the I category (see Table 14.2).

The data was then divided into the activity categories by date to determine if there were any changes in behavioral patterns from day to day over the course of the study. No significant difference was found in the proportion of time spent by Chessie in each activity category from day to day (see Table 14.3). Although there was significant fluctuation in the proportion of time spent in each activity from day to day for Cobie, these fluctuations did not form regular patterns or trends over the course of the study (see Table 14.3).

Overall, since the only significant difference in the daily activity patterns throughout the day or from day to day that was found was an increase in Cobie's activity between 12:00 p.m. and 2:00 p.m., all observations in one activity category were lumped together (see Table 14.4). In this way, the comparison of the behavior of the two juveniles by activity categories was possible. The total number of observations

Table 14.3.
Observations of Chessie and Cobie for Each Day

Activity	X^2	df	P	Results
Chessie (female)				
Infant	6.89	9	> 0.50	No sig diff
Quiet	2.12	9	> 0.975	No sig diff
P,C,M,T,O	12.61	9	> 0.10	No sig diff
Cobie (male)				
Infant	20.79	9	< 0.025	Sig diff
Quiet	15.50	9	> 0.05	No sig diff
P,C,M,T,O	30.56	9	< 0.005	Sig diff

Note: The number of observations on each day were noted, and the play, chase, mouth, touch, and other (P, C, M, T, O) categories' values were combined because of small sample size. The expected frequency for a given activity category on a certain day was P(A) x number of observations for that day. The proportion of time devoted to a particular activity did not vary significantly over the course of the study for Chessie. Cobie did not vary in the proportions of time spent in quiet time over the course of the study. However, he did show a significant decrease from expected values in infant activity on September 26, 1995, and a significant increase in infant activity on November 21, 1995. He also exhibited significant differences from expected values in P, C, M, T, and O behavior categories combined. These differences included an increase in these activities on September 5, 1995, September 26, 1995, and October 31, 1995, and decreases on October 24, 1995, and November 21, 1995.

Table 14.4.
Observations of Chessie and Cobie for Each Time Period and
Over All Observation Days

Activity	X^2	df	P	Results
All	23.24	6	< 0.005	Sig diff
P,C,I,O	1.61	3	> 0.50	No sig diff
M,Q	0.01	1	> 0.90	No sig diff
P,C,I,O, and M,Q	8.54	1	< 0.005	Sig diff
P,C,I,O, and T	9.78	1	< 0.005	Sig diff
M,Q, and T	18.32	1	< 0.005	Sig diff

Note: Observations for each individual were tallied for each time period and over all observation days. The proportion of time in each activity category differed significantly for Chessie (female) and Cobie (male) by contingency table analysis. The juveniles did not differ significantly in the proportion of time devoted to P, C, I, and O. Nor did they differ in the amount of time devoted to M and Q when these activities are pooled. When groups of activities were compared, Chessie displayed more M and Q activities, and Cobie displayed more touch activities.

in each activity category was used to examine behavioral patterns by comparing the proportion of time spent in each activity category. The percentage of time spent in each activity category by Chessie and Cobie was compared visually using pie charts (see Figure 14.1). Both juveniles spent 60% to 65% of their time in some sort of resting behavior (I or Q).

A contingency table analysis showed that there was a significant difference between the two juveniles in the proportion of time they spent in the different activity categories. The categories were then divided into groups by which juvenile had more observations. Cobie had more C, I, and O observations, while Chessie had more P, M, and Q observations. There was no significant difference within each group of activity categories. The T category was considered separately because of the large difference between the two juveniles in the number of observations. There was a significant difference between the two juveniles in the proportion of time spent touching compared to the other two groups of activities; Cobie spent a significantly larger proportion of time in the T category (see Table 14.5, Figure 14.2).

Once their overall behavior patterns were determined, the interactions of each of the juveniles with the other individuals in the pool were examined. Each activity count total for P, C, M, T, and TS (play aggression categories) was categorized by the individual with which the juvenile interacted (other juvenile, Nani, Hailey, or Shiloh). The I and Q categories were not included because they, by definition, involved interactions with specific individuals. The O category was excluded because it included a variety of very different behaviors (such as sexual play), and therefore the interaction results for observations in this category would not have any reflection of the individual behaviors combined in the category. The interactions with the three adults were combined together because of small sample numbers, and then compared with those of the other juvenile. Tail slapping, a behavior that frequently

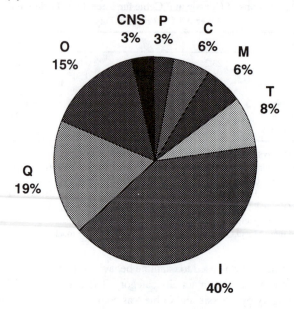

(a) Cobie: % of Time Observed in Each Activity

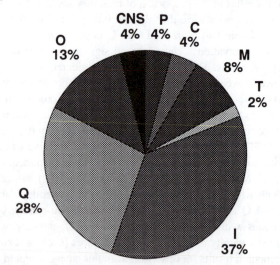

(b) Chessie: % of Time Observed in Each Activity

FIGURE 14.1. Percentage of time that Cobie (a) and Chessie (b) were observed in each activity category; 60% to 65% of both juveniles' time was spent in "infant" and "quiet" behaviors.

Table 14.5.
Interactions Between the Juveniles and Adults or Each Other

	# of Interactions					
Subject	Juvenile	Adult	X^2	df	P	Results
Chessie	57	25	86.65	1	< 0.005	Sig diff
Cobie	58	36	67.53	1	< 0.005	Sig diff

Note: The juveniles spent more time with each other than with the other three adults combined, based on Chi square analysis where the expected frequency of a juvenile meeting another juvenile is 0.25, and 0.75 for a chance meeting with an adult.

Table 14.6.
Influence of the Type of Interaction on the Proportion of Interactions Spent with an Adult or Another Juvenile

	# of Interactions					
Subject	Juvenile	Adult	X^2	df	P	Results
Chessie			3.08	4	> 0.50	No sig diff
Play	6	2				
Chase	10	6				
Mouth	22	6				
Touch	12	5				
Tail slap	7	6				
Cobie (All activities)			11.97	4	< 0.025	Sig diff
(w/o Touch)			1.151	3	> 0.05	No sig diff
Play	6	3				
Chase	15	8				
Mouth	24	8				
Touch	8	16				
Tail slap	5	1				

Note: The proportions of interactions between a juvenile and an adult is not influenced by the type of interactions for Chessie, but Cobie has significantly more touch interactions with adults than with Chessie (contingency table analysis).

occurred with mouthing, chasing, and touching, was then considered and included among the categories being compared. If it was possible to determine, the instigator of each interactive behavior was noted.

Chi square analyses then showed that both of the juveniles primarily interacted with each other in the play aggression categories, rather than with any of the adults (see Table 14.5 and Figure 14.3). Contingency tables showed that the selection of interaction partners in activities was independent of the type of activity in all activity categories for Chessie. This, however, was not true for Cobie; the selection of interaction partners was not independent of the type of activity until the T category was removed (see Table 14.6). Cobie spent more time "touching" adults.

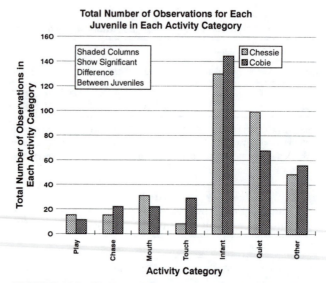

FIGURE 14.2. Total number of observations in each activity category for Chessie and Cobie. The shaded columns show a significant difference between Chessie and Cobie in total number of observations of "touch."

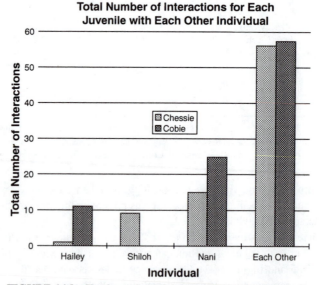

FIGURE 14.3. Total number of interactions with other individuals for Chessie and Cobie. Both juveniles spent significantly more time interacting with each other than with the three adults combined in play aggression categories.

The instigator was determined for the activity categories of T, C, M, and TS. The proportion of instigations in each activity was independent of which juvenile was being considered (see Table 14.7). Since TS was the only category in which Chessie

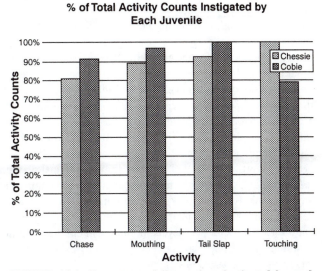

FIGURE 14.4. Percentage of interactions instigated by each juvenile in "chase," "mouthing," "tail slap," and "touching." Both juveniles instigate significantly more interactions in these categories than the three adults combined.

TABLE 14.7.
Instigations of Activities by the Two Juveniles

| | # of Instigations | | | | | |
Activity	Chessie	Cobie	X^2	df	P	Results
Touch	17	19				
Chase	13	21				
Mouth	25	31				
Tail slap	13	6				
All			0.56	1	> 0.10	No sig diff
T and M			0.49	1	> 0.10	No sig diff
C and TS			4.44	1	< 0.50	Sig diff

Note: Chessie and Cobie instigated equivalent interactions, assuming that each animal would instigate half of all instigations (Chi square analysis). Instigation of T & M activities did not differ significantly for Chessie and Cobie. However, Cobie instigated more C activity, and Chessie displayed more TS behavior (contingency table analysis).

instigated a greater number of interactions, TS and C (which also showed a rather large numerical difference between the two juveniles) were compared in a Chi square test. This did show significantly that Cobie did more of the chasing, while Chessie instigated more tail slaps, which is a response to being chased. T and M were then compared, but they remained independent of the juvenile being considered (see Table 14.7). A Chi square test then showed no significant difference between the two juveniles in the total number of interactions instigated (see Table 14.7 and Figure 14.4).

Also noted was a tendency for the mother-calf pairs to show a typical captive marine mammal rotational tendency of swimming in a counter-clockwise direction (Sobel, Supin, & Myslobodsky, 1994). This counter-clockwise rotation occurred 97% of the time when direction was noted (172 of 177 observations). Nani, the dominant female, swam in the opposite direction.

Many similarities in play behavior between human children and juvenile bottlenose dolphins were found using the Piaget (1962) and Parten (1932) categories of play. On the Piaget cognitive levels of play, both exhibit functional play, constructive play (using objects such as bubbles to make something like a hoop), and dramatic play (role-playing, such as sexual play). Detailed and extensive studies would be required to determine if dolphins enact the fourth cognitive category, which is games with rules. On the Parten social play levels, both human children and juvenile dolphins exhibit solitary and group play. Dolphins also may exhibit parallel play, but this type of play was not observed in this study.

DISCUSSION

The influence of daily environmental fluctuation is evident in all animals. River dolphins are more active during the day, with faster swimming preceding feeding and play following it (Renjun, Gewalt, Neurohr, & Winkler, 1994). This is also true of Atlantic White-sided dolphins (*Lagenorhynchus acutus*), whose social activity is more frequent in the middle of the day (Nelson & Lien, 1994). Cobie followed this pattern and Chessie did not, but this discrepancy could have resulted from a number of different factors given the small sample size. Although significant differences in the proportion of time Cobie spent in each activity from day to day occurred, there were no real trends in the patterns over the course of the study, as might be expected from a study that had a duration of less than a year. A longer study may have shown seasonal changes as well as developmental changes.

Although they spent the most time overall in infant swimming, Chessie and Cobie did not differ significantly in the proportion of time spent in any of the activity categories, except for T, in which Cobie spent more time. This follows a pattern from their first nine weeks after birth, in which Cobie was found to be more dependent upon his mother (spent more time infant swimming) than Chessie was on her mother (Reid, Mann, Weiner, & Hecker, 1995). This difference may have resulted because touching often occurs during infant swimming or sexual play, the latter of which Cobie displays more interest in as time passes.

This preference for one's mother did not, however, carry over into the play aggression categories for Cobie or Chessie. Wild nursery groups may have little or no contact with roaming bands of adult males, but high-ranking bottlenose dolphin females usually have a dominance relationship (Johnson & Norris, 1986). This proved true in this study, as the juveniles, after each other, spent the most time in play aggression activities interacting with Nani, rather than with their mothers.

Which individual is the instigator in an interaction is often determined or influenced by the dominance hierarchy. In a study of captive Atlantic White-sided dolphins involving one adult male and one adult female, the female was found to initiate more total interactions (Nelson & Lien, 1994). However, in bottlenose dolphins, the male usually initiates more interactions (McBride & Hebb, 1948; Tavolga & Essapian, 1957). In this study, there was no significant difference between the two juveniles in the number of activities instigated. This could have been because neither of the two are fully mature, nor have they reached reproductive age.

Social interactions are an integral part of everyday activities because they are important in the maintenance of the dominance hierarchy of the nursery group. In captivity, the oldest female is basically a focal point on which the social activity of the tank centers (Johnson & Norris, 1986). However, despite being the center of attention, Nani did definitely display and retain her dominant position in many ways. One way, in particular, was her consistent manner of swimming in a clockwise direction around the pool, in a direction opposite to that of the other dolphins in the pool. The majority of *Tursiops* and *Delphinus* species show a distinct preference for swimming in a counter-clockwise direction in captivity. This is especially true for resting behaviors. This intrinsic, typical directional choice may be the result of brain lateralization or right eye preference and is not affected by the positioning of the dolphins when admitted to a pool, or the direction of water circulation. However, it can be temporarily affected by "poolmate subordination." In such a case, a single dominant member of a group might lead the rest of the group to rotate in the direction opposite to their intrinsic preference, but if that dominant animal is removed, the animals will revert to their original counter-clockwise rotation (Ridgway, 1986). This counter-clockwise preference has even been observed in Amazon river dolphins, although Chinese river dolphins were observed to spend equal time swimming in both directions (Renjun, Gewalt, Neurohr, & Winkler, 1994).

A number of conclusions can be drawn from the results of this study. First, only the second of the three hypotheses, based on initial observations, was confirmed by the results. More play behavior did occur between the juveniles themselves and with Nani than with their mothers. The other two hypotheses were found to be in error, at least concerning these individuals. The juveniles spent most of their time in resting behaviors, rather than play behaviors. When they were playing, more interactions occurred between the two juveniles than between the juveniles and Nani. In addition, the following conclusions were made.

1. Cobie had a significantly larger proportion of observations than Chessie between 12:00 p.m. and 2:00 p.m. in all activity categories except "infant," but there were no significant differences between the two juveniles in the other time periods.
2. No overall changes in the activity patterns of either juvenile over the course of the study were found, although there were significant fluctuations in Cobie's activity patterns.
3. Cobie spent a significantly larger proportion of time "touching" than Chessie, but there were no significant differences between the two in the proportion of time spent in any other activity category.
4. Both juveniles interacted with each other more frequently than with the three adults combined in all play aggression activity categories, except that Cobie "touched" adults more frequently than he "touched" Chessie. Of the three adults, Nani, the dominant female, was the primary partner in play aggression.
5. Cobie instigated more "chases," while Chessie responded with more "tail slaps," but there was no significant difference between the two in instigating "mouth" and "touch." There was no significant difference between the two juveniles in the total number of instigations.

CONCLUSION

This study has provided a look into the behavioral patterns of two juvenile captive bottlenose dolphins. Analysis of the amount of time spent in different behavior categories allows one to begin to determine the importance of certain play behaviors in the physical and social skill development and future success of the individual. A comparison with the intellectual and social development of human children may offer additional insight, given the highly complex behavior and potential cognition of bottlenose dolphins, and the exhibition of almost all of the human intellectual and social developmental categories described by Parten and Piaget (Rubin, Maioni, & Hornung, 1976; Rubin, Watson, & Jambor, 1978).

Further research on this data set could include sequence analysis of play aggression and sexual play, the frequency with which bubble blowing accompanies play aggression, and signals that may initiate play interactions (such as vocalizations or posturing). A continuing study of these individuals, or other captive juveniles, could examine the effect of play upon the social interactions of the nursery group as the juveniles mature to the age of leaving the group. Once again, the effects of captivity must be considered, and intense observations of wild individuals, if possible, would be preferential.

REFERENCES

Breland, K., & Breland, M. (1966). *Animal behavior.* New York: Macmillan.

Chalmers, N., & Locke-Haydon, J. (1985). Correlations among measures of playfulness and skillfulness in captive common marmosets (*Callithrix jacchus jacchus*). *Developmental Psychology, 17,* 191–208.

Dufran, R., & Pryor, K. (1980). The behavior and training of cetaceans in captivity. In L. M. Herman (Ed.), *Cetacean behavior: Mechanisms and functions* (pp. 319–362). New York: John Wiley.

Fagen, R. M. (1981). *Animal play behavior.* New York: Oxford University Press.

Fagen, R. M. (1984). Play and behavioural flexibility. In P. K. Smith (Ed.), *Play in animals and humans* (pp. 159–174). Oxford, England: Basil Blackwell.

Hughes, F. H. (1991). *Children, play, and development.* Boston: Allyn and Bacon.

Johnson, C. M., & Norris, K. S. (1986). Delphinid social organization and social structure. In R. Schusterman, J. Thomas, & F. Wood (Eds.), *Dolphin cognition and behavior: A comparative approach* (pp. 335–346). Hillsdale, NJ: Lawrence Erlbaum.

McBride, A. F., & Hebb, D. O. (1948). Behavior of the captive bottle-nose dolphin, *Tursiops truncatus. Journal of Comparative and Physiological Psychology, 41,* 111–123.

Meaney, M. J. (1988). The sexual differentiation of social play. *Trends in Neuroscience, 7,* 54–58.

Meckley, A. M. (1995). Studying children's social play through a child cultural approach: roles, rules, and shared knowledge. *Advances in Early Education and Day Care, 7,* 179–211.

Nelson, D. L., & Lien, J. (1994). Behavior patterns of two captive Atlantic white-sided dolphins, *Lagenorhynchus acutus. Aquatic Mammals, 20*(1), 1–10.

Parten, M. B. (1932). Social participation among pre-school children. *Journal of Abnormal & Social Psychology, 27,* 243–269.

Pellegrini, A. D. (1989). Categorizing children's rough-and-tumble play. *Play & Culture, 2,* 48–51.

Piaget, J. (1962). *Play, dreams and imitation in childhood.* New York: W. W. Norton.

Reid, K., Mann, J., Weiner, J., & Hecker, N. (1995). Infant development in two aquarium bottlenose dolphins. *Zoo Biology, 14,* 135–147.

Reiss, D., & McCowan, B. (1993). Spontaneous vocal mimicry and production by bottlenose dolphins (*Tursiops truncatus*): Evidence for vocal learning. *Journal of Comparative Psychology, 107*(3), 301–312.

Renjun, L., Gewalt, W., Neurohr, B., & Winkler, A. (1994). Comparative studies on the behaviour of *Inia geoffrensis* and *Lipotes vexillifer* in artificial environments. *Aquatic Mammals, 20*(1), 39–45.

Ridgway, S. H. (1986). Physiological observations on the dolphin brain. In R. Schusterman, J. Thomas, & F. Wood. (Eds.), *Dolphin cognition and behaviour: A comparative approach* (pp. 31–59). Hillsdale, NJ: Lawrence Erlbaum.

Rubin, K. H., Maioni, T. L., & Hornung, M. (1976). Free play behaviors in middle- and lower-class preschoolers: Parten and Piaget revisited. *Child Development, 47,* 414–419.

Rubin, K. H., Watson, K. S., & Jambor, T. W. (1978). Free-play behaviors in preschool and kindergarten children. *Child Development, 49,* 534–536.

Schustermann, R., Thomas, J., & Wood, F. (Eds.). (1986). *Dolphin cognition and behaviour: A comparative approach.* Hillsdale, NJ: Lawrence Erlbaum.

Slijper, E. J. (1976). *Whales and dolphins.* Ann Arbor, MI: University of Michigan Press.

Slooten, E. (1994). Behavior of Hector's Dolphin: Classifying behavior by sequence analysis. *Journal of Mammalogy, 75*(4), 956–964.

Sobel, N., Supin, A. Y., & Myslobodsky, M. S. (1994). Rotational swimming tendencies in the dolphin (*Tursiops truncatus*). *Behavioural Brain Research, 65*, 41–45.

Symons, D. (1978). *Play and aggression: A study of rhesus monkeys.* New York: Columbia University Press.

Tavolga, M. C., & Essapian, F. S. (1957). The behavior of the bottle-nosed dolphin (*Tursiops truncatus*): Mating, pregnancy, parturition and mother-infant behavior. *Zoologica, 42*(1–14), 11–31.

Vanderschuran, J. J. M. J., Niesink, R. J. M., Spruijt, B. M., & Van Ree, J. M. (1995). Influence of environmental factors on social play behavior of juvenile rats. *Physiology & Behavior, 58*(1), 119–123.

part V

Other Conceptions of Play

15

Evolving a Consilience of Play Definitions: Playfully*

Brian Sutton-Smith

PREFACE

In this article, I want to show that we cannot trust most of our contemporary psychological definitions of play. But that as a step towards something more universal that will apply to animals and humans as well as to culturally different forms of play, we should look for parallels between biology, neurology, anthropology, and psychology. It makes sense that because play characterizes both animals and humans, it has something to do with evolution. With this as a lead, we can look next for the neurological, cultural, and psychological phenomena that seem most relevant to the suggested evolutionary paradigm. This is the procedure that will be followed here, though the formulations are, of course, quite speculative. Still, we may hope that they prompt similar attempts at creating a homogeneity of definitional layerings across different disciplines, and that as a result, we can rise above the rather simplistic psychological essentialisms that have dominated the field. We have borrowed the term "consilience" from E. O. Wilson, which he defines as "a jumping together of knowledge as a result of the linking of facts, and fact based theory, across disciplines to create a common groundwork of explanation" (1998, p. 53).

---

* A footnote to *The Ambiguity of Play* (1997).

THE CONTEMPORARY RHETORICS OF DEFINITION

What practically all theorists of this century have had in common has been the desire to show that play is useful in some way or another. Presumably, this has been a reaction against the 300 prior years of play being seen as a waste of time for either religious or economic reasons. The major 20th-century paradigms for rehabilitating play from its former lower status have been, in turn, that it makes contributions to conventional socialization, to the players' sense of personal freedom, to the self-actualizing character of the players' subjective experiences, or, most recently, to the development of professional adult play careers.

Thus, psychology's major contribution to theorizing on play has been its focus upon it as essentially *a form of conventional socialization*. Whether the Enlightenment's concern with progress, or Evolution's concern with skill preparation, has had the most influence in promoting this concept is hard to say. Basically, in these theories play is said to be useful because it contributes to other kinds of development: moral, social, emotional, and cognitive. However, the resulting psychological play concepts are generally little more than intuitive guesses about play's socialization functions as the terms "rehearsal," "preparation," "recapitulation," "mastery," "learning," "flexibility," "symbolic interactionism," "subjunctivity," "assimilation," "transformation," "transition," "proximal development," "affect regulation," "symbolic usage," "divergent thinking," "practice of subroutines," and "exploration" all imply. The more collective anthropological concepts such as play being a civilizing force, mediating conflict, establishing communal identity and group hierachy, as well as reflecting major economic and military affairs through game simulation, are like the psychological theories insofar as they reflect a similar progress-oriented strain. They are also about how play contributes to the collective socialization and social problem solving of the larger society. Whether the great variety of these concepts owes simply to our confusion or reflects the great variability of play phenomena will be taken up later in this chapter.

As far as the notion that play socializes is concerned, it is empirically true that more complex forms of play do sometimes correlate with higher levels in any of the psychological or cultural "functions" previously listed. So it follows that play may instigate such functions. However, the direction of the causal relationships is seldom clear. Players over time typically improve the quality and complexity of their own play performances, regardless of these other developmental or cultural complexity associations. Such improvements in play skill are one of its major characteristics and coaches, educators, and therapists, for their part, organize children's play tendentiously so that these play improvements will occur and will transfer to athletic awards, other kinds of knowledge (such as literacy) and, in the therapy case, to mental health. But this interventionist work, important as it is in its own right, only tells us how play can be manipulated for other purposes. It does not tell us what the primary function of play may be, except that once again (as in the multiple theories above) it implies a great lability in the phenomenon of play itself. It is odd to think of play being regarded by theorists for most of this century mainly as a support to conventional individual and collective socialization when the commonsense about play is largely that it is for the satisfaction of personal or collective desires, rather than for personal or collective obligations.

Second, because our civilization in earlier centuries made a clear contrast between play and work, one of the other directions of more recent play theory has been to turn this notion of play as wasteful and useless on its head, and make these apparently wasteful play characteristics instead the *valued symbols of modern freedom*. Concepts of play that may be interpreted this way are the varied notions of play as catharsis, nonproductivity, autotelia, active not passive, voluntary, indeterministic, anarchic, inversive, grotesquely realistic, intrinsically motivated, oriented to a means rather than an ends, noninstrumental, creative, and as an escape. Freudianism is a special case of such arguments for play's freedom, insofar as through play, one is said to abreact conflicts, compensate for inferiorities, and obtain therapy, all of which are messages of escape from the burdens of the family romance. In this definitional category of play as freedom, however, the major play vehicle has been the imagination, which in the past 200 years has formed romantic company historically with art and poetry, both of which are often also said to be dignified by their nonpragmatic nature, "arts for arts sake," and so on. What is typically missing in the modern advocacies of the imagination, however, are its linkages to the more Dionyesian or irrational elements of modern society and personality (Spariosu, 1989).

Another problem with the advocacy of play as freedom is that throughout history, play's practice has often been obligatory, not optional, and typically fused with pragmatic cultural rhetorics and functions. Examples of such obligatoriness are easily found today in festivals, sports, in professional kinds of play as with comedians and actors, and indeed also in children's own playground play as forms of childhood power politics. Much childhood social play is motivated more by a desire to be accepted by the other children than by any especial desire for freedom of play choice. Furthermore, it is the very obligational aspects of play (the routines and the rules) that makes it so difficult for maladjusted children to either master the play performances or be accepted by their peers. Clearly, play is itself a compound of voluntary and involuntary elements, not totally one or the other. Some have claimed indeed that the essence of games is that they play you, rather than that you play them—a concept easily allied to the notion that their compulsoriness to the player is an essential part of what play is about. A more cynical view of this kind of play as a freedom metaphysic, however, is that it actually derives mainly from the increased role of consumerism in modern recreation, and, therefore, of the value given to the ability to make free choices in modern capitalism.

Third, the concept of play as *self-actualization* derives from the same romantic and individualistic historical sources as the concept of play as freedom. They are overlapping concepts. However, the definitional emphasis in this category is upon the particular qualities of experience that make play into a kind of personal self-actualization or even transcendence. Emphasis is on certain selected kinds of play as the only pure kinds, such as the "play of children" or "infinite play," "the well-played game" or "flow," the "play of being" or "ecstatic play," and "aesthetic play." The focus can be also on particularly valuable affects that are said to especially characterize play, such as confidence, communitas, optimism, methexis, monstration, effectance, self-actualization, and even "playfulness." Or the reference can be to supposedly self-evident experiences, such as excitement, fun, light-heartedness, joy, spontaneity, wit, and enthusiasm. Obviously, play cannot be all of these things at the same time, unless its functions are so variable that everything can still count somewhere. Indeed perhaps it is appropriate to stop thinking of play as a unified kind of activity. Maybe child play and imagination, adult contests, festivals, gambling, and folly have less in common than we tend to assume.

Fourth, there is the model of Howard Gardner's *Frames of Mind* (1983), in which he puts aside the notion of one unified kind of intelligence (the IQ) and refers instead to the different kinds of mental ability in which geniuses show their stuff (linguistic, musical, logical, spatial, kinesthetic, and social). It is possible likewise to give up thinking only of a unified function of play and instead to nominate multiple divergent *frames of play*. Such differences have seldom, if ever, been investigated by play scholars (Slade & Wolf, 1994). Yet all players, to some extent, and some with great intensity, display their variant play forms through such behaviors as clowning, exploration, athleticism, narrative, pretending, hosting, fashion modeling, and through any and all forms of art such as acting, singing, and so forth. Each of these has its place in childhood play and sometimes in adulthood leads to individuals who are professionals at play. What is unique to our times is that now some of the most outstanding of these professional players receive incomes in the hundreds of millions, as can be observed by mentioning such illustrative names for each of the above play types as Jerry Seinfeld, Carl Sagan, Michael Jordan, John Grisham, Julia Roberts, Oprah Winfrey, and Princess Diana. All of these persons have become celebrity players. So in modern society today, it is not unreasonable, even if surprising, to define play not as a search for what it does for other forms of reality (cognition, affect, etc.), but in terms of what it does for professional players like those mentioned here. Play has apparently moved closer to the center of what this society is about and these kinds of players have become celebrities by being outstanding at what they do. Perhaps it is high time that the social sciences investigated the childhood development and vicissitudes for children following these divergent ludic paths. It is certainly something of a shock for play theorists to realize that their life's concern with the object called play has suddenly moved to the center of modern culture, instead of being on the periphery where they have been used to studying it. Still, the focus of this paper is on what all kinds of play have in common, if indeed such a phenomenon can be discovered.

Play as Adaptive Variability

The general case for evolutionary issues being important to the understanding of play is based first on humans playing more than all other species, upon the size of the cortex across species being positively correlated with the time spent in play, and on the amounts of energy available being much larger in the playing animals than in the nonplaying reptiles. It has been difficult in this light not to suppose that play serves some evolutionary purpose. There have been many evolutionary theories of play suggesting, for example, that ontogeny recapitulates phylogeny and in doing so dissipates its cruder influences; that play activity is a direct preparation for survival, the fittest in play being more likely to survive; that play maintains high levels of energy, its availability being a necessary aspect of organic complexity; that play relaxes an otherwise stressed organism; that it exercises optimal levels of neurological arousal; and that it provides metabolic recuperation. And there are more of such evolutionary theses (see Bekoff, 1998; Burghardt, 1998). The serious examination of animal play as functioning universally as a form of skill training, fighting rehearsal, bonding, flexibility training, or of affective maturation, however, has not gained much support when all of the evidence has been carefully considered, even though some of these functions often seem to be of key importance in particular species (Fagen, 1981; Smith, 1982). This means we must look elsewhere for a general evolutionary explanation, if there is to be one.

More recently (taking a cue from Gould, 1996a, 1996b), we have mooted the notion that play may be itself primarily a manifestation of adaptive variability (Gould, 1997). Gould (1997) argues that evolution depends upon the availability of variable responses and that these variable responses, occasioned by the organism's basic flexibility, occur with surprising quirkiness and redundancy. Although he is not talking at all about play, one notices immediately that these characteristics seem to describe play very well. Play is *quirky*, often being called inversive, paradoxical, fragmentary, disorderly, and nonsensical. Play is *redundant*, often being called repetitive, stereotypical, compulsive, and ritualistic. Consider the repetitive character of sports programs, soap operas, and recess pastimes. But underlying both of these, says Gould, play is *flexible*, translating again to notions of play as imaginative, improvisational, and constantly open to new strategies, new tactics, and new festival displays . Gould's main argument in favor of the importance of variability is that the greater the repertoire of such variable responses, the less the likelihood that an organism will fall heir to its own habit-forming, but rigidifying, successes. Just how such variability in play might provide feedback to the general organism for this purpose is not as yet clear.

Play as a Simulation of the Struggle for Survival

To this point, the discussion has been about variability in a fairly mechanical or mathematical kind of way, in the sense that more variability is a good thing and less is a bad thing. This is not entirely false because without variability, choices are limited and flexibility is impossible. But there is a sense also that this approach in evolution only confirms variability as a mechanism rather than a promise. Variability is no promise of progress, it is merely the means by which progress might be achieved in the best of circumstances, which is to say that the stress on play as adaptive variability is not a statement that it makes progress inevitable. That would be similar to the older view that play is inevitable for various kinds of socialization. The present statement, to the contrary, merely says that without variability, progress would be impossible, but still it is no guarantee that progress will occur; most of the variability that play contributes is not functional in the progressive sense. For the greater part, play is just as crazy as it seems.

There is more to variability than these mathematical considerations. The variability under discussion is itself a part of the basic processes in the struggle for survival, for life or death in the biological case, and for success or failure in the cultural evolutionary case. Of course, much, but not all, of the biological case is handled by the reproductive processes. But in either biological or cultural processes, variability enters into the existential predicaments the responses that might be available to provide effective solutions. Given that the history of the human species, whether *homo erectus* or otherwise, is a history of considerable anarchy (Auguet, 1972; Diamond, 1997; Keeley, 1996), makes it not improbable that play and its variabilities have been selected over time to model and mollify this ever-present chaos. That is to say that the persistence and universality of play may depend on it being hooked into these most universal of life experiences.

The key point is that although play generates simulations of existential predicaments, it does so generally (but not always) within relatively safe packages. The predictable elements of play that attempt to keep the players safe are those governed by metacommunications, frames, routines, rules, cooperation, stylized performances, and the inhibition of hurtful responses. These all provide boundaries against danger and allow excitement to take place without too much anxiety. On the other hand, within the play, there are contrary means to excitement, such as the kinds of variability termed risk taking, wishful thinking, impulse indulgence, nonsense, and exaggeration, all of which typically take place within ways of intensifying experience through laughter, noise, music, inebriation, grotesquerie, and so forth. There is, in addition, the attempts of sporting opponents to create further unpredictabilities of mind and body for the player by their oppositional strategies and tactics (Myers, 1997). The notion that play has evolved as such a simulation of the struggle for survival is perhaps assisted by two contrary kinds of evidence. One is that some societies seek to completely inhibit play because they wish to maintain a rigid code of economic or religious behavior. Their prohibition of play is an implicit testimony that they believe play promotes a real diversity or is itself a diversity they do not wish to have entertained by their children. The details of this point of view will be discussed in the anthropology section later in this chapter. The opposite extreme are the examples of what is called "deep play," such as rock climbing or heavy gambling, where the outcomes can involve physical or economic damages. Here, what is sometimes called play is undertaken partly because it risks not being playful at all. There are, for example, many varieties of war-like play and games that vary in their degrees of play versus real-life dangers. Some wars are total. Some are moderate, as when the warriors return home when an accepted number on each side has been killed. Some are sham battles as when Zulu war games were fought with spears the tips of which were blunted by wooden blocks. Some are contemporary war games where no one is meant to be killed. Then there are games of physical skill and strategy (chess and football), which may be a simulation of those other forms of existential reality. The point is to show that in some domains there is a great variety of inter-mediate survival forms versus clear-cut play forms (Chick, Loy, & Miracle, 1997). This very variety supports the view that indeed some forms of play are simulations of the struggle for survival; there is a kinship running across these various forms.

Forms of play, it is argued here, package the variable existential contraries of everyday life in their own unique and quirky, yet redundant, syntheses, known cul-turally as simply playing, passing the time, playing games, fantasizing, partaking of contests, being festive and making celebrations, or being humorous. What is nice about this formulation of play as an internal balance between equilibrating and dis-equilibrating (safe yet exciting) elements is that these apply as well to animal as to human behavior and thus gives this evolutionary formulation structural cogency that it might not otherwise have. Animal play is just as quirky (disorderly, fragmentary, and repetitive) as is human play (Fagen, 1981). We might talk metaphorically of this packaged and internal binariness of sense and nonsense as a *ludic dialectic* (Sutton-Smith, 1978a, 1978b).

But, in addition to this internal binary relationship of safety and risk within play, there is also an external binary relationship between play and the rest of society. In this latter formulation, play is not only an intrinsic dialectical form in its own right, but it also always stands in a special dialectical relationship to the rest of society. After all, play exists between what might on the one hand be the simulation of a dis-aster (evolutionary or otherwise), and on the other hand, what is always habitual and mundane as everyday life. It is the great intermediary between the one and the other. It mirrors, mocks, and diminishes the greatest concerns of existence for life and suc-cess, but it also relieves the boredom of our everyday succession of habitual events. This external binariness might be spoken of as an *adaptive dialectic* because it speaks to the function of play in society, rather than just to how it functions within itself (Sutton-Smith, 1978a, 1978b).

However, remembering that, as it stands, talking "dialectics" is just metaphoriz-ing about the possible meaning of given empirical structures, it follows that these might also be referred to as paradoxes (Bateson, 1972). Although Bateson is refer-ring to how the play form is, and is not that which it seems to represent, we would say that he was concerned only with an adaptive dialectic, an adaptive paradox, or what might be called a virtual paradox, because virtual reality is always in some way meant to be representative of some reality. What Bateson doesn't do is talk about the ludic paradox, which is the intrinsic paradox between the sense and the nonsense within the play itself. So talk can be in terms of adaptive and ludic dialectics or in terms of virtual and ludic paradoxes, depending on one's preference for structuralist or literary metaphors.

What we have shown elsewhere is that on the adaptive level, most societies have their own "rhetorics" that they apply to play, attempting to rationalize it in ways that suit their own culture (Sutton-Smith, 1997). Thus, play is said on the one hand to be a form of socialization, on others to be forms of power, unity, creativity, fate, or nonsense. In each of these adaptive dialectics, the supposed play function is encouraged or discouraged in one way or another and the rhetorics themselves sometimes closely parallel the kind of play (as contestive sporting rhetoric is not unlike sport as a ludic contest), and sometimes fail to parallel the play (as when adults talk about moral development in play and it has little to do with, say, "Hide-and-Seek"). It is, of course, difficult to imagine how even animals have invented this enactive play poetry to mimic or mock the actual stringencies of their realistic struggles for survival, yet they have done so clearly in their play fighting, play pursuit, play bonding, and play flexibility. It is even stranger to know that the cortex and culture between them once created this primordial simulative ludic map of their own existential predicaments on their evolutionary way towards creating animal sign systems and, much later, towards creating human symbol systems including language.

The Brain is Itself a Variable Field

Two new kinds of data about the brain seem to amplify the explanations of variability and existential predicaments presented above. The first is about the brain's incredible variability, the second is about its character as a jungle of connections. First, contemporary magnetic imaging resonance research shows the brain to be a phenomenon of trillions of synapses with an early infant potential for behavior much of which will atrophy without usage. There are about 50% more synapses in infancy than there will be in maturity (Huttenlocher, 1994). A famous example is how easy it is to learn many languages in the early years of life when the brain has multiple possible sound connections with which to assimilate the variety of languages, and how difficult it is to do so later, when this variety in the brain has been much reduced by nonusage. In the present terms, it is possible to see this infant potential brain as predicting greater actual neurological variability for those who have the opportunity to play most widely with its synaptic resources. Play, like multiple languages, may actualize more of these potentials of the brain than could be actualized by relatively narrow, mundane, everyday behaviors. Intriguingly, play, like this early synaptic brain, is itself a form of potential rather than actual behavior, a kind of variability waiting for its evolutionary moments. Paradoxically, play's "unreal" realizations (which are only potentials for ordinary behavior) are actualizations for the potentials of synaptic neurology. On these grounds, play does the prefatory work of the future, it doesn't just put together the past as it is said to do in more imitative theories of the nature of play (Sutton-Smith,1966) .

Second, modern neurological descriptions of the brain may be construed also as supportive of the evolutionary ludic paradigms presented above. Thus, the brain has been described as a jungle of potentials, 80% of the time concerned with its own internal associations. It has also been described as a value-driven labile correlator, meaning that drive (value, angst, or whatever) instigates variable associative processes, which bring into the field of dreams or consciousness any and all directly or barely relevant matters for thought (Edelman, 1992). As Rudolfo Llinas describes it:

> Essentially the brain is a dreaming instrument. At night it dreams in the absence of sensory input, and it is free to be as crazy as it wants to be ... in the day it dreams in a more limited fashion because the senses serve to limit the types of images that you can generate ... sometimes our mental maps get so elaborate we get lost in them, or we hide from ourselves.... Humans are probably the only self delusional animal. (qtd. Hilts, 1997, p. B9)

Clearly, following these mental descriptions, play might well derive much of its variable associative character from the very nature of mental activity. Dreams and play may share much in common, being variable ways individuals express their desire for fictional power over their life events. On this reading, the parallels between our evolutionary discourse and our neurological discourse are meant to be mutually supportive of the play theory being evolved in these pages, both with respect to the concept of variability and the characterization of the existential realm within which these variabilities are embedded (Damasio, 1994). It follows, in turn, that much of play is daydreaming, vicarious and empathic not unlike the passively experienced dreams from which it derives. The preference for more "activist" theories of play in the 20th century has more to do with our own entrepreneurial attitudes than with the nature of the phenomenon itself. Play is probably more empathic (consider all spectator activities) than it is active, more of a social obligation or private compulsion than it is a freedom.

The Role of Culture in the Development of Play

The next issue for consideration is to what extent, in cultural terms, play can be envisaged as a kind of variability/redundancy, or a kind of pseudo existential excitement. There is clearly cultural data which could be read as supportive of this possibility but also cultural data that seems to be contradictory. First, the supportive data: Western civilization, particularly the United States, is unique in its attention to the variability of individual child play. Nowhere else in world history have so many toys been produced for so many children and so much effort put in to having these children preoccupy themselves imaginatively with these multiple objects, as well as spend solitary time in play apparatus, playpens, play rooms and play computers In addition, there are joking relationships as well as endless negotiations and dialogues between parents and children. The child is expected to develop independence in relationship with people, with objects, and in fantasy play. The ideal child is highly imaginative and is, in consequence, an excellent student, who produces few behavior problems and does well in school. This child, described for us so well by the 30-year research program of the Singers (Singer, 1966, 1973; Singer & Singer, 1992), is a demonstration that play can be a field of great variability and of engaging life-like excitements. Its main features are, in sum, the variability of toy objects, imaginative behaviors, and of much-associated independent solitary play.

But, with some exceptions, the other 70% of the world does not so generally entertain this kind of "individualism" (Tudge, Lee, & Putnam, 1998). As Triandis (1997) says "the 70% lives in cultures in which a group is the figure and individuals are in the background while in the remaining cultures the autonomous individual is the figure and groups are in the background. This contrast has been given different names such as collectivism and individualism, an interdependent versus independent self, group focused and self focused cultures and many others" (p. 789). This difference is found even when play contrasts are made with other complex civilizations. Thus, although playful stimulation between parents and children is found throughout India and Asia, there is also often a much greater physical closeness to the more obedient baby through massaging and washing it throughout infancy and childhood. Unlike the Western patterns of separate sleeping from infancy onward, children often sleep with other members of these families from an early age. Where there is parent-stimulated imaginative play, it is more often about pretence of a social or interdependent sort, where the mother helps the child to playfully adopt attitudes and behaviors which are to be held towards significant extended family, including teachers. This valuing of social interdependence manifestations in play rather than object-related independence manifestations is also widesread throughout the rest of the non-Western world (Greenfield & Cocking, 1994; Haight, Wang, & Fung, 1995; Sutton-Smith & Heath, 1981).

Clearly, this older world presents a contrast to the present theoretical focus here on play as a kind of variability and existential challenge. And yet, it is necessary to recall that the other characteristic of adaptive variability stressed by Gould (1997), as well as quirkiness, was redundancy. Throughout most societies, what is most emphasized about play is its traditions rather than its novelty. What one finds in general in most, but not all, earlier societies (band, tribal, and chieftan) is generally much more emphasis on play as a collective rather than as an individualistic activity. Ernst Mayr, noted evolutionist, explains this preference:

> One of the most important developments in human cultural evolution was social integration in the hominid group. Among the primates some species, such as orangutans, are more solitary, and others, such as chimpanzees and baboons live in much larger social groups. The shift by the time of homo erectus (1.9 millions years ago) to a strictly terrestrial mode of living was accompanied by an increase in group size. The evident advantages were better protection against predators, greater ability to cope with other competing groups of conspecifics and an improved efficiency in the search for new resources, especially food. (1997, pp. 241–242)

It is not hard to believe, on Mayr's (1997) grounds, that the great role of social integration in human play has been for the survival advantages that it has. It's not hard to think of group play as a fairly low cost way of celebrating social integration.

But still, as a play form, social play is always paralleled by simpler forms of motor and object play in animals and, in modern times, it is often secondary to various forms of solitary physical and mind play. All of which means that important as such collective behavior is to the development of human adapation from band, to tribe, to chieftan, and to state societies, it is still not sufficient for a universal definition of play's function. In modern times, although cooperation underlies every form of social play that there is, we tend more to emphasize individual achievements because our collectivity is less likely to be under threat. But what this analysis does show is that the type of play (collective or individual) is produced because of its relevance to the type of society. The kind of existential threats that are most valued in society find expression in the appropriate forms of play. While we don't see as much variability in the older traditional forms as in modern forms, their play is nevertheless amongst the more variable of cultural forms that they possess, whether it serves social integration or not. Consider for example the randomness of games of chance, or the uncertain outcomes in games of physical or strategic contest. Clearly, such variability is as intrinsic to traditional play forms as is the redundancy of their forms.

But there is yet a greater threat to this discussion's attempt to ground play in culture. What is surprising anthropologically is to find societies that attempt to prevent play taking place, that punish or limit play where it is observed, or that do not regard children as worthy of attention until they have acquired either language or apprentice work capacities. Furthermore, what is often inhibited is largely the more variable imaginary play of the children, though the physical play may be allowed (Feitelson, 1977; Miracle, 1977). While this kind of negativity towards child play is common throughout the world, it appears most often to be connected with low subsistence urban or agricultural societies where there is a great need for the labor of the children , or alternatively is connected to fundamentalisic belief systems where there is felt to be a great need for conformity to the collective ideology. Typically, child play, where it exists in such cultures, is mostly imitative of adult daily work activities and there is "little elaboration or introduction of variation or complexity during the course of the play. Scripts and roles are repeated over and over, almost ritualized," writes Susan Gaskins (Gaskins & Göncü, 1992). She continues:

> Mayan children do not pretend to be something other than people. They do not pretend to be babies or anyone younger than they are. They do not create imaginary people or things in their play.... In addition adults do not participate in or seem to be entertained by children's symbolic play." (p. 33)

Giving considerable support for Gaskins and Göncü's (1992) finding of these low-level, ritualistic kinds of play in some cultures (see also Wilson, 1974) is the long available data in the six-culture study of Whiting (1963) from the Nyansongo group of Kenya, where the children played the least of all the six world groups studied. Subsistence agriculture prevails with this group; children must help with the work and the care of younger children. Under the mother's control, both boys and girls have many chores, such as collecting firewood, fetching water, preparing food, cooking, cleaning and sweeping, harvesting vegetables, grinding grain, gardening, and herding (see also Lancy, 1996). In addition to this kind of example, Feitelson (1977) has detailed the kinds of religion-based negativity towards signs of child imaginative play in a number of Middle East cultures.

What we have here perhaps is the assertion that social integration by work routines or by religion is more important than any support that may be given by socially integrative play forms in these stringent societies. They have developed a rigidification of behavior in the narrow strand that they must occupy in order to survive. One might suggest that the negation of play by societies that do not countenance much variability in work or belief systems is indirect evidence that play is itself a system of variability and, therefore, a potential source of deviance for them. Their position is not unlike that of European working-class parents in the 18th- and 19th-century Industrial Revolution whose children went off to work in factories and were discouraged from wasting their time at play. Cultures have varied enormously throughout history in their flexibility in the face of external conquest. There are innovative societies and there are conservative societies, the former adapting quickly to conquest and the others not at all (Diamond, 1997). It would be interesting if research could show that the innovative kinds of society had more highly variable play than the conservatives.

The question is whether these kinds of information can assist a cultural evolutionary thesis about play by showing that play's absence can be as powerful as play's presence in support of the appropriate cultural behaviors. The above data at least would seem to indicate that adults in these cultures assume that play can either promote or interfere with that which they wish to teach. It certainly shows that patterns of play variability are deemed relevant to the adjustment patterns of the larger, more complex cultures, a not surprising finding in light of earlier studies of the relationship between child rearing and games, and between technology and games. Games of strategy, for example, are found chiefly in complex cultures (Roberts & Sutton-Smith, 1962). The very rigidity that play is meant to circumvent, in the Gould (1997) view of variability, is in these low play societies, exercised to reverse that effect; which reminds us also of the danger of only emphasizing the contribution of play to variability when it is clear that much of play has highly redundant characteristics on both animal and human levels. Play's own internal ludic variability between repetitive and innovative characteristics permits the kind of varying uses of play in different cultures, as previously described. If play does serve evolutionary variability, perhaps the emphasis should be on the particular ludic way in which this occurs because the play medium is itself labile to these variable uses. There is, after all, a ludic as well as an adaptive dialectic, an internal as well as an external set of relationships to be considered. Adaptively, play serves variability by its lability to variant usage rather than by any necessity for innovation alone; but then, this is to say again that play creates a range of variability rather than any necessary usage. Its function is to increase the range of simulated possibility, even if what is created is rather ritualistic forms of expression.

PLAY AS STRUCTURE

What has been achieved to this point is to say that despite the great variety of psychological definitions of play given earlier, and despite the variety of approaches—biological, neurological, and anthropological—which give further support to the reality of play's variability, there is nevertheless considerable data given here to support a formulation of play as having a universal equilibrial-disequilibrial structure. Table 15.1 defines the structure of play. It argues that all the various disciplines show some parallel conciliative tendency towards the parallelism of structures, which is to say that whether it is a young child at play or a comedian on television, there is always a balancing between everyday real expectations and their defiance in these playful acts (the virtual paradox), and, further, there is a balancing between the ludic sense so established and the nonsense to which it may still lead (the ludic paradox).

In frankness, however, it cannot at this point be known whether these parallels across disciplines legitimize the notion that there is here a common evolutionary and cultural descent of ludic forms, as this table suggests, or whether this is merely a fortuitous listing of analogies. Or even worse, as the author is the one who has chosen the table's contents, there is always the possibility of an "experimenter" bias

TABLE 15.1.
Play's Structural Definition

Discipline	Equilibrium	Disequilibrium
BIOLOGY		
Flexibility	Redundancy	Quirkiness
	Cooperation	Unpredictability
Metacommunication	Signals, frames	Virtual Paradoxes
Animals	Repetition	Disorder,
	Inhibition of hurting	fragmentariness
NEUROLOGY	Value-driven correlations	Delusional fantasies
		Synaptic variability
ANTHROPOLOGY	Collective traditions	Celebratory disorders
	Rituals, hierarchies	Ludic paradoxes
	Mediations	Intensifications (noise)
	Communal identity	Inebriation
PSYCHOLOGY	Rules, referees	Excitement, risk taking
	Stylized actions	Wishful thinking
	Exaggerations	Impulse indulgence
	Illusions of mastery	Laughter, nonsense
		Grotesquerie
		Unrealistic optimism
		Egocentricity, lability
		Fantasy

in that selection. Countering these attenuations of the argument, however, much greater differences might well have been expected across the time span reflected in these disciplines. The notion of such a fixed ludic structure is not, therefore, entirely untenable.

THE FUNCTIONS OF VARIABILITY

There are two kinds of variability to be dealt with, the biological and cultural or the psychological. First, what can be said about the evolutionary function of the ludic variability presented above? These are some of the possibilities:

First, real variability might be served by the fact that play itself is a major and visible *exemplification of variability*. The immediate joy of playful variability lies in its own improvisational moves to defy convention by trying to jump farther, run faster, laugh louder, have good luck, sing more heartily, display oneself well, and win contests. There is little question that play exemplifies novel forms of variability, even though we are also struck with the repetitive and apparently stereotyped character of the play forms of others. My wife, for example, has done two newspaper crossword puzzles every morning for over 20 years before arising from bed. Surely that is stereotyped. From an outside observer's point of view, it might seem so. But from her point of view, quite the contrary, every puzzle presents a novel predicament and requires novel associations to render it conquered. We might speculate, perhaps, that it is not impossible that those who lead lives of some such degree of exemplary playful liveliness are less likely be committed to stereotypy of body or mind, in the arenas of their fickle play involvement, in this case, with words. This is a speculative argument that there might be some kind of neurological feedback from one form of variabilty (ludic) to other forms (neurological). Alternatively as mentioned earlier, play as variability may be the best reinforcer and sustainer of neurological synaptic variability. This would be the greatest biological gift of all. Societies that repressed early such ludic synapsis reinforcement would presumably have a more limited citizenry.

Second, although the major function of play does not seem to be the immediate enduring service that it renders to conventional forms of adaptation, it nonetheless seems likely that transfer can take place. My wife often used to ask me to tell her the meaning of this word or that word. Nowadays, after her 20 years of verbal puzzle play, it is just as likely that it is *I* who will have to ask *her* the meaning of obscure words, as well as the location of obscure geographical places. More darkly, but similarly, it is also probable that the baseball or cricket players of peace time were amongst the most facile grenade throwers of war time. Biologically speaking, a useful function has only to serve probabilistically to be adaptive, a concept which I once labeled *adaptive potentiation* (1975). This inherent randomness of play/life relations would also explain why scholarly attempts to envisage tight causal relationships between play and transfers beyond play have not had much

success. On the other hand, this concept of play's potentiation of novel compe-
tences would fit better into the small amount of research that shows long-term,
generalized productive consequences from earlier experiences going to "playway"
preschools and "playway" elementary schools, and from having a wider range of
nonacademic "playful" commitments in high school than others with comparable
academic skills.

Third, if it could be shown that those societies that were more variably playful
were also more viable on the world scene because of their openness, flexibility, and
perhaps even highly maintained energy levels, then the multiple modern cultural and
psychological ludic forms might well be supposed to have biological consequences
because of the long-term greater survival of the capitalistic societies within which
these forms of play are taking place. One might suppose, in this vein, that the contemporary tendency of psychologists to define play as a form of special freedom or
as a unique form of self-actualization, when conjoined together with the new kinds
of monetary eminence being given to some professional players (such as novelists,
actors, comedians, athletes, hosts, film directors, etc.) might augur an even greater
importance for the role of play's stimulative variability training in the modern societies of the future.

Fourth, there are all those other contemporary definitional phenomena that call
attention to play's role in promoting persistence, optimism, excitement, fun, display,
laughter, triumph, and so on. They are presumably the names for the pleasures that
play's variable paradoxes promote. These might be presumed to be the consequences
of play that undoubtedly then also become its reinforcers and, therefore, need to be
incorporated into any definition of play.

A DEFINITION OF PLAY

Putting together all of the above materials with some optimism, we have a definition
of play:

> Play, as a unique form of adaptive variability, instigates an imagined but equilibrial
> reality within which disequilibrial exigencies can be paradoxically simulated and give
> rise to the pleasurable effects of excitement and optimism. The genres of such play are
> humor, skill, pretence, fantasy, risk, contest, and celebrations, all of which are selective
> simulations of paradoxical variability.

PLAYFULLY

What the function-shift phenomena warns us is that while this all sounds very
interesting, it is quite possible that these biological rumors are no longer the relevant issues for modern play forms. It may be, after all, a further distance than it
seems from animals play fighting to the capers of Jerry Seinfeld and his cohorts.

What were once serious cortical considerations of imagined dangerous existential scenarios have been changed into nonserious cortical considerations of nonsense. In play, these earlier existential neurological maps have now come to function as the enjoyment that can be had by simulative derivations from those earlier adaptive alternatives. Which is to say one gets quite different rewards than was formerly the case. Now perhaps one finds in play not just a variability exercise, but instead a parody on the vicissitudes of our mortal existence. In such a case, play would now bring a redemption from earthly inadequacy. It would function more like a religion in offering alternatives to the everyday life, even though in the case of play these would be relatively temporary. Still, the opposite of play—if redefined in terms which stress its reinforcing optimism and excitement—is not work, it is depression. Players come out of their ludic paradoxes, whether as participants or fans, with renewed belief in the worthwhileness of merely living. The cry of "We're number one!," or that I climbed Mount Everest, or that I have 10 Barbie dolls, or that I have another successful novel, or that I have a Motion Picture Academy Award, or that I am a master at chess, or that I won the lottery, or that I am a beauty queen, are all exultant cries, and they convince most of us, for a while at least, that the world is not such a bad place to be living in. Perhaps play, while it may continue biologically to be about energizing and making us more flexible, now psychologically is more like a branch of existential utopian philosophy, carrying us absurdly forward with optimism and confidence in the life we are leading. Perhaps as Baktin said so mysteriously about the Rabelaisian carnivals that he studied, play works because it is refructifying.

Finally, of course one does need to be playful about all of this. It is too tenuous and too complex to be taken too seriously, and yet there's no hope at all if we don't practice what we preach and believe somewhat in the adaptive or refructifying value of all of this paradoxical variability.

REFERENCES

Auguet, R. (1972). *Cruelty and civilization: The Roman games*. London: Allen & Unwin.

Bateson, G. (1972). *Steps to an ecology of mind*. New York: Ballantine.

Bekoff, M. (1998). Playing with play: What we can learn about cognition, negotiation and evolution. In D. Cummings & G. Allen (Eds.), *The evolution of mind* (pp. 162–182). New York: Oxford University Press.

Burghardt, G. M. (1998). Play. In G. Greenberg & M. Haraway (Eds.), *Comparative psychology: A handbook* (pp. 757–767). New York: Garland.

Chick, G., Loy, J., & Miracle, A. (1997). Combative sport and warfare: A reappraisal of the spillover and catharsis hypotheses. *Cross Cultural Research, 31*(3), 249–267.

Damasio, A. R. (1994). *Descartes error*. New York: Grosset Putman.

Diamond, J. (1997). *Guns, germs and steel*. New York: W. W. Norton.

Edelman, G. M. (1992). *Bright air, brilliant fire*. Boston: Beacon.

Fagen, R. (1981). *Animal play behavior*. New York: Oxford University Press.

Feitelson, D. (1977). Cross cultural studies of representative play. In B. Tizard & D. Harvey (Eds.), *The biology of play* (pp. 6–14). London: Heinemann.

Gardner, H. (1983). *Frames of mind*. New York: Basic Books.

Gaskins, S., & Göncü, A. (1992). Cultural variation in play: A challenge to Piaget and Vygotsky. *The Quarterly Newsletter of the Laboratory of Comparative Human Cognition, 14*(2), 31–35.

Gould, S. J. (1996a). *Full house*. New York: Harmony Books.

Gould, S. J. (1996b). Creating the creators. *Discover, 17*(10), 43–54.

Gould, S. J. (1997, October 9). Evolutionary psychology: An exchange. *New York Review of Books, 45,* 56–57

Greenfield, P. M., & Cocking, R. R. (Eds.). (1994.) *Cross cultural roots of minority child development*. Hillsdale, NJ: Lawrence Erlbaum.

Haight, W., Wang, X.-L., & Fung, H. (1995). *The ecology of everyday pretending in three cultural communities*. Paper presented at the Biennial Meeting of the Society for Research in Child Development, Indianapolis, IN.

Hilts, P. J. (1997, May 27). Listening to the conversation of neurons to study the mind. *New York Times*, p. B9.

Huttenlocher, P. (1994). Synaptogenesis in human cerebral cortex. In G. Dawson & K. Fisher (Eds.), *Human behavior and the developing brain* (pp. 137–152). New York: Guilford Press.

Keeley, L. H. (1996). *War before civilization*. New York: Oxford University Press.

Lancy, D. F. (1996). *Playing on the mother ground*. New York: Guilford Press.

Mayr, E. (1997). *This is biology*. Cambridge, MA: Harvard University Press.

Miracle, A. (1977). Some functions of Aymara games and play. In P. Stevens (Ed.), *Studies in the anthropology of play* (pp. 310–328). West Point, NY: Leisure Press.

Myers, D. (1997). *Is play random?* Paper in progress.

Roberts, J. M., & Sutton-Smith, B. (1962). Child training and game involvement. *Ethnology, 1*(2), 166–185.

Singer, J. L. (1966). *Daydreaming*. New York: Random House.

Singer, J. L. (1973). *The child's world of make-believe*. New York: Academic Press.

Singer, D., & Singer, J. L. (1992). *The house of make believe*. Cambridge, MA: Harvard University Press.

Slade, A., & Wolf, D. P. (1994). *Children at play*. Oxford, England: Oxford University Press.

Smith, P. K. (1982). Does play matter? Functional and evolutionary aspects of animal and human play. *The Behavioral and Brain Sciences, 5,* 139–184.

Spariosu, M. (1989). *Dionysus reborn*. Ithaca, NY: Cornell University Press.

Sutton-Smith, B. (1966). Piaget on play: A critique. *Psychological Review, 73,* 104–110.

Sutton-Smith, B. (1975). Play as adaptive potentiation. *Sportswissenschaft, 5,* 103–118.

Sutton-Smith, B. (1978a). *Die dialekitk des spiel*. Schordorf, Germany: Verlag Karl Hoffman.

Sutton-Smith, B. (1978b). The dialectics of play. In E. Landry & W. Oban (Eds.), *Physical activity and human well being* (Vol. 2; pp. 759–770). Miami, FL: Symposia Specialists.

Sutton-Smith, B. (1997). *The ambiguity of play*. Cambridge, MA: Harvard University Press.

Sutton-Smith, B., & Heath, S. (1981). Paradigms of play. *The Quarterly Newsletter of the Laboratory of Comparative Human Cognition, 3*(3), 41–45.

Triandis, H. C. (1997). Human development in the majority world. *Contemporary Psychology, 42*(9), 789.

Tudge, J., Lee, S., & Putnam, S. (1998). Children's play in sociocultural context: South Korea and the United States. In M. C. Duncan, G. Chick, & A. Aycock (Eds.), *Play and culture studies: Explorations in the fields of play*. Greenwich, CT: Ablex.

Whiting, B. W. (Ed.). (1963). *Six cultures*. New York: John Wiley.

Wilson, C. (1974). *Crazy February*. Berkeley, CA: University of California Press.

Wilson, E. O. (1998, April). The biological basis of morality. *The Atlantic Monthly, 281*(4), 53–70.

16

Play as Ascending Meaning: Implications of a General Model of Play

Thomas S. Henricks
Elon College

The following chapter presents a general model of play. Because of the myriad understandings of play that have developed in the social sciences, such a project may seem either too ambitious or worse, wrongheaded. After all, the various academic traditions regarding play have been well explored by others (see, for example, Ellis, 1973; Levy, 1978; Rogers & Sawyers, 1988; Sutton-Smith, 1997); and it can be argued that diversity of viewpoint (under whatever conceptual framework) ensures fuller attention to the various issues surrounding play.

This chapter does not attempt to ignore or reduce this diversity, but rather tries to place it within a wider framework. Initially, the author will bring together some commonly held tenets about play into a general definition. This definition will be set within a broader model featuring three other fundamental kinds of human activity (namely, "work," "ritual," and "communitas"). A view of play as "ascending meaning" will then be developed and illustrated at the different levels of analysis common to the social sciences (i.e., at the levels of psyche, social system, culture, organism, and environment). In a concluding example, the utility of the approach will be examined. In general, this chapter "locates" play as a category of human relationship and displays the potential settings of that relationship in a broader way than has been done before.

EXPLORING PARADOX: ISSUES IN DEFINING PLAY

Most play scholars are familiar with the idealist and romantic traditions (see Sutton-Smith & Kelly-Byrne, 1984c) that have influenced the rise of play studies. As expressed most famously by Huizinga (1955), play is often thought to be freer or more voluntary than other types of activity. One aspect of this freedom is the predominance of intrinsic rather than extrinsic motives (see Gottfried, 1985). Players "make up" and sustain actions for reasons that are primarily psychological or even physiological. Furthermore, the process of playing itself seems to be more important than the outcome of the activity; products or consequences may be deemed irrelevant. For such reasons, play is often contrasted with work. However, play may also be matched against "routine" or "real" life. As a number of authors have noted (see Bateson, 1972; Herron & Sutton-Smith, 1971), play typically has a profound "as-if" quality that separates it from the rest of what people do. And players (or at least the older ones) are well aware when they are "at play."

For such reasons, play is sometimes seen as a wellspring for spontaneity, imagination, and creativity (see Lieberman, 1977). Play cultivates the possibilities of personal accomplishment. Players "assimilate" reality (Piaget, 1962); they seek out new kinds and levels of stimulation (see Berlyne, 1960). They plot a thousand futures.

Set against the position that play exemplifies spontaneity and personal freedom is an emphasis upon the ways in which play seems restricted or limited. Huizinga (1955) himself described the extent to which play is "rulebound"; and other scholars (for example, Caillois, 1961; Mead, 1934; Piaget, 1962) have described the restrictive and obligatory aspects of the more social forms of play. Indeed, many recent sociological and anthropological commentators on play (for example, Gruneau, 1983; Henricks, 1991) have been emphatic about the degree to which players and play events are entangled by broader societal values, norms, and institutional patterns. By such lights, players typically do not "escape" society, but rather participate in it in strategic, publicly sanctioned ways. Simple frivolity gives way to the complicated commitments that characterize other portions of people's lives.

The apparent tension between these themes in play studies—between freedom and restriction, spontaneity and order, frivolity and seriousness, and so on—has tended to give play a contrary, even paradoxical character. Huizinga's *Homo Ludens: A Study of the Play Element in Culture* (1955) revels in the apparent contradictions of its subject matter; and several other scholarly works (Gruneau, 1980; Kline, 1995; Loy, 1982) describe play as a "paradox" in their titles. As Levy (1978) puts it: "To play means to accept the paradox of what is at once essential and inconsequential" (p. 1). A similar tack is taken by Sutton-Smith and Kelly-Byrne (1984b), who point to a "fundamental bipolarity" (p. 30) in most accounts of play. At the same time, play manages to be both equilibrating (i.e., restoring various kinds of order) and disequilibrating (i.e., introducing disruption and novelty and irrationality into the world).

There is something appealing about a concept that embraces opposites and thereby defies scrutiny. And it fits a certain vision of players (and some of the academics

who study them) as romantic and rebellious spirits who defy a constraining and formal world. Having acknowledged this, the author would argue that there is little to
be gained by confirming the status of play as paradox. Instead, it is the task of the
play scholar to identify the elements that pose these seeming contradictions. If play
is said to be both serious and nonserious, in what ways and for what reasons does
each term apply? If play is both rulebound and spontaneous, what are the issues associated with each description? Surely, play both confirms social order and challenges
it—but in what ways? Such questions suggest the value of returning to issues surrounding the nature and dimensions of play. This chapter participates in that project.

LOCATING PLAY WITHIN THE DIMENSIONS OF REALITY

Attempting to define play means first of all determining what domain or dimension
of reality play inhabits. Several possible sites for the study of play will be considered
here: play as form, play as activity, play as disposition, and play as experience.
Choices made at this point are fateful in that they determine, by a process of elimi-
nation, the kinds of research questions that can be asked.

Play as Form

One possibility for the definition of play is to see it as a set of material and symbolic forms that guide the activity of individuals. In this sense, games like Monopoly or
baseball or festivals like Carnival or the county fair become objectified as cultural
patterns. People can anticipate with some confidence the nature of a hockey game or
a high school dance; such forms have a "life of their own" in public consciousness.
For his part, Huizinga (1955) identified a variety of cultural forms in the West (such
as law, poetry, etc.) as essentially "play forms" (i.e., as frameworks which not only
express but foster human creativity). A slightly different version of this viewpoint
sees play as a form that has been *institutionalized*—that is, established and accepted—in society (see Loy, 1968, for an application of this idea to the definition of
sport). In this context, it is only the more important and popular forms that achieve
the status of true play. By such criteria, baseball is a recognizable play-form in the
United States; knurr-and-spell is not.

There are certain advantages to defining play as a form or set of forms because
this position opens up many interesting questions about the various activities and
experiences that actually occur during, for example, carnivals or bingo games.
Nevertheless, common usage protests against defining play in this way. There are
other words like "game" or "fair" that better describe the forms people recognize.
Aside from the familiar reference to dramatic presentations as "plays," play itself is
more commonly understood as something one does. One "plays" the form or plays
"at" or "in" it.

Play as Activity

In this viewpoint, play is understood as a process or "mode of relating" to the world. Play is not a framework for action but the activity itself. Scholars taking such a view (see, for example, Levy, 1978) insist that human activity is a dynamic, and some-times unpredictable, series of happenings. Expressed differently then, play refers to a special quality of relationship between actors and their environments, or between "subjects" and the objects of their apprehension. These objects may be external to the actor (where the term "behavior" is an appropriate description) or they may be elements in purely mental activity.

Even if one agrees that play refers to some pattern of subject-object relations (itself a conception with a rather "Western" tinge), it is unlikely that he or she will agree on the specific kind of pattern that characterizes play. For example, does play refer to some characteristic way that the subject approaches or renders the world (the approach taken by Piaget, 1962) or is play better understood as a way of seeking and then responding to stimuli (the behaviorist orientation of, for example, Ellis, 1973; Hunt, 1961)? Is play to be understood as a special "dialec-tical" interplay between the elements of the world (the approach of Sutton-Smith, 1978)? Or does it refer to some "deep engagement" where the entire notion of challenge and response, of subject-object opposition, becomes subordinated (the position advanced by Csikszentmihalyi, 1975, 1990)?

The view of play as an activity or process is appealing because it opens up a num-ber of questions about the relationship of human beings to the various "forms" they inhabit. For example, what does it mean to "play" baseball, charades, or house? Should we deem everything that happens during the game to be acts of play or are some actions playful while others are not? Do some structures or circumstances gen-erate more play actions than others? Furthermore, this approach exposes the activi-ty-experience relationship as especially problematic. Do behaviors that seem "playful" to external observers yield emotional states that are at all equivalent in the various players?

Play as Disposition

A third viewpoint emphasizes the elements that players bring to events. Play is not something that happens to people (like "falling in love"); rather, players create and sustain the activity through the pursuit of their own interests, motives, or purposes. People may seek optimal levels of arousal, discharge, or ego support (see Ellis, 1973). Play begins for such reasons and continues until these conditions are met or abandoned. Not surprisingly, this view of play as intrinsically motivated or at least psychologically generated has been popular with psychologists (see, for example, Levy, 1978). An interesting extension of this approach is Lieberman's (1977) con-cept of "playfulness," which she describes as the "play element in play." Some chil-dren, she argues, bring more to the play setting than others. Their activity is characterized by spontaneity, energy, enthusiasm, wit, and social engagement. Such emotional-intellectual buoyancy is, in her words, "an ingredient of the creative individual's cognitive style" (p. 108). Clearly, this viewpoint serves as a bridge between what people do (play as activity) and what people feel (play as experience). Nevertheless, dispositions are shifting things that are hard to measure. The motives for entering a game may be different from the motives that sustain it. Purposes may be half-recognized or hidden entirely from players and observers. To summarize, play is less a simple expression of the playful spirit than a complicated interaction between orienting individuals and their environments.

Play as Experience

A final viewpoint is that play is some quality of experience that is generated and sustained by certain actions. To play is to discover excitement. Play is often characterized by smiling, laughter, or at least by the "glow" of psychic fulfillment. In this sense, the activity is consummatory; there is a pattern and pace to events that permits emotional completion. This quality of embeddedness or "flow" has been emphasized by both Csikszentmihalyi (1990) and Goffman (1961). However, it is worth noting that neither author restricts this quality of focus or entrancement to play; under the right conditions, a person may be lost in work or love as well.

Furthermore, there is considerable disagreement about the *level* and *type* of excitement that is characteristic of the play experience. Is play characterized by modest or "optimal" excitement (see Berlyne, 1960), or can players be more lethargic or frenzied in their experience? To further complicate matters, some play scholars (see Pellegrini, 1995) have accompanied Freud "beyond the pleasure principle" to examine the range of emotions that are associated with aggressive playful encounters. Still others (for example, Bogue & Spariosu, 1994; Spariosu, 1989) have returned with Nietzsche to the mixtures of power and pleasure exhibited in pre-Socratic Greece. To push the "dark side" argument to its extreme form, is play not about the pursuit of modest pleasure at all, but rather (or at least equally) about the pursuit of opposition, misery, and fear? At any rate, it seems safest to conclude that the emotional states generated by play are more diverse and complicated than is generally acknowledged.

TOWARD A GENERAL MODEL OF PLAY

It would certainly be possible to develop a definition of play that embraces elements from all four dimensions previously noted. In this sense, play could be seen as a certain *form* (for example, specific culturally-prescribed games or events) that cultivates a certain type of *activity* (for example, social confrontation) that entails specific *dispositions* (for example, motives defined as acceptable by the event) that generate a certain type of experience (for example, an "optimal" level of excitement). However, the definition would be so specific as to eliminate most interesting human activities from consideration. Furthermore, if one defines play as a specific form (for example, games) or experience (for example, joy), he or she can not ask questions about other forms or experiences that might be pertinent to the event. Clearly, choices must be made. In this chapter, then, play will be defined as a distinctive kind of *activity*. Matters of *form*, *disposition*, and *experience* will be seen as variables related to but not defining play events.

Although the previous pages have emphasized the different ways of understanding play, it is argued that most treatments of the concept can be reduced to two sets of characteristics: 1) separation or boundedness; and 2) control or transformation. In so doing, the author wishes to revisit the much-abused notion that play is somehow about freedom. As may be apparent, the two categories above refer to the two sides of freedom: negative and positive. Freedom as a negative phenomenon refers to the separation of the person (i.e., subject) from entanglement or interference. Freedom in its positive mode refers to the subject's ability to control or render the world. Together, these elements constitute two interlacing themes of human capability.

Separation/Boundedness

Although there remains a sense in which the play of young children is also their "work," for the most part, players are aware that their activity is somehow discontinuous with the normal stream of events. As Huizinga (1955) emphasized, players work with the "stuff" of ordinary life, but they do it in settings that are sheltered in a variety of ways. Some of these separating devices include: the separation from external consequences, the separation from external purposes, the separation by distinctive cultural elements, and the separation by awareness.

Separation from external consequences. Play activity is commonly seen as having few or no consequences beyond the event itself. Of course, all of us know that playful activity may result in the creation of some product (variously defined) or in other (short or long term) effects on the contexts surrounding the action—on the body, psyche, society, environment, and so on (see Goodale & Godbey, 1988). However, in general, play activities are notable in that the scope and intentionality of consequences are restricted.

Separation from external purposes. A special case of (anticipated) consequence is the consciously recognized goals of individuals and organizations. While it does not seem profitable to interpret any consciously regulated activity (including play) as entirely aimless, it does seem clear that purposes may be distinguished in terms of their location. To put this as a question: Are anticipated goals or end-states located within the time-space frame of the event itself, or are they external to it? Although human activities feature a great range of agendas by participants, many definitions of play (see, for example, Levy, 1978) have emphasized the extent to which players either keep (or are encouraged to keep) their focus within the event. In this sense, activities directed toward long-term or beyond-the-playground ends (for example, earning money, building endurance, or fostering national pride) lose some of their playful character.

Separation by distinctive cultural elements. Commonly, play is separated from other activities by special norms that guide the action or otherwise regulate the demeanor of participants. Indeed, play often occurs (and is recognized by observers) within a framework of extremely artificial but jealously defended rules. Furthermore, players may adhere to a variety of norms (regarding tone of voice, gait, posture, appropriate emotional expression, etc.) to indicate that they are entering the play sphere and sustaining their interest in it (see Miller, 1973). Other devices, some of which include special costumes, equipment, redefinitions of time, names for participants, playing terminologies, specially prepared playing fields or courts, all contribute to the sense of being apart. Indeed, the more elaborate or pointlessly silly these contrivances, the more the player signifies his or her commitment to the play sphere.

Separation by awareness. Social forms of play typically depend on signals of play-commitment from participants (see Bateson, 1972). Humans and animals adopt special "play-faces," postures, or movements to let others know the character of their intentions. However, even in solitary play, there is often an awareness that the player has moved into a special "zone" demanding certain kinds of attention and skill (see Singer, 1995, for a description of "paratelic" awareness). This experience of periodicity, of time broken free from the long stream of events, is commonly part of the charm of play (see Rahner, 1972).

To summarize, play represents activity separated from the various demands or entanglements of life. Players center their attention by consciously cutting off or ignoring wider considerations. They may take special liberties with time (by disavowing past and future) and with space (by creating a distinctive limited world of objects and gestures). They permit themselves (or are permitted) to be "intrinsically" involved. These intrinsic considerations may be of various types (for example, accomplishing certain ends as defined by a game, experiencing certain feeling-states, gaining social recognition or approval by other players or viewers, and so on). Of course, many of the motives of real people at play spill over into the realm of the "extrinsic" (e.g., social approval beyond the time-frame of the event) and the two kinds of motives may be curiously raveled. For such reasons, activities may be only more or less play-like. However, it is argued here that events with significant extrinsic elements be recognized as "mixed" events or be described by names other than "play."

Control/Transformation

The second general category in conceptualizations of play is the element of voluntarism or freedom. Individuals at play actively engage the world; they seek out new challenges or sources of stimulation. They explore a range of alternative futures.

Once again, this general theme can be broken into various components or aspects. These include: control of access, ability to initiate action sequences, ability to control the activity, and freedom as spontaneity. As may be apparent then, control may be exerted in different ways at different stages of the action sequence.

Control of access. Huizinga (1955) emphasized that players have a conspicuous freedom to enter and exit the playground. They take up play for largely psychological or physiological reasons and head on to other venues when the play spirit departs. As noted previously, this viewpoint has been criticized by sociologists and anthropologists who demonstrate the degree to which all human activity is constrained. Certainly, any behavior is limited to the extent that cultural expectations and the intentions of other actors get in the way of individual desire. And, as Simmel (1950) pointed out, increasing the people involved introduces new kinds of complexity and constraint. Furthermore, as a historical phenomenon, play has often been hedged around by a great range of gate-keeping devices (related to issues of propriety, wealth, knowledge, and power). Nevertheless, play activities generally are thought to provide relatively freer access than other types of human endeavor.

Ability to initiate action sequences. Entering the playworld is one thing; directing the course of behavior once there is something else. Sociologists of sport (see, for example, Coakley, 1996) commonly have distinguished informal or play-oriented sport from more formal versions by, among other things, the ability of players to control the pace and pattern of the action. In youth sport, this has meant challenging coaches and parents in their roles as authoritarian, rulebound, outcome-oriented directors of activity (see Orlick & Botterill, 1975).

From a more psychological perspective, it does seem that play follows a pattern in which individuals (i.e., subjects) initiate or seek out encounters with the object-world. Certainly, behaviorist accounts of play (Berlyne, 1960; Ellis, 1973) tend to emphasize the extent to which players seek out stimuli to maintain optimal levels of arousal. This stimulus seeking may trigger a long series of reverberations between the environment and the subject; such interaction is surely part of the entrancement of play. Nevertheless, it is the players themselves who initiate these moments. The surfer seeks her wave; the skydiver throws himself into jeopardy. Indeed, socially-oriented contests typically employ the terminology of being one's "play" or "move," an alternating opportunity for individuals to begin the action-sequence.

Ability to control the activity. A more extensive type of control is the ability to direct the course of action once begun. In this particular context, "voluntarism" means the imposition of will upon the objects of one's environment; players objectify and "take on" the world in ways that, in other settings, may be too consequential.

Although Huizinga (1955) emphasized the role of human assertion and even creativity in play, Piaget (1962) is probably the outstanding contributor with regard to this particular theme. In play, individuals "assimilate" reality instead of adjusting to it. Piaget's point means somewhat different things as children grow older and enter some of the more social (and thereby obligatory) forms of relationship. However, in general, he argues that players attempt to manipulate objects or forms by setting them within subjectively-generated schemas or action-patterns. Players discover the nature of the world by rendering it—through simple mechanical behaviors (characteristic of the sensory-motor stage) or later by symbolic manipulations (featuring increasingly abstract, mental activity).

Freedom as spontaneity. A final element for a model of play is the theme of spontaneity (see Klinger, 1971). Play is commonly seen as a protest against routine and is often surprising, tense, and unscripted. The outcome is usually in doubt, not only in terms of the final relationships discovered by the process, but also in terms of the moment when the activity will end.

Unfortunately, the term "spontaneity" has many related meanings. Is play "impulsive" (the product of sudden psychological inspirations), "unpremeditated" (i.e., unplanned), or "unpredictable" (i.e., impossible to foretell)? Is play "natural" or "instinctive" in ways that defy social order? Is it instead "unconstrained" (i.e., not influenced by external agencies or forces of any sort)? Although play is typically a rebellion of behavior against external forms, the term "spontaneity" seems to mystify that relationship more than elucidate it. Again, it seems more useful to try to specify the various ways in which the subject either honors or challenges specific forms through activity than to paint the entire affair as an exercise in unpredictability.

Having illustrated the roles of both separation and control in most accounts of play, the author offers the following definition: Play is *activity exhibiting the subject's efforts to control or transform the conditions of its existence. Such activity is guided and comprehended by purposes, consequences, and characteristics confined to the space-time frame of the event itself.* Activities are then considered "play-like" to the extent that they exhibit the aspects of separation and control previously described.

PLAY AS ASCENDING MEANING

The remainder of the paper will assess the implications of this particular definition for the study of play. To begin, it is argued that the study of play would profit from a stricter identification of activities conceived as its opposites. Simply to contrast play with the all the phenomena that are nonplay (i.e., eggplant, toasters, sleeping, etc.) seems particularly unproductive (see Bateson, 1971). For that reason, this paper will analytically oppose play to three other profoundly important modes of relating to the world: work, ritual, and communitas. In so doing, the author reasserts Huizinga's (1955) key insight that play is central to human civilization.

In the definition developed above, play was described as transformative, separated activity. This approach can be generalized in terms of these two variables (i.e., transformation and separation) to yield the typology represented in Figure 16.1.

As the reader can easily see, the position of play is now contrasted with that of "work," an activity that is structurally indistinguishable from play, except for the role of extrinsic purposes, consequences, or qualities in instigating or guiding the event (see Goodale & Godbey, 1988). Workers are hounded or inspired by visions of future

STANCE OF SUBJECT TOWARD OBJECT–WORLD

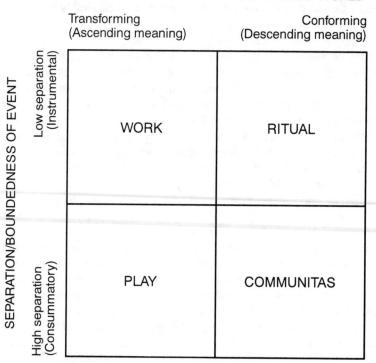

FIGURE 16.1. A typology of human experience.

states-of-affairs beyond the workplace; players are not. Although work is a more commonly exhibited category of life than play, most transformative activity is guided by purposes and contingencies of both types (i.e., internal and external). In other words, many events are simultaneously worklike and playlike with regard to their treatment of different issues.

The distinction between play and the conformitive modes of relationship (i.e., ritual and communitas) is more interesting—or, at least, is less-worked territory. As noted above, "ritual" is the term used to refer to conformitive, connected (i.e., non-separated) activity (see Handelman, 1977; Henricks, 1980). Whereas individuals test or transform the object-world in work-play, so the object-world tests or transforms individuals in ritual. This antithesis is extended in other ways, in that ritual celebrates order and play challenges it. Ritual emphasizes compliance and self-denial; play emphasizes resistance and self-assertion. In rituals, order creates and sustains individuals; in play, individuals create and sustain order.

The term used here to describe conformitive, separated activity is "communitas" (for the best known, if somewhat different, use of this term, see Turner, 1969).

Whereas rituals are activities expressing realms of order that connect people to both past and future, "communitas" immerses people in a present disconnected from historical time. Rituals (like work) have purposes and consequences beyond the event itself; communitas, on the other hand, focuses on the experience of order itself. Rituals create or realign status in the world beyond the event. By contrast, personal changes in communitas events are limited to the space/time-frame of the event itself.

In both ritual and communitas activity, people surrender themselves to something greater or more transcendent. The intentions and effects of communitas are simply more curtailed. In that sense, events like festivals, parades, proms, pageants, and fairs commonly feature elements of communitas (see Manning, 1984). Like play, such events represent moments stolen from the ordinary reaches of life. However, the "experiment" usually ends with the completion of the activity; routine is restored the following hour or day.

It must be acknowledged that the decision to treat the subject's enactments of transcendent structures as ritual/communitas rather than play differs from the approaches of a number of post-modern theorists (see, for example, Hans, 1981; Spariosu, 1989). Furthermore, it stands against the prevailing treatment of festivity by anthropologists. After all, traditional societies or subcultures commonly mix festivity with obligation or even self-effacement (see Schwartzman, 1978; Sutton-Smith & Kelly-Byrne, 1984a). When play occurs in such settings, it is often part of a more complicated journey into the meaning of collective relationship. Having said this, it is argued that the obligatory, formal, and conforming aspects of festivity should be called something else. In other words, the term "play" should cease being an all-purpose designation for whatever happens at festive events. To the contrary, festivity is typically an organization of opposing themes (for example, playful versus ritualistic elements) or an alternation between them.

To this point, the reader has been asked to consider a view of relationship in which people either willfully objectify and transform their environments (i.e., work-play) or submit to objectification and transformation themselves (i.e., ritual-communitas). However, terms like "environments" or "object-worlds" are spectacular in their vagueness. If the nature and dimensions of play are to be identified, some clearer architecture of human possibility is required. Figure 16.2 represents such a model.

The model itself draws its inspiration from Erich Kahler's (1960) distinction between "descending" and "ascending" symbolism in the interpretation of works of art. For Kahler, artistic meaning in earlier times (for example, the European Middle Ages) featured an interaction between the images themselves and some more important and transcendent level of reality that typically preceded and provided a context for the viewer's interpretation. For example, early paintings were often "about" great historical personages or events; they were bridges to established cultural (and metaphysical) verities. In this sense, such works featured "descending symbolism." By contrast, modern paintings tend to feature ascending symbolism; that is, they draw the interpreter's mind toward a quite different level of reality—the subjective expe-

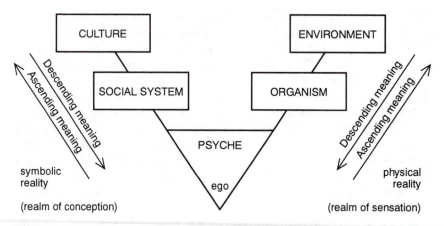

FIGURE 16.2. Contexts for human experience (the ascending-descending meaning perspective).

rience of the artist. Earlier works invited people to consult publicly articulated concepts and accounts as frameworks for human experience; later works (typically) ask people to consult personal experience itself as a vantage point for evaluating and responding to the world.

Figure 16.2 extends Kahler's (1960) general insight by elaborating on some of the different contexts in which "meaning" (defined as the capacity of patterns to recognize and respond to other patterns) occurs. As the reader will note (and perhaps disapprove), the notion of "meaning" is being applied to both the symbolic or mental plane of relationship (culture/society/psyche), as well as to the physical plane of relationship (environment/organism/psyche). Human consciousness itself (the ego) is placed at the center of the figure, where it assists people in recognizing and responding to patterns from various contexts.

To return to Kahler's (1960) metaphor, some events are understood better as an act of subjectivity expressing itself upon the world (i.e., by recognizing and transforming external patterns). This is ascending meaning. Descending meaning, by contrast, features the adjustment of subjectivity to external patterns. In this sense, the position resembles the assimilation-accommodation distinction of Piaget (1962).

However, the model also argues that the different contexts of reality (psyche, organism, society, culture, and environment) can be arrayed in terms of their relative "transcendence" (i.e., spatial scope and temporal abstraction) from the here-and-now moments of conscious decision making by the ego. In other words, the ascending-descending model pictures the psyche as being embedded in society, which is then embedded in culture on the symbolic plane. On the physical plane, psyche is embedded in the organism, which in turn is embedded in the wide physical environment. The ego attempts to recognize and negotiate patterns from these contexts—both intrapsychically (i.e., through the negotiation of various psychobiological demands and culturally influenced ideas/images) and externally (through the psyche's object-relations with culture, society, the body, and the environment).

What is perhaps unusual about this approach is its attempt to see play not merely as a psychologically generated event (i.e., as a rebellion of consciousness against the conditions of its existence), but also as a quality of relationship between patterns at different levels or contexts of reality. In other words, just as the psyche may rebel against the human body by testing and transforming it in play, so the body itself may rebel against its environment through its treatment of external objects. On the symbolic side of Figure 16.2, play embraces not only the rebellion of the psyche against social form, but also the eruption of social form itself against cultural order. It is in this sense that the model aspires to be "general" in scope and significance. Some comments about the different levels of playful interaction follow.

THE CONTEXTS OF PLAY

Play as an Intrapsychic Phenomenon

As the figure indicates, the ego opposes and negotiates the demands from two rather different sources—physiologically influenced impulses or needs and culturally influenced ideas and images. The point in saying this is not to saddle the reader with the trappings of a Freudian viewpoint, but simply to indicate the extent to which human experience is a negotiation of both sensation and conception. Furthermore, emphasizing the role of the ego in this way is not the same as suggesting that play is somehow "rational" or calculating in character. "Play" occurs to the extent that the ego opposes and transforms its own psychic patterns for the sake of experience itself. Imagination, daydreaming, and other forms of symbolic manipulation are examples of play under the terms stipulated above; i.e., 1) that this mental activity is disconnected from long-term purposes and consequences and 2) that the ego succeeds in controlling the flood of psychic material. To the extent that the ego is merely in the service of these internal patterns (for example, in various forms of imitation and mimetic indulgence), concepts other than play apply.

Play as an Interaction Between Psyche and Organism

As Freud and his followers emphasized, the other role of the ego is to negotiate the demands of external reality. Like other elements, our own bodies may become objectified. In this sense, play is a subjectively generated testing or teasing of physical abilities and limits (see Winnicott, 1971). A child (or adult) tests how well she can run or skip or hold her breath. Play interrupts ordinary functioning in a way that heightens awareness of both the process of challenge and its immediate consequences. As play more generally is the opposite of ritual, so physical play is the enemy of habit. And, as may be apparent to the reader, activity that is ritualistic at the intrapsychic level (for example, skills practicing) may be playful in terms of the individual's manipulations of the object world.

Play as an Intraorganismic Phenomenon

Can the body be set against itself? While functionalist images of body (i.e., as a system of interdependent parts operating in mutually adjusting or equilibriating ways) remain powerful in biology, it is worth pursuing the extent to which individual body elements may challenge one another or even the organism as a whole. As in the other cases previously described, this process of objectification and opposition helps the psyche become aware of these parts as differentiated entities and, even more importantly, of their relationship to one another.

Play, in this sense, may feature all manners of twisting, leaping, and tensing of muscles. In skipping, for example, the person not only challenges her body to perform a relatively complicated set of movements, but each leg challenges the other. One leg is made to wait while the other does its work; then it must adjust to the force of the movement created by the other. Spinning until dizzy and running until breathless are similar examples. Activity by certain parts of the body set the rest of the body (or at least certain parts of it) into a mad scramble of adjustment. In so doing, people expand their understanding of the nature and limits of physical capacity.

Play as an Interaction between Organism and Environment

Most play involves the manipulation of or resistance to material objects or patterns. Even the most abstract symbolic manipulations or games (for example, chess or mathematical puzzling) involve material elements as vehicles of communication or objects of play. However, physical play is distinctive from symbolic manipulation in that the "object" or focus of play is the player's ability to interrupt and redirect physical processes in the external world. Players hit fastballs, return serves, and make putts. To that extent, play is an exercise in object mastery. However, in a much profounder sense, players (as they hit, run, and jump) confront the laws of physical relationship itself. To extend professional golfer Ben Hogan's observation about golf and science, every sportsman is also a physicist.

Play as an Interaction between Psyche and Society

Although much of play seems to be a tussling with the objects and orders of the physical world, social scientists are (predictably) interested in other types of encounter. Of special interest is the interaction of the individual with social objects and patterns. As the reader will already have noted, the ascending-descending meaning model posits a distinction between the "social" and the "cultural." Following a tradition in sociology (if not some other disciplines), "culture" refers to the patterning of humanly created resources (both symbolic and artifactual) available to members of societies. "Society," on the other hand, refers to the patterning of human inter-relationship. Unlike cultural patterns (which are basically edifices of human conception), social patterns describe interactions between differentially located "actors" (persons-in-positions or other social "units"). Culture and society meet in the concept of "social structure." That is, a structural element (for example, an organization or a role) is "cultural" to the extent that it exists as a form or entity in public consciousness. It is "social" to the extent that it reflects a dynamic arrangement of people-in-positions. As is often noted, animals, even insects, can be social; however, the culture-creating capacities of animals (even other mammals) is less well-developed than our own.

By these terms, social players rebel against the arrangements of public life and their own positions in these orders. In play, children (or adults) try out new roles (like "teacher" or "nurse") and explore the possibilities therein. As Mead (1934) emphasized, such role-playing not only gives a person new vantage points for social experience, but also shows them how such role-players might see themselves in the more characteristic roles they play. That is, by playing "mommy," a child can view how that role might see a "child" who behaves a certain way. As in the other contexts of play previously described, play at this level is a trying-on of possibility.

As Mead (1934) and Piaget (1962) described, social play may also entail more thoroughgoing inquiries into the nature of social order itself. In Mead's famous example of the baseball game, the child must learn not only his own role, but also the roles of every other player and their simultaneous relationship to one another. In games, older children learn about social obligation—to one another and to the group. While Mead did not stress the way in which players may "play" with these obligations, Simmel, in his great essay on "sociability" (1950) did just that. Sociability, for Simmel, is a play-form of social life in which individuals cut themselves loose from customary roles and obligations. Within the settings of parties, maskings, and so on, people push the boundaries of civility. A profound "what would happen if..." attitude prevails. In so doing, social arrangement itself is made precarious.

Play as an Intrasocial Phenomenon

Just as the units of physical body may pit themselves against one another, so social units (for example, organizations and persons as role-actors) commonly oppose each other in play. Such encounters (for both humans and animals) are sortings-out of social relationship, both from the viewpoint of the individuals involved (who experience their abilities in new contexts) and from that of the group as a whole (which becomes more conscious of its own diversity). Even sham-fights (perhaps the best example of these activities) are not just tests of physical strength between individuals, but instead are collisions of socially conditioned expectation or will (see Pellegrini, 1995). In other words, social play is "minded". That is, players consciously explore the meanings of advantage and disadvantage, of rights and responsibilities within the group. In this sense, intrasocial play is about the fleeting experiences of public entitlement.

While agonistic activities like sport perhaps show these themes best, the experience of advantage-disadvantage, challenge-response is prominent in most forms of teasing, flirting, and joking (see Groos, 1976). In each, players attempt to manipulate or demonstrate their powers over the "other." In (typically) alternating scenes of dominance and submission, players generate and then address status anxiety.

Play as an Interaction between Society and Culture

Yet another level of play is the situation where social form itself erupts against its cultural frameworks. As previously noted, social arrangement is dependent both on more or less widely shared patterns of symbolic order (i.e., culture) and on the inspirations of differently situated actors. This latter aspect can, under certain circumstances, overwhelm established symbolic order.

Durkheim (1972) described this phenomenon as "collective effervescence" (p. 228). As the name implies, collective will seems to bubble forth. Old orders are obliterated and new visions are created. Within the restricted confines of the play world (events cut loose from long-term consequences and purposes), such activity is experienced as an affirmation or burgeoning of human possibility. Sociologists sometimes refer to these events under the category of collective behavior (i.e., the sudden dissolution and re-erection of social arrangement). However, these same sociologists are quick to remind us that many of these events are not as spontaneous as they seem. That is, many riots, rumors, crazes, panics, and so on are fairly controlled phenomenon—directed by the calculations of specific individuals or by the quick substitutions of other cultural "customs" onto an ambiguous situation. Nevertheless, the spectacle of emerging social order (what is sometimes termed "crescive" behavior) is of much importance to play studies. There is a sense that children (and adults) at play "make a new world" with each moment of their interaction. Indeed, play is perhaps the great site of social life becoming discovered as process rather than as structure.

Play as an Interaction of Psyche and Culture

One final site for play studies is the objectification and rendering of symbolic objects and patterns. Play with language—i.e., making up words, fracturing syntax, creating unusual juxtapositions and metaphors, attaching novel intonations to spoken words, and so on—is an important example of this (see Athey, 1984). To reverse anthropology's Sapir-Whorf hypothesis, personal thought patterns create and disorder linguistic structure. Furthermore, much intellectual and artistic work falls into this category of activity. Creative people impose their personal conceptions upon communities of discourse. To the extent that this is done for purposes of symbolic manipulation itself (and the experiences that derive from those efforts), the term "play" applies. Essays of the type you have been reading illustrate this principle. A body of knowledge is shoved (more or less successfully) into categories of the author's own scheming; the result is something that is usually more satisfying to the author than to the reader, who tends to have his own categories.

FINAL REFLECTIONS (AND AN EXAMPLE)

The preceding passages have pictured human behavior (and the subject matter of the social sciences) as an interaction or interpenetration of patterns at different levels or "contexts" of reality. The ascending-descending meaning metaphor has been used to locate these contexts (particularly in their relationship to the "ego") and to describe the extent that patterns at higher or lower levels predominate (i.e., require adjustment and response at other levels). In this perspective, play-work refers to an "ascending" mode of relationship in which the ego (or other agent) transforms "external" patterns. Communitas-ritual refers to modes of compliance or submission by these same agents.

Despite the effort to distinguish more or less pure types of human activity, it should be apparent that most events feature significant portions of all four modes—play, work, ritual, and communitas—and that differences between events are largely differences in the importance or predominance of each mode. Indeed, for play—as a challenge to specific forms—to come most brilliantly into focus, it is important that a great range of external forms from other contexts be accepted or complied with. In other words, ritual-communitas at some levels of relationship is the groundwork of work-play at other levels. Stated again, acquiescence in some contexts (for example, giving in to personal desire, accepting the responsibilities of a new social role, and so on) is the armament for battle at others. This is not to argue that play is in any sense "paradoxical," but rather to state that researchers should be more specific about which issues exhibit compliance and which exhibit transformation. To illustrate this point, an example is needed.

"Take Me Out to the Ball Game"

Play and sport researchers readily acknowledge that any game—in this example, a professional baseball game—admits of many different kinds and levels of interpretation. Even if one confines the analysis to the actual event itself (and excludes related activities in newspaper offices, television studios, parking lots and public thoroughfares, homes with televisions and radios tuned to the event, and so on), the possibilities for description are profound. Players, umpires, coaches, spectators, vendors, announcers, technicians, mascots, and so on are involved in the event in different ways; and the variety of actors playing these positions (for example, star players versus benchwarmers, fanatic spectators versus demure ones) are interesting and important. Any event of this sort is based upon the role enactments of individual actors moving through multitudes of changing predicaments; every game (and every moment of every game) is different. Having said this, the author will comment about the participation of two broad categories: players and fans. To what extent is their activity "playful"? Are the other modes of relationship—communitas, ritual, and work—important as well?

As stated above, ritual-communitas is commonly the groundwork for play-work. Sporting events are, for the most part, exercises in public order. For the players themselves, there is the ceremonial acceptance of the "rules" at the beginning of the event; players appear in "uniforms," run out to their "positions" on the field, and assume their status in a batting "order." Authority is granted to the umpire; and players have very closely supervised limits (such as no inappropriate touching, gestures, and language) with regard to these umpires and to each other. Fans accept their places in similar ways; they find their assigned seats, wait in lines, observe the requirements of vendors, and make a fairly predictable range of gestures and calls at more or less appropriate times. In other words, the game itself follows a very closely prescribed order that both players and fans understand and anticipate. Such "descending meaning" is especially important on the symbolic plane (psyche-society-culture relationships); however, there are also countless examples of physical acquiescence (psyche-organism-environment relationships), in which individuals accept and adjust to equipment, landscape, weather, and their own physical limitations.

To the extent that acquiescence to these physical and symbolic orders is characterized by purposes and consequences that stay within the event itself, the term "communitas" applies. Sporting events are largely sites for communitas; and much of the thrill of the game is the enactment of cherished traditions by tens of thousands of people. Players and fans alike draw energy from being part of something greater than themselves. The term "ritual" applies when this activity transforms lives beyond the ball park—for example, fans or players learn values that abide for a lifetime, communities attain prestige by the magnificence of the event, the "old game" itself prospers in the public imagination.

Nevertheless, games like baseball are generally distinguished as play-work events—i.e., as occasions when oppositional or transformative activity predominates. These transformations are most apparent at the physical level (where people test themselves against material objects and the "laws" of relationship). However, these physical challenges have implications at social and cultural levels as well. Games differ from more ritualized activities not only in that the specific actions and outcomes are relatively unscripted, but also in the sense that private aspiration or struggle actually creates order. Games feature the negotiation of social hierarchy (i.e., winner and loser) instead of its conferral by well-placed officials. For such reasons, games are key elements within societies that have achievement-based mythologies (see Henricks, 1991).

Games, however, are not philosophies; rather, the appeal of the game lies in the series of specific confrontations it generates. Batters facing pitchers, coaches screaming at umpires, runners and fielders frantically working against each other. In this sense, games highlight a specific kind of human aspiration—when the subject's efforts to achieve or control are blocked by the circumstances of the world. Thus, every nuance of the game (i.e., how the batter cleans his spikes at the plate or the pitcher holds the ball before winding up) is a prelude to battle. And the best moments are those when the play element is perfectly distilled—when 50,000 people are straining to see whether the runner's foot beat the catcher's tag by an eyelash in the last moments of the last inning.

While fan participation is by and large an expression of communitas, fans may become "players" to the extent that they do not merely observe or enact the forms, but instead transform them. While much fan behavior is fairly ritualized, fans can play with the forms of the event by unusual antics, signs, and costumes. The rowdiest and most creative will influence the experience and behavior of the crowd around them—if not the game itself. Role-playing in this sense is true playing and not merely the enactment of public expectation.

As previously noted, work and play are distinguished from each other by the degree to which the event is separated from the remainder of personal or social life. Professional athletics is an entertainment spectacle with tremendous economic ramifications. Participants are well-paid workers whose future contracts depend on success. Somewhat surprisingly, this work-like quality (i.e., that there are external consequences for the players and teams, such as bonuses, trophies, improvement in league standings, or continuation in a tournament) actually enhances the drama of the event by framing the commitment of players and fans. In the same way, investments of personal identity in a team's success or desperate money wagers (see Geertz, 1972) bring spectators more "deeply" into the event.

One effect of such stakes is to move the game from play-communitas to work-ritual (i.e., to rescue the event from triviality). However, it must be acknowledged that most baseball games are not connected to society in any particularly important way. Few lasting consequences occur for the players, the audiences, or even the physical objects or environments that are used. Even as symbolic events, the effects are indeed fleeting. Great plays, flashing tempers, spectacular failures—all typically are left upon the field. Hierarchies of winner and loser evaporate as the day passes and another game or season begins.

REFERENCES

Athey, I. (1984). The contributions of play to development. In T. Yawkey & A. Pellegrini (Eds.), *Child's play: Developmental and applied* (pp. 9–28). Hillsdale, NJ: Lawrence Erlbaum.

Bateson, G. (1971). The message: This is play. In R. E. Herron & B. Sutton-Smith (Eds.), *Child's play* (pp. 261–269). New York: Wiley.

Bateson, G. (1972). *Steps to an ecology of mind.* New York: Ballantine.

Berlyne, D. (1960). *Conflict, arousal, and curiosity.* New York: McGraw-Hill.

Bogue, R., & Spariosu, M. (Eds.). (1994). *The play of the self*. Albany, NY: State University of New York Press.

Caillois, R. (1961). *Man, play, and games*. Glencoe, IL: Free Press.

Coakley, J. (1996). Play group versus organized competitive team: A comparison. In D. Eitzen (Ed.), *Sport in contemporary society: An anthology* (5th ed., pp. 53–61). New York: St. Martin's Press.

Csikszentmihalyi, M. (1975). *Beyond boredom and anxiety*. San Francisco: Jossey-Bass.

Csikszentmihalyi, M. (1990). *Flow: The psychology of optimal experience*. New York: Harper and Row.

Durkheim, E. (1972). *Selected writings* (A. Giddens, Ed.). Cambridge, England: Cambridge University Press.

Ellis, M. (1973). *Why people play*. Englewood Cliffs, NJ: Prentice-Hall.

Geertz, C. (1972). Deep play: Notes on the Balinese cockfight. *Daedalus, 101*, 1–28.

Goffman, E. (1961). *Encounters: Two studies in the sociology of interaction*. New York: Bobbs-Merrill.

Goodale, T., & Godbey, G. (1988). *The evolution of leisure: Historical and philosophical perspectives*. State College, PA: Venture Publishing.

Gottfried, A. E. (1985). Intrinsic motivation for play. In C. C. Brown & A. W. Gottfried (Eds.), *Play interactions: The role of toys and parental involvement in children's development*. Skillman, NJ: Johnson and Johnson.

Groos, K. (1976). The play of man: Teasing and love-play. In J. Bruner, A. Jolly, & K. Sylva (Eds.), *Play: Its role in development and evolution* (pp. 68–83). New York: Basic Books.

Gruneau, R. (1980). Freedom and constraint: The paradoxes of play, games, and sports. *Journal of Sport History, 7*, 68–85.

Gruneau, R. (1983). *Class, sports, and social development*. Amherst, MA: University of Massachusetts Press.

Handelman, D. (1977). Play and ritual: Complementary frames of meta-communication. In J. Chapman & H. Foot (Eds.), *It's a funny thing: Humour* (pp. 185–192). London: Pergamon.

Hans, J. (1981). *The play of the world*. Amherst, MA: University of Massachusetts Press.

Henricks, T. (1980). Ascending and descending meaning: A theoretical inquiry into play and ritual. *Sociological Inquiry, 50*, 25–37.

Henricks, T. (1991). *Disputed pleasures: Sport and society in preindustrial England*. New York: Greenwood Press.

Herron, R. E., & Sutton-Smith, B. (1971). *Child's play*. New York: Wiley.

Huizinga, J. (1955). *Homo ludens: A study of the play element in culture*. Boston: Beacon.

Hunt, J. (1961). *Intelligence and experience*. New York: Ronald Press.

Kahler, E. (1960). The nature of the symbol. In R. May (Ed.), *Symbolism in religion and literature*. New York: Braziller.

Kline, S. (1995). The promotion and marketing of toys: Time to re-think the paradox. In A. Pellegrini (Ed.), *The future of play theory: A multidisciplinary inquiry into the contributions of Brian Sutton-Smith* (pp. 165–186). Albany, NY: State University of New York Press.

Klinger, E. (1971). *Structure and functions of fantasy*. New York: Wiley Interscience.

Lieberman, J. (1977). *Playfulness: Its relation to imagination and creativity*. New York: Academic Press.

Levy, J. (1978). *Play behavior*. New York: Wiley.

Manning, F. (1984). Carnival in Canada: The politics of celebration. In B. Sutton-Smith & D. Kelly-Byrne (Eds.), *The masks of play* (pp. 24–33). New York: Leisure Press.

Loy, J. (1968). The nature of sport: A definitional effort. *Quest Monographs, 10,* 1–15.

Loy, J. (Ed.). (1982). *The paradoxes of play.* West Point, NY: Leisure Press.

Mead, G. H. (1934). *Mind, self, and society.* Chicago: University of Chicago Press.

Miller, S. N. (1973). Ends, means and galumphing: Some lietmotifs of play. *American Anthropologist, 75,* 87–97.

Orlick, T., & Botterill, C. (1975). *Every kid can win.* Chicago: Nelson Hall.

Pellegrini, A. (Ed.). (1995). *The future of play theory: A multidisciplinary inquiry into the contributions of Brian Sutton-Smith.* Albany, NY: State University of New York Press.

Piaget, J. (1962). *Play, dreams, and imitation in childhood.* New York: W. W. Norton.

Rahner, H. (1972). *Man at play.* New York: Herder and Herder.

Rogers, C., & Sawyers, J. (1988). *Play in the lives of children.* Washington, DC: National Association for the Education of Young Children.

Schwartzman, H. (1978). *Transformations: The anthropology of children's play.* New York: Plenum.

Simmel, G. (1950). *The sociology of Georg Simmel* (K. Wolff, Ed.). New York: Free Press.

Singer, J. (1995). Imaginative play in childhood: Precursor of subjunctive thought, daydreaming, and adult pretending games. In A. Pellegrini (Ed.), *The future of play theory: A multidisciplinary inquiry into the contributions of Brian Sutton-Smith* (pp. 187–220). Albany, NY: State University of New York Press.

Spariosu, M. (1989). *Dionysus reborn: Play and the aesthetic dimension in modern philosophical and scientific discourse.* Ithaca, NY: Cornell University Press.

Sutton-Smith, B. (1978). *Die dialetik des spiels.* Schorndorf, Germany: Verlag Karl Hoffman.

Sutton-Smith, B. (1997). *The ambiguity of play.* Cambridge, MA: Harvard University Press.

Sutton-Smith, B., & Kelly-Byrne, D. (Eds.). (1984a). *The masks of play.* New York: Leisure Press.

Sutton-Smith, B., & Kelly-Byrne, D. (1984b). The phenomenon of bipolarity in play theories. In T. Yawkey & A. Pellegrini (Eds.), *Child's play: Developmental and applied.* Hillsdale, NJ: Lawrence Erlbaum.

Sutton-Smith, B., & Kelly-Byrne, D. (1984c). The idealization of play. In P. Smith (Ed.), *Play in animals and humans* (pp. 305–321). London: Basil Blackwell.

Turner, V. (1969). *The ritual process: Structure and anti-structure.* Chicago: Aldine.

Winnicott, D. (1971). *Playing and reality.* New York: Tavistock.

Author Index

Subject Index